The Exorbitant

John D. Caputo, *series editor*

PERSPECTIVES IN
CONTINENTAL
PHILOSOPHY

Edited by KEVIN HART
and MICHAEL A. SIGNER

The Exorbitant

*Emmanuel Levinas Between Jews
and Christians*

FORDHAM UNIVERSITY PRESS
New York ■ 2010

Library of Congress Cataloging-in-Publication Data

The exorbitant : Emmanuel Levinas between Jews and Christians / edited by Kevin Hart and Michael A. Signer.
    p.   cm.— (Perspectives in continental philosophy)
  Includes bibliographical references and index.
  ISBN 978-0-8232-3015-0 (cloth : alk. paper)
  ISBN 978-0-8232-3016-7 (pbk. : alk. paper)
  1. Lévinas, Emmanuel.   2. Christianity and other religions—Judaism.   3. Judaism—Relations—Christianity.   4. Christianity.   5. Judaism.   6. Philosophical theology.
I. Hart, Kevin, 1954–   II. Signer, Michael Alan.
B2430.L484E96 2010
194—dc22

                                                                                            2009034004

Printed in the United States of America
12 11 10   5 4 3 2 1
First edition

In memoriam:

Michael A. Signer
and
Edith Wyschogrod

Contents

Acknowledgments

This book grew out of a conference entitled The Exorbitant: Emmanuel Levinas Between Jews and Christians, organized by the editors, that was held at the University of Notre Dame from April 17 to April 19, 2005. It was made possible by the generosity of the Departments of English, Philosophy, and Theology, the Program in Religion and Literature, the Dean of the College of Arts and Letters, the Dean of the Graduate School, the Nanovic Institute, the Notre Dame Holocaust Project, the Office of the Provost, and the Henkels Lecture series. Scott Moringiello provided expert assistance before, throughout, and after the conference.

One of the pleasures of organizing the conference and editing the papers for this volume was working closely with Rabbi Michael A. Signer. Michael was involved in every stage of the book, and discussions with him made it a richer and stranger collection than it would otherwise have been. It is melancholy to have to say that Michael went to God on January 10, 2009, and will not see this book in print. The world of Jewish scholarship has lost a noble spirit, and the world of Jewish-Christian dialogue has lost one of its most articulate and passionate advocates. The contributors to this volume, and its surviving editor, have lost a friend. Adieu, Michael.

KH

The Exorbitant

Introduction

Levinas the Exorbitant

KEVIN HART

The word *exorbitant* takes us deeply into the thought of Emmanuel Levinas (1906–95). On first hearing the word, and letting it return to its native strangeness, we are likely to remember from school or college the Latin masculine noun *orbis*, meaning "disk, ring, circle," even "eye." We may also recall *orbis terrae*, the globe on which we live, *orbis lacteus*, the Milky Way, and images of the whole such as *orbis doctrinae* or encyclopedia. We may think too of *orbita*, the track of a wheel or the circuit of a planet or a moon. A planet, comet, or asteroid is exorbitant when it departs from its regular path around a star. We are exorbitant when we stray from our circle of action, perhaps eating or drinking more than we should, or spending more money on something than we usually do. And we can be exorbitant in a positive sense: remember Nietzsche's sentence in the prologue of *Thus Spake Zarathustra* (1891), "I tell you: one must still have chaos in one, to give birth to a dancing star."[1] Yet Levinas prompts us to hear an older voice speaking through the word, a voice that did not originally speak Latin, any Romance language, or German, a voice that upsets the word's settled modern sense. It will take us a little while to hear it, and in the meantime there is much to learn from the Latin.

We are to understand that we are exorbitant, and rightly so, when we cut any link we may have to cosmological powers, even when this link is weak, as when we casually consult a horoscope, or when it strikes us as benign, as when we respond almost instinctively to a sense of the sacred in the rebirth of the year in spring. We are also to think of ourselves as exorbitant when we resist the lure of the totality of the whole, of hearing the satisfying mental click that comes when everything is at last connected to everything else, whether that is in philosophy, politics, art, religion, or in a systematic articulation of them all. And we are to think of ourselves as exorbitant when we distance ourselves from metaphors of vision in metaphysics, epistemology, and theology. Accordingly, we begin to listen well to Levinas when we hear him inviting us to break completely with the pagan world in which the gods are simply the highest beings in the cosmos, up there in the constellations, and to learn to practice an adult religion in which God is outside cosmology and ontology. For God never "comes to mind [*vient à l'idée*]," Levinas tells us, in our attempts to prove His existence or in thinking of Him as the Creator of the cosmos. Nor does God come to mind when we engage in Hasidic prayer and lose ourselves in ecstasy or when we participate in charismatic liturgies and speak in tongues. Nor does God approach us when we piously affirm the Good, as when reciting a creed, singing an anthem, or vouching for international humanitarianism.[2] Rather, God comes to us in banal acts that are nonetheless genuinely holy, such as sharing a piece of bread with someone in a time of desperate need or offering an enemy a drink from one's canteen in wartime.[3] And God also draws close on perfectly ordinary days when we give up our money, time, or energy to help someone who neither attracts nor pleases us. As we approach the other person, so we find ourselves in the trace of God.

To detach our selves from the influence of a star—*astrum* in Latin—is, quite literally, to court disaster. In contemporary French thought the word *disaster* is most closely associated with Levinas's lifelong friend Maurice Blanchot (1907–2003). His late work *The Writing of the Disaster* (1980) is a series of fragmentary remarks that reflect partly on the disaster and partly on the later work of Levinas. "Disaster" for Blanchot has several senses: writing that has been cut off from any determinate end; the process of dying when it seems never to terminate in death; the endless approach of the neutral space of images that is neither being nor nonbeing; and the Shoah, when, ironically, Jews in the death camps were forced to wear the Star of David. Levinas approvingly quotes a line from the first of Blanchot's fragments: "we have a premonition that the disaster is thought."[4] Just as we began to think anew when, with Copernicus, we jettisoned the old cosmology, so too we start to think freshly when, with some cosmologists today, we start to ponder reality as a multiverse with galaxies apparently without end and without the overarching unity we once found in the universe.[5] Also, we think anew when we release ourselves from any fixed star, principally metaphysics understood as the study of the ground of being. Levinas glosses Blanchot's fragment by adding that this new thought has nothing in common with the "measure, the correlative, the repose, and the identity of the *astronomic* positive."[6] What binds Levinas the observant Jew and Blanchot the Gentile atheist is the conviction that there is no longer any star, any fixed point in the heavens, that can guide us here on earth and that the planets and the stars offer us no model of transcendence that we can trust. Levinas's own thought is exorbitant not in its literary form—he does not write fragmentary prose, for example—but in what it contests in philosophy. Like Franz Rosenzweig's *The Star of Redemption* (1920), to which it is indebted, Levinas's mature thought sets itself against a strain in philosophy that runs from Parmenides to Hegel and beyond, a desire for the unity of thought and being.[7]

In the preface to his first major work, *Totality and Infinity* (1961), Levinas notes that "We were impressed by the opposition to the idea of totality in Franz Rosenzweig's *Stern der Erlösung*, a work too often present in this book to be cited."[8] And then he immediately says, "But the presentation and the development of the notions employed owe everything to the phenomenological method" (28). The two debts are equally important. One is to what Rosenzweig called "the new thinking." In his 1925 essay of that name, he contrasts the old style of philosophizing with the new. "When, for instance, the old [thinking] poses the problem of whether God is transcendent or immanent, the new [thinking] tries to say how and when He turns from the distant to the near God and again from the near to the distant one."[9] As Rosenzweig sees it, "The new philosophy does nothing other than turn the 'method' of common sense into the method of scientific thinking" (83). Only when the old philosophy, used to brooding on essences, comes to an end can the new philosophy begin. Rosenzweig calls this new thinking "experiential philosophy" [*erfahrende Philosophie*] (75).

Yet Levinas plainly does not subscribe to all that Rosenzweig teaches, for his second debt is to another new style of thinking, phenomenology, which is a science of eidetic essences. A little care is needed here, for these essences or principles, *eidē*, are not those that interest Plato in the dialogues or Hegel in *The Science of Logic*. The essences Husserl has in mind can be seen, he says, by which he means that a phenomenon's distinct way of being can be directly grasped. A child looks at several triangles, for example, and *sees* that the essence of a triangle is that its internal angles must add up to 180 degrees. A teenager goes to a performance of *Othello* and *sees* what sexual jealousy is. So phenomenology is not an example of what Rosenzweig calls the old thinking. Yet phenomenology needs to be adjusted lest it become entranced by the dream of a reduction to pure consciousness, itself (at times) a figure of totality. There is a Cartesian attitude in Husserl, as is well known to readers of the "Paris Lectures," delivered in 1929, and the *Cartesian Meditations* (1950).[10] However, there is another, more pronounced Cartesianism in Levinas. For him, it is infinity that challenges the imperious claim of totality, and it is the task of a new phenomenology to locate and describe the effects of this unity. This phenomenology will be new—a "newer thinking," one might say— because it has learned from Edmund Husserl and Martin Heidegger without being bound by the former's intellectualism or the latter's preoccupation with the forgetting of being. It will be suspicious of totalities even in, especially in, the new thinking of phenomenology. In *Totality and Infinity* we are told that infinity is always and already at the back of human consciousness; it disturbs our moral complacency by reminding us day and night that there are other people outside our circle of being who nonetheless have a claim upon us, even though we may never have met them or agreed at any time to be responsible for them. Responsibility precedes my freedom, Levinas says, and modifies it very considerably. We are enjoined to be exorbitant in our ethical dealings with one another. With Levinas we may be in the world of postwar Paris, but we are a very long way from Jean-Paul Sartre's philosophy of the subject, with its accent on the primacy of freedom.

Finally, Levinas's thought is exorbitant in that it resists the theoretical sense of vision, its correlation in light, and its origin in the sun. Ocular metaphors have covertly organized Western philosophy since Plato's allegory of the cave in book 7 of *The Republic*, Levinas thinks. One might add that they permeate Christian theology. Think of Augustine's figuring of justice as light, Saint Gregory of Nyssa's metaphors of the "light of divinity," Saint John Chrysostom's conviction that God not only dwells in unapproachable light but is unapproachable light, and Pseudo-Dionysius's prizing of Light as one of the divine names.[11] Think too of the entire theology of light devised by Saint Bonaventure and passed on to later theologians.[12] "Light illuminates and is naturally understood; it is comprehension itself," Levinas writes in *Existence and Existents* (1947).[13] Later in the same book he points out that "Light, whether it emanates from the sensible or from the intelligible sun, is since Plato said to be a condition for all beings. Thought, volition and sentiment, however far they may be from intellection, are first experience, intuition, clear vision or clarity seeking to come about" (47). Writing a quarter of a century later, Jacques Derrida implicitly confirms Levinas's claim and pushes it a little further: "The sun does not just provide an example, even if the most remarkable one, of sensory Being such that it can always disappear, keep out of sight, not be present. The very opposition of appearing and disappearing, the entire lexicon of the *phainesthai*, of *aletheia*, etc., of day and night, of the visible and the invisible, of the present and the absent—all this is possible only under the sun."[14] No metaphors of vision, light, and sun, then no philosophy, it seems—or at least no philosophy as we have traditionally learned it. Derrida continues: "Insofar as it structures the metaphorical space of philosophy, the sun represents what is natural in philosophical language. In every philosophical language, it is that which permits itself to be retained by natural language. In the metaphysical alternative which opposes formal or artificial language to natural language, 'natural' should always lead us back to *physis* as a solar system, or, more precisely, to a certain history of the relationship earth/sun in the system of perception" (251).

Certainly phenomenology is caught up in this play of metaphor. It is the conversion of the naïve gaze of common sense to the phenomenological gaze that gives us the concrete situation in which something appears to me. In performing the transcendental reduction I am turned around to examine the *mise-en-scène* of my original contact with the phenomenon and can now see the ways in which its manifestation to me has been constituted by my intentional relationship with it. The old duality between subject and object has yielded to a more complex dynamic in which, as Levinas nicely puts it, "Objects are uprooted from their dull fixity to sparkle in the play of rays that come and go between the giver and the given."[15] This procedure leads to dazzling results when I am concerned with the things of the world. Yet if another person, *Autrui*, enters the orbit of my gaze and becomes a phenomenon for me, I have thereby reduced his or her otherness to a modification of my intentional consciousness. Like Buber, who in *I and Thou* (1923) distinguished the "thou" from the "it," Levinas insists on the irreducibility of the other person. Unlike Buber, though, Levinas affirms that the other person is in an asymmetric relation with me, speaking to me always from above.[16] The other person is not given to me as a phenomenon but faces me as an enigma. And so Levinas proposes that we pass from metaphors of vision to metaphors of hearing. I hear the voice of another person, forever demanding my attention and my consideration, and am pointed to the exemplary response to that voice as given by Samuel to the Lord: "Here I am [*Hineni*]" (1 Sam. 3:4). In responding to this voice, even to the point of compromising my *conatus essendi*, my desire to persist in being, I am following in the trace of God.

⌇

In fact, the word *exorbitant* can take us more deeply into Levinas's thought than its Latin origin suggests, with respect both to what he says and to how he says it. Content and form can never be neatly distinguished, yet, for ease of exposition, let us begin with what Levinas says. To do so we must take a step or two back and retrace his intellectual itinerary. Apart from a period of exile in the Ukraine (1916–20) during World War I, Levinas spent his childhood in Kaunas, Lithuania, where he "breathed in Judaism with the air" and imbibed Russian literary culture.[17] In 1923 he left Kaunas for Strasbourg, the closest city in France to Lithuania, in order to study Latin and, after this preparation, philosophy. There his professors were Charles Blondel, Henri Cateron (succeeded after his early death by Martial Guéroult), Maurice Halbwachs, and Maurice Pradines, people whose teaching and moral integrity he respected throughout his life. And there one day in 1925 or 1926 he met Blanchot, a student of philosophy and German, who would introduce him to French literary culture, especially Proust and Valéry.[18]

At the university in Strasbourg phenomenology was already in the air, though perhaps it could not be so easily breathed in as the Judaism in Kaunas. Freiburg-im-Bresgau, over the Rhine and only sixty-five kilometers away, was "*the city of Phenomenology*," as Levinas was to put it in 1929.[19] Jean Hering, a former student of Husserl in his Göttingen days and now teaching Protestant theology at Strasbourg, had published his *Phenomenology and Religious Philosophy* in 1926, when Levinas was an undergraduate. It was the first study of phenomenology to appear in France. And Gabrielle Peiffer, in Strasbourg's Philosophy Institute, suggested that her friend read Husserl's *Logical Investigations* (1900–1), which he did, German being a language he had known since the upper grades of Hebrew school in Kaunas. He found in the second volume of the *Investigations* not just one more speculative system (like that of Hermann Lotz or Wilhelm Windelband) but a fresh way of thinking and chose as the topic of his thesis, "The Theory of Intuition in the Phenomenology of Husserl." A spell in Freiburg was plainly desirable, and he studied with the master for two semesters, the summer of 1928 and the winter of 1928–29, quickly making a good impression. As early as July 13, 1928, Husserl wrote to Roman Ingarden, saying, "Hering has sent me a very talented Lithuanian student."[20] At Freiburg Levinas also encountered Martin Heidegger, whose *Being and Time* (1927) had just been published and who in his lectures and seminars was resetting phenomenology from within and giving a new, powerful impetus to philosophy. "I went to see Husserl," Levinas would muse in later life, "and I found Heidegger."[21] Blanchot would reflect in 1980 that, when talking with Levinas at that time, "I persuaded myself that philosophy was life itself, youth itself, in its unbridled—yet nonetheless reasonable—passion, renewing itself continually and suddenly by an explosion of new and enigmatic thoughts or by still unknown names, who would later shine forth as prodigious figures."[22]

Husserl taught Levinas that meaning is to be found within our lived experience, while Heidegger showed him exactly how concrete and coruscating phenomenological analyses could be. My consciousness has an intentional structure, Husserl argued, following his teacher Franz Brentano; it is always a consciousness *of* something.[23] This "something" may be external to consciousness, like a football, or internal to it, like the concept of a centaur; it makes no difference, since the judgment whether reality is internal or external is bracketed in order to attend to the experience at issue. Consider a football. I may perceive it, desire it, remember it, and so on. By returning to the implicit horizons of my consciousness, I can reflect critically on my rapport with it and can see it situated with respect to horizons of which I was unaware. For my intention exceeds the football, containing it in a web of pre-predicative intentions. Without being able to walk up to the football, without having a foot that can kick it, a hand that can pick it up, and an arm that can throw it, and without being able to remember scenes from playing football as a teenager, now all deeply layered in my ego, I would not be able to represent the football to myself. So the football, though caught in my intentional gaze, is nonetheless embedded in horizons that are not thematic projects of my subjectivity. Its being is neither inside my consciousness (as in idealism) nor outside it (as in realism). Phenomenology indicates a genuine third way in philosophy: hence the excitement surrounding it in the 1920s and hence too its power to keep renewing itself ever since. Given that representation is placed within horizons that I have not willed but that are needed for it to be possible, the primacy of representation for philosophy, especially idealism, is called into question. This is what Levinas means by "the ruin of representation."[24] It follows from this ruin of a venerable cornerstone of philosophy that *Sinngebung*, bestowal of meaning, is broader than that availed by transcendental subjectivity. Levinas will therefore propose "a *Sinngebung* essentially respectful of the Other," in which one passes from a thought *of* the other to a thought *for* the other.[25]

Respect for the other person does not follow directly from the ruin of representation. Levinas needs to add two steps to his argument before that conclusion can be drawn. First, he must bracket the God of confessional religion and thereby stop Him from directly occupying this extension of the field of meaning. The God of Judaism and Christianity so radically transcends the world, Husserl noted in *Ideas I* (1913), that no immanent correlatives are to be found for Him in consciousness.[26] Phenomenology must restrict itself to *originäre Gegebenheit*, originary givennness, Husserl insists. Levinas respects this protocol and accordingly fastens onto the concrete situation of transcendence, the face, and not the transcendent deity as such. It is the other person, standing before me in originary givenness, who transcends me insofar as I am unable to fathom his or her otherness; and this transcendence is a movement without term rather than a higher state of being. Throughout his work, Levinas is indebted to Nicolas Berdiaeff's distinction between transcendence considered as an "absolute reality" and considered as an "existential experience."[27] It is the latter, philosophical rather than theological, sense of the word upon which he draws.

Now the exact relation between the God of Abraham, Isaac, and Jacob, and the God who comes to mind in moral action, is less than clear in Levinas. Is the latter the former considered only as an eidetic possibility? Can one pass from the latter to the former by an act of faith? Is the God of Abraham, Isaac, and Jacob a metaphor of religious consolation, while the God who comes to mind is a figure of philosophical meaning? Or is the God who comes to mind best grasped as a metaphor for the reticence Jews feel about talking directly of God? These are difficult, central questions, and they are variously approached in this collection of essays. For now, though, let us watch Levinas take his second step. He distinguishes two modes of nonreligious transcendence, one appropriate to the things of the world and one specific to human beings. I can bring the things of the world into my consciousness as immanent correlates. Not so with the other person, who remains enigmatic to me, inaccessible in his or her otherness, and whose transcendence has to be accounted for.[28]

One way in which Levinas proposes to account for this transcendence is by a direct appeal to Descartes' claim, in the third of his *Meditations on First Philosophy*, that "in some way I have in me the notion of the infinite earlier than the finite—to wit, the notion of God before that of myself."[29] This notion of the infinite, of that which is irreducible to my acts of consciousness, has its correlate in the otherness of the other man, woman, or child. My consciousness is perpetually disturbed by the infinity it somehow contains; it is exposed to more than it can think. Levinas construes this disturbance in terms of me being accused by the other person, even though I have committed no fault. There never was a present moment in which I obligated myself to be responsible for him or her. (The situation is much like when, at home, the one who comes across a mess in the house is the one who has to clean it up.) The infinity in question comes from an "immemorial past."[30] This strange expression has a twofold sense: first, infinity precedes my selfhood, having been given to my consciousness before I have had any experience of the world (and hence any memory of it); and, second, I did not know the other person before he or she impinged on me with a call for help. Either way, I am responsible for the other person before I can represent him or her to myself. Without a doubt, the world of representation will claim him or her once again, but there is a moment when its power is arrested, a moment in which, as Levinas will put it in his later work, the Saying exceeds the Said.[31] Instead of phrasing the priority of infinity negatively, in terms of a past that was never present, the matter can be stated affirmatively: I have metaphysical desire for the other person, a desire without the concupiscence that would inevitably try to turn the infinite into the finite and thereby satisfy my desire. Perhaps Paul Celan best expresses the two claims, negative and affirmative, in one sublime line from his late lyric "Great Glowing Vault" when he says, "Die Welt is fort, ich muß dich tragen [The world is gone, I have to carry you]."[32]

The other person is to be figured, Levinas thinks, by way of what Jean Wahl calls "transascendance," an elevation without any possibility of termination in another, higher immanence.[33] This transascendance does not provoke a negative theology of the other person, removing him or her from the world, although it is near enough to doing so that the other person and God need to be disentangled from one another. I am placed in the position of acting concretely for my fellow human being, my neighbor, here and now. The other person speaks, indeed commands, "Thou shall not kill," which we are to hear in all its harmonic notes (respect me, allow me to live, do not murder me, be with me when I die, and so on). Faced with this vulnerability I may be tempted to destroy the one who stands before me. And yet, if I act well, I recognize that I am uniquely called to be of help. "Here I am," I say in response to his or her exposure to hunger, suffering, and death. In *Totality and Infinity* Levinas chose the powerful metaphor of the face, the most naked and exposed part of the body, to capture this sense of human vulnerability. And then, realizing the danger that the metaphor may be taken literally and that the other may be understood only as the one physically before me, replaced "face" with "proximity" in his second major work, *Otherwise than Being, or Beyond Essence* (1974).[34]

Transascendance does not raise the other person above and beyond the realm of human meaning but rather requires us to extend that realm so as to find another mode of meaning that is irreducibly ethical, that precedes the meaning associated with propositions, and that cannot be translated into them. "Truth presupposes justice," Levinas says tersely.[35] It is by helping the stranger, the widow, or the orphan that I find myself in the trace of the living God, whose otherness is of a completely different mode than that of the other person. I cannot approach God directly, nor should I wish to do so, since God deflects any and all advances by always putting the neighbor between Himself and me. As Levinas observes in an important essay of 1957:

> A face can appear as a face, as a proximity interrupting the series, only if it enigmatically comes from the infinite and its immemorial past. And the infinite, to solicit desire, a thought thinking more than it thinks, cannot be incarnated in a desirable, cannot, qua infinite, be shut up in an end. It solicits across a face, the term of my generosity and my sacrifice. A you [*Un Tu*] is inserted between the I [*le Je*] and the absolute He [*Il absolu*]. Correlation is broken.[36]

It is always broken and never restored: religion is a "relation without relation," which means in part that I am in relation with God if and only if I am taking responsibility for my neighbor.[37] I can never be done with this responsibility and turn to purely spiritual concerns. My responsibility is exorbitant, exceeding any bounds that I might wish to assign it in advance. It is limited not by reference to any principle but only by the advent of a third person, who requires me to distribute my powers and resources between the two who now stand before me asking for my help.

Ethics precedes politics and prevents it from becoming a totality, while politics clamps down on ethics and retards the Kingdom of God, which, as Levinas says, is ethical rather than spiritual.[38] All of Levinas's thought, it might be said, keeps open the crack between human life and politics in a world that, as history shows us, is grimly determined to ignore the humanity of the other person: a crack kept open only by rare acts of goodness. "The crack—that's the face," as Michael Levinas, the philosopher's son, beautifully puts it.[39] For many philosophers there is an unbroken line that joins ethics and politics; the latter is an extension of the former and an almost endless supply of examples for it. If this is so for Levinas, it is not as a consequence of his main ideas, which elaborate an ethics before ethics, even an ethics of ethics, and not a system of first-order morality. Can this *Ur*-ethics underpin and work with deontologism, divine command theory, or virtue ethics? Levinas makes no direct remarks about this, and readers are often perplexed as to which ethical systems, if any, square with Levinas's ethics and which do not. Some remarks suggest an affinity with divine command ethics, others with deontologism, and others with neither.

Nor does one find any attempt to link his ethics of ethics with concrete political events. The objection that his thought is utopian is one that he credits. Responding to this question, he replies, "its being utopian does not prevent it from investing our everyday actions of generosity or good-will towards the other: even the smallest and most commonplace gestures, such as saying 'after you' as we sit at the dinner table or walk through a door, bear witness to the ethical."[40] They may also merely testify to the fact that one has been taught good manners, however, and as we know, good manners and good morals are not quite the same. Nor are politics always the same as good morals. Yet Levinas prizes aspects of Marx's thought before Stalinism compromised it. In Marx's critique of capitalism we find, he says, "an ethical conscience cutting through the ontological identification of truth with an ideal intelligibility and demanding that theory be converted into a concrete praxis of concern for the other" (69). And so we do, although we also find a theory of class and a theory of economic exchange, among other things that Levinas does not mention. An anecdote sums up Levinas's response to concrete political action: "I remember meeting once with a group of Latin American students, well versed in the terminology of Marxist liberation and terribly concerned by the suffering and unhappiness of their people in Argentina. They asked me rather impatiently if I had ever actually witnessed the utopian rapport with the other which my ethical philosophy speaks of. I replied: 'Yes, indeed, here in this room'" (68). But what those students should or should not do when they get back to Argentina is passed over without comment. Hence the charges heard from time to time that Levinas's ethics leads to an anemic politics.

Doubtless Levinas's method of philosophizing will sometimes strike the reader as utterly exorbitant, falling far outside the normal course of philosophy. An analytic philosopher who reads *Totality and Infinity* or *Otherwise than Being* will almost certainly not find anything there that passes for an argument. Indeed, a coercive argument of the sort that would satisfy an analytic philosopher would run against the general intention of Levinas's writing, which is to alert the reader to a meaning prior to that offered by knowledge. Each reader must be individually converted, as it were, to ethics rather than metaphysics as first philosophy by reading one or another of Levinas's essays or books. Closer inspection will reveal that Levinas launches a transcendental argument (if there is to be ethics, then it must be based on the priority of the other person) that is filled out with an account of the limits of phenomenology (meaning exceeds the meaning of representation) and concrete descriptions that are nonetheless inspired by phenomenology (albeit a phenomenology that eschews the transcendental reduction).[41] The language of this philosophy becomes increasingly exorbitant: Levinas speaks of the "I" as the *hostage* of the other person, as being *obsessed* with the other, and as being *persecuted* by him or her.[42] We have a new philosophy of the subject that in its very presentation is methodologically committed to exorbitance. We might find support for this in *Otherwise than Being*: "In subjectivity the superlative is the exorbitance [*démesure*] of a null-site, in caresses and in sexuality the 'excess' [*surenchère*] of tangency—as though tangency admitted a gradation—up to contact with the entrails, a skin going under another skin."[43]

Can the use of superlatives constitute a philosophical method? It would seem so if the aim were to shock us out of our habit of regarding ethics as centered on the self and requiring reciprocity from the other person. Elsewhere, Levinas reflects on his rhetorical strategy: "Emphasis signifies at the same time a figure of rhetoric, an excess of expression [*un excès de l'expression*], a manner of overstating oneself, and a manner of showing oneself. The word is very good, like the word 'hyperbole': there are hyperboles whereby notions are transmuted. To describe this mutation is also to do phenomenology. Exasperation as a method of philosophy!"[44] One might say that the whole of Levinas's philosophy is supported by the word *exorbitant*, even though *démesure, exorbitant,* and related words appear only rarely in his writings. In content and form, Levinas invites us to practice what in Hebrew is called *hesed,* unrestrained and generous charity, given without thought of return. One gives *gemilut hasadim* not by way of alms but by performing a service for the one who needs it. The word *exorbitant* comes to us from Latin and becomes a word in its own right only in the medieval Christian Latin *exorbitant,* and yet as it guides us when reading Levinas an ancient Hebrew voice speaks through it.

༃

The Exorbitant: Emmanuel Levinas Between Jews and Christians began life as a conference that Rabbi Michael A. Signer and I convened at the University of Notre Dame in April 17 to 19, 2005. All the papers gathered here either were given at that conference or, if pregnancy or sickness prevented a speaker's attendance, were written specifically for it. In giving the conference the title we did, Rabbi Signer and I wanted to keep in play all that I have said about the word *exorbitant* and thereby focus attention on the infinite relation and metaphysical desire as central to his religious thought. We also wanted to mark the word *between.* We had in mind Levinas's discernment of a "new modality of between-the-two," which would exceed ontology, a thinking of "the *between (Zwischen)*" as "an origin that disposes the I as I and the You as You."[45] Especially, we wanted to see in what ways Levinas's writings facilitated a dialogue between Jews and Christians, between the two worlds of Hebrew and Latin. This dialogue would differ from the one that Rosenzweig invited us to take part in: that much was clear. But where would it take us? In one sense, Levinas stands exactly between Jews and Christians: ethics, as he conceives it, is a space in which the two religious traditions, along with other world religions, can meet. When talking with Christians, he liked to remind us of Matthew 25, when Jesus tells his disciples about the Judgment. The Son of man shall come in his glory, Matthew's Jesus says, and shall tell the unjust that they did not care for him when he was hungry, thirsty, naked, sick, and without shelter, and then hear their blank denial that they failed to help him. Jesus' response is Levinas's favorite verse in the New Testament: "Verily I say unto you, Inasmuch as ye have done *it* unto one of the least of these my breathren, ye have done *it* unto me" (Matt. 25:40).[46] Ethics as first philosophy is to be found not only in the Hebrew Bible but also in the Gospel.

At the same time, though, Levinas's ethics seems to flatten out discussion between Jews and Christians even before it begins, putting out of play questions about the particularity of revelation that are so important to observant Jews and practicing Christians. Religion is to be examined in its phenomenological concreteness, the human face, and this examination will cut across the phenomenality of revelation: the giving of the Law to Moses on Mount Sinai, the Resurrection of Christ, and so on.[47] All the same, Levinas does not speak solely as a philosopher. No one can read a page of one of his essays, speeches, or books without hearing a Jewish voice as well as a philosophical one. Sometimes this voice bypasses any claims about the particularity of the Jews, as when we are told that "Judaism is an essential modality of all that is human."[48] At other times, at least to Christian ears, Levinas's talk of substitution in *Otherwise than Being* seems to resonate with Christological themes. It does so explicitly when he talks of the "passion" of Judaism in the Shoah.[49] Levinas speaks of the West having two languages, Hebrew and Greek, the one being the language of the holy and the other being the language of philosophy and, more generally, the university. (Latin, for Levinas, *is* Greek.) To what extent does Levinas use a language that is Christian as well as Greek? The question must be allowed its point; it must resist being blunted, though, by Christians who try simply to appropriate Levinas's thought.

On other occasions, Levinas sharply distinguishes Judaism from Christianity. We hear him saying that "the infinite . . . cannot be incarnated" and find there a confessional response to Christianity interlaced with a philosophical position. Needless to say, Christians—especially Catholics who know their Aquinas—will object that the divine nature was not coiled physically *in* Jesus of Nazareth, as though competing for space with His human nature, for the divine *esse* cannot be localized at a particular point in the cosmos.[50] Yet Levinas would also remind us that John-Paul II taught that "God would be incarnated not solely in Christ, but through Christ in all men."[51] Would this attention to different sides of the doctrine of the Incarnation help Jews and Christians achieve a better understanding of the central issue that divides us without dissipating into tepid platitudes? More generally, could issues such as these be proposed and perhaps developed in a dialogue between Jewish and Christian scholars of Levinas so that the result would not be just another discussion of an important philosopher but a contribution to mutual understanding in a world fraught with religious difference?

We thought it a risk well worth taking. Certainly Levinas himself had been cautiously interested in dialogue between Jews and Christians, as becomes clear especially in some of the interviews he granted in the last stage of his writing life. Caution was necessary, since neither the Crusades nor the long history of anti-Semitism in which they took place can or should be forgotten. As he would sometimes say, in words that must pierce any Christian, "the executioners of Auschwitz—Protestants or Catholics— had all probably done their catechism."[52] They had almost certainly all been baptized. Yet Levinas does not stop with this justified rebuke: "Nevertheless, what we experienced within the civilian population—simple believers and members of the hierarchy who welcomed, helped, and often saved many of us—is absolutely unforgettable, and I have never stopped reminding others of the role played—with a lot of ruses and risks—in the rescue of my wife and daughter, by the monastery of Saint Vincent de Paul near Orléans" (41).

Levinas knew little of Christianity before moving to Strasbourg, but he learned much about it from Henri Carteron, doubtless from his example as well as from his lectures. Later, in the 1930s, *The Star of Redemption* impressed Levinas, even though he was not to follow Rosenzweig's vision of the mutuality of Judaism and Christianity, as developed there.[53] Certainly Levinas had taken heart from reading Vatican II's declaration on the relation of the Church with non-Christian Religions, *Nostra Aetate* (October 1965). The earlier drafts of the document were assuredly the more heartening for Jews, yet in the final version, which disappointed many Catholics committed to dialogue with the other world religions, the Vatican nonetheless recognizes, as he puts it, "a permanent signification of religious Judaism in the Christian perspective" (69).[54] Also, he had meditated on the ten points about Jewish-Christian relations that were formulated by the International Council of Christians and Jews at their conference on anti-Semitism at Seelisburg, Switzerland, in 1947. On the twentieth anniversary of that conference, he reflected that Jewish-Christian relations had passed "beyond dialogue" and that now there was perhaps "a new maturity and earnestness, a new gravity and a new patience, and, if I may express it so, *maturity and patience for insoluble problems*."⁵⁵ There can be no resolution of the dialogue between Jews and Christians; the task cannot be completed, and yet, as the Talmud teaches us, this does not give us the right to desist from the task.

۶

It is important to recognize in any dialogue that the participants will bring different traditions to the discussion, even different traditions folded into the one writer. No one who reads an essay or a book by Levinas can doubt that he was trained as a philosopher in the tradition of phenomenology. It is clearest in *Totality and Infinity*, *Otherwise than Being*, and the collections of essays that circle around them. Yet different emphases, different lightings of questions, perhaps even different questions, at times, will become prominent if one approaches Levinas from *Difficult Liberty* and the Talmudic commentaries gathered together in *Nine Talmudic Readings*, *In the Time of the Nations*, *Beyond the Verse*, and *New Talmudic Readings*. It is in these books that one recognizes what the Jewish Bible means for Levinas, not just what philosophy means for him. As he says in a discussion of Jewish philosophy, "The Bible *signifies* for all authentically human thought, for civilization *tout court*, whose authenticity can be recognized in peace, in *shalom*, and in the responsibility of one man for another."⁵⁶ Perhaps philosophy and the Bible were never meant to harmonize.⁵⁷ That, though, would be an argument for keeping the Bible ever before us, along with Plato and the rest, and one that Levinas is glad to advance.

Not all the contributors to this volume draw the distinction between Judaism and Christianity in the same way. Some are inclined to draw it more firmly than others, and some are inclined to draw it more extensively than others. For some writers, what is immediately of interest is a teaching that divides Jews and Christians (the Incarnation); for others, it is a concept that brings the two traditions closer together (substitution). Jeffrey Bloechl and Edith Wyschogrod focus on the motifs of excess and expenditure, surely of deep interest to both faiths, and do not engage directly with Jewish-Christian debate. And yet Dana Hollander finds an interesting point of entry precisely in Jewish-Christian polemic. Robyn Horner wonders what Christian theology can learn from Levinas's distinctively Jewish thought, and Michael Purcell seeks to rethink the Catholic teaching of the prevenience of Grace by way of Levinas's notion of the posteriority of the anterior. For some contributors, the important distinction is less between Judaism and Christianity than between Judaism and philosophy, especially philosophy as practiced in the German university. Thus a Jewish philosopher (Hermann Cohen or Franz Rosenzweig) becomes for some contributors the appropriate figure for understanding a motif in Levinas, while for others—principally Leora Batnitzky, Jeffrey L. Kosky, and Jean-Luc Marion—it is Martin Heidegger, a thinker with roots in Christian theology (and with much to answer for in the 1930s) who is central to making sense of Levinas. For some contributors, the word *religion* is more significant than either "Judaism" or "Christianity," while for others it is the word *God* that provides the focus. Richard A. Cohen looks to Levinas for a way of thinking God without theodicy. Still others attend to traditions of exegesis. Robert Gibbs finds that the best question to ask of Levinas is how he can guide us in reading scripture, while Elliot Wolfson reads Levinas and discovers a relation with Jewish esoteric teaching that has been carefully hidden.

In choosing our speakers, we did not want to stage a confrontation of Jewish and Christian scholars for whom Levinas has been and remains important. We did not want appropriation. We did not want reductive speech. We wanted, if it was possible, for our contributors to keep one eye on Levinas and another on the possibilities and impossibilities of Jewish-Christian dialogue. To that end, we asked Paul Franks and Merold Westphal to comment on each paper as it was presented and to keep before us the figure of Levinas between Jews and Christians. Their interventions were decisive in the recasting of several papers, and their reflections at the end of the collection sum up and keep in play the live options for reading Levinas and for maintaining a conversation between Jews and Christians. That conversation is one that must be kept alive, one that, if it is to live and breathe, must itself be free to be exorbitant, outside the expectations and protocols that we bring to it. The concluding reflections by Rabbi Signer underline the importance of maintaining the conversation, and of keeping historians as well as philosophers and theologians involved in it.

Doubtless the conversation between Jews and Christians has many other possibilities that are not marked here, and doubtless in time it will be transformed (it may include Islam, for example, without which all that Jews and Christians say about monotheism can be only partial). This collection is, as it were, a snapshot of a dialogue at a particular point of time—ten years after the philosopher's death—and in a place, the United States, where many Jews and Christians are absorbing his thought and learning lessons from it that do not always converge with one another. The debate at the conference produced more light than heat, and it ranged widely, beyond the normal academic boundaries of some contributors, as though the proper name *Levinas* itself encourages exorbitance.

Levinas Between German Metaphysics and Christian Theology

LEORA BATNITZKY

Emmanuel Levinas is most famous for his claim that "ethics is first philosophy." By this he means primarily to criticize the priority given to ontology, to the question of being as such, in Martin Heidegger's philosophy in particular and in the Western philosophical tradition more generally. Levinas aims to show that my obligation to another person constitutes the starting point of all truth. Philosophy cannot fully grasp what Levinas calls the "face of the other." Philosophy can, however, by way of a phenomenological retrieval, recover what ontology—the quest for the meaning of being—has forgotten: namely, the way in which the subject has already been "called" into responsibility by the revelation of the other's moral authority. In this sense, Levinas's thought challenges the "totalitarian" impulse of Western ontology, which constitutes much of the Western philosophical tradition. And it is "Judaism," or "Hebrew," as opposed to "Athens," or "Greek," that, Levinas maintains, allows him to challenge philosophy's hegemony from within.

As is well known, in opposing philosophical totality by way of revelation's alterity, Levinas professes a strong debt to the thought of the German-Jewish philosopher Franz Rosenzweig (1886–1929). Levinas's first major philosophical work, *Totality and Infinity*, includes the following now-famous note in its preface: "We were impressed by the opposition to the idea of totality in Franz Rosenzweig's *The Star of Redemption*, a work too often present in this book to be cited."[1] As both Robert Gibbs and Richard A. Cohen have shown, an appreciation of Levinas's claim about his debt to Rosenzweig takes us far in appreciating the theological-ethical import of his thought.[2] For Levinas, Rosenzweig's *The Star of Redemption* "is a Jewish book, which founds Judaism in a new way."[3] While Levinas affirms that "Rosenzweig is one of the rare Jewish philosophers who has . . . acknowledged Christianity's fundamental place in the spiritual evolution of humanity," he also insists that Rosenzweig "acknowledged it [Christianity] by refusing to become a Christian."[4]

Rosenzweig's break with totality would seem to issue in what Levinas calls elsewhere "a religion for adults," which "does not exalt a sacred power, a *numen* triumphing over other numinous powers but still participating in their clandestine and mysterious life."[5] In this sense, for Levinas, "Judaism . . . [does] not cross the same landscapes as the Christian paths."[6] Judaism, Levinas maintains, rejects wishes for supernatural intervention for the sake of a view of reality that insists on bettering the world in the here and now. As he puts it:

> If Judaism is attached to the here below, it is not because it does not have the imagination to conceive of a supernatural order, or because matter represents some sort of absolute for it; but because the first light of conscience is lit for it on the path that leads from man to his neighbor. . . . To be without being a murderer. One can uproot oneself from this responsibility, deny the place where it is incumbent on me to something, to look for an anchorite's salvation. One can choose utopia. On the other hand, in the name of spirit, one can choose not to flee the conditions from which one's work draws its meaning, and remain here below. And that means choosing ethical action.[7]

For Levinas, Rosenzweig's break with totality is at the same time a turn toward the neighbor. In this way, Levinas's reading of Rosenzweig would seem to encapsulate simultaneously his criticism and redirection of philosophy, on the one hand, and his Jewish corrective to Christian theology, on the other. Seen in this context, Levinas would seem to reject both German metaphysics and Christian theology. He would seem to be *between* neither. Given the preceding descriptions of Levinas's project, it would seem that the title of this paper ought to have been "Levinas Beyond German Metaphysics and Christian Theology" or, perhaps, "Otherwise than German Metaphysics and Christian Theology."

Yet against these well-received characterizations of Levinas's project and Levinas's self-description described above, I argue in this essay that Levinas's positive relation to the Western philosophical tradition is far more complex than Levinas's interpreters have allowed. At the same time,

Levinas's relation to Judaism is also far more complex than Levinas and his interpreters suggest. Analyzing Levinas's messianic claims for philosophy in the context of the historically religious roots and *aspirations* of modern German philosophy, this paper considers some broad affinities between Levinas's philosophy and Christian theology, in terms of both form and content. Drawing on the recent work of intellectual historians Ian Hunter and Walter Sparn, I maintain that the development of modern metaphysics historically transformed what had been the *social* function of Christian theology. In this sense, I contend, Levinas's positive use of the term *metaphysics* is akin to the historical function of Christian theology, as well as to the historical function of what became post-Christian (or post-Protestant) metaphysics.

To make this argument, I reconsider Levinas's interpretation of Rosenzweig to shed light on Levinas's conceptions of "philosophy" generally and his conception of "incarnation" in particular. I argue that Levinas's attempt to harmonize philosophy and theology is in keeping with the attempt of the early modern metaphysicians through Kant to keep secular knowledge within the orbit of what Levinas would call revelation and what I am suggesting would be more appropriately called Christian revelation, or Christian theology. Rather than being seen as a straightforward interpretation of Rosenzweig's notion of revelation, Levinas's conception of incarnation is best understood in the context of the metaphysical attempt of both Leibniz and Kant to transform and generalize Luther's metaphysical view of Christ's two natures. While broadening the possibility of conversation between Levinas and Christian thinkers, this reading of Levinas also complicates two mainstays of contemporary Levinas interpretation: one that sees Levinas as a distinctively Jewish thinker and one that sees Levinas as a distinctly secular thinker. In conclusion, I consider briefly the relation between these historical and philosophical analyses as they relate to the question of what it means to call a thinker "Jewish," "Christian," or otherwise.

Levinas's Reading of Rosenzweig

When Levinas claims that Rosenzweig introduced an opposition to the idea of totality, he claims that Rosenzweig's system of philosophy undoes itself as a philosophical system by way of his claims about revelation. Indeed, we need but note the title of Stéphane Mosès's seminal work on Rosenzweig, *System and Revelation*, to which Levinas wrote the introduction.[8] From Levinas's perspective, Rosenzweig's consideration of revelation bursts what he claims is the totalizing and systematic tendency of

Western philosophy, which is the premise that reason can know everything. Revelation undoes reason for Levinas in that it ruptures our ability to cognize everything.

Yet revelation does not signify the end of philosophy for Levinas. In fact, Levinas attributes this insight also to Rosenzweig, claiming that Rosenzweig's philosophical opposition to the idea of totality not only does not diminish the relevance of philosophy but signifies the beginning of an era in which "everything is philosophy."[9] Levinas suggests that Rosenzweig's opposition to totality yields two significant metaphysical insights: the first concerns the nature of the self and the second concerns the relation between the self and another person. Levinas uses the term *metaphysics* to signify a basic structure of experience that makes possible and *is* in fact the ethical relation. As he puts it, "Metaphysics, transcendence, the welcoming of the other by the same, of the Other by me, is concretely produced as the calling into question of the same by the other, that is, as the ethics that accomplishes the critical essence of knowledge. And as critique precedes dogmatism, metaphysics precedes ontology."[10] Rosenzweig's opposition to totality should, for Levinas, be understood in terms of ethics. I cannot cognize or assimilate another person into myself. The other person's rupture of my idea of totality is, for Levinas, the proper and true meaning of revelation. Ethics, for Levinas, is my response to the other person. The possibility of ethics rests on my irreducible uniqueness. Simply put, if I couldn't respond to the other, ethics would not be possible. So, while the other person ruptures my freedom from the perspective of my totality, this rupturing also truly frees me from the perspective of ethics.

From Levinas's perspective, Rosenzweig's views of the atheistic self prior to revelation and this same self in the throes of revelation give expression to what he argues are the metaphysical "facts" about human subjectivity. From the perspective of Levinas's philosophy, Rosenzweig's account of the meta-ethical self (in part 2 of *The Star of Redemption*) points to the radical distinctness of the irreducibly separate self. Levinas follows Rosenzweig in claiming that once the sediments of culture and history have been brushed away, an irreducible surplus remains of the self. Levinas claims that this irreducible separateness makes ethics, which he claims is the meaning of revelation, possible.

As is well known, Rosenzweig begins his discussion of revelation in *The Star of Redemption* by quoting the Song of Songs. He writes:

Love is strong as death. Strong in the same way as death? But against whom does death display its strength? Against him whom it seizes.

And love, of course, seizes both, the lover as well as the beloved, but the beloved otherwise than the lover. It originates in the lover. The beloved is seized, his love is already a response to being seized.[11]

Let us explore briefly a number of Levinasian themes in the preceding quotation. Rosenzweig's explication of "Love is strong as death" serves from Levinas's perspective as the quintessential response to Heidegger. Death displays its strength against him whom it seizes. In the context of Levinas's philosophy, Rosenzweig's formulation would describe the limitation of Heidegger's view of the self and of death. The power of death is that it is the end of being oneself. This is what it means to die: to no longer be living. Love is as strong as death because love is as transforming as death is. But love, Rosenzweig suggests, is more complicated than death. Love seizes both the lover and the beloved. For this reason, love breaks open the notion of totality even more profoundly than death does because love concerns the relation between two subjects, while death concerns only one subject.

From Levinas's perspective, Rosenzweig's account of the dynamic of revelation also describes the dynamic of the ethical relation, which is one of asymmetry. The experience of revelation, Rosenzweig claims, is a two-stage process, which consists of two statements made by the beloved to the lover (who, again, is the initiator of love). These two statements are "I have sinned" and "I am a sinner." What Rosenzweig describes as the acknowledgement of sin in the present, Levinas would describe as the ethical situation in which I transform my present (and not only recognize the error of my past) by virtue of my relationship to the other. Rosenzweig's description of the response of the lover to the beloved's second acknowledgment would seem to confirm Levinas's view. Rosenzweig claims that, in response to my acknowledgment of my sin, the lover says to me, "You are mine."[12] As Rosenzweig continues, this "is a sentence which does not have 'I' for a subject."[13] From Levinas's perspective, I am now for the other because I am now a "you." But in responding to the other, in becoming a "you," I truly become myself.

Levinas transforms Rosenzweig's consideration of divine revelation into an ethical theory. Calling what Rosenzweig describes as revelation "the Good," Levinas writes:

> Has not the Good chosen the subject with an election recognizable in the responsibility of being hostage, to which the subject is destined, which he cannot evade without denying himself, and by virtue of which he is unique? A philosopher can give to this election only the signification circumscribed by responsibility to the other.

This antecedence of responsibility to freedom would signify the Goodness of the Good: the necessity that the Good choose me first before I can be in a position to choose, that is, welcome its choice.[14]

Levinas understands himself to be a philosopher and Rosenzweig to be a philosopher also. Hence he contends that the meaning of revelation is "the necessity that the Good choose me first."

That Levinas reads Rosenzweig philosophically or ethically does not mean, however, that Levinas does not have recourse to theological concepts. Indeed, Levinas is at times more theological than Rosenzweig, as when he describes what I called above Rosenzweig's two stages of revelation with reference to "incarnation":

The body is not only an image or figure here; it is the distinctive in-oneself of the contraction of ipseity and its breakup. This contraction is not an impossibility to forget oneself, to detach oneself from oneself, in the concern for itself. It is a recurrence to oneself out of an irrecusable exigency of the other, a duty overflowing my being, a duty becoming a debt and an extreme passivity prior to the tranquility, still quite relative, in the inertia and materiality of things at rest . . . . Here what is due goes beyond having, but makes giving possible. This recurrence is incarnation. In it the body which makes giving possible makes one other without alienating. For this other is the heart, and the goodness, of the same, the inspiration or the very psyche of the soul.[15]

Like Rosenzweig, Levinas describes the self's ability to respond to the other as a remaking of the self for the sake of the other. Levinas describes this process as incarnation in order to emphasize the concrete particularity of the self who is now for the other.

Yet while Levinas appears to be far more theological than Rosenzweig in his choice of vocabulary, the important thing to notice is that while Rosenzweig suggests in his discussion of the Song of Songs that we can understand divine love through human love, Levinas's analysis reverses this order. For Levinas, we can understand ethics through theological concepts such as "incarnation." Again, we can appreciate Levinas's articulation of his own project, which is to understand theology, revelation, and even incarnation from the point of view of the philosopher.

The reading I have just offered of Rosenzweig through Levinas (a reading that has a number of contemporary advocates) is not a claim for the historical accuracy of such a reading, both in terms of what Levinas says about Rosenzweig and in terms of what Rosenzweig actually says. As Samuel Moyn has shown, it is quite possible, if not likely, that Levinas projects his debt to Rosenzweig back onto his own philosophical claim about ethics.[16] What is interesting about this historical point, however, is that this fact would not make a difference from Levinas's point of view. Nor would the fact that Rosenzweig, in his discussion of revelation, may have meant something different from or at least in tension with Levinas's claims about interhuman relations. Indeed, we need but mention Rosenzweig's 1914 essay "Atheistic Theology," in which Rosenzweig sharply criticizes the attempt of nineteenth- and twentieth-century Christian and Jewish thinkers to make of revelation only a human matter. Rosenzweig defines "atheistic theology" as the denial of the "hard mark of the divine that actually entered into history and is distinct from all other actuality."[17] Atheistic theology makes the concept of God's election "immanent to the human."[18] While the crux of Levinas's philosophy is an attempt to rethink the possibility of transcendence, he nonetheless also denies the possibility of what Rosenzweig calls the "hard mark of the divine" actually entering into history. And while Levinas insists that "the Good choose me first before I can be in a position to choose," supernatural interventions of any sort (which he associates with utopia) are anathema to his conceptions of religion and ethics. As we have seen, particularly in regard to Levinas's use of theological concepts such as "incarnation," the hard mark of the divine for him concerns only the relation between human beings.

From Levinas's perspective, neither the historical record of the development of his own thought nor the answer to the question of what Rosenzweig himself was really up to would change what he claims is the philosophical significance of Rosenzweig's claims about revelation. For Levinas, it is not philosophically relevant whether or not he gets Rosenzweig qua Rosenzweig right because, as Kant famously suggested in connection with his reading of Plato, it is possible to understand an author better than he understood himself.[19] It is here that we find the confluence between Levinas's reading of Rosenzweig and his own claims about the meaning of philosophy. It is the work of philosophy, from Levinas's perspective, to disregard extra-philosophical matters, such as historical, cultural, literary, or even theological context. The significance of Rosenzweig's philosophy, Levinas would maintain, is this philosophical insight, both about the content of philosophy, which for Levinas is the ethical relation, and the scope of philosophy, which for Levinas is to articulate clearly and definitively the ultimate meaning of our humanity (which, he argues, is ethics). In the conclusion of this essay, we will return to the question of the ultimate philosophical relevance or irrelevance of historical contextualization for understanding Levinas's philosophy, but before doing so we turn first to further contextualize Levinas's thought within the context of the history of early modern debates about the teaching of metaphysics in the German university.

Levinas and the Historical Rise of the German Metaphysical Tradition

Despite the ways in which Levinas often presents himself and despite the ways in which he is often received, I suggest that Levinas's expansion of the task of philosophy—in which "philosophy" becomes "everything" and is revealed through nonphilosophers—is of a piece with a particular Christian and post-Christian philosophical project that historically does not, as is often argued, secularize theology but instead makes philosophy theological. In making this argument I rely on the historical analyses of Ian Hunter, who, in his recent *Rival Enlightenments: Civil and Metaphysical Philosophy in Early Modern Germany*, shows the religious roots and, even more importantly, the religious aspirations of modern German philosophy.[20] Levinas's philosophy, despite his claims to the contrary, reenacts the very Christianization of philosophy that defines German metaphysics and, again despite claims to the contrary, also marks post-Kantian moral and political philosophy. My suggestion is that, rather than a turn away from philosophy toward Judaism, Levinas's reading of Rosenzweig and transformation of some of Rosenzweig's themes are instances of this modern, historical Christianization of philosophy.

Before turning to Hunter's historical analysis, it may be helpful to consider the claim of Levinas's contemporary Leo Strauss (1899–1973) regarding the different historical statuses of philosophy for Judaism and Islam, on the one hand, and Christianity, on the other. Strauss writes:

> we are touching on what, from the point of view of the sociology of philosophy, is the most important difference between Christianity on the one hand, and Islam as well as Judaism on the other. For the Christian, the sacred doctrine is revealed theology; for the Jew and the Muslim, the sacred doctrine is, at least primarily, the legal interpretation of the Divine Law (*talmud* or *fiqh*). The sacred doctrine in the latter sense has, to say the least, much less in common with philosophy than the sacred doctrine in the former sense. It is ultimately for this reason that the status of philosophy was, as a matter of principle, much more precarious in Judaism and in Islam than in Christianity: in Christianity philosophy became an integral part of the officially recognized and even required training of the student of the sacred doctrine.[21]

Strauss's assertions about Christianity are certainly not comprehensive. Nevertheless, even though these assertions do not do justice to the full array of Christian traditions, Strauss's contention about the status of revealed theology for the Christian tradition is useful not only for appreciating broadly one important difference between Judaism (along with Islam) and Christianity but also for understanding the development of modern metaphysics as it relates to Levinas's philosophy. While the standard story of the development of Enlightenment philosophy suggests that modern philosophers properly separate philosophy from revelation and that medieval theologians do not make such a separation, the recent work of Hunter, along with a number of other intellectual historians, shows that that this misleading account of the historical circumstances in which the modern study of metaphysics arose is in fact the outcome of how deeply embedded we are in what has became and remains the religious aspiration of the development of the discipline of modern philosophy.[22]

Hunter begins his study by noting that it was in fact Martin Luther who called for the *exclusion* of university metaphysics. As Luther put it: "Virtually the entire Ethics of Aristotle is the worst enemy of grace. This is in opposition to the scholastics. . . . It is an error to say that no man can become a theologian without Aristotle. Indeed, no one can become a theologian unless he becomes one without Aristotle."[23] Contemporary philosophers and historians of philosophy attack Luther for irrationalism,[24] but, as Hunter notes:

> As soon as we . . . reinstate the specific anthropology underpinning Luther's . . . position . . . then the true character of the "two truths" doctrine becomes apparent. . . . [Luther] was not irrationally rejecting philosophy. Rather he was attempting to exclude philosophers (university metaphysicans) from the role of mediating the Christian mysteries, treating their rationalist pursuit of salvation through ascent to transcendent knowledge as incompatible with the mode of acceding to salvation through biblical faith.[25]

Arguments against university metaphysics introduced by Luther were, ironically, defeated by the Protestant academy.[26] This Lutheran argument was taken up by civil philosophers such as Christian Thomasius and Samuel Pufendorf, who, in advocating the separation of politics from philosophical claims to the good, put forward an alternative anthropology to what became the post-Kantian anthropological view of the human being. These civil philosophers, historical critics of the rise of modern metaphysics, in fact criticized the metaphysical school as sectarian because of its commitment to a particular view of human nature. First and foremost, this metaphysical view of human nature implied, in the words of Thomasius, that "it is within human capacity to live virtuously and happily."[27]

There is much to say about the historical conditions of the rise of German metaphysics, as well as the ways in which post-Kantian philosophers and intellectual historians have rewritten this history, but this is of course an enormous subject beyond the scope of this essay. However, two aspects of this historical debate between the metaphysical and civil philosophers are directly relevant for our consideration of Levinas. The first aspect, on which we have already touched, is the anthropological vision of the early German metaphysicians, who saw human beings as being able to create and sustain the conditions for their own happiness. Clearly, this anthropological assumption remains at the core of Kantian and post-Kantian metaphysics and moral philosophy. The civil philosophers were critical of the metaphysical philosophers not only for this assumption but also for implying that the problems of all human beings are the same and require the same solution.[28] Thomasius, for example, rejected the premise of the metaphysical philosophers that "man is a single species and that what is good for one [person] is good for another."[29] This premise about the natural equality of all human beings and all human problems is of course at the heart of what became the post-Kantian liberal political project.

It is this notion of natural equality as the first premise of political, social, and ethical life that Levinas criticizes. As he put it in the 1990 preface to the republication of his article "Reflections on the Philosophy of Hitlerism," first published in 1934, "we must ask ourselves if liberalism is all we need to achieve an authentic dignity for the human being."[30] Or, as Levinas puts it in *Totality and Infinity*, "The Other is not transcendent because he would be free as I am; on the contrary his freedom is a superiority that comes from his very transcendence."[31] As we have seen, in his reading of Rosenzweig Levinas questions precisely a conception of freedom predicated on an autonomous subject. For Levinas, all human beings are not equal. The basis of ethics, instead, is the recognition of the other's superiority to me. While the modern liberal tradition of Western political theory contends that human equality confers equal rights on each individual, Levinas maintains that our duties precede our rights. In his words, "commands are the political condition of freedom."[32] Or, as he puts it in *Otherwise than Being*, "The equality of all is borne by my inequality, the surplus of my duties over my rights."[33] For Levinas, Rosenzweig's description of the dynamics of revelation exposes the totalizing myth of human equality. For Rosenzweig, according to Levinas, I am not one self among other, equal selves. Rather, I am irreducibly unique in my being for another. In the context of Levinas's philosophy, this irreducible, unique being for the other would be the meaning of Rosenzweig's notion of "sin."

In terms of philosophical content, that is, in terms of the very definitions of human individuality and equality, Levinas would seem to be deeply critical of the implications of the development of modern metaphysics. But it is in connection with a second, perhaps more basic theme related to the rise of German metaphysics that Levinas shares in the implicit Christian assumptions, in both form and content, that went along with the development of German metaphysics. As Walter Sparn argues, rather than attempting to free philosophy from the shackles of theology, the fusing of philosophy and theology in university metaphysics had theological aims and used theological tools to achieve these ends.[34] The basic goal of university metaphysics was not to rationalize theology (as most of its subsequent histories would have it) but to keep secular subjects within Christian academic culture. This historical point raises an important philosophical point that has been lost in most histories of the rise of German metaphysics. The metaphysical philosophers, rather than moving beyond theology, in fact created a new theology of metaphysics. As Hunter succinctly puts it, "the metaphysical philosophers regarded their 'natural theologies' as *new moral theologies for public life,* shifting the locus of salvation to metaphysics itself" (emphasis added).[35] Modern metaphysics arose as a spiritual exercise that recommended itself not just to individuals (as was the case for ancient philosophy) but to society at large. In arguing and eventually triumphing philosophically against the civil philosophers, the metaphysical philosophers championed a new vision of, to borrow a term from Levinas, a messianic future in which metaphysics as philosophy becomes "everything" and saves society.

Seen in historical context, Levinas's messianic claims for philosophy do not represent a break with the aspirations of modern metaphysics (neither do, for instance, Derrida's religious claims for philosophy). Like the early modern German metaphysicians, Levinas regards philosophy as a spiritual exercise, which is designed to perfect not just our understanding of philosophical matters but the kind of person we may become. As Hunter puts it, "From a purely historical perspective . . . it is the *paideia* of metaphysics itself—inculcated in religious or academic institutions dedicated to grooming the spiritual elite—that is responsible for inducing the desire for metaphysical knowledge."[36] But a historical look at the development of early modern metaphysics also points to something more important than this common quest for spiritual improvement (common also to ancient and medieval philosophy), which much of the subsequent reception of the modern metaphysical tradition has eclipsed. Levinas's deepest formal affinity with the rise of modern metaphysics is in ascribing moral and social authority to, in Hunter's words, "the self-transformative function of university metaphysics."[37] Prior to the rise of modern metaphysics, moral and social authority came from the Church (and scholastic philosophy). The development of modern metaphysics historically transformed what had been the social function of Christian theology.

In this sense, Levinas's positive use of the term *metaphysics* is akin to the historical function of Christian theology as well as to the historical function of what became post-Christian metaphysics. Referring to Plato and describing his use of the term *metaphysics* as the subsuming of theology by philosophy, Levinas writes: "The very dimension of height is opened by the metaphysical Desire. That this height is no longer the heavens but the Invisible is the very elevation of height and its nobility. To die for the invisible—that is metaphysics. This does not mean that desire can dispense with acts. But these acts are neither consumption, nor caress, nor liturgy."[38] For Levinas, metaphysics means, to return to his reading of Rosenzweig, that everything, including *theology*, is philosophy. Philosophy does not dispense with theology but rather uses the philosophical truths of theology for salvific purposes.

But the kinship between Levinas's philosophy and Christian and post-Christian philosophy goes deeper than this formal structure of ascribing moral and social authority to university metaphysics. The content of Levinas's attempt to harmonize philosophy and theology is in keeping with the attempt of the early modern metaphysicians through Kant to keep secular knowledge within the orbit of what Levinas would call revelation and what I am suggesting would be more appropriately called Christian revelation or Christian theology. Let us turn to one aspect of this historical objective that is particularly relevant for understanding the meaning of Levinas's philosophy in general and his transformation of Rosenzweig in particular.

According to Sparn and Hunter, the metaphysics of both Leibniz and Kant should be understood as a transformation, indeed a generalization, of Luther's metaphysical view of Christ's two natures.[39] Summing up Kant's employment of Luther's metaphysical doctrine, Hunter writes: "In fact Kant superimposes the Christological doctrine of Christ's divine and human natures onto the metaphysical doctrine of man's noumenal and phenomenal natures, thereby conceiving of moral renewal as a kind of secular spiritual rebirth taking place via philosophy within the person."[40] In this context, I'd like to suggest that Levinas's use of Christological terms, such as *incarnation*, is not insignificant. Hunter's description of the

Kantian project as attempting a "moral renewal as a kind of secular spiritual rebirth taking place via philosophy within the person" could equally apply to the role that "incarnation" plays in Levinas's philosophy. Incarnation, for Levinas, is the way in which I am for the other. As the ethical relation, incarnation also fuses the human with the divine. The trace of the other is divine, and the only meaning the divine trace can have, for Levinas, is an ethical meaning. In this important sense, ethics, Levinas's main theme, is the fusing of divine and human nature. Incarnation is my spiritual rebirth, but this rebirth is at one and the same time secular in that it can and does concern only human relations. For Levinas, as for Kant, philosophy is the mediating force that affects this spiritual change.

Levinas might reply that it is actually the other person and not philosophy that affects this change within me. But this reply would only beg the question of why Levinas finds the highly technical, metaphysical, and indeed philosophical language of phenomenology necessary for describing the ethical relation. And why does Levinas, in his confessional writings, also insist upon recourse to philosophical points and arguments in attempting to articulate the true meaning of the Talmud? We need but mention Levinas's own dictum, taken not from his philosophical writings but from his confessional writings: "Philosophy derives [*dérive*] from religion. It is made necessary by religion adrift [*en dérive*], and in all likelihood religion is always adrift."[41] Or, as Levinas puts it in an interview, "Despite the end of Eurocentrism, disqualified by so many horrors, I believe in the eminence of the human face expressed in Greek Letters and in our own, which owe the Greeks everything. It is thanks to them that our history makes us ashamed."[42] There can be no question that Levinas ascribes to the philosophical, indeed metaphysical enterprise the very prestige and even more so the *social* importance assigned to it by the university metaphysicians in the early modern German university. And while many subsequent histories of the modern metaphysical tradition, as well as many subsequent philosophies premised on these histories, continue to deny the religious claims of modern European philosophy, the continuity of Levinas's thought with this tradition can help us to rethink the reception of this history as well. Indeed, we might say that Levinas's very attempt to return philosophy to its ethical origins is a return to the origins of modern metaphysics itself.

Conclusion: Philosophy Between Judaism and Christianity

As I mentioned at the beginning of this paper, the reading I have offered of Levinas complicates two mainstays of contemporary Levinas interpretation: one that sees Levinas as a distinctively Jewish thinker and one that sees Levinas as a distinctly secular thinker. I have not suggested that Levinas is a German metaphysician, nor have I suggested that he is a Christian theologian. Rather, my claim has been that Levinas's philosophy remains *between* these two forms of thought. On the one hand, Levinas rejects some of the basic tenants of the German metaphysical tradition, such as its devotion to reason and the individual rights that ensue from the purported equality of all human beings. Yet on the other hand, Levinas shares in the German metaphysical tradition's attempt to use philosophy for social, indeed, in Levinas's vocabulary, *messianic* purposes and to subsume, philosophically, basic Christian theological concepts for the purposes of so doing. At the same time, while Levinas is not a Christian theologian, he does implicitly claim, like many of his Christian predecessors, that, to use Strauss's terms, philosophy is "an integral part of the officially recognized and even required training of the student of the sacred doctrine." It is for these reasons that I have claimed that Levinas is *between* German metaphysics and Christian theology.

But to leave the matter at this is perhaps to raise as many questions as it is to answer any. Just what does it mean to characterize a thinker as "Jewish" or "Christian" or anything else? Is this a philosophical question or is it a historical one? I mentioned at the end of the first section that, from Levinas's perspective, neither the historical record of the development of his own thought nor the answer to the question of what Rosenzweig himself was really up to would change what he claims is the philosophical significance of Rosenzweig's claims about revelation. So too, from Levinas's perspective, neither the historical record of the development of his thought in relation to German metaphysical tradition nor an answer to the question of how Judaism has historically understood the relation between philosophy and law would change what he claims is the philosophical significance of Judaism. Yet Levinas's answer would only beg the question of whether his philosophy is not better understood as an attempt to make religious claims for philosophy (which is what Hunter and others have suggested is the innovation in the rise and historical triumph of German metaphysics) than as a return to Judaism.

As a tentative attempt to get beyond this impasse, I would suggest that while historical accuracy may not be the sufficient condition for philosophical truth, it is nevertheless a necessary condition. In other words, a philosophical claim has to at least cohere with the historical record. In this sense, Levinas's philosophical description of Judaism does not cohere with classical Judaism, which, as Strauss rightly argues, understands revelation primarily (though not exclusively) in terms of law and not philosophy or theology. In making his messianic claims for philosophy, does

Levinas really mean to understand, as Kant did with Plato, the Talmud and, indeed, the Hebrew Bible better than they understand themselves?

On this issue, Levinas could perhaps take a cue from Rosenzweig, who claimed not to articulate the original meaning of the timeless, philosophical truths of both philosophy and Judaism but to consider how *modern* Jews, in fact, modern people, might reorient themselves toward revelation through a *negotiation* with the past.[43] For Rosenzweig, this reorientation institutes a "new thinking" that is marked first by contemporary awareness not of our timeless relation to the past but of our distance from the past.[44] Perhaps Levinas would want to suggest that in the modern era, that is, in an era in which Jewish communities and individual Jewish people are not constituted first and foremost by a legal system (which is also an era in which the Christian community, in its various forms, has also lost its historical constitutions), *philosophy* provides the door into a lost world, not to regain its original meaning but to create *new* meaning. An acknowledgment of historical change would thus constitute a philosophical opportunity to ask what is perhaps the most basic of philosophical questions: What is the meaning and scope of philosophy? In an important sense, this is Levinas's very question. Yet, as I have suggested, his answer that philosophy is ethics begs the question of the role of philosophy, at least as it relates to Judaism, in bettering, if not saving society. In asking this basic philosophical question about the meaning of philosophy as it relates to the sacred doctrine of Judaism, Levinas would also be between Jewish philosophy and Christian theology, for, as we have seen in our all too brief discussion of the work of Hunter and others, the role of philosophy and its relation to sacred doctrine has historically been and perhaps ought to remain at the very heart of debates about what it means to be a Christian.

The Disincarnation of the Word

The Trace of God in Reading Scripture

ROBERT GIBBS

Philosophy and *theology* are not only terms that are open to renegotiation in each generation, they are also terms that fit different religious communities differently. Levinas was never a theologian, but that means something quite different from saying that Kant was never a theologian (although Hegel was) or that Frege was never a theologian. It means something quite different from asking what theology continued to mean for Heidegger throughout his philosophical thinking. For Jewish thought is not oriented by the specific opposition between theology and philosophy that one can surely find in Augustine and cannot quite escape today. Indeed, I would add that both terms, therefore, are inflected by the theological community in which they are used. There is no philosophy per se, only Jewish philosophy, Protestant philosophy, neo-pagan philosophy, and of course, Catholic philosophy. Philosophy is not-yet universal, and so it bears within it an index of the way that thinking about God and metaphysics and about ethics and community transpires in the different communities in which it occurs. In that sense, Levinas is a Jewish philosopher—his thought bears many indices of its Jewish soul.

Whether there is anything called theology per se is even less likely, and less likely to have any claimants, except for the most rigorous dogmatic theologians. For each of them, there is only one proper way to think about God, and their communion knows or aspires best to that way. But if our task is to reconstruct, to imagine, or even to discipline how a Jewish philosopher can contribute to Christian theology, we must see that Levinas cannot view the discourse about God in the way that the Christian theologians do, nor do his protests against seeing himself either as a theologian or even as a Jewish philosopher mean what they might for Jean-Luc Marion or Heidegger. Later, I will return to this indexicality of our disciplines, and indeed, to the question of how the singularities of intellectual traditions interact with one another. But if we will end up with a question about how to read scripture, that is, how a Jewish reading of scripture might be of value for a Christian theological reading of scripture, part of what we will need to see is not only that the term *theological* is ambiguous but that of signal interest in reading scripture is attention to the indexicality of the community and its tradition of reading.

But long before we can ascend to the complex question of how a translation from Jewish to Christian readings of scripture can occur, we will first have to explore the relation of Jewish scriptural hermeneutics to Levinas's philosophy, and before that, we must set forth a basic account of that philosophy, indeed, see there a specific intervention against Christian theology. Levinas takes his distance from one of the central doctrines of Christianity: incarnation. Indeed, despite what you may find in some of the secondary literature, Levinas does not view the other person, particularly his face, as an incarnation of God or of the infinite. His account of the face portrays how it disrupts the reification that our judgments impose both on the other person and on God.

There, with the other's face, I would begin, except for a short word about my own practice. For some time, I have been devoted to commentary, and there is little that can explain disincarnation of the word better than asking you to join my performance by reading along with me. I will attempt to free these words from the page before you, to let Levinas's saying readdress in my commentary upon those words.

1. The Face and Disincarnation

I will begin with a great text from *Totality and Infinity*. I will cite it at length, then comment upon it by re-reading. The numbering is my own addition; the translation, like all those in this essay, is my own, though occasionally adapted from Lingis's.

> [1.1] Ethics is the spiritual optics. [1.2] The subject-object relation does not reflect it; in the impersonal relation that it leads to, the invisible but personal God is not approached outside of all human presence. [1.3] The Ideal is not merely a being superlatively being, a sublimation of the objective, or, in lovers' solitude, a sublimation

of a You. [1.4] It requires the work of justice—the uprightness of the face to face—in order to produce the breach that leads to God— and "vision" here coincides with this work of justice. [1.5] Hence metaphysics is performed where the social relation is performed—in our relations with men. There can be no "knowledge" of God separated from the relationship with men. [1.6] The other person is the place itself of metaphysical truth and is indispensable for my relation with God. He does not perform the role of mediator. [1.7] The other person is not the incarnation of God, but precisely by his face, in which he is disincarnate, the manifestation of the height in which God is revealed.[1]

The question is: Where do we find the spirit and spirituality?

[1.1] Ethics is the spiritual optics.

Levinas insists that all appearance of the spirit will be in ethical media—in the relations between people. Levinas's ethics is not one of self-perfection but only of interhuman relation. Hence there is spirituality in the relation neither to the natural order, to supernatural beings, nor to myself alone—but only in the relation to other people. Levinas does not deny that there is spirit, but asserts that its medium is ethics. As a result there is no access to a relation to God outside of ethics. A cognitive relation with an object will not lead to God.

[1.2] The subject-object relation does not reflect it; in the impersonal relation that it leads to, the invisible but personal God is not approached outside of all human presence.

Notice here, however, that God is both personal and invisible. For Levinas the face is a *visage*, something to do with *vision* (visible or encountered as seeing me). But God can be personal because God is invisible. What is visible is like an object of my intentionality. Here already is a critique of a theology of incarnation—God is visible neither in the stone statue in the Temple nor in the visible face of a human being. And God is still personal. The relation that leads to God is through the human. We see the spirit through the human; through the neighbor, and never without a human being.

The modes of access are, surprisingly, not objective but, surprisingly, neither are they ontological or even dialogic.

[1.3] The Ideal is not merely a being superlatively being, a sublimation of the objective, or, in lovers' solitude, a sublimation of a You.

Levinas rejects a move that would see sublimation as a way to the spirit. The dismissal of the ideal as a mode of being recognizes that God must transcend entities and even their way of being (in the substantive sense of being and the Heideggerean verbal sense). One does not ascend to God through the orders of being. But more striking here is the refusal of Buber's Eternal You. Indeed, by focusing on lovers' solitude and the intimacy of the relation to a *Toi*, Levinas limits Buber's I-you dialogue to a relation of withdrawal from the world. The disqualification of God from the role of a private, intimate relation with a "you" points back to a distinctive sense of ethics.

[1.4] It requires the work of justice—the uprightness of the face to face—in order to produce the breach that leads to God—and "vision" here coincides with this work of justice.

Access to the spiritual is through the work of justice: not a private intimacy with God and not an ascent to the highest mode of being, but spirit at work in the world. God will be found through doing justice (an interesting echo of Jeremiah 9:23). But that relation itself requires a kind of directness, an uprightness [*droiture*] of the face to face. And what we see in this face to face is a breach opening, a gap between God and myself, between God and human beings, between God and the world. Unlike a smooth motion that sublimates from being or from a "you," the work of justice presupposes an absolute, a God who is invisible and separated from the world. The face to face of another person holds things apart, is spiritual because it produces the breach between God and me. "To see God" is to work justice in a world that dwells separated from God—and only in working justice can we have access to the spiritual realm.

[1.5] Hence metaphysics is performed where the social relation is performed—in our relations with men. There can be no 'knowledge' of God separated from the relationship with men.

Metaphysics is the spiritual, exceeding the objectivity of the physical and the visible. It is performed, or played out, only in relations between people. The claim is that metaphysical knowledge depends not on *knowledge* of human beings but rather on relationship—in playing out the work of justice. Here knowledge is bound to ethics—and knowledge of God most of all has its dignity through working justice amongst men. Hence *Autrui*, the other person, steps forward here.

[1.6] The other person is the place itself of metaphysical truth and is indispensable for my relation with God. He does not perform the role of mediator.

The other, not as the sheer metaphysical other of alterity [*Autre*], now yields to the otherness of another person—who is where we find metaphysical truth. That is, while ethics is an optics for the spiritual, the truth that we seek there is found only in another person. To come into relation with God requires an other person. Relations with others are indispensable for more than access. We cannot have relations with God without other people. But the other is not the one who allows us to relate to God, thus becoming merely a means of access. The relation with God is not mediated through the other—as though the two final terms of the relation were simply God and me. Rather, the relation with the other person is itself primary—indispensable. He is not merely the medium for gaining access to God but is constitutive of the relation to God. The ethical relation is a relation of difference that allows two different things to remain different.

[1.7] The other person is not the incarnation of God, but precisely by his face, in which he is disincarnate, the manifestation of the height in which God is revealed.

We must consider just what Levinas is rejecting here and, moreover, what the positive value on disincarnation contributes. For whatever reason, readers tend to see the infinite relation with the other as one in which God becomes incarnate in the other's face—not a mere image, but a dwelling or presence of God. Levinas rejects this emphatically because he finds that the other person becomes disincarnate, loses his sheer immanence in facing me, becomes something other than the dwelling of God within human form. What happens here is the production of that very breach—the other person breaks apart the realm of vision and material immanence, the realm of the objective, then also the realm of ontology, and then even the intimacy of a "you"—instead, otherness breaks apart the horizon of incarnality, the world of embodiment. The radical transcendence of God exceeds incarnation and is made manifest in the face of the other person—a facing where my cognition of the other person is exceeded and called into question.

The theology advanced in this first text then places a premium requirement on ethics as a mode of access to relation with God—as relations that cannot be incarnated but in fact require a rupture of the incarnate order. God does not become human, and neither my neighbor nor Jesus can be God incarnate. Rather, the infinity of responsibility opens up by absolutizing the difference between me and the other person, and thence of me and God. The neighbor or, again, the Son does not mediate this absolute difference—rather, the other person is where the difference opens up.

Justice requires the impossibility of overcoming this breach. Levinas regards all efforts to ascend or to close the gap, whether through Platonic participation or a doctrine of incarnation, as fundamentally reducing ethics and as a result reducing God.

2. The Infinite and the Other

If disincarnation of the other person opens up the gap that allows a relation with a transcendent God, a relation that is ethics, then the metaphysics we are thinking about here is a specific mode of infinity. Again, incarnating the infinite, bearing the divine within the human, is not an option for Levinas. Instead, we have a relation of otherness that does not negate or violate the one whom it addresses. There are numerous texts that address the infinite in the book bearing the infinite in its title. Let us look at one from the section entitled "Ethics and the Face."

> [2.1] The idea of the infinite, the overflowing of finite thought by its content, carries out the relation of thought with what exceeds its capacity, with what in each moment it learns it is not shocked.[2]

The infinite is an idea that overflows our capacities to think. The spontaneity and agency of intentionality, of thinking, is put in check because something occurs to me that I cannot grasp. The idea of the infinite calls my grasping into question, but it also allows me to learn. Totality presumes the dyad *take or be taken*: that all knowing is a capture and assimilation, an overcoming of the otherness of the other. But the infinite exceeds me without shocking me or taking me; rather, it is a moment of learning that preserves the otherness of what is learned.

> [2.2] This is the situation we call welcoming the face. The idea of the infinite is produced in the *opposition* within discourse, within sociality.[3]

The infinite now appears as facing, as social interaction with another person. Conversation [*discours*] depends on opposing voices, on a relation that harbors difference and even disagreement. The idea of the infinite is produced in that situation. It is not a question of solitary meditation or self-imposed intellectual discipline but comes to me in welcoming the face.

> [2.3] The relation with the face, with the absolutely other other that I cannot contain, with the other in this sense [is] infinite, is nonetheless my Idea, a commerce.[4]

I enter into a relation that is infinite or even infinitizing. The absolute otherness of the other person cannot be contained. Such an "encounter," such a "radical experience" exceeds my ability to think or to grasp. The relation, as an idea that is more than I can conceive, as Anselm also says, is also an intercourse, a kind of dealing with another. The idea of the infinite is not a thought in my mind but a quality in a relation, a relation that is not possible from my powers. A relation to which I am summoned by the other in his welcome. My Idea *in* this intercourse.

[2.4] But the relation is maintained without violence—in peace with this absolute alterity. The "resistance" of the Other does not do violence to me, does not act negatively; it has a positive structure: ethical.[5]

To learn without shock is to be put in question but not to be assaulted. This is not the consuming fire but rather a dimension of peace in conversation. Levinas does not stipulate that we have purely peaceful discussions, that discourse be utterly free of violence, but only that in discourse the requirement of otherness and opposition includes a pacific dimension. There is a positive structure and not merely the dyad of take or be taken.

[2.5] The first revelation of the other, presupposed in all the other relations with him, does not consist in grasping him in his negative resistance and in circumventing him by ruse. I do not struggle with a faceless god, but I respond to his expression, to his revelation.[6]

And so we arrive at a strong claim: that revelation of the other is presupposed in all relations with another person. Prior to any of my efforts to control, manipulate, resist, grasp, or even murder the other person there is a revelation from him—a revelation that is not an incarnation of God but a revelation to me of the Idea of the infinite. Revelation here precedes my own maneuvering. It occurs in a social drama, when the other person addresses me, welcomes me, faces me. Because it is not the presence of an entity that is infinite but a relation with what exceeds my power to relate, it is not a moment of incarnation. The disincarnation of the other person opens the gap to God but also opens a gap in conversation. Her otherness exceeds me and leads me to a relation across a gap I cannot close. This is revelation, where my passivity, my inability to constitute the relation, allows me to learn without being absorbed. The distance is maintained from the other side: not a mediation, not an incarnation, but a relation that depends on the breaking apart, a separation between God and the world, produced in the radical separation between the other person and me, performed in a conversation, in the moment of address when the other person welcomes me, invokes me, calls me to speak.

The location of ethics as an intersubjective (and asymmetrical) space is one of discourse, of conversation, of address and response. But it is just here that a striking question for Levinas arises, one that is brought into focus by Blanchot at least as vividly as by Derrida: What about the written text? If the disincarnation of the other person opens up the relation to God, can a written text, where the other person is not present and therefore not facing me, not engaging me in the polarized space of conversation, also be a revelation? And if the objectivity of the other person is not itself what opens the gap, then what of the writtenness, the engraved or printed words? In Hebrew, language is *lashon*, "tongue," but the alphabet is called *gufen*—"body." A written text is embodied in an alphabet (or by ideograms). What is the status of the alphabet, of the embodied physical text itself?

3. The Infinite Meaning in the Text

Levinas engages in close reading of Talmudic texts in contexts at first quite removed from philosophy. Indeed, he reiterates within his published works the difference between theology and philosophy when he separates his philosophical from what he calls, adopting the French term, his *confessional* writings. I will not justify here my drawing together of these two sets of work, nor will I explore the internal as well as rhetorical reason for his choice to bifurcate his writings. I will only comment that it was Derrida who first and most regularly insisted on interfacing and interweaving the two sets of writings. In any case, the problem of the relation to God in a written text for Levinas is treated in works that are singularly Jewish but at the same time allow him to develop a theory of reading in general and of the revelatory possibilities of all great texts (perhaps simply of all written texts). Later I will briefly explore the possibility of generalizing from a Jewish reading to a more general reading or, perhaps at least for this volume, to a Christian reading.

Levinas is exploring a Talmudic comment upon a scriptural passage. The question is not how the comment works as a text but rather how it reads the scriptural passage. What is the relation of meaning to written text? Again we have language resembling the infinite.

> [3.1] The processes of reading that we have just seen at work suggest, at the outset, that the statement commented upon exceeds the intending to say whence it originates; that its ability to say goes beyond its intending to say, that it contains more than it contains; that

a surplus of meaning, perhaps inexhaustible, remains enclosed in the syntactic structures of the sentence, in its groups of words, in its actual words, phonemes, and letters, in all of that materiality of the saying, always virtually significant.[7]

The intended meaning [*vouloir-dire*] is an origin of a written word. The saying of the writer is exceeded by the ability to say [*pouvoir-dire*] of the statement. Hence we have an infinite structure: containing more than it contains. Indeed, the excess is inexhaustible. There is more and more meaning in the written text. The oddness of this passage for readers familiar with Levinas, I suspect, is not the excess of saying but rather that the written itself is viewed as *a saying* and not as *a said*. The said normally would seem to the content, the script, what could be written down or made explicit in a conversation. The saying is the place of opposition that opens the breach. Here Levinas asserts that there is a materiality of the saying (which is the written text). He explains that the syntax, the grouping of words, the words, including phonemes and letters, are an enclosure for infinite meaning. The body of the written text bears within it an excess of signification.

Here is a fascinating parallel with the mind thinking more than it can think. The mind cannot contain its own contents and so is called by the infinite toward the other person. The infinite does not devastate the mind but comes in a passive mode. But what is interesting about the written text bearing a surplus is that the excess also moves beyond the intention of the author. Intentionality is exceeded. The author's intention is surpassed by the meaning of the text, a saying that is infinite. All that is required is a reader—that is, the commentary itself solicits this excess. Another (even if the author later in the day) comes to read and finds more saying than the self intended.

[3.2] Exegesis would come to free, in these signs, a bewitched significance that smolders under the characters or that is coiled up in all this literature of letters.[8]

Hence exegesis gains a vital role. It frees the meaning that is bound to the written words. That meaning smolders, waiting for breath to ignite it again. Or it lies coiled like a snake in the very letters of literature, in its literariness. Here are images of meaning waiting to strike, waiting to break into flame. The issue is that exegesis does not disembody the text—does not draw from it the essential meaning, the proper meaning, the author's intended meaning. The text is not merely a casing for a fixed meaning. On the contrary, the text is fixed in order to bear multiple meanings. But the embodiment itself has to be broken out of, set on fire, etc. Exegesis infinitizes the embodied text. Exegesis is a mode of disincarnation of the word.

4.1 God and Letters

In a commentary from 1985, Levinas explores a passage from the Talmud, Sanhedrin 99a-b. This is a key passage and has been subjected even by Levinas to commentary on previous occasions. The Mishnah's question is: Who are the exceptions that among Israel have no share in the world to come? One answer is he who denies that the Torah is from heaven, denies that the text is divinely inspired. The Gemara digresses into questions about the attitude of those who study the Torah, and so this exclusion becomes one for not reading well. Levinas then inserts his own interest: Torah as the antithesis of idolatry. Idolatry would be a different way of reading or would be not to read at all. But the address to and from the text is a protection against idolatry.

> [4.1] To claim to be a Jew thus, from the teaching of a book, is before all to recognize oneself as a reader, which is to say, a student of Torah; it is to exclude oneself from idolatry by true reading or study. [4.2] Reading or study of a text that is protected from the eventual idolatry of that text itself, in renewing by an exegesis that cannot stop—and exegesis of that exegesis—the fixed letters and hearing there the breath of the living God. [4.3] Of a God certainly not incarnate, but somehow inscribed, living His life—or a part of His life—in the letters, in the lines and between the lines, and in the exchange of ideas between readers who comment on them, where these letters are animated and are renewed by the prescription of the book—commandment without enslaving, like truth—to respond to the neighbor in justice, which is to say, to love the other person.[9]

The relation between the Jew and the book does not depend on the mere object. To be a people of the book for the Jews is to read. Indeed. For Levinas, to be Jewish is to be such a reader. Jewish identity, for Levinas, is a matter of reading and reading in a specific manner. But to belong to Torah is to engage it, to solicit meaning, to read it.

> [4.1] To claim to be a Jew thus, from the teaching of a book, is before all to recognize oneself as reader, which is to say, student of Torah; it is to exclude oneself from idolatry by true reading or study.

Hence, idolatry is not merely prohibited by the book. Idolatry is avoided by *studying* the book. Study or true reading is a manner of thinking and behaving—and the Torah teaches us to avoid idolatry not merely as its content but by the performance of reading. Idolatry, in this sense, would not only extend to how we treat statues or objects in general. It would, per force, also be a way of relating to the *sefer Torah*, to the material book itself. Thus the material text must, as we saw above, contain more than it contains, must break open inexhaustible meaning.

[4.2] Reading or study of a text that is protected from the eventual idolatry of that text itself, in renewing by an exegesis that cannot stop—and exegesis of that exegesis—the fixed letters and hearing there the breath of the living God.

The destiny of the book is to become an idol. By renewing the text, exegesis prevents idolatry. The premise of exegesis is that it does not unearth the final meaning but that reading will continue. Indeed, to stop the exegesis would be to idolize a final interpretation. Hence, there must be not only anti-idolizing interpretation of the text but also an exegesis of the exegesis, preventing the most recent exegesis itself from becoming an idol. The overflowing of meaning itself overflows the vessels in which it is received. They too become fountains of meaning, not merely because there is always more there but because to not seek that more is to reduce first the scripture and then the tradition of interpretation to idols. There is an ethical need here to keep going.

And there is also a specific theology of the word: fixed letters and the breath of the living God. Again: fixed letters lest there be the idolatry of a fixed meaning. But what is this "breath of the living God"? Again the spirit appears in Levinas. Renewal of the text allows us to hear not God's word, but God's breath to receive inspiration. But not incarnation.

[4.3] Of a God certainly not incarnate, but somehow inscribed, living His life—or a part of His life—in the letters, in the lines and between the lines, and in the exchange of ideas between readers who comment on them, where these letters are animated and are renewed by the prescription of the book—commandment without enslaving, like truth—to respond to the neighbor in justice, which is to say, to love the other person.

No, not incarnated in the written word, but dwelling, inscribed. A part of God's life occurs in the written text. And the text is a written set of letters, letters on lines. This most material sense we ever get of God in

Levinas then yields to the animation and renewal of a process of exegesis. We have not only comments, as in a process of deciphering, but also exchange of ideas. There is never only one interpretation but a plurality of interpreters, and that plurality is constitutive of the work of exegesis. Moreover, it is not merely a community of interpreters; the renewal arises through the normativity of the text: the reading is directed to prescription, to ethics. And here we have a specific linking of the most familiar themes in Levinas to the part of God's life that occurs in the study of the text. The text renews by commanding without enslaving. Here is the metaphysics of our first quote: truth is an assignment, a commanding that enables, that capacitates me to respond—respond to the other person, to the neighbor. Meaning is found as the assignment of doing justice. Because the work of justice is an infinite responsibility, so, too, the text's renewals are inexhaustible, providing instruction through exchange with current readers and through the anti-idolizing reading of both the text and its tradition. God's living is the life of this renewal of instruction, of the commandments.

Here is a pneumatology at the expense of a view of the full revelation of the word. The word as a material text works to break open to new and renewing interpretations. The text is not an incarnation of God, but it is poised as a relation between the materiality of the text and a breath. Readers find instruction, but renewing and renewed instruction. Such reading prevents idolatry—which here would be the notion that God became fully present and determined in the text, or even in a previous exegesis. This tension between a fixed text and the spirit as a reading that reveals the command to respond to the other person is what I am claiming as disincarnation, in parallel with the first text.

But how can we relate to what is not merely only partially present, but is somehow so lacking in full presence/real presence? Here we must go to the philosophical interpretation of face and illeity. If you recall the argument that the face was not the sublimation of a you (a *Toi*), then it may be of interest to note that originally Levinas preferred to name the other person a *Vous*. But in his later thought, he developed the concept of *illeity*—a kind of thirdness that was even less intimate than the *vous*. Indeed, illeity as the otherness of the other person is not invocable, not suitable as an interlocutor. This abstracting, absolving motion from conversation into a more radical otherness is linked in Levinas's later thought with a theological claim about how God is not a *tu* but also not a *vous*, or not for long. Instead, God has passed by and is not present.

5. Trace of God

I turn to a text from the essay "Meaning and Sense."

> [5.1] The face is on its own visitation and transcendence. But the face, wholly open, because it is in the trace of illeity, may at the same time be in itself. Illeity is the origin of the alterity of being, which the *in itself* of objectivity both participates in and betrays.[10]

The face, as we have seen, is a confrontation, a visitation. It is an opening up to transcendence. There is, in the face, a trace of illeity. That otherness does not appear, is neither interlocutor nor object. But as the anarchic origin of alterity, illeity (like the infinite) also makes possible the realm of presence, of objectivity, of materiality. Illeity does not threaten or annihilate the objective order—it questions it. Indeed, it also invokes it and so makes possible the *in itself* of the face, the possibility for me to be for myself and not only for another. Were illeity a counter-force or a necessary cause of beings, it would act on a plane that could not tolerate or generate differences, indeed, differences that become objective. Illeity instigates a realm that is independent from it and as such is capable of betraying it. But this is then a theological dimension.

> [5.2] The God who passed is not the model of which the face would be the image. To be in the image of God does not mean to be an icon of God but to find oneself in His trace.[11]

This is, I believe, the most explicit statement Levinas makes about the supposed analogy of God and the other. The face is not the image of God. The other does not resemble God, and in a pique of iconoclasm, the face is not an icon. Perhaps here is the place to see the refusal of incarnation at its most polemic. Moreover, the God who passed is not the God incarnate, not the God who is present to us, in full and real presence. The other is no sign of God. But such an aniconic, disincarnate God is one in whose trace I find myself. Tracing is not a mode of presence or of signification. It is an absenting, a withdrawal. To find myself in this withdrawal of God is, indeed, to become assigned to the other and to run the risk of becoming a betrayal: the modern subject in itself. There is no resemblance with God, only this practice of withdrawal, commission, and response.

> [5.3] The revealed God of our Jewish-Christian spirituality keeps all the infinity of his absence, which is in the personal "order" itself. He shows himself only by his trace, as in Chapter 33 of Exodus.[12]

Instead, God keeps absent, for the infinite cannot be present. Revelation, following at least Schelling and Rosenzweig, and probably Heidegger and also Kabbalah, depends on an absence and precisely on keeping absence. God "appears" in the personal order as missing, as an absence. Not one, moreover, that can be reduced to the presence of absence, but an absence that remains absent in its presence, in its trace. The trace of God is not the promise of presenting what is absent in God but the opposite: the keeping absent of what is absent, the infinite as withdrawal. The trace, as illeity, is the sign only of withdrawal, not a sign of an absent being or principle. I reserve Exodus for a moment.

[5.4] To go toward him is not to follow this trace that is not a sign. It is to go toward the Others who stand in the trace of illeity.[13]

Hence, again we find ethics as the optics for spirituality. We follow after the withdrawn God, the one who has passed, not by addressing or acting in relation to God but by going toward other people. By responding to their needs. They, too, stand in the trace and do not resemble God. The other, as much as myself, does not look like God but instead is the one for whom I must respond. God is traced in the face, not imaged, but the trace commissions me to the other person.

It seems inevitable that we must at least once recall a scriptural text—and it is oddly fitting that it is one cited in a "philosophical" work. There are several key texts of Torah that govern Levinas's thought (consider Genesis 33:10, Jacob to Esau, for instance), yet for us today the trace of God as the revelation of a God who has passed is most challenging in Exodus 33:18–23:

And he said, "Please let me behold your glory."

And He said, "I will make all of my goodness pass before your face and I will proclaim the name of the NAME before you, and I will grant the grace that I will grant and show the compassion that I will show. But," He said, "you cannot see my face because man cannot see me and live."

And the NAME said, "Behold there is place with me. Station yourself on the rock. And when my glory passes, I will put you in a cleft in the rock and I will hide you with my hand until I have passed by. Then I will take back my hand and you will see my back, but my face is not seen."

Moses pleads for a vision of God, and God agrees to pass by Moses so that Moses may see, but Moses is not permitted to see the face of God. To see how complicated this is, we need only go back to verse 11, "the

NAME spoke to Moses, face to face, as when a man speaks with his neighbor." The prohibition on seeing God's face is often repeated in Torah, and it bears the most basic sense that the authority of God would be devastating for a human being. God, or so it seems, cannot appear to a person. But God does converse with Moses, and more importantly, there are various texts in which God does appear. It seems that Moses in this text is permitted to see the back, and that varies in the history of interpretation (my favorite is *the past and not the future*), but were Levinas to weigh in on just this, I doubt he could resist the link in Hebrew between my back [*achorai*] and my other [*acheri*]. Indeed, one might translate the last line as "see my illeity, but not my face."

But perhaps more interesting for our purpose is the procedure for not seeing God's face. To not see the face requires an intricate hiding. Moses is to be inserted into the rock, indeed, inscribed, in a bored-out hole or cleft. In the context of these chapters, it is hard not to think about the carving of the tablets and the inscriptions on the tablets. Moses has a hiding place, and God's hand covers him there. To not see God is to see the hand (not the face), and when the hand is removed, the back is revealed. I need hardly tell you that these anthropomorphic terms are among the most interpreted in Jewish tradition, but Levinas is gesturing here to the possibility of the human being hidden in order to make revelation possible. What we see, after the work of hiding us, is only the God who has passed by. Only the trace in which we stand, the cleft carved from the rock. We are inserted into the word, or perhaps are the word that God writes (with his finger?), occluded from the revelation. We are not incarnate words but the place where disincarnation allows the gap for response to occur. We find ourselves standing in the trace of the back/illeity.

6. The Disincarnation of the Word

Among all words, the name of God, which I have just translated as the NAME, is clearly an exceptional one. In Hebrew it seems to point out the tension between writing and speaking, because although it is written, it is not pronounced. Indeed, it is a capital offense to pronounce the name! When we look at the process of renewing and hearing the breath of this name, we see that it breaks apart the bondage of word to material inscription. Levinas looks at a set of quite difficult texts about the name, and I will limit myself to a paragraph—but I must recall that vast ranges of Jewish tradition are devoted to the NAME and to the problems of writing and reading that name.

[6.1] The name Adonai—which in its turn must not be pronounced in vain—is the name of the Tetragrammaton. The name has a name.[14]

Even the euphemism (*Adonai*) is not to be used in vain. It means "my Lord," but it is used precisely as a euphemism, a nickname, and so the NAME has a name, a word we use to refer to the name that cannot be uttered. Traditional Jews often name this name *haShem*, the name. The Tetragrammaton, *yud heh vav heh*, needs a name, and "my Lord" works, but it seems that we need to utter something about the way that names work, particularly proper names.

[6.2] The name shows itself and conceals itself. Whatever comes in the context of meaning must always also be an anchorite and a holiness; the voice that resounds in speech must also be the voice that fades and that falls silent. The proper name may have this modality.[15]

But the written name does not "work" like a normal word. As a name it must both conceal and reveal at the same time. Levinas beautifully evokes both the anchorite, the person who withdraws, and the voice that falls silent. What appears requires a withdrawing—and so meaning is surrounded by a hiddenness, permeated by the tracing, which is not a sign of what is absent but only the residue of withdrawal. A proper name can indeed work this way—not leading to the one we call by name but also leading to absence, the withdrawal of that person. We use a name because the person is not fully present. The name we use invokes absence—it reflects the disincarnation that happens in facing the other person.

[6.3] It is the name that "sticks" to that which it names, totally otherwise than the common name, clarified by the system of language, that designates a species but does not stick to the individual and reunites him, if one may say, in indifference.[16]

Levinas contrasts the proper name with the common one. And here the philosophy of language gets a specific twist. For the common noun is the focus of most of our thinking about language. And what is most characteristic of names is the way that the singularity of the named stands in one of two very different relationships to the name. The proper name seems bound to the singularity of what is named, while the common noun has a kind of indifference to the particular entity to which it refers. This indifference in reference characterizes objectivity and the conceivability of reality. What does it mean for a name to somehow stick to its referent if not that it indicates the trace itself, the absence, the incompleteness of the naming to the named? But this is not merely the replacement of a species with a particular (which leaves aside the detritus of accidents), rather, this is the invocation of another in his otherness, the awareness of a nonsignifying withdrawal, of the hidden in the revealed. To call by name, to call to another, is also to invoke the absence we saw above, which keeps its absence.

> [6.4] But the proper name, near to the named, lacks a logical con-
> nection with it and as a result, despite this nearness, is an empty
> shell like a permanent revocation of what it evokes, a disincarnation
> of what is incarnated by it.[17]

And so a proper name, like the face and indeed like the reading of a text, performs a disincarnation. The name both calls into presence and, because it has no logical link to the named person, also absolves the other—or perhaps better, revokes (unvoices like Levinas's unsaying) the name itself. The name both becomes incarnate and then disincarnates. This is a logic of vocation. The name is a word that stands as a kind of incarnation, signifying the other person, but it also must revoke that signification, must become a trace.

> [6.5] By the prohibition of being uttered, it is held in this interval:
> Tetragrammaton that is never pronounced the way it is written.[18]

The Tetragrammaton is held not between a common and a proper noun but rather between incarnation and disincarnation. How? Somehow the tension between inscription and euphemism represents both incarnation and disincarnation—with a strong beat on the latter. That it is written means that the materiality of the characters stands on the side of embodiment, but that we cannot "trust," cannot grasp that written form as the proper name but must disrupt its very materiality with a different pronunciation disincarnates. Indeed, it challenges the possibility for written language to stand as a secure manifestation of what it names. To prohibit the utterance of the written name is to disincarnate the written text—and to submit all writing to a specific questioning. If the NAME disrupts the incarnation of the written word, the securing of the written in the oral, then a proper name also disincarnates the incarnation of invocation, leaving us in the trace of the other person and not with a grasp on him in his presence. Thus all words undergo a specific series of disincarnations through this structure of proper names and writing. The written text depending on the writing of the name of God disincarnates the word—and the word of God most of all.

7. Translation

I have promises still to keep. Obviously the theory of language, of spirit, and of ethics, and even the philosophical theology I have developed here is in sharp engagement with Christian theology. If someone responded that everything I have said makes perfect sense to Christian theologians, I would be happy but surprised. After all, to have chosen my title was to be at least a little provocative, maybe a little unorthodox. But if there is some sense that Christian theology might reappropriate these reflections, might hear a call that suits it, there is a different question of why Jewish philosophy should offer this call. I leave it to others to judge how to hear this call as Christians, but my penultimate reflections offer a justification for making the effort to offer Jewish philosophy to Christian theology.

The problem, in part, is how to interpret the embodiment and singularity of the Jewish textual tradition. The standard logic has opposed Jewish particularity to the universal truth of philosophy (and often enough of Christianity). Levinas does not accept the terms of this opposition. Just as the relation of a proper name to the person invoked is different from the indifference of a common noun to any singular referent, so Judaism has a singularity that need not be a matter of indifference, nor a matter of hostility. But can it also offer something to an other that is not a sublimation into a totality?

Translation moves from one singularity to another singularity. There is no language so disembodied, so eternal, that it escapes utterly from its singularity. Similarly, there is no philosophy that also escapes utterly. But translation is not simply dwelling in one's own singularity, but is disincarnating that in the hope of being heard in another singularity. Levinas often reflects on translation, most of all on that between Hebrew and Greek, where Greek is a specific mode of philosophy and Hebrew is the reading of Jewish texts. The university (and not the yeshiva or the madrasa) speak Greek (even in French—or English!).

But what happens to Jewish singularity in the university?

[7.1] In the singularity of Israel a peak is reached that justifies the very perenniality of Judaism. It is not a permanent relapse into an out-of-date provincialism.[19]

Israel here is a mode of nonconformity, of withdrawing into ourselves, rather than a political situation. But singularity, living and thinking and speaking differently (Hebrew), is not merely being out of step with the times. It is not a romanticism of identity politics. The persistence of Judaism arises in relation to this singularity, which we might well describe as the reading of scripture, as this way of standing in the trace by reading.

[7.2] But a singularity that the long history from which we are just coming out has left in a condition of feeling and faith. It needs to be made clear for thought. It cannot furnish rules for education right away.[20]

But the twentieth century and the whole romance of modernity have left Jews with a clearer feeling, and at times a clearer faith in Jewish singularity. It has razed not only the culture of Eastern Europe but also the intellectual traditions of Jewish studies—both of the university and in the community. Writing in 1980, Levinas issues a call for a new thinking about singularity within the Jewish community. That strong feeling needs to be clarified in thought.

[7.3] It still needs to be translated into that Greek that, thanks to assimilation, we have learned in the West. We have the great task of expressing in Greek the principles that Greece did not know. Jewish singularity waits for its philosophy.[21]

If ever there were a mandate for my work, and indeed, for my colleagues in Jewish philosophy, this would be it. Because we are Western, raised in modern assimilated Judaism, we have learned to think Greek. But there are principles that were not accessible to Greeks, to philosophy so far. And the principles of Greek philosophy are not adequate to grasp the ethical and metaphysical truth of singularity—again, specifically the singularity of a way of reading. A singularity that persists in attention to the materiality of texts and to the disincarnation of the word in the call to justice. That singularity requires a new philosophy.

[7.4] Servile imitation of European models is no longer enough. Research for references to universality in our scriptures and in the texts of the oral law reinstitute the process of assimilation again.[22]

But such a philosophy is not merely an application of the methodologies of the humanities in order to discern where in our texts there is a call for universality and where there are moments of effacement of singularity, where the singular can be treated as common and thus with indifference. Such a universality only reapplies the assimilation of modernity again. It will not offer the West anything that the West does not have already. This would not be a translation that offered a new way of thinking singularity—a new insight into the ethics that arises in reading.

[7.5] These texts, through their two thousand years of commentaries, still have something else to say.[23]

Thus, Levinas concludes that there is something new to be heard here. Philosophy can learn a new logic of reading, a way of seeing the trace of God in scripture, or at least of attending to the responsibility for the other. But we are then thrown back on the original question: the relation of philosophy and theology. For clearly what Levinas hopes the singularity of Jewish reading can offer the West is also offered to Christian theology. Offered, again, without reducing the singularity to an instance of an indifferent generality. Offered from one singularity to another. The costs for Christian theology are exorbitant: a focus on disincarnation, a trace replacing full presence, a recognition that Christianity is singular and not the totality, a heightened attention to scripture and commentary as traces of God—with a plurality of voices and acknowledgment that there is no final interpretation—an infinite that is social and not held in the mind, and a radical ethics of responsibility for others. How Christian theologians will hear this is a great concern—not just in the present context but for the Church.

As a final thought, I would like to emphasize what has occurred in this essay. I have staked out a position that is singular and attempted to frame a conversation that retains opposition. Any hope for standing in the trace of God today depends on maintaining singularities and not confusing the logic of totality and indifference for one of the infinite. Reading texts, attending to their embodiment and freeing the spirit in them without overcoming their materiality—this is the path of a philosophy that tries to attend and respond to singularity. Such reading is neither a consolidation of truth and closing of the question nor a disembodiment that seeks angelic insight. It opens a conversation through the materiality of the texts I have offered for commentary.

Secrecy, Modesty, and the Feminine Kabbalistic Traces in the Thought of Levinas

ELLIOT R. WOLFSON

Various scholars have discussed the possible affinities between Levinas and kabbalistic tradition,[1] despite his unambiguous critique of mysticism on the grounds that the experience of union it presumes effaces the transcendence beyond ontology[2] that grounds the radical difference between human and divine, the basis for the alterity that serves as the foundation for the ethical responsibility that one must bear for the other.[3] The focus of the scholarly discussion has been on certain key terms and ideas, largely drawn from the teachings transmitted in the name of the sixteenth-century master Isaac Luria, to wit, the notion of withdrawal of the infinite (*şimşum*) and the trace (*reshimu*) of light left behind in the primordial space (*ţehiru*) as a consequence of that withdrawal, the task of rectification (*tiqqun*) that ensues from the diminution of the contracted light, the emphasis on secrecy, and the utilization of gender to account for the metaphysical principles of being.

To date, the most extensive and affirmative treatment of Levinas and kabbalah has been proffered by Oona Ajzenstat. I am doubtful of many of Ajzenstat's claims due to her questionable views about both the prophetic kabbalah of Abraham Abulafia and the theosophic kabbalah of Isaac Luria—she is hampered, unfortunately, by her dependence on secondary sources—but I am nevertheless persuaded by her surmise that Levinas was guided by the esoteric nature of kabbalah "to occult the kabbalistic images in his own text and to protect them under a layer of antimystical argument."[4] In my judgment, this is a keen insight, and my own engagement with Levinas has led me to a similar conclusion regarding the need to posit an esoteric use of Jewish esotericism on his part, even though I will nuance the argument in a different way. As I will propose in this study, the antitheosophic interpretation of kabbalah proffered by Levinas accords with his polemical depiction of Christianity as a form of idolatry.

The influence of kabbalah on Levinas, it may be presumed, can be explained primarily, if not exclusively, by his study of and admiration for the compilation of eighteenth-century ritual piety, *Nefesh ha-Ḥayyim*, written by Ḥayyim of Volozhyn, the disciple of Elijah ben Solomon, the imposing Lithuanian rabbinic authority better known as the Gaon of Vilna.[5] Levinas maintained, dubiously in my opinion, that in this treatise Ḥayyim of Volozhyn rejected mysticism or at least the mystical impulse "in its Hasidic excesses."[6] Predictably, therefore, the focus of scholarly attention, following the assessment of Levinas himself, has been on the ethical implications of R. Ḥayyim's treatise, the "spiritual meaning" as opposed to the "outdated cosmology,"[7] that is, the demand imposed on the human to strive to be divine—indeed to be united with the divine—not through theosophic gnosis but through action that is for the sake of the other, on the way to drawing near God, drawing near by turning toward as opposed to becoming one with the transcendent—for the spiritual ideal of *devequt* embraced by R. Ḥayyim, based on earlier sources, especially zoharic literature, entails that the human agent is conjoined with and hence juxtaposed to the divine person.[8]

Levinas's attempt to adduce a universal ethical principle on the basis of the pietism enunciated in *Nefesh ha-Ḥayyim* should be seen as part of his larger project to demonstrate (perhaps in response to the dichotomy proposed by Lev Shestov[9]) that Athens and Jerusalem are not to be set in binary opposition, that philosophical concepts are implicit in rabbinic texts, and that talmudic discourse betrays a speculative mode of argumentation.[10] As Levinas puts it in one context, "If the Talmud is not philosophy, its tractates are an eminent source of those experiences from which philosophies derive their nourishment."[11] The paradigm, therefore, is that of the "Western Jew," the Jewgreek or Greekjew,[12] prophetic and contemplative, midrashic and speculative, equally adept in textual exegesis and deductive reasoning. Predictably, Levinas relates the "synthesis of the Jewish revelation and Greek thought" that he embraces to the religious philosophy of Maimonides.[13] It seems to me, however, that Levinas articulates something fundamentally different from his medieval predecessor. According to Maimonides, philosophic truths have been scattered in rabbinic dicta, and it is therefore possible for one to adduce these truths exegetically by applying them eisegetically to relevant texts. By contrast, according to Levinas, it is not simply a matter of discerning philosophical content encoded in talmudic passages, whether halakhic or aggadic, but a matter of recognizing that talmudic argumentation accords with the way of philosophy, and that the goal shared by both is the enunciation of an ethical truth that is truly universal and hence singularly "applies to every reasonable being."[14]

Anyone remotely familiar with Levinas knows well that his talmudic readings advocate for the particularism of the Jewish tradition, expressed especially in its ritual laws, but without compromising its universalism. According to Levinas, the "absolutely universal," which constitutes the essence of spiritual life, albeit an essence that is essentially inessential, "can be served in purity only through the particularity of each people, a particularity named enrootedness."[15] The contribution of rabbinical Judaism, which Levinas refers to as the "primordial event in Hebraic spirituality,"[16] is the consciousness of a "universalist singularity," a universalism that is predicated on the principle that "to be with the nations is also to be for the nations."[17] As he puts it elsewhere: "That is our universalism. In the cave that represents the resting-place of the patriarchs and our mothers, the Talmud also lays Adam and Eve to rest: it is for the whole of humanity that Judaism came into the world."[18]

From a number of comments in his *oeuvre*, we may deduce, moreover, that Levinas's repeated emphasis on the compatibility of the particular and universal is a response to the age-old polemical charge of Christianity against Judaism, the pitting of the catholic in opposition to the provincial, a bias that assumed a particularly poisonous and perilous effect in light of the neo-pagan framing displayed in Nazi rhetoric and conduct.[19] Thus, in many of his lectures and essays, Levinas insists that it is the particularism of Judaism that promotes the universal idea of one humanity and the ensuing ethical obligation to bear infinite responsibility for the other. Tackling the notion of Israel's election, one of Jewish civilization's most vexing ideas, Levinas insists that chosenness is not a "scandal of pride and of the will to power" but a "moral conscience itself which, made up of responsibilities that are always urgent and non-transferable, is the first to respond."[20] The "particularism" of Judaism "conditions universality," writes Levinas, as "it is a moral category rather than a historical fact to do with Israel, even if the historical Israel has in fact been faithful to the concept of Israel and, on the subject of morality, felt responsibilities and obligations which it demands from no one, but which sustain the world."[21] The destiny of Israel, therefore, is not determined by conflict with the other but rather by contrast to the other, standing in a distinctive role vis-à-vis the other. In the brief essay "The Spinoza Case," Levinas addresses this point passionately:

> Israel is not defined by opposition to Christianity, any more than it is defined as anti-Buddhism, anti-Islam, or anti-Brahminism. Instead, it consists in promoting understanding between all men who are tied to morality. It seeks their understanding, in the first instance, with Christians and Muslims, who are its neighbors or companions in civilization. But the base of this civilization is the Reason that the Greek philosophers revealed to the world. We are completely convinced that, in an autonomous and even more glorious way, the Mosaism prolonged and interpreted by rabbinism led Israel there; we are completely convinced that we still have more chance of finding an unsullied rationalism in Plato and in Aristotle than in Spinoza.[22]

In "Religion and Tolerance," Levinas goes so far as to say that "the idea of Israel as a chosen people, which seems to contradict the idea of universality, is in reality the founding of tolerance." The sense of being chosen "expresses less the pride of someone who has been called than the humility of someone who serves. Being chosen is no more appalling as a condition than being the place for all moral consciousness." In the case of Judaism, "the certainty of the absolute's hold over man—or religion—does not turn into an imperialist expansion that devours all those who deny it. It burns *inwards*, as an infinite demand made on oneself, an infinite responsibility." Levinas concludes, therefore, that Judaism is responsible for the "rehabilitation of tolerance in Christian and Islamic thought, and has brought such a message to the whole of the modern world."[23]

Although both Christianity and Islam—"neighbors" or "companions" of Judaism in civilization—are implicated by Levinas, and the latter is especially relevant to comments that he made frequently about Zionism and the modern state of Israel, many of the remarks concerning the universalism and/or ritual formalism of Judaism are meant as responses to the longstanding Christian critique of a presumed Jewish parochialism and ceremonialism.[24] In one context, for instance, he notes, continuing on the path set by Rosenzweig but also diverging from him by subsuming the theological under the stamp of the ethical,[25] that Israel, the "people of the book," are also the "people of the continued revelation," in order to lay aside the charge that "rabbinic hermeneutics is rashly considered as neglecting the spirit."[26] Levinas does not mention Christianity by name, but I think it reasonable to surmise that he is responding to the stock charge of Christians against the Pharisaic/Rabbinic orientation that privileged the letter to the detriment of the spirit. Levinas, expectedly, counters that text study and ritual performance are occasions to experience revelation anew. The revelatory moment—for Levinas, as for Rosenzweig,[27] the spiritual texture of revelation arises from and gives rise to an "essential moment,"[28] the instant, the blink-of-the-eye (*Augenblick*),[29] which escapes the temporalized ontology of the specious present[30] presumed by a spatialized conception of time,[31] the temporality of the saying that is genuinely open to the transcendence of the other beyond the ontological difference of sayer and said, the subject/object dichotomy of Western metaphysics, the alterity that accounts for the chronic discontinuity of time[32]—cannot be isolated from what may be called the compulsion of the universal demand to do justice.[33] The transcendent meaning that breaks through the text is discerned in the ethical task par excellence,[34] the "order that orders me to the other . . . through the trace of its reclusion, as a face of a neighbor."[35]

En passant, I suggest that within the contours of this infinity, which comes to life in the irreducible relation of the face to face,[36] one can discern a residuum of incarnational thinking in the philosophy of Levinas though it assumes a character quite different from the Christological instantiation of this theme. The embodiment of which Levinas speaks, the concretization of the transcendent infinite, is not manifest in the divine becoming human or even in the human becoming divine, but in the self that assumes its moral stance vis-à-vis the other.[37] One's own materiality can be considered the locus of infinite transcendence in the sense that it is dependent on the immediacy or proximity of the other, on the sensibility of being there for the other, a mode of contact that extends beyond the exteriority of "an ego assimiliating the other in its identity, and coiling in over itself."[38]

It is of interest to note, moreover, that Levinas identifies the common ground shared by Judaism and Christianity as the "idea of an omni-human universality."[39] As I noted above, what Judaism uniquely contributes to this conception is emphasis on the teaching that the universal is best preserved by the individual, or, as Levinas puts it in one context, the Jewish mentality is characterized by a consciousness of "universalist singularity,"[40] a perspective that is congruent with the conception of ethical discourse proffered by Levinas, which seeks to strike a balance between particularity and universality.[41] Levinas insists, accordingly, that the scriptural idea of election or chosenness imparts to the people of Israel the responsibility of illumining the world in the affirmation of the infinite worth of each and every person. In "The Temptation of Temptation," he candidly surmises that even though "all Western Jews" are drawn by the "dramatic life" that is central to Christian doctrine, "the person of Christ still remains remote for us Jews, or at least the vast majority of Jews, remain particularly indifferent to Jesus. This Jewish unresponsiveness to the person who is the most moving to Christians is undoubtedly a scandal for them."[42] What did Levinas intend by the terms "remoteness," "indifference," and "unresponsiveness"? To comprehend this we would do well to recall another comment of Levinas, where he acknowledges that the teaching regarding humanity that he found in the Gospel accounts resonated with the Jewish perspective,[43] but with respect to the theological doctrines there is a fundamental difference between the two faith communities:

> Having learned later the theological concepts of transubstantiation and the eucharist, I would tell myself that the true communion was in the meeting with the other, rather than in the bread and the wine, and that it was in that encounter that the personal presence of God resided. . . . And, if I may be so bold, it was also the understanding of the person of Christ. What remained incomprehensible was not the person, but all the realist theology surrounding him. The whole drama of his theological mystery remained unintelligible. It is still so today, whereas concepts such as God's kenosis, the humility of his presence on earth, are very close to Jewish sensibility in all the vigor of their spiritual meaning.[44]

Levinas credits Rosenzweig for imparting to him the "very possibility of thinking, without compromise or betrayal, in two forms—the Jewish and the Christian, that of Christian lovingkindness and that of the Jewish Torah," which, in turn, allowed him "to understand the relation between Judaism and Christianity in its *positivity*."[45] The conciliatory tone of the dialogical sentiment notwithstanding, Levinas was not reticent to mark the insurmountable disparity separating the two Abrahamic faiths: The basis of Jewish religiosity is a contempt for idolatry, a condemnation that is manifest in the practice of studying Torah relentlessly, a text that "demands, in opposition to the natural perseverance of each being in his or her own being (a fundamental ontological law), care for the stranger, the widow and the orphan, a preoccupation with the other person. . . . We do not have as much awe as we should at this reversal of ontology into ethics."[46] For Levinas, the Christological mystery of incarnation (not to speak of the even more scandalous mystery of the Trinity) is a reversal of this reversal, a transformation of the ethical into the ontological, a privileging of faith over action, sacramental belief over ritual obligation. The attuned ear will discern in the following passage a tacit polemical jab against the Christian doctrine of incarnation:

The love of God in the love of one's neighbor. This original ethical signifying of the face would thus signify—without any metaphor or figure of speech, in its rigorously proper meaning—the transcendence of a God not objectified in the face in which he speaks; a God who does not "take on body," but who approaches precisely through this relay to the neighbor—binding men among one another with obligation, each one answering for the lives of all the others.[47]

The "idea of infinity," when divested of ontological implications, signals the "metaphysical relation," a moment that points the way to "the dawn of a humanity without myths." Levinas was astute enough to realize, however, that a "faith purged of myths," which he identifies as the "monotheist faith," invariably "implies metaphysical atheism." The traditional dogma of the Church falls short of this ideal, as it persists in being "obstinately mythological."[48] The Jew must steadfastly stand against the desire of Christianity to assimilate it or to behave as if its time had come and gone. By acknowledging irreducible difference the possibility of unconditional tolerance for the other is effectuated:

Our feeling for Christianity is wholehearted, but it remains one of friendship and fraternity. It cannot become paternal. We cannot recognize a child that is not ours. We protest against its claim on the inheritance and its impatience to take over, since we are still alive and kicking.[49]

What has been less appreciated by Levinas scholars, and what I propose to investigate in the remainder of this essay, is the utilization of kabbalah, or at least the reading of the kabbalah offered by him, in rejecting what he considered to be the theologically erroneous core of Christianity. To ascertain this point, we will need to explore in greater depth the nexus of secrecy, eros, and modesty in his thought. The image of the secret is treated most fully by Levinas in his account of the phenomenology of eros in *Totality and Infinity*. To state the matter simply, the secret is associated with the transcendent, the *"essentially hidden"* that *"throws itself toward the light, without becoming signification."*[50] To be thrown toward the light, on the way to being seen, without, however, becoming signification, the light that illumines the horizon, the radiance of the beyond that "has meaning only negatively, by its non-sense,"[51] the "trace of a withdrawal which no actuality had preceded" and whose "essence is undone in signification, in saying beyond being and its time, in the diachrony of transcendence." This transcendence is "not convertible into immanence," for it is "beyond reminiscence, separated by the night of an interval from every present . . . a time that does not enter into the unity of transcendental apperception."[52] It is precisely at this spatial-temporal dislocation that the secret is displayed, a showing of the nonphenomenalizable that translates into an inherent and incontrovertible dissemblance: the secret, if it is to persist as secret, can be revealed only as what is hidden and hidden only as what is revealed. Levinas has this dissimulation in mind when he writes that the secret "appears without appearing" and the clandestine "exhausts the essence of the non-essence."[53]

But what does it mean to speak of something that "appears without appearing," and what are we to make of the reference to an "essence of the non-essence"? Levinas pushes at the boundary of reason and language to heed the "echo of the *otherwise*" issuing from the "*hither side of ontology.*"[54] Rejecting the traditional metaphysical binary, he insists that the secret is neither something nor nothing, but rather the enigma of the face that cannot be faced, the disfiguration of all figuration,[55] "the ambiguity of an event situated at the limit of immanence and transcendence,"[56] the "epiphany of the Beloved," which is the "*way* of the tender," which "manifests itself at the limit of being and non-being, as a soft warmth where being dissipates into radiance." The superfluity of eros signifies the "non-signifying" of the other, the alterity that defies objectification, reification, or thematization, the "exorbitant ultramateriality" that

> does not designate a simple absence of the human in the piles of rocks and sands of a lunar landscape, nor the materiality that outdoes itself, gaping under its rent forms, in ruins and wounds; it designates the exhibitionist nudity of an exorbitant presence coming as though from farther than the frankness of the face, already profaning and wholly profaned, as if it had forced the interdiction of a secret. *The essentially hidden throws itself toward the light, without becoming signification.*"[57]

The matter can be expressed in temporal terms as well:[58] "Not nothingness—but what is not yet. This unreality at the threshold of the real does not offer itself as a possible to be grasped; the clandestinity does not describe a gnoseological accident that occurs to a being."[59]

The secret, however, is not to be construed as the unrepresentable fullness, the *hyperousios*, according to the apophatic current of Neoplatonic metaphysics,[60] the excess of being beyond affirmation and negation; it is, rather, the unreality, the not-yet, positioned at the threshold of the real. The secret provides "the way of remaining in the *no man's land* between being and not-yet-being," the "way that does not even signal itself as a signification, that in no way shines forth,"[61] the surplus of the given that does not present itself as a visible spectacle and hence cannot be an object of predication or denial. We may surmise that the conception of the not-yet is indebted to Rosenzweig's notion of the future that is present always as what is yet to be,[62] as Levinas himself puts it, "the obscure light coming from beyond the face, from what *is not yet*, from a future that is never future enough."[63] Summarizing his position, Levinas reiterates that the secret is "not a hidden existent or a possibility for an existent," the hidden is "what is not yet and what consequently lacks quiddity totally."[64] The caress of the erotic, accordingly, "consists in seizing upon nothing, in soliciting what ceaselessly escapes its form toward a future never future enough, in soliciting what slips away as though it *were not yet*. . . . It is not an intentionality of disclosure but of search: a movement unto the invisible."[65]

The phenomenology of eros expounded by Levinas, in contrast to the phenomenological reflections of Husserl, presumes an "*intentionality without vision*," a "discovery" that "does not shed light," for "what it discovers does not present itself as *signification* and illuminates no horizon."[66] Levinas refers to this intentionality without vision as "voluptuosity," the advance of consciousness that "goes without going to an end," the "pure experience" that is "irreducible to intentionality" insofar as it cannot be schematized in terms either of the subject-object structure or the I-thou structure.[67] Thus Levinas concludes, "Eros is not accomplished as a subject that fixes an object, nor as a pro-jection, toward a possible. Its movement consists in going beyond the possible."[68]

The inessentiality of the secret is cast by Levinas in gender terms: "The simultaneity or the equivocation of this fragility and this weight of non-signifyingness [non-significance], heavier than the weight of the formless real, we shall term *femininity*."[69] The link that Levinas forges between the secret and the feminine rests on the correlation of the feminine and the other. It goes without saying that this correlation is not an invention of Levinas or even of modern philosophy; its roots lie deep in scriptural and philosophical traditions that have sustained and informed human thinking from time immemorial. The manner in which it is thematized in Levinas, however, does reflect the strategy of some contemporary thinkers to correlate the epistemological rejection of totality and the sociocultural role of the female. Thus in one context Levinas explicates the "mystery of the feminine" as the "essentially other": "The pathos of love . . . is a relationship with what always slips away. The relationship does not *ipso facto* neutralize alterity but preserves it. . . . The other as other is not here an object that becomes ours or becomes us; to the contrary, it withdraws into its mystery."[70]

It should come as no surprise that Levinas would associate the transcendence of the other, the "contrariety that permits its terms to remain absolutely other,"[71] with the feminine. The correlation of woman and alterity points to the sexual differentiation inherent to the human condition, a point that Levinas exegetes with alacrity in his talmudic lecture "And God Created Woman."[72] Gender difference is one of the primary ways that the "division" or "rupture" in the depth of the "human substance" is expressed, the fact that the human being is "*two* while remaining one."[73] Levinas elaborates: "The creation of man was the creation of two beings in one but of two beings equal in dignity: difference and sexual relations belong to the fundamental content of what is human."[74] Levinas draws the following conclusion from the debate between Rav and Shmuel regarding whether the side (or rib) of man from which woman was fashioned (Gen. 2:22) relates to a face or to a tail: "The fact that a woman is not merely the female of man, that she belongs to the human, is an assumption shared by both disputants: woman is from the first created from that which is human. According to the first sage, she is strictly contemporary with man; according to the dissenter, to come into being, a woman required a new act of creation."[75]

In my judgment, the gender construction underlying the rabbinic text interpreted by Levinas is far more androcentric than the egalitarian approach he proffers, and thus I would question the validity of ascribing his notion of sexual identity to the rabbinic sources. I concur with the observation of Derrida that, according to Levinas, "alterity as sexual difference" (the other as the other sex) is subordinate to the "alterity of a sexually non-marked wholly other" (the other beyond or before sexual difference), a subordination that leads to the conclusion that "the wholly other, who is *not yet marked* is *already* found to be marked by masculinity (he before he/she, son before son/daughter, father before father/mother, etc.)."[76] The drift of Derrida's thinking accords precisely with what I have found independently to be the case in sundry compositions espousing the rudiments of traditional kabbalah.[77] The overcoming of gender dimorphism is realized through the restoration of the female to the male. Consequently, I cannot accept the distinction that Levinas draws between the Platonic privileging of union and the rabbinic preference for difference.[78] Be that as it may, Levinas was convinced that Judaism does offer a view of the feminine that affirms the inherent link between alterity, secrecy, and femininity. The feminine signifies the "being not yet," which "is not a this or a that," but the clandestinity that "exhausts the essence of this non-essence."[79]

To be even more precise, Levinas links virginity to the not-yet of the mystery insofar as it is always inaccessible, the quality that renders a woman potentially "forever inviolate."[80] The feminine represents (though language here is cumbersome, as the precise point is that there is no presence to be represented) that which is "simultaneously uncovered by *Eros* and refusing *Eros*."[81] For Levinas, this dual gesture, uncovered and recovered, is denoted as profanation, which signals the discovery of the hidden as hidden, the uncovering of the mystery recovered wherein "the hidden is not disclosed, the night is not dispersed. The profanation-discovery abides in modesty, be it under the guise of immodesty: the clandestine uncovered does not acquire the status of the disclosed. To disclose here means to violate, rather than to disclose a secret."[82]

By way of summation, we might say that the secret is associated with the feminine insofar as the latter signifies that which resists thematization, the essentially other, the "presence of non-signifyingness in the signifyingness of the face,"[83] the term that Levinas employs to mark what cannot be visibly configured except as the disfigured, the "face that goes beyond the face." Rendered semiotically, the feminine delineates the margin of expression, the "refusal to express," the "end of discourse and of decency," the "abrupt interruption of the order of presences."[84] The repudiation of ontology that is characteristic of the feminine, the "refusal of the concept," the "resistance to generalization," accounts as well for the connection that Levinas makes between the feminine and interiority, though interiority in its most interior sense, the "ipseity of the I," is beyond all generalizing concepts, "outside the distinction between the individual and the general," and thus it cannot be placed under the category of either masculinity or femininity. The feminine is nonetheless an apt metaphorical signifier of what eludes signification, the "secrecy of the I," the "breakup of totality" that "leads to the presence of the absolutely other."[85] It is precisely this connection, moreover, that accounts for the characteristic of modesty and its relation to secrecy.[86] Inherent to the secret, the essence of the non-essence, is the gesture of concealment, though, as we have seen, this gesture entails the concomitant disclosure of the concealed and the concealment of the disclosed. The quality of modesty is ascribed, therefore, to the "simultaneity of the clandestine and exposed."[87] Immodesty, on this score, is unabashed and complete disclosure, whereas modesty presupposes the disclosure of the hidden as concurrently hidden and disclosed.

A remarkably similar connection of eros, secrecy, modesty, and the feminine is found in traditional kabbalistic sources. Needless to say, in his strictly philosophical works, Levinas makes no explicit or implicit reference to the Jewish mystical tradition. My contention nevertheless is that he may have been influenced by the interrelatedness of these motifs in kabbalistic lore, and especially by the zoharic tradition as it was mediated through the prism of *Nefesh ha-Ḥayyim*. For the kabbalist—and in my estimation this is a feature that is shared by the different schools of Jewish esotericism that have flourished since the high middle ages—the secret is what cannot be reified, the essence that cannot be essentialized, a movement toward transcendence envisioned as the invisible and declaimed as the ineffable. As I have argued in several previously published studies, the distinctive view of secrecy promoted by kabbalists is such that the inability to communicate the secret is not due to the unworthiness of a particular recipient but is associated rather with the inherent ineffability of the truth that must be kept secret. This is not to suggest that kabbalists have not also embraced the rhetoric of esotericism based on the presumption that secrets must be withheld from those not fit to receive them, a form of esotericism attested in classical rabbinic and medieval philosophical texts. The esoteric hermeneutic attested in many kabbalistic sources does indeed resonate with this elitist posture, but it goes beyond it as well, inasmuch as the concealment of the secret is inextricably linked to its disclosure. Simply put, the utterance of the mystery is possible because of the inherent impossibility of its being uttered. It follows that, even for the adept who demonstrates unequivocally that he deserves to be a recipient of the esoteric tradition, something of the secret remains in the act of transmission. Expressed differently, the secret has an ontic referent that is separate from the phenomenal realm and thus transcends the limits of human understanding and modes of conventional discourse.

Here it is incumbent upon me to note as well that in kabbalistic lore an inherent connection is made between secrecy, modesty, and the feminine. As I have argued previously, for the most part the juxtaposition of the secret and humility is presented from an androcentric perspective, a point that is underscored by the nexus affirmed by kabbalists between circumcision, secrecy, and concealment, an idea that can be viewed as an embellishment of the rabbinic emphasis on the need to conceal the circumcised phallus, an aspect of the etiquette of modesty (*ṣeniʿut*) required of the Jewish male.[88] Symbolically, circumcision embodies the hermeneutical play of secrecy, which rests on the presumption that the wisdom that encompasses a hidden mystery (*ṣeniʿuta*) will be disclosed exclusively to the humble (*ṣenuʿin*), for they know the art of concealing the concealment

Secrecy, Modesty, and the Feminine ■ *63*

in disclosing the disclosure.[89] This art is tied uniquely to circumcision, the sacrament through which the Jew enacts the role of dissimulation by cutting away the foreskin to create the sign, a presence that is re/presented through its own absence.

In addition to this complex of themes, however, kabbalists also associated the feature of hiddenness with the genitals of a woman, an idea that is based on the pietistic virtue of modesty promulgated in classical rabbinic literature, which demands of women that they conceal themselves from the phallic gaze, an attitude informed by a longstanding exegetical connection between the feminine and interiority, which fostered the figural representation of women in tropes that denote sheltering as well as the disproportional allocation of domestic responsibilities to the mother of a household. This metaphorical depiction, for instance, underlies the zoharic idiom of "fixing the house" applied to the woman when she prepares herself to be the abode to receive the seminal fluid of the male donor.[90] The vagina is thus referred to as the "holy of holies," the most interior space of the Temple complex, wherein the ineffable name was pronounced by the high priest on Yom Kippur, the most solemn day of the Jewish calendar. On account of the kabbalists' belief in the natural propensity of the female to be seductive, women are bridled with the virtue of modesty and implored to stay inside, to prepare the house for the entry of the man, and not to flaunt in a public display of sensuality or erotic enticement.

Without ignoring or downplaying the intertextual links that bind the kabbalists to their rabbinic ancestors, it is worth noting that their approach in this matter accords well with the stance toward the female body propagated in medieval society, itself based on tropes that stretch back to antiquity, especially the connection that is drawn between chastity and the occlusion or enclosure of the woman in a domicile setting.[91] The theme of secrecy associated with female genitalia in zoharic and other kabbalistic literature should be seen against the background of the accentuated gynecological use of the concept of secret to refer to women's private parts and diseases related thereto beginning in Europe in the twelfth century.[92] Monica Green, who has studied this phenomenon in detail, astutely surmised that this semantic shift may have been due in part to the fact that men were "presumed to constitute the principal audience for gynecological literature . . . and it is therefore men's perspective on women's bodies that renders the topic 'secret.'"[93] I submit that one can apply these words without qualification to the symbolic representations of the secrecy of women, especially in the portrayal of the genitals, in kabbalistic literature, which was informed by contemporary philosophic, scientific, and medical modes of discourse. In the last analysis, it is a matter of men's perspective on women and the anatomical generalities they presumed to be in order that is reflected in their construction of femininity, a construction that in the end bolstered misogynist structures of traditional authority that empowered men and impaired women.

Having established some of the thematic affinities between traditional kabbalah and the thought of Levinas, we need to ask to what extent we can assume that these affinities bespeak an actual appropriation or misappropriation of the kabbalah by Levinas. Let me approach this question by stating plainly that I take issue with Ajzenstat (and come closer to the view of Mopsik) inasmuch as I do not think traditional kabbalists eschewed ontology.[94] Even though they posit an excess of being beyond affirmation and negation as the source whence all beings emerge and whither they shall return, this being-that-is-more-than-being, the otherwise-than-being, is being nonetheless in line with the Neoplatonic conception of the One that is "being-not" as opposed to "not-being," the manifest (un)seen in the splintering of the four-letter name YHWH through the filter of the ten *sefirot*. I cannot accept Ajzenstat's assertion that the rejection of the ontological in Levinas accords with both the prophetic kabbalah of Abulafia and the theosophic kabbalah of Luria. Even the venerated Ḥayyim of Volozhyn does not depart from his kabbalistic predecessors when he asserts that the zoharic contention that God and Torah are one implies that the semblance of difference is merely apparent since, in truth, there is but one divine reality, which seems from our perspective to be multiple in nature.[95]

Given the importance of this point, it is worthwhile comparing the statement of Levinas concerning the contraction of infinity, a passage cited by Mopsik and Ajzenstat,[96] and the language of Ḥayyim of Volozhyn referring to the same doctrinal point. In the formulation of Levinas, infinity is produced "in a contraction that leaves a place for separated being."[97] The critical point for Levinas is that this "separated being" is truly separate and therefore cannot be subsumed under the category of the same. By contrast, Ḥayyim of Volozhyn insists that ontologically there is no being that is truly separate from the divine; alterity is merely an accommodation to our limited epistemic perspective. Consider the following comment from *Nefesh ha-Ḥayyim*:

> Concerning the future to come it says "All the flesh together will see that the mouth of the Lord has spoken" (Isa 40:5), that is, our comprehension will be purified to the point that we will merit to comprehend and to see with the physical eye the matter of the dissemination of his word [*dibburo*], blessed be he, in every thing in

the world [*be-khol davar ba-olam*], just as there already was a comprehension of this sort in the time of the revelation of the Torah. . . . Therefore, [God], blessed be his name, began the ten commandments "I am the Lord your God" (Exod 20:2), for this is the entire essence of the foundation of faith [*kol iqqar yesod ha-emunah*], that every man in Israel must establish in his heart that only [God], blessed be his name, is the true agent, the soul, vitality, and root of his essence and of all the created entities, powers, and worlds. This is the matter and explanation of the name *elohim*, the master of all the powers. Notwithstanding all of this, according to the explanation and matter of the name, one may infer that there is also in the whole of reality worlds and powers created from his simple will, blessed be he, for he constricted his glory and left a place, as it were, for the existence of the powers and the worlds, but he, blessed be he, is their soul and the source of the root of the power of their vitality that they receive from him, blessed be he, for he is expanded and hidden within them, as it were, in the manner of the expansion of the soul in the body of man, for even though [the soul] expands in every part and in every particular point in [the body], it cannot be said that the body is nullified in relation to [the soul] as if it were not in existence at all. Similarly, with respect to every power and supernal world that expands in all the strength of power in the world beneath it, even so the power and lower world have existence, and thus it is from our perspective in the matter of our comprehension. But the essential name, YHWH, instructs about the aspect and the matter as it is from his side, blessed be he . . . the worlds are nullified in existence in relation to him, blessed be he [*mevuṭṭalim bi-meṣi'ut negdo yitbarakh*], from the perspective of this glorious name . . . and therefore the essential name is called the unique name [*shem ha-meyuḥad*], blessed be he.[98]

Ḥayyim of Volozhyn distinguishes between the two divine names, Elohim and YHWH. The description of the former at one point seems to support a Levinasian orientation: the worlds in relation to the divine have an independent existence just as the body in relation to the soul has autonomy. The matter is expressed in terms of the Lurianic teaching of *ṣimṣum*, the withdrawal of the infinite light to create a space wherein the chain of being can be unfurled: "he constricted his glory and left a place, as it were, for the existence of the powers and the worlds." And this is precisely how Levinas presents the idea of *ṣimṣum*, the "originary contraction," as interpreted in *Nefesh ha-Ḥayyim*: whereas this idea was originally intended by kabbalists to resolve "the antinomy between God's omnipresence and the being of creature outside God," the contraction of God "from Creation in order to make space, next to self, for something other than self," according to Ḥayyim of Volozhyn, denotes "a gnoseological event" that consigns the Infinite to concealment and obscurity but thereby allows for the "possibility of thinking of the Infinite and the Law together, the very possibility of their conjunction." The mythopoeic idea of contraction, therefore, does not convey the "antinomy of reason" but a "new image of the Absolute."[99] When one looks carefully at the text of *Nefesh ha-Ḥayyim*, however, it becomes clear that even in the place of the withdrawal the only matter that is real is that light, the one true agent, soul, and root of all that exists. The worlds and powers appear independent solely from the perspective of our comprehension. The matter is rendered even more explicit in the depiction of the Tetragrammaton, which is called *shem ha-meyuḥad*, the "unique name," since it signifies that there is one true reality in virtue of which all the seemingly autonomous worlds are nullified.

In another passage from *Nefesh ha-Ḥayyim*, the point is linked more specifically to the nature of the Torah: "Even though by way of its descent and concatenation from gradation to gradation, and from world to world, it contracted itself [*ṣimṣemah aṣmah*] to be garbed in each world [*lehitlabbesh be-khol olam*], to communicate in the matters of that world in accord with the matter and value of that world, so that its holiness and light could be endured."[100] The Torah in this world is the condensation of the infinite light, and thus it is clothed in narratives and laws that reflect the natural conditions of the spatiotemporal world. The one who apprehends the secrets encoded in the text discerns, however, that contained therein is the infinite light of the divine, which is the one true reality. From that perspective, none of the worlds in the cosmic chain can be considered separate from God, even if our language misleads us into thinking that way. The manifestation of what is hidden, the ostensible creation of an other for that which has no other since it comprehends everything within itself, is a rupture of the primal, nondifferentiated one, the articulation of the name by which the nameless is to be called. The process of delimitation can be viewed in textual terms as the constriction of the limitless within the boundaries of the Torah, an idea that logically ensues from the zoharic identification of the Torah and God.

To savor the mystical intuition of the divine as the coincidence of being and nothing, one must reclaim the middle excluded by the logic of the excluded middle, for it is only by positioning oneself in that middle between extremes that one can appreciate the identity of opposites in the opposition of their identity, that a thing is not only both itself and its opposite, but neither itself nor its opposite. Even nondiscrimination must not be treated as the antinomy of discrimination; true insight into the oneness of everything requires that one transcend all distinctions, even the distinction between distinctiveness and indistinctiveness, unconditional unity and conditional multiplicity. From a phenomenological standpoint, the path of the inclusive middle engendered by the ontological coincidence of opposites is discerned experientially in knowing that the invisible (the use of the definite article is unfortunate, as it might convey a sense of being qua substance; what is marked semiotically as "invisible" can only be seen as not seen if it is not seen as seen) is rendered visible by the cloaking of invisibility, the secret exposed in the obfuscation of secrecy. In kabbalistic lore, there is symmetry between emanation and esoteric hermeneutics: the one as the other entails a process of uncovering preexistent roots by laying bare the complex simplicity of the simple complexity of Ein Sof. That which is without limit can be revealed only when concealed, for if not concealed, it could not be revealed as the concealed being it appears (not) to be. All that exists, therefore, is simultaneously a manifestation and an occlusion of the divine essence.

It follows that for kabbalists, including Ḥayyim of Volozhyn, the ontological assertion that the world is the garment through which the divine is concomitantly revealed and concealed converges with the hermeneutical assertion that the literal meaning of the text overlaps with the secret meaning. From the kabbalistic perspective, therefore, apprehension of the secret does not resolve the apparent conflict between the external and the internal meaning, *peshaṭ* and *sod*, but it forges the paradoxical awareness that the external veil and the internal face are identical precisely because they are different. We would do well to consider the following remark of Levinas against this background: "But the word *sod*, or mystery, in talmudic symbolism signifies the ultimate meaning of the scriptures, the one reached after searching for the literal meaning, or *pochate*, which then raises us to the allusive meaning, or *Remèz*, from which we reach the symbolic meaning, or *Drache*. But the true mystery stays within the original simplicity, more simple again than the literal meaning."[101] In this passage, Levinas utilizes the four levels of meaning developed by kabbalists beginning in the late thirteenth century: the literal, allegorical, homiletical, and mystical, encoded acrostically in the word *pardes—peshaṭ, remez, derash*, and *sod*.[102] What is most significant for the purposes of this analysis is the insight expressed by Levinas with regard to the confluence of the exoteric and esoteric, or, in his words, "the true mystery stays within the original simplicity, more simple again than the literal meaning." The position articulated by Levinas with regard to the enigmatic nature of the plain meaning, a hermeneutical task that invites one "to extricate, from within the meaning immediately offered by the proposition, those meanings that are only implied,"[103] is clearly indebted to kabbalah.

The appropriation of the kabbalistic hermeneutic nevertheless entailed a major revision, since Levinas was clearly uncomfortable with the full ontological implications of the Jewish esoteric tradition. As I have noted, from the kabbalistic vantage point, the inner meaning of the text relates to the unveiling of the potencies of the divine, but the infinite Godhead remains concealed in the very act of self-manifestation. The secret, therefore, is not merely cognitive or epistemological in nature; it is decidedly ontological insofar as it signifies an aspect of the divine that is most appropriately referred to in paradoxical terms as the disclosed concealment. "Ontological," in my understanding, entails an experiential component, for access to being comes by way of intimate experience, which in the case of the medieval kabbalist involved primarily contemplative study, prayer, and fulfillment of traditional rituals. These are the major paths that lead the kabbalist to the goal of *devequt*, communion with the sefirotic potencies of the divine. The secretive nature of that which is deemed a secret is thus allied with the potential experience of that grade of being to which the secret is related. Such a conclusion is inevitable if one begins, as one must, from the premise that God and the Torah are ontologically equivalent, a principle that is often expressed as well in terms of the mystical identification of the Torah as the Tetragrammaton. To gain knowledge of the mystery is an act of ultimate empowerment, for through such an acquisition one contemplatively visualizes the imaginal form of God, which is rendered possible on the basis of the assimilation of the soul into the divine nature through hermeneutical penetration to the sign that is hid beneath the veil of the text.

The degree to which this is modified by Levinas can be gauged from his comment that God is "not incarnate, surely, but somehow inscribed, whose life, or a part of it, is being lived in the letters: in the lines and between the lines and in the exchange of ideas between the readers commenting upon them—where these letters come alive and are echoed in the book's precepts—ordering without enslaving, like truth—to answer in justice to one's fellow, that is, to love the other."[104] The underlying intent of this passage may be ascertained by recalling the title of the essay wherein it appears, "Contempt for the Torah as Idolatry." Levinas argues that the Jewish emphasis on "continual exegesis" facilitates the possibility of hearing the breath of the living God in the words of scripture without presuming that the divine is incarnate therein. On the contrary, according to Levinas, the Jewish belief in the inscription of God in the text yields an ethical as opposed to an ontological focus. I remarked above that it is likely that in this comment is a tacit polemic against the Christological doctrine of the incarnation of the Word. I would add at this juncture that Levinas utilized the kabbalistic tradition as well in his effort to translate the ontological into the ethical. In my mind, this is precisely the spot where one can speak credibly of an esoteric reading of Jewish esotericism, a reading that, ironically enough, divests the secret of its secretive potency. But perhaps in so divesting the secret of its secrecy, Levinas does, after all is said and done, preserve the esotericism, albeit in a philosophical key appropriate to his own historical moment.

I conclude with what seems to me to be an excellent illustration of the concealing the concealment at play in Levinas from his lecture "The Name of God According to a Few Talmudic Texts." In describing the Tetragrammaton, Levinas writes: "The name is revealed and is hidden."[105] The note that is cited in conjunction with this passage points the reader to the Babylonian Talmud, Qiddushin 71a. In that context, one can find the textual source for the liturgical practice not to pronounce the Tetragrammaton as it is written but rather by means of the circumlocution *Adonai*, an epithet that preserves the ineffability of the name. The statement of Levinas, however, is a verbatim rendering of a formula that appears in several zoharic contexts, which would have been known to him through the *Nefesh ha-Ḥayyim*,[106] "the holy name is hidden and revealed," *shema qaddisha satim we-galya*.[107] The kabbalistic background does not remain hidden for a long time, as Levinas himself explicitly reveals the source he kept hidden: "But is not this withdrawal, contemporaneous with presence, maintained in the proximity of prayer? Throughout this talk we have avoided conceptions taken from the Kabbalah. Let us make an exception here, for it is an illuminating one."[108]

Levinas goes on to delineate the kabbalistic explanation of the traditional formula of all blessings, which involves placing the Tetragrammaton in between addressing God in the second person and addressing God by the third person. The grammatical shift signifies the "essential ambiguity—or enigma—of transcendence,"[109] that is, the aspect of the divine that lies beyond human comprehension. In the note to this passage, Levinas offers the following explanation:

The Kabbalah is a way of thinking whose traces and sources can admittedly be found in the Talmud, but the Talmud is quite distinct from it. In the Kabbalah the names constitute a sort of objective sphere—or at least, a sphere which is not subjective—of the revelation of an inaccessible, non-thematizable God. There exists a kind of world of names that determines a separate speculation. A world of names in which names and letters offer to thought their own dimension and order. I am not capable of leading you into this.[110]

Can there be any more convincing proof that Levinas well understood the spiritual force of kabbalah than his concluding statement that he is not capable of leading the reader into the intricacies of this religious philosophy? The admission can be read as a sincere declaration of his limitations, but it can also be decoded as evidence that Levinas apprehended the tenor and texture of kabbalistic esotericism, the need to hide what must be hidden, a doubling of secrecy that prevents one from giving in to the temptation of the impulse to idolatry that stubbornly lingers in the heart of any theism, especially pertinent in the domain of liturgical practice. To be sure, this impulse is mitigated by the ultimate paradox that if the God seen is not the invisible God, then it is not God who has not been (un)seen. From the kabbalistic perspective, the yearning to image what has no image lies deep in the poetic sensibility of the Jewish soul, with its unique propensity for prophecy. Every image of God conjured in the imagination—and that would include, most poignantly, the theosophic symbols crafted by kabbalists themselves—may be considered an "icon of the invisible God."[111]

The turn of Levinas from the ontological to the ethical may well have been inspired by the kabbalistic notion of poetic con/frontation—facing the face that cannot be faced in saying the name that cannot be named—a facing that entails both encounter and resistance, embrace and rebuff, approach and withdrawal, revelation and occlusion, communication ensuing from the incommunicable absence that is presently absent in a presence that is absently present. The Tetragrammaton, as Levinas understood, is the model to convey the paradoxical confluence of the hidden and revealed that must always be held together in the middle excluded by the logic of the excluded middle: the prohibition of pronouncing the name as it is written secures the fact that the epithet preserves the ineffability of the name, just as the veil conceals the face it reveals by revealing the face it conceals. The main objective of the contemplative path is to be conjoined to the transcendent, the limitless beyond all representation, but the only way to attain that end is through the agency of the name, which is the ladder that connects the finite to the infinite, the image to the imageless.

In spite of the instrumental role that kabbalah played in informing the thought of Levinas, his rejection of the mythological led him to misrepresent the incarnational tendency of medieval Jewish esotericism, a tendency that significantly narrowed the gap between Judaism and Christianity.

The incarnational theology that informed the kabbalistic standpoint is predicated on a distinctive understanding of corporeality. "Body" does not denote physical mass that is quantifiable and measurable, but the phenomenological sense of the corporeal as lived presence. Medieval kabbalists, due to the influence of the philosophical thinking that had informed the general cultural trends of European societies in the high middle ages, adopted a negative view of the corporeal body (indeed, according to some passages in zoharic literature, the physicality of the human is linked to the demonic other side[112]) and thus considered the contemplative life a way to escape the bonds of carnality. This explains the adoption of ascetic forms of piety by kabbalists, with special emphasis placed on sexual abstinence.[113] The positive valence accorded the body in kabbalistic symbolism, reflected in the repeated use of anthropomorphic images to depict God, images that on occasion embrace an intense erotic tone, is related to the textual nature of bodiliness, which, in turn, rests on an assumption regarding the bodily nature of textuality. The linguistic comportment of embodiment accounts as well for the theurgical underpinnings of the kabbalistic understanding of ritual epitomized in the saying "limb strengthens limb," that is, the performance of ceremonial acts by human limbs fortifies the divine attributes, which are imaginally envisioned as bodily limbs.[114] Alternatively expressed, insofar as Torah is the name YHWH and the latter takes the form of an anthropos (an idea buttressed by the numerical equivalence of the four letters of the name written out in full and the word *adam*), it follows that each commandment can be represented as a limb of the divine body.[115] Such a perspective reverses the generally assumed allegorical approach to scriptural anthropomorphisms promoted by medieval rabbinic exegetes, for instead of explaining anthropomorphic characterizations of God as a figurative way to accommodate human understanding,[116] the attribution of corporeal images to an incorporeal God indicates that the real body, the body in its most abstract tangibility, is the letter,[117] a premise that I have dubbed the principle of poetic incarnation.[118] When examined from the kabbalistic perspective, anthropomorphism in the canonical texts of scripture indicates that human and divine corporeality are entwined in a mesh of double imaging through the mirror of the text that renders the divine body human and the human body divine.[119] Phenomenologically speaking, the life-world of kabbalists revolves about the axis of the embodied text of textual embodiment.

The secret of poetic incarnation imparted by masters of Jewish esoteric lore, beholding the luminous flesh from the word, may be seen as a counter-myth to the image of the word/light made flesh in the Johannine prologue, a mythologoumenon that played an inestimable role in fashioning the hermeneutical aesthetic of medieval Christendom. This is not to deny that in the history of Christian devotion the incarnational theme did express itself in terms of textual embodiment.[120] My point is, however, that the mythologic basis for this form of embodiment in Christianity is always the incarnation of the Word in the person of Jesus, whether this is understood veridically or docetically. In consequence, medieval Christian piety has been informed by the exegetical supposition that incarnation of the word in the flesh had the effect of removing the veil of the letter as expounded by Jews, who steadfastly refused to accept the spiritual interpretation that the Christological understanding demanded; the literal meaning, intricately bound to the carnal law, thus killed the spirit by obstructing the true knowledge of the Last Things.[121] By contrast, in the kabbalistic wisdom that materialized in the course of the twelfth, thirteenth, and fourteenth centuries, incarnation of the flesh in the word preserved the veil of the letter, given that the only credible means to apprehend the inner meaning of the law was thought to be through its outer covering, to behold mysteries of Torah from underneath the garment, to see the image of the imageless embodied iconically in the text that is the textual embodiment of the name.

Against Theology, or "The Devotion of a Theology Without Theodicy"

Levinas on Religion

RICHARD A. COHEN

The sentence in which God gets mixed in with words is not "I believe in God." The religious discourse that precedes all religious discourse is not dialogue. It is the "here I am" said to a neighbor to whom I am given over, by which I announce peace, that is, my responsibility for the other.
          —**Emmanuel Levinas, "God and Philosophy"**

This obligation is the first word of God. For me, theology begins in the face of the neighbor. . . . To recognize God is to hear his commandment "thou shalt not kill, which is not only a prohibition against murder, but a call to an incessant responsibility with regard to the other.
          —**Emmanuel Levinas, Interview with Bertrand Revillon**

The doctrines which flowed from the lips of Jesus himself are within the comprehension of a child; but thousands of volumes have not yet explained the Platonisms engrafted on them; and for this obvious reason, that non-sense can never be explained.
          —**Thomas Jefferson, letter to John Adams, October 28, 1813**

Theology is a notoriously difficult term to define, owing both to the depth of its meaning and to its long and varied usage in the West. Etymologically, the term is a combination of two classical Greek words: *theos*, referring to the divine, and *logos*, referring to word, speech, manifestation, reason, science, or logic. Both of these words are perhaps no less difficult to define. We can nevertheless say that the term *theology* is commonly used to mean reasoned speech about God. In this way it is a term akin to such words as *biology*, *anthropology*, and *etymology*, except that common sense also understands that the term *theology*, unlike these scientific terms, usually includes an aspect of special pleading or apology.

For the most part,[1] Levinas usually uses the term *theology* in three different senses, two of them strict and one of them relatively loose. The loose sense is as a synonym for religiosity (as in the second epigraph above) or, somewhat more narrowly, for the intellectual or discursive dimension of religion or spirituality, as when Levinas speaks of "rabbinic theology" or "Jewish theology." What it refers to varies according to context, and Levinas attaches no strong evaluative judgment to it. For obvious reasons, this loose usage is not our concern.[2]

The first and broader strict sense in which Levinas uses the term *theology* refers to "formulations of articles of faith."[3] Here Levinas has in mind a person's or an organized religion's *representations* of God, whether as testimony, prescription, description, or dogma. Here theology means *discursive truths* articulating belief or faith in God.

The second strict sense in which Levinas uses the term *theology* is actually a subset of the first, but, as we shall see, we must treat it separately according to its specific difference. By "theology" here Levinas will refer specifically to Christian dogmas and doctrines, that is to say, Christian representations articulating, expressing, and, above all, *performatively* actualizing faith in God.[4] Theology as performative utterance, in this instance, occurs when a Christian verbally professes his or her articles of Christian faith. Here, verbally to express one's faith is to have faith, to have proven it, to bear witness to its reality. To say "I believe in God" or to say "I acknowledge Jesus as my Lord and Savior" is to be a believer and to be saved by Jesus. And it is only in the saying of these statements, in *using* them and not merely *mentioning* them, that these testimonials become true. Since no other human (but only God) can verify the sincerity with which one enunciates such theological formulations, the issue of whether one means it or not, in contrast to the question of whether one is using or mentioning these dogmas, is *objectively* not at stake. Theology in this narrower but still strict sense, regardless of the degree of its intellectual sophistication—from the magisterial *Summa Theologica* of Saint Thomas Aquinas, on the one hand, to the emotionally charged outpourings of a simple American Southern Baptist, say, on the other—is both witness and apology, that is to say, performatively self-justified Christianity. To declare one's faith in God is to be faithful to God.

Levinas boldly criticizes both these versions of theology—*doctrinal representation* of religion and *verbal performance* of Christianity—as essentially inadequate, as approaches unfaithful, indeed traitorous, to the very religious dimension they claim discursively to enunciate. For Levinas, theological formulations eclipse rather than express true religion. Furthermore and of utmost importance, for Levinas the critique of theology, the putting into question of theology, is itself a constituent moment of a genuine religious consciousness. Theology, in other words, is not an accidental aberration of religion but one of its permanent if pernicious and dangerous temptations. The subversion of theology, then, is not merely a negative enterprise but in fact a necessary and ever to be renewed positive component of true religion. The critique of theology aims to puncture the pretensions of theology precisely in order to awaken theology from its slumbers, to awaken theology to religion.

It is with the two strict meanings of the term *theology* and with the reasons for Levinas's rejection of them that this essay is concerned. Nevertheless, I underline that its aim remains primarily positive rather than negative. It is only by seeing why theology is inadequate, where precisely it fails, that we can glimpse what for Levinas is the genuine core of religion. Levinas opposes theology not by rehearsing the usual enlightened attacks that prove its internal inconsistencies and hence its basic incoherence, which is no doubt the case,[5] but rather and more essentially, Levinas opposes theology because it is a compelling but nevertheless inadequate means of grasping the religious dimension that Levinas defends. In sum, Levinas is against theology not because he is against religion but because he is for it.

Excursus: The Sacred and the Holy

Before turning to theology, however, let us first clarify the place of Levinas's critique within the broader architecture of his thought. This is important for our purposes because we must distinguish his critique of theology from his critique of the sacred.[6] Levinas opposes the "holy" to the sacred and rejects the latter because it interprets religion in terms of participation, ecstasy, rapture, enthusiasm (Greek: *en-theos*), and the dissipation of the self that these states induce. Indeed, Levinas entitled the second collection of his annual Talmudic readings, published in 1977, *From the Sacred to the Holy [Du sacre au saint]*.[7] The third of the five readings included in this volume, entitled "Desacralization and Disenchantment," addresses directly the distinction between "The Sacred and The Holy," which is also the title of its first subsection.

Briefly, for Levinas "holiness" (which is expressed in Hebrew by the term *kedushah,* whose noun form is *kadosh,* "holy,"[8] and which is another notoriously difficult term to define in any language) means "separation or purity."[9] Here Levinas is following the classic definition of this term given by the great Jewish French medieval commentator Rabbi Solomon ben Isaac (1220–93; better known by his Hebrew acronym "Rashi"). The holy is that which is separated from the profane, the vulgar, the ignoble, the "unclean," the forbidden, and certainly from evil and injustice. As for the "sacred," which in this particular Talmudic reading Levinas discusses in terms of "sorcery" and "magic," the exegesis is complex, but the heart of the matter lies in it manifesting a loss of identity. Characteristically referring both to the ancient and to the contemporary at once, Levinas writes: "Nothing is identical to itself any longer. That is what sorcery is: the modern world; nothing is identical to itself; no one is identical to himself; nothing gets said for no word has its own meaning; all speech is magical whisper; no one listens to what you say; everyone suspects behind your words a not-said, a conditioning, an ideology."[10] The sacred, then, in this sense, is the loss of the sincerity of meaning ("saying") and the initiative of selfhood ("responsibility") through the "proliferation" of anonymous significations and personae.[11] In *Totality and Infinity*, Levinas calls this loss of identity the war, violence, or violation effected by "totality,"[12] ending ultimately in the totalitarian state. To refer only to the dissipation of meaning and identity, however, is too broad a way to specify what Levinas means by the sacred in contrast to the holy. For our purposes, then, we will limit the meaning of the sacred to pagan idolatry, that is to say, to the loss of the identity of both meaning and selfhood through a proliferation that occurs at the levels of sensations and praxis in a dizzying paroxysm, effusion or enthusiasm of ecstatic participation. In a word, it is Dionysian frenzy—carnal intoxication, enchantment, mystification in speech and action.

The overall point of bringing up the opposition of the sacred and the holy is to distinguish Levinas's critique of theology from his opposition to the sacred in terms of the levels at which each occurs within the architecture of his thought. His rejection of the sacred opposes totality from "the bottom," as it were, at the level of sensations and praxis, where Levinas rejects the lure of sensuous or sentimental dissipation of identity into the dark anonymity of the "there is," an existence without existents. His critique of theology, in contrast, as we are about to see, opposes totality from "the top," at it were, at the level of representation and knowledge. So, if we distinguish, as I think is appropriate, three levels in Levinas's phenomenological analysis of meaning and selfhood—namely, the sensational, the practical, and the theoretical—the sacred operates primarily at the level of the sensational, as the sensuous seduction to succumb or to lose oneself in the "there is," while theology operates at the level of the theoretical, as the intellectual seduction to remain at or lose oneself in the cognitive level. Worship as the sacred and worship as theology both have broad practical consequences, to be sure, but their primary locus of operation lies in sensations and contemplation, respectively. Notice that I do not say that the holy, like the sacred, operates primarily at the level of sensation. There is no simple symmetry here. Levinas opposes the holy to both the sacred and theology. With these distinctions in mind, we are now better able to take a closer look at Levinas's critique of theology.

Theology as Representation

Like all other contemporary philosophers, Levinas began his intellectual career with a critique of representation, although in his case this means a critique of the contemporary phenomenology of Husserl. On the concluding pages of his celebrated expository book of 1930, *The Theory of Intuition in Husserl's Phenomenology*, which introduced Husserlian phenomenology to France, after having shown the nature and centrality of intuition as the key to the phenomenological method, Levinas argues that Husserl, despite himself, continues to privilege representation and theory. "This admission of representation as the basis of all acts of consciousness," Levinas writes, "undermines the historicity of consciousness and gives intuition an intellectualist character."[13] Here, in speaking of "the historicity of consciousness," Levinas is not at all reverting to the historicist relativism which Husserl had refuted so definitively in the "Prologomena" to the *Logical Investigations*, but rather to Heidegger's account of the temporality and historicity of Dasein published a few years earlier in *Being and Time*.[14] But Levinas is far from being a Heideggerian or even following Heidegger.

His critique of Husserl in *The Theory of Intuition in Husserl's Phenomenology* continues by invoking the "phenomenological reduction," which is meant to neutralize humanity's naïve realism and is for Husserl the very beginning of the "presuppositionless" or disinterested quest for truth that is the mark of philosophy. Levinas writes: "by virtue of the primacy of theory, Husserl does not wonder how this 'neutralization' of our life, which nevertheless is still an act of our life, has its foundation in life."[15] The issue raised in these few seemingly obscure and apparently abstract words about method is the fundamental question of the origin of philosophy. Levinas is asking how in beings such as humans the disinterested quest for truth begins. He is asking what it is that jolts a person out of his or her self-interests, desires, and prejudices in order to engage in the quest for truth. It is a fundamental question, one that all philosophers must and do answer, whether implicitly or explicitly. If Husserl did not provide a precise or clear account of the origin of the phenomenological reduction, his students, by contrast, did, and they differed from Husserl and from one another about what precisely shocks or disabuses the naïve individual out of his or her naiveté. In addressing this issue, Levinas joins Heidegger and all of contemporary philosophy by seeking and discovering a nonrepresentational and nontheoretical ground for representation and theory. But quite unlike Heidegger, whose answer lay in the historicity of "fundamental ontology" and hence, more generally, in the aesthetic path already trodden by Bergson and Nietzsche, among others, Levinas, beginning in 1930, but even more originally in 1935 and continuing throughout all his subsequent intellectual career, will answer this question by turning to the unique significance of the impact of the other person. That is to say, he will turn to the primacy not of the world of things but of the world of people, of intersubjectivity, and there, even more importantly, he will discover that intersubjectivity is from the first not a derivative aesthetic event, an event of being (as is Heidegger's *Mitsein*), will, or history, but an irreducibly *moral* event, and hence that first philosophy must be ethics.

To return more directly to our topic, theology, we leave behind Levinas's first book and turn to his last, *Otherwise than Being or Beyond Essence*, published in 1974. The "germ" of this entire book, as Levinas calls it, is chapter 4, entitled "Substitution," which is a modified version of a paper Levinas gave on November 30, 1967, at the University of Saint-Louis in Brussels. As he had been doing with an ever more refined precision since the 1930s, Levinas is once again addressing the topic of the unique encounter with the other person in moral proximity. Once again, too, he is discussing phenomenology and its limitations. The link between these two topics—the surplus of morality and the limitations of phenomenology—parallels the link that joins and separates what is positive and what is negative in Levinas's critique of theology.[16] Of the moral encounter with the other person, Levinas writes: "Here there is proximity and not truth about proximity, not certainty about the presence of the other, but responsibility for him without deliberation, and without the compulsion of truths in which commitments arise, without certainty."[17] Though truth, deliberation, certitude, commitments—representations—do arise in the need for justice, here Levinas is discussing their condition and justification, namely, morality. Morality, for Levinas, is a function of an inalienable responsibility, of selfhood in the first person singular—me, myself—responsible for the other prior to self-interest and self-esteem. The rhetorical effort of Levinas's argument is to *intimate and emphasize* not only the prerepresentative or precontractual character of this responsibility: "proximity and not truth about proximity," but also, relatedly and no less importantly, its preactive, presynthetic, preintentional character, what Levinas calls "the absolute passivity of the self . . . more passive than any inertia."[18] The latter, the exceptional passivity of a moral self, its extreme receptiveness, Levinas describes in social-moral terms as "accusation, persecution, and responsibility for the other,"[19] or, borrowing from psychology, the self's "obsession" with and "insomnia" over the other, the other whose very alterity "traumatizes" the self. The surplus of the other short-circuits and overloads the reflexive intrigues of a self-interested selfhood. It "de-nucleates" the self, to use another Levinasian expression, so that the self is without its own principle, is an-archic, for-the-other before itself, turned "inside out" for the other, and yet is not lost in or annihilated by the other.

Regarding the exceptional passivity of the moral self accused and responsible in moral proximity to and for the other, and regarding the danger of representation to this responsibility, Levinas writes: "To thematize this relation is already to lose it, to leave the absolute passivity of the self." Accordingly, must we not ask whether Levinas (and I myself, right now), as a philosopher and author of books, thematizes morality? The answer is yes and no. Yes, as the author of a book of ethics, a book about morality, one indeed presents an exposition, a thematization, a propositional representation of morality. But no, too, because the four-dimensional nature of morality as Levinas conceives it—the irreducible transcendence of the other, the inordinate proximity of I and you, my infinite responsibility, and the exceptional passivity of the moral self—is that which occurs outside of thematization, outside of representation, indeed, more deeply (or, one can also say, "higher" or "more nobly") than the freedom of thought or action. This "excess" is in no way "guilty" of an unjustified and unjustifiable "empiricism" (or "external relations"), for such a charge comes only from a philosophical idealism (Hegelian or deconstructive) no less naïve (or adamant, or ingenuous) about its own totalizing presuppositions. Moral proximity makes thematization possible and not the other way around. Writing, like speaking, is already an act of communication, and hence already a moral response to others. Thus even to represent is, as Levinas once put it, "the ruin of representation,"[20] that is, a deposing of representation's sovereign pretensions, an infusing of representation with the trace of morality's proper authority—a "saying" and not merely a "said."

The matter is complex. To thematize, and thereby to misrepresent morality, is also to bring into play—to trace—a moral proximity beyond thematization. But thematization tends, by virtue of its own temporal structure of re-presenting—which places the anterior posterior, or the prior later, or the philosopher before the prophet[21]—to deny this "beyond." To thematize the position (or, more precisely, the nonposition, because it is "de-posed") of the moral self ("proximity and not truth about proximity"), there, in that first person singularity, there where alone morality occurs and nowhere else, would be inappropriate to the morality, to the obligations and responsibilities of the moral relation undergone. Morality is not stupefying; one does not become an idiot, not at all. But its imperative is not initially an intellectual representation of what one "ought to do." Therefore, what Levinas thematizes in his ethical writings is a morality that precedes, traumatizes, and subtends representation, but at the same time it is a thematization that also shows how morality, in requiring justice (equality), also requires thematization—including an ethical account of morality. In this sense Levinas's writings are at once concrete works of justice, products of the quest for truth, and "transcendental" writings, exceeding their propositional statements, even though in the latter function they point to a condition—moral proximity—that is a noncondition, indeed a nontruth, because it transcends, disrupts, and exceeds what it nevertheless makes possible, including truth. Moral "saying," from the other or from my own mouth, is only "traced" in any ethical thematization, in what is "said."[22] But far from making ethical thematizing worthless, precisely this—requiring an unsaying and resaying of whatever is said ("exegesis of exegesis"), animating a saying that alone makes the said significant—is what makes such thematizing imperative.

The contrast with Kantian morality is instructive. For Kant, to be moral the self must indeed thematize, must ask itself if its potential actions are following maxims (i.e., rules) that can be universalized. Only maxims that can be universalized, and in this way be thematized, can be good. Universalization is indeed the standard by which the moral agent determines which maxims are moral rules and which are not. The good is therefore subordinated to rationality, must pass the test of rationality in order to be good in the first place. Levinas rejects this priority, whether explicit or implicit, given to knowledge (and hence, in philosophy, to epistemology), despite the long and venerated Western tradition of giving priority to intellect in all things.

What has this to do with theology? Theology, as I have indicated, is first of all a rational account of God, or, more specifically, since theology, unlike philosophy, is apologetic (i.e., the committed defense of a particular religion's vision of God), it is always a particular religion's rational defense of God. Reason, in this instance, serves as the handmaiden of religion, as a tool to coordinate, bolster, and render convincing its beliefs. In a word, it is "monstration," an obsolete term in English, which is defined as "the act of demonstrating proofs of an asserted conclusion." The term *monstration* derives from the same Latin root as the word *monstrance*, which is the receptacle, usually made of gold or silver, in which the consecrated host is publicly exposed for adoration during Mass in the Roman Catholic communion. (Curiously, too, it also derives from the same Latin root as does the word *monster*.) With this in mind we turn to another citation (and a footnote) from the section of *Otherwise than Being or Beyond Essence* that we have been examining. Having explained that phenomenology, which aims at descriptive rather than deductive disclosure, necessarily requires and yet is exceeded by ethics, because only the latter, beyond thematization, is able to point to the trace or surplus of moral proximity, Levinas writes the following:

> This trace is significant for behavior, and one would be wrong to forget its anarchic insinuation by confusing it with an indication, with the monstration of the signified in the signifier. For that is the itinerary by which theological and edifying thought too quickly deduces the truths of faith. Then obsession is subordinated to a principle that is stated in a theme, which annuls the very anarchy of its movement.[23]

To this he appends the following footnote: "Thus theological language destroys the religious situation of transcendence. The infinite "presents" itself anarchically, but thematization loses the anarchy which alone can accredit it. Language about God rings false or becomes mythic, that is, can never be taken literally."[24] Here we see Levinas's critique of theology. Theology, because it is monstration, interprets the trace of the other as a relationship of signifier to signified, as a kind of "proof" by "witness," as if the terms of moral proximity were amenable to thematization. But it is precisely because they are not amenable to thematization that the one-for-the-other relationship is a moral relationship in the first place, a relationship of command and responsibility, an asymmetric relationship whose terms exceed their relationship while maintaining a relationship. Such a peculiar relationship, neither wholly external, nor wholly internal, nor dialectical, can only make "sense" in moral terms. And it is this relation that Levinas, in *Totality and Infinity*, calls "religion."[25]

One cannot reason or even speak about God in a religiously genuine way because God is not a subject matter, not a "signified," and least of all is He (or what Levinas calls "illeity," the third person) the conclusion of a demonstrative proof. Transcendence—which always absents or absolves itself—can only be pointed to, hinted at, indirectly in thematization. And this can only be done in an ethical discourse, which points to the situation of moral proximity wherein absolute alterity transpires (to once again refer to its unique four-dimensionality): the irreducible otherness (transcendence) of the other person; the inexhaustible passivity of the self ("here I am"); the inescapable exigency of the other's commanding destitution (mortality, suffering); and the nonsubstitutability (election) of the self's responsibility for the other person. This relation, and not by any deduction, demonstration, manifestation, revelation, or disclosure, is the "way" in which transcendence transpires on earth. "There is only His word in the face of the Other," Levinas said in 1982 in an interview with Edith Wyschogrod about theology, ". . . the essential thing is not to appear, not to show itself, not to be thought, not to be witnessed. It is to go toward the other human being who is God's divinity."[26] Theology, by reducing transcendence to a theme, even if a *via negativa*, even if a creedal witnessing, by its very nature as thematization occludes the genuine and prior transcendence that marks the interhuman proximity that requires a going toward the other, giving to the other, kindness.

Christian Theology

Before turning to Levinas's critique of Christian theology, let us mention several positive aspects of Christianity that Levinas has noted. First and at the personal level, it is well known that his wife and daughter were hidden in a convent of the Sisters of Saint Vincent outside Orléans during the Vichy-Nazi persecution of Jews in France and that Levinas, in addition to being grateful to them, has expressed his gratitude to the many priests and clergy who at risk to their own lives provided safety for Jews throughout the Nazi period. Second, more broadly, and reflecting the traditional Jewish perspective on this matter, Levinas acknowledges the virtue of Christianity as a monotheistic religion for the Gentiles. Third, Levinas's thought, like all modern European thought, is permeated by references to Europe's Christian heritage, from citations taken from Pascal to the appropriation and reinterpretation of religious terminology now usually associated with Christianity, such as *kenosis, parousia,* and *the passion.* Of course, much of Christianity is itself permeated by the influence of its Jewish origins, and often Levinas is simply reminding Christianity of, or attempting to reinvigorate it with, forgotten Jewish significations. Finally, independent of Christian theology, Levinas has expressed his closeness to many of the teachings of the Gospels, for instance, Matthew 25, "where," Levinas writes, "people are quite astonished to learn that they have abandoned or persecuted God, and are told that when they turned away the poor who knocked on their doors, it was really God in person they were shutting out."[27]

Of course, too, Levinas also has several important reservations regarding Christianity. It is clear, and again in keeping with Jewish tradition, that Levinas has no sympathy whatsoever with Christianity's claim to have superseded Judaism. Jews and Judaism are full-fledged contemporaries and not simply antiquated ancestors of Christians and Christianity.[28] Second, Levinas, along with everyone else who is not Christian, does not accept Christianity's hubristic claim to be the exclusive path to salvation: *Extra Ecclesiam nulla salue*; "Outside the Church there is no salvation."[29] For Judaism, by contrast, the path to salvation is open to "the righteous of all nations." For Islam (excepting, apparently, Wahabi Islam, which is also exclusivist) it is open to all monotheists. For Hindus it is open to all spiritual seekers. Indeed, no other world religion outside of Christianity, however deeply attached to its own spirituality, takes itself to be an exclusive path to God as does Christianity. Or, as I tell my students, Christianity is the only religion that thinks it is the only religion.[30] Finally, Levinas holds European Christendom culpable for not having had the moral fiber during the long and dark years of persecution and Holocaust to "love your neighbor as yourself" (Leviticus 19:18). We can think back to the Inquisition, to the Crusades, more recently to the Holocaust, and really to so much else to understand why Levinas is disturbed by "the fact that, properly speaking, the world was not changed by the Christian sacrifice."[31] This colossal failure, this Himalayan lack of love, which has yet to be fully acknowledged, let alone rectified, along with Christian exclusivism, is directly related to Levinas's critique of Christian theology, to which we now turn.

The moral failure of Christianity has everything to do with theology, with the place held by theology within Christian spirituality. We must realize that it is no accident that theology and Christianity in particular are intimately entwined if not synonymous. Indeed, in the final account, one can say that Christianity does not simply *have* a theology, but *is* a theology. Christianity, in any event, is the theological religion par excellence. What this means is that Christianity is based on right adherence to doctrine or what the Church explicitly calls "dogma." Its "faith" is "creedal," the affirmation of correct doctrine. This, as I indicated earlier, is religion as theology, theology as performative utterance: to declare one's faith in Christ is to be faithful to Christ and hence the very accomplishment of personal salvation. While Jews are a "people" or "the children of Israel," Christians are "believers" or "the faithful," and their clergy are one and all "theologians." Christians are in this sense, whether explicitly, as with clergy, or implicitly, as with laypersons, all theologians. For Levinas, however, because he takes the ethical redemption of the world to be religion's first priority, "personal perfection and personal salvation are, despite their nobility, still selfishness."[32] It is a strong statement, to be sure, but it needs to be said. Personal salvation permits him or her who is saved to opt out of the larger redemptive enterprise, regardless of the state of the world, regardless of immorality and injustice, regardless of the suffering of the "widow, the orphan, the stranger."

Although Heidegger is certainly a philosopher and not a theologian, he has, however, articulated the theological essence of Christianity. He is also Levinas's great protagonist. In his lectures of 1937–38 entitled "Phenomenology and Theology," he summed up the intimate relation between Christianity and theology as follows:

> For the "Christian" faith, that which is primarily revealed to faith, and only to it, and which, as revelation, first gives rise to faith, is Christ, the crucified God. The relationship of faith to the cross, determined in this way by Christ, is a Christian one. The crucifixion, however, and all that belongs to it is an historical event, and indeed this event gives testimony to its specifically historical character only in the scriptures. One "knows" about this fact only *by believing*. . . . The occurrence of revelation, which is passed down to faith and which accordingly occurs only through faithfulness itself, discloses itself only to faith. . . . *Presupposing* that theology is enjoined on faith, out of faith, and for faith, and *presupposing* that science is a *freely* performed, conceptual disclosure and objectification; theology is constituted by thematizing faith and that which is disclosed through faith, that which is revealed. . . . Insofar as theology is enjoined upon faith, it can find sufficient motivation for itself only through faith.[33]

The fundamentally "Barthean" elements of this description of theology are, of course, its grounding of theology in faith and faith alone, and then, even more specifically, its grounding of faith in scripture and scripture alone, meaning, of course, the New Testament, as supplemented by the Old Testament.

The "Heideggerian" element of the description, by contrast, is not especially evident in this citation, but it is alluded to in Heidegger's use of the term *science*. For Heidegger, theology is an "ontic" science, an account of beings (and not of the being of beings), what Heidegger calls an "onto-theology," and as such it stands in contrast to and remains ultimately determined by and dependent upon "fundamental ontology," which does raise the "question of being" (*Seinsfrage*). Insofar as theology sees itself as fundamental, however, Heidegger's recontextualization cannot be satisfying to Christian theologians. Nevertheless, there are theologians (most notably the Heidegger scholar, ordained Jesuit priest, professor, and psychoanalyst William Richardson[34]) who believe that Heidegger's notion of "fundamental ontology" is itself more theologically satisfying than the ontic notions of theology it displaces.

For Levinas, however, whether one takes fundamental ontology to be a better expression of Christian theology than what Heidegger considers its ontic and merely onto-theological expressions, as Levinas agrees,[35] or whether one believes that onto-theology is more deeply rooted than Heidegger takes it to be, in either case what disturbs Levinas is that in the equation of Christianity and theology, religion in both cases is reduced to *disclosure*. For Levinas, as we know, the domain of the divine is morality and justice, not disclosure, or, to the extent that it is disclosure, it is disclosure serving justice, what Roger Burggraeve has recently called "the love of wisdom in the service of the wisdom of love."[36]

One can see the centrality of disclosure in Christian theology in the thought of Jean-Luc Marion, who while acknowledging Levinas's great influence on his thought, remains, in the end, a Catholic philosopher-theologian in the very sense that Levinas rejects. Marion continues to makes Logos and its disclosure the highpoint, indeed, the very essence of Christianity. In his book *God Without Being*, despite its title, he goes so far as to characterize the central and defining moment of Christianity—in this case, Roman Catholic Christianity—as an "absolute hermeneutic," one that "culminates in the Eucharist," a Eucharist that itself culminates in theology. "The theologian," he writes, "find his place in the Eucharist because the Eucharist itself offers itself as the place for a hermeneutic. . . . This place—in Christ in the Word—is opened for an absolute hermeneutic, a *theo*logy."[37] Monstrance becomes monstration. Marion's "beyond being" remains within the orbit of Heidegger's ontological hermeneutics; and let us remember that Heidegger too, in his later thought, also (and literally) crossed out being without thereby departing from the question of being.[38] Again we see confirmed Levinas's contention that at the heart of Christianity is theology, and that the significance of the centrality of theology is the centrality of disclosure, understanding, hermeneutics, comprehension, as the key to religious consciousness. It is precisely this, of course, that Levinas contests. Keeping alive the surplus trace, the anarchy of morality through discourse—the ever-renewed exegetical resaying of the said—however tempted by knowledge, is never reducible to the disclosure of knowledge, conceptual or hermeneutic.

Early in his career, and in reference to Heidegger, Levinas had challenged the Christian equation of religion and theology/disclosure in an article of 1951 entitled "Is Ontology Fundamental?" There he first shows that, far from contesting philosophy's traditional predilection for knowledge, truth, and intellection, the existential or ontological analysis that Heidegger proposes in contrast to onto-theology merely deepens it. "Understanding," he writes of Heidegger's account of *Dasein* and fundamental ontology, "is the very event that existence articulates. All incomprehension is only a deficient mode of comprehension. It turns out that the analysis of existence and of what is called *haecceity* (*Da*) is only the description of the essence of truth, of the condition of the very understanding of being."[39] If anyone has the slightest doubt that Heidegger's analyses of *Dasein* and fundamental ontology lead to the comprehension of being as the truth of being, I recommend reading his 1930 lecture entitled "On the Essence of Truth," where this connection can hardly be made clearer.[40] For Levinas, by contrast, religion is not ultimately a matter of being or—since being is equivalent to the disclosure of being—with disclosure, whether ontic or ontological, but rather of the transcendence that transpires in the relationship of *beings as beings to other beings*, a relation whose adequate expression is found in morality and justice rather than in ontology or theology. In this way, as I have indicated, Levinas takes seriously the notion of creation, not as an illusory or provisional phenomenon, but as the irreducibly multiple scene of a "Divine Comedy"[41] lived in all the seriousness of the first person singular, in responsibility for the other and for all others, or, to recall the title of this paper, lived in "the devotion to a theology without theodicy."[42]

The transcendence proper to religion, for Levinas, is not that of Logos, which is always reducible to immanence, whether personal and existential or world historical and ontological, but rather the otherness of the other person encountered morally. Indeed, the otherness of the other person, hence irreducible transcendence, is only encountered when encountered morally. Morality, in other words, is not added to intersubjective relations as a gloss or luxury or bonus. It is what first makes intersubjectivity possible, or, more precisely, morality is the first significance by which such a relation occurs. It is for this reason, because religion is relation with absolute transcendence, that Levinas locates religion within the proximity of moral intersubjectivity rather than in any form of the disclosure of self-understanding, which is a product and not the source of the original significance of moral proximity.

After showing Heidegger's conformity to philosophy's and theology's time worn privileging of ontology and knowledge, in "Is Ontology Fundamental?" Levinas writes: "Religion is the relation with a being as a being."[43] Of course, as I have already mentioned, in *Totality and Infinity*, thirteen years later, Levinas defines religion in the same basic way, as "the bond that is established between the same and the other without constituting a totality." In his 1951 article, Levinas writes of his choice of the word *religion* that in "choosing the term *religion*—without having pronounced the word *God* or the word *sacred*":

> Nothing theological, nothing mystical, lies hidden behind the analysis that we have just given of the encounter with the other . . . the object of the encounter is at once given to us and in *society* with us; but we cannot reduce this event of sociality to some property revealed in the given, and knowledge cannot take precedence over sociality. If the word *religion* should, however, announce that the relation with human beings, irreducible to comprehension, is itself thereby distanced from the exercise of power, whereby it rejoins the Infinite in human faces, then we accept the ethical resonance of that word.[44]

Or, in the same article: "this tie to the other, which does not reduce itself to the representation of the Other but rather to his invocation, where invocation is not preceded by comprehension, we call *religion*."[45]

In his early writings Levinas associates religious consciousness with morality, that is, the face to face relation, the responsibility of one for the other. In his later writings, by contrast, he links the "presence" of God more specifically to justice, which is to say, to the laws, to legislative, judicial, and executive institutions, to courts, police, army, and schools, which are required in society by morality. Regarding the theological implications—and calling to mind our present title, *The Exorbitant: Emmanuel Levinas Between Jews and Christians*—Levinas once declared, with a certain irony and constructive honesty: "The direct encounter with God, *this* is a Christian concept. As Jews, we are always a threesome: I and you and the Third [i.e., the call for justice] who is in our midst. And only as a Third does He reveal Himself."[46] This comment, which recalls Buber's critique of Kierkegaard, was made at an academic conference held in Israel in July 1972. Levinas was responding—in Hebrew—to what he called "a fundamental question," asked by Professor Jacob Petuchowski (1925–91) of the Hebrew Union College in Cincinnati. Professor Petuchowski had wondered, in Levinas's words, why or how Levinas passes "from ethics to divinity" and had raised the question: "Is morality possible without God?" Levinas responded (again, with some humor and much profundity): "I answer with a question: Is divinity possible without relation to a human Other? Is such a thing possible in Judaism? Consider Jeremiah,

Chapter 22, or Isaiah 58:7: 'to bring to your house the poor who are outcast.'" It is then that Levinas made the statement just cited about direct encounter with God being a Christian concept, in contrast to the prophetic idea that only in justice does God reveal Himself. Jeremiah, in fact, is far braver than Levinas, who is speaking to fellow academics. In the text to which Levinas refers, Jeremiah is castigating the king of Judah and the throne of David, as well as their servants and the people Israel, in the name of God: "Execute judgment and righteousness, and deliver the robbed out of the hand of the oppressor, and do no wrong, do no violence to the stranger, the fatherless, or the widow, neither shed innocent blood in this place." (Jer. 22:2–3). And, as is characteristic of Jeremiah, he threatens dire consequences if these things are not done.

For Levinas, God is found in morality and justice, in what little there is of both in our world, rather than in theology, whose representations, even with the best good will, obscure and deflect the imperatives of God's love. Levinas has written:

Religion is the excellence proper to sociality with the Absolute, or, if you will, in the positive sense of the expression, Peace with the Other. . . . The obligation of responding to the unique, and thus of *loving*. . . . The love of God in the love of one's neighbor. This original ethical signifying of the face would thus signify—without any metaphor or figure of speech, in its rigorously proper meaning—the transcendence of God not objectified in the face in which he speaks; a God who does not "take on body," but who approaches precisely through this relay to the neighbor—binding men among one another with obligation, each one answering for the lives of all the others.[47]

Religion, prior to knowing and yet as the support of knowledge, is an ethical service, a devotion to others in what Levinas has called the "wisdom of love." It is by serving the imperatives of the wisdom of love that the propositions of the "love of wisdom"—philosophy, science, theology—emerge and find their true significance.

Is the Other My Neighbor?

Reading Levinas Alongside Hermann Cohen

DANA HOLLANDER

"Der Ferne ist der Nahe geworden"; "The distant one has become the near one." This statement represents a key claim from a 1910 essay by the German-Jewish philosopher Hermann Cohen entitled "Conviction" ("Gesinnung"), an essay that belongs to a series of works by him concerning the question of love of the neighbor. The claim that it represents is—like all the arguments made by Cohen in his writings on "the neighbor"[1]—both a matter of Jewish-Christian polemic and part of a philosophy of morality, sociality, law, and politics.

As an observation concerning something that "has" occurred (that the distant one *has become* the near one), the statement "the distant one has become the near one" applies to a development that Cohen often highlights in the Bible: the elaboration of the love of God as at the same time love of the neighbor and love of the stranger. Its immediate inspiration, in the passage that I am quoting from, is a line Cohen cites from Isaiah 57:19: *shalom, shalom la-rahok ve-la-karov*, "Peace, peace to the far and to the near." For Cohen, this means that the "nearness" of the neighbor does not admit of degrees and that, in accordance with the duty to love one's enemy, I must become conscious of "God's nearness" not only in view of those who treat me well but even in the face of my enemy. The nearness of God is thus produced by human proximity, conceived necessarily at the same time as a distance.[2] And this, we will learn elsewhere in Cohen's corpus, is oriented ultimately toward a solidarity across humankind, associated with the "idea of the messiah" and with peace.

The verse "Peace, peace to the far and to the near" is also frequently cited by Emmanuel Levinas, notably in chapter 5 of *Otherwise than Being or Beyond Essence*, a work that, among other things, examines the condition of responsibility as one of "proximity." Levinas had frequent occasion to reflect on the relationship between the Bible, or God, and philosophy in his own writings and in general, and he routinely did so by highlighting the fact that for him God, or the infinite, as an "ethical exigency,"[3] represents a requirement of being "for the other," or for the "neighbor." Thus, in "God and Philosophy" Levinas elaborates on the *me voici*, the "here I am," as implying a relation to the infinite that is distinct from any thematization or representation of God:

> The infinite is not "in front of" me; it is I who express it, but I do so precisely in giving a sign of the giving of signs, of the "for the other" in which I am dis-interested: here I am [*me voici*]. Marvelous accusative: here I am under your gaze, obliged to you, your servant. In the name of God. Without thematization! The sentence in which God comes to get involved in words is not "I believe in God." The religious discourse that is prior to all religious discourse is not dialogue. It is the "here I am," said to the neighbor [*prochain*] to whom I am given over, and in which I announce peace, that is, my responsibility for the other. "In making language flower upon their lips . . . Peace, peace to him who is far off, and to him who is near, says the Eternal.[4]

For Levinas, the idea of God is a naming, is God "getting-involved in words"—which is why he cites also from the verse that leads into the pronouncement about peace in Isaiah 57:19: "In making language flower upon their lips . . ."). Like Cohen, then, Levinas sees in the idea of God the value of a peace that means responsibility to another.

To cite from one of the many interviews in which Levinas was asked to comment on the relationship of his philosophizing to Judaism or to religion, here is a related passage from the 1985 interview "On Jewish Philosophy": "The Jewish Bible I quote is not the originality of an ethnic particularism, no more so than is the Hellenic rationality of knowledge. The Bible means something for all authentically human thought, for civilization *tout court*, whose authenticity can be recognized in peace, in *shalom*, and in the responsibility of one man for another. 'Peace, peace, to him who is far off and to him who is near.'" Here the line from Isaiah represents for Levinas a questioning of the category of the human being as a self-sufficient "subject of perception" that is "master of what is not itself" in being "the one who *originally knows* [originellement connaît], grasps and owns." This calling into question of knowing mastery issues from the neighbor, the *prochain* or "near one," whose nearness is at the same time, in accordance with the concept of "proximity" that is developed extensively in *Otherwise than Being* and other works, undone by the fact of its being the *inconnu*, the unknown or the stranger: "Or is not the I precisely as I [*moi*] already hateful to itself, that is, already obliged to the neighbor [*au prochain*], to the first person to come along [*au premier venu*, to the "first-comer"], to the stranger [*à l'inconnu*]? To the neighbor who, in one way or another, is not merely of the world!"[5] At the same time, in this interview—and this too accords with the analyses in *Otherwise than Being*—the pronouncement in Isaiah 57:19 is also taken to be an expression of the equivalence between the "neighbor" as "not merely of the world" and the "neighbor" as the "third": that is, to name a kind of proximity that poses the problem of sociopolitical obligation, as opposed to the condition for an ethical responsibility that is always conceived as exclusive:

> "Peace, peace to the one who is far off [*éloigné*] and to the one who is near, says the Eternal" (Isaiah 57:19). Outside the near one, or before/prior to him, the one who is far off [*lointain*] imposes himself; outside the other, there is the third party, who is also an other, also the neighbor. But where is the closest proximity [*la proximité la plus proche*]? Is it not always exclusive? Who then is the first one to whom I must respond, the first to be loved?

To ask such a question is to return to asking questions of "knowledge," which had previously, in seeking to conceive of the *ethical* responsibility to the neighbor, been excluded as forms of mastery.[6] It is to leave behind, or proceed past, the possibility that the first to be loved is the first-comer, the first to come along, the *premier venu*, in order to ask about the relationship between the sphere of alterity, the ethical, and the sphere of the third, which is for Levinas the political.

From this brief juxtaposition, it is clear that both Cohen and Levinas had occasion to take the biblical concept of the neighbor as a resource, or as evidence, for an understanding of ethical and political obligation. As we will see, for both thinkers appropriating this notion requires understanding love of the neighbor not as a form of love in general but as aligned with the idea of justice. For Cohen, to elaborate the concept of the "neighbor" in such a way that it can be mobilized for ethical and sociopolitical philosophy is explicitly also a problem of Judeo-Christian difference. For Levinas, the appearance of the "neighbor," along with related terms of biblical provenance or with theological connotations, can, on the one hand, be read as allied with the kinds of analyses that Cohen elaborated. But on the other hand, his oblique, transformative use of this term seems calculated to sidestep any possible contemporary counterpart to the kind of Jewish-Christian polemic in which Cohen, as a thinker active in Wilhelmine Germany, was engaged.

In what follows, I will continue in the manner of juxtaposition, beginning with a look at the moments in Cohen's and Levinas's works at which each rejects love of the neighbor as an ethically productive concept. I will then look at how the neighbor "returns," in a sense, in each of their philosophies and examine both what makes possible such a return and its implications for their views of ethics and politics. In doing so, I hope to show how the "neighbor" in Cohen's and Levinas's works can be read as exemplifying each thinker's broader strategies for taking account of Judaism in his philosophy.[7]

అ

By the time Martin Buber published a selection of Cohen's writings entitled *The Neighbor* (*Der Nächste*) in the book series Bücherei des Schocken Verlags in 1935—during the last years of Jewish publishing in Nazi Germany[8]—Cohen's studies of love of the neighbor had become a canonical reference point for a modern Jewish understanding of the significance of this command to love. But though Cohen produced a rich corpus of texts devoted to showing the significance of this biblical concept for the ethics and politics that issued from Jewish monotheism, there is one crucial point in what is generally deemed to be a somewhat separate corpus—his philosophical system—at which he appears to hold a decidedly negative view of the philosophical potential of this category. As part of an extended argument, along Kantian lines, for the autonomy of ethics from religion, Cohen emphasizes that "systematic ethics must go its own way; it must not allow itself to be led by the nose by the language and the expressions of religion." Thus, although "love," "the highest expression with which religion is able to operate," has made a monumental contribution to the history of ethics in having "given birth to the fellow human being [*Nebenmensch*]," it is also necessary to treat the expression "love" with caution and call it into question.[9]

In proceeding cautiously where love is concerned, Cohen is following the lead of his philosophical teacher, Kant, who in the *Critique of Practical Reason* narrowly circumscribes the sense in which love can be involved in the morality of an action. Moral actions imply a relationship between the agent and the principles under which they may be judged moral, but whether that relationship is one of love or inclination (Kant cites "love of man" and "love of order" as examples) is not relevant to whether they are moral. Those who think of themselves as "volunteers [*Volontäre*]" in acting morally, rather than as doing their duty, are engaged in the self-flattery of imagining themselves the "sovereign" of the "kingdom of morals" rather than its subjects, and this is itself a "defection in spirit" from the "holy law." The double commandment to "love God above all and your neighbor as yourself" is consistent with this requirement only in the sense that what it commands is "respect for a law." It is with respect, as the only properly "moral feeling," that we should aspire to comport ourselves toward the law, and not with love.[10] Neither love of God nor love of the neighbor, in the sense of "pathological love" or "inclination," can be commanded, since God is not an object of the senses and thus cannot be an object of such love, and we are not capable of loving a human being on command. Thus, the love in question must be a "practical love," which is to say that love is not a disposition or conviction (*Gesinnung*) one can "have"—namely, that of obeying God's commandments and doing one's duties toward one's neighbor "gladly [*gerne*]"[11]—but rather one toward which one must strive. In this sense, the moral precepts of the Gospels are merely a representation of "moral *Gesinnung*" in its perfection, an ideal of "holiness" that is unattainable by finite creatures.[12]

Cohen on a number of occasions cites this passage from the Second Critique. In his study *Kant's Foundation of Ethics* (1877/1910), he praises the "sober solidity [*Gediegenheit*]" with which Kant in this passage locates morality in the "feeling" of respect, or duty. "At this point," he comments, "rational ethics touches by a hair's breadth" ethics that is *schwärmend* ("raving," "fanatical"[13]), in that it explicitly avoids love as a basis for morality.[14] In his 1910 lecture "Inner Affinities of Kant's Philosophy with Judaism," Cohen underscores the centrality of "law" for understanding Kant's line about the "volunteers of morality": He explains that autonomy[15] may mean we are free, but with respect to our will this means only that we may "impose on it a universal law." In saying that we must not be "volunteers of morality," Cohen writes, "it is as if Kant had heard this expression from a Jewish philosopher and in the Talmud itself," which he illustrates with a citation from Tractate Kiddushin 31a: "One who is commanded and fulfils [the command] is greater than one who fulfils it though not commanded [*gadol metsuve ve-oseh me-mi she-eino metsuve ve-oseh*]."[16]

Cohen's endorsement of both Kant's de-emphasis of love and his use of the concept of law is continued in his own systematic work on ethics, *Ethics of the Pure Will* (1904/1907). At the point in that work at which

Cohen introduces one of his core (and best-known) ideas, that ethical action is made possible by a "correlation" between the I and its counterpart, a nonempirical "other"—that indeed the I as moral agent itself originates in the correlation with that other person, or alter ego[17]—Cohen announces: "We are standing at a crossroads of systematic ethics," namely, the very point "at which it diverges from religion." To be sure, Cohen writes, the one God of monotheism corresponds from the start to a unity of humankind across the multiplicity of individuals and peoples. But this has meant that the problem of the other has been understood in a way that is misleading from the point of view of the ethics that Cohen is seeking to develop: the other in the religious context is the stranger or foreigner, initially encountered as a challenge to the unity of humanity, in that the stranger "initially appears foreign as such; he appears different from one's own people and from one's own faith." This is why the Bible seeks to dispel this appearance, this prejudice, by decreeing that "the stranger shall be to you as the native among you."[18] Cohen concedes that such pronouncements evoke sympathy—the same sympathy, he adds, that the biblical prophets call for when they evoke, together with the foreigner, the figures of the widow and of the orphan—and that, based on such sympathy, they are supposed to engender a hospitality that allows the native to extend the scope of the law to encompass the foreign. These are "sublime ideas," capable of captivating us and reverberating in our hearts, but, Cohen writes, a sober look at the contemporary political hostility to foreigners makes evident that they have had no impact at all. Similarly, the idea of love that is employed by religion is admirable as far as it goes, but insofar as it is an affect, it cannot serve as the basis for ethics. If the other or the stranger is ethically significant, this is not because they are objects of love but because they are concepts of law (or legal science) and thus belong to the political realm from the outset.[19] The self-other correlation is better viewed along the lines of a legal action (*Rechtshandlung*) than as driven by affect.[20]

Furthermore, Cohen adds that the danger of appealing to love is nowhere as evident as in the command to love thy neighbor—or at least in the discourse surrounding this command—since "neighbor," in German *der Nächste*—has traditionally been misconstrued as the one who is "nearest" to me, that is, in terms of proximity or nearness. But surely, Cohen protests, ethical obligation cannot be a matter of degrees of nearness, or of "more or less." This, he adds, is evident in the history of mistranslations of the command to "love your neighbor [in Hebrew: your *re'a*] as yourself." While *re'a*, according to Cohen, means simply "other" or "another," the Septuagint renders it as *plesios* ("neighbor"), the Latin Vulgate with *amicus* ("friend"), and Luther's translation goes so far as to use the superlative *der Nächste* ("the nearest"). All of these translations suggest that the other whom I shall love is someone who is close to me, related to me in some way, and for Cohen this misinterpretation simply mirrors the failure of ethics throughout the history of politics. Wherever differences of degree are invoked, wherever nearness is a criterion, ethical rigor is endangered.[21]

We can place this argument alongside Levinas's arguments in *Totality and Infinity* and related works, in which the image of the "neighbor" and the command to "love thy neighbor" are also rejected as models for understanding the ethical relationship. In the discussion following his 1962 presentation to the Société Française de Philosophie published under the title "Transcendence and Height," Levinas is pressed on his understanding of the self-other relation as one of "transcendence." In a challenge that is at the same time leveled at Levinas's view that traditional philosophical language is, or has been, limited in its ability to grasp what he is trying to grasp, Eugène Minkowski wonders, for example, whether, instead of conceiving of the other as transcendent, it would not be more productive to use the everyday terms *autrui* ("other person"), *semblable* ("fellow human being") or *prochain* ("neighbor"). He continues: "On the phenomenological plane, each of them provides us with particular givens and tends to diminish the initial distance and opposition which can exist between the Same and the Other, which leads to the proximity, an immediate given, that we find in the 'neighbor.' Seen from this angle, it is an essential given, namely the primitive human solidarity upon which our existence rests." Minkowski, a psychologist, wants to suggest that to proceed from an essential notion of the "human" takes into account the "essential phenomenon of the echo or reverberation in which all affective movement finds or tries to find its natural accomplishment." Rather than the dimension of height that is represented by transcendence, which he finds "too static and too spatial," Minkowski recommends paying attention to the "primitive dynamism of existence," which, as an "expanding or opening out," "has a more vital importance" than the idea of something extended.[22]

In his answer, Levinas insists on the primacy of transcendence for understanding the Other (*Autrui*) and thus on understanding *Autrui* as "*not* initially the *semblable* [fellow human being] or the *prochain* [the neighbor or near one]" but as *le très lointain*, "the very distant," as *l'Autre*, "the Other," that is, "the one with whom initially I have nothing in common," and thus "an abstraction." Responding to Minkowski's references to empirical psychological experiences, Levinas continues: "It is precisely in all this affirmation of the concrete from which philosophy today lives, that one fails to recognize that the relation with the other (*autrui*) is an element of abstraction which pierces the continuity of the concrete, a relation with the Other qua Other, denuded, in every sense of the term." Levinas concludes from this that "it is necessary to avoid the words *pro-chain*/neighbor and *semblable*/fellow human being," because they "consecrate between myself and the other so many things in common—I always have a lot of things in common with my neighbor [*voisin*], and so many resemblances to my *semblable*; we belong to the same essence."[23] To use such terms is thus to proceed from a conception of human essence of the kind we see in Minkowski's question about human solidarity.

As for Cohen, then, for whom the criterion of "nearness" in the concept of the "neighbor" renders the latter ethically suspect, Levinas here voices concerns, for different reasons, about the commonality that is connoted by the term *neighbor*. The other in the ethical relation, which is a relation of transcendence, is not a figure who inhabits the same space as myself but is "absolutely different" from me. "Absolute difference" does not refer to any amount of particular qualities that the I and the other happen not to share, as could be discovered by means of an empirical psychology or a sociology. It doesn't refer to quality at all, but rather to the fact of my being "absolutely unique" vis-à-vis the other, an "initial difference" that refers only to itself.[24]

The dimension of "height" referred to in the 1962 discussion is in *Totality and Infinity* the dimension of an "inordinate" "metaphysical desire," which is explicitly opposed to "love," understood as having the capacity to be satisfied.[25] This desire is not directed at "return" or at some sort of complete recuperation of its object but is, Levinas explains near the beginning of the book, "desire for a land not of our birth, for a land foreign to every nature, which has not been our fatherland and to which we will never transport ourselves."[26] This strangeness or foreignness to which desire aspires corresponds to a transcendent other whose "eminence [and] height . . . in its concrete meaning includes his destitution, his exile [*dépaysement*], and his rights as a stranger [*droit d'étranger*]."[27] Indeed, *Totality and Infinity* is punctuated throughout by the refrain of "the stranger, the widow, the orphan," sometimes also accompanied by "the poor one,"[28] biblical figures for the obligation that issues from a condition of absolute poverty, destitution, and need.[29] The command issues from an absolute distance, but there are also hints that this distance is, even in *Totality and Infinity*, also a proximity, that is, that the stranger is not completely dissociated from the neighbor:

A relation with the Transcendent that is however free from all captivation by the Transcendent [*libre de toute emprise du Transcendant*]
is a social relation. It is here that the Transcendent, infinitely other,
solicits us and appeals to us. The proximity of the Other, the proximity of the neighbor, is in being an ineluctable moment of the revelation, of an absolute presence (that is, disengaged from every
relation), which expresses itself. His very epiphany consists in soliciting us by his destitution in the face of the Stranger, of the widow,
or of the orphan.[30]

This passage appears in a section entitled "The Metaphysical and the
Human," whose primary purpose is to explain why the ethical or metaphysical relation is "atheistic" even though it is a relation to transcendence. Traditionally, God is the source of the command to love the
neighbor or the stranger. The dimension of "atheism" put forward by
Levinas is a way to avoid "theologies" or "thematizations" of God. Understood "atheistically" in this sense, the social relation, as a "relation
with the Transcendent," is supposed to be "free from all captivation [*emprise*] by the Transcendent." Understood "atheistically," the proximity of
the neighbor is no longer a proximity in a common space that we inhabit.
This is a nonspatial dimension, a name for the "justice rendered to human
beings" to which "God" is a "correlative" or as which "God" is "accessible."[31] Recalling that Levinas in his later writings (like Cohen before him)
will at times use "peace" to name the task of justice, we can say that we
are here approaching the proximity that is at the same time a distance,
represented in the verse from Isaiah that we began with, "Peace, peace to
the far and to the near."[32]

Cohen likewise does not stop at rejecting the "neighbor" based on its
corruptibility as a term that denotes "degrees of nearness." Indeed, in the
writings on the "neighbor," he develops a full-fledged argument for why
the biblical neighbor must essentially be understood as the stranger or the
distant, the foreign one. Cohen returns to the question of the neighbor in
several essays that engage with representatives of the Protestant biblical
criticism of his time to expose its Christian-supersessionist biases. In these
essays, it is thus also a matter of envisioning the "neighborhood," as it
were, of Judaism as a living, constitutive force in the world, rather than
as a philological artifact. Let me trace out Cohen's thinking about this
question as he develops it in his 1914 essay "The Neighbor," which begins with a look at the notion of peoplehood represented by the Israelites
in the Hebrew Bible.

The Old Testament, writes Cohen, is a "national literary product," but
one that is to be credited with thinking the people of Israel always "within

its environment." Citing Genesis 12:3 (which has God saying to Abraham, "in you all the families of the earth shall be blessed") and Isaiah 49:6 (which contains the famous idea of Israel as a "light to the nations"), Cohen highlights the Bible as a resource for opposing nationalism and particularism in a way that is nevertheless—paradoxically, I would add—rooted in what he calls a "naiveté" that is the stylistic mark of all epics, a "freedom from concern about everything that is otherwise going on in the world." This universalism Cohen contrasts with that of the New Testament, which proceeds not from "naiveté" but from a people's reflective self-critique aimed at surpassing the national religion. But for Cohen, Judaism already contains such a surpassing of the national, in its foundation of a messianic world religion.[33] This is the aspect of Judaism that he is continually at pains to assert against supersessionist interpretations: that its "neighborhood" has essentially world-wide, rather than tribal or national, dimensions. In his 1914 essay "The Neighbor," Cohen responds to a contemporary newspaper opinion piece by the linguist Karl Otto Erdmann in which the latter coins the word *nosism* as an alternative to *egoism*. Erdmann points out that, while people condemn egoistic behaviors, understood as individuals acting in their own individual self-interest, numerous sociopsychological phenomena attest to a far greater tolerance of behaviors that favor one's own relatives or social group, a "we [*nos*]"—hence his coinage for this class of behaviors: "nosism." His piece thus suggests a relativistic ethics according to which the "altruism" that, as he puts it, is "preached" by moral philosophers and religious leaders is perhaps worthy of striving for but utterly unrealistic, because group loyalties cannot be eradicated. Erdmann points out that *altruism* was originally coined by Auguste Comte as a technical term, before, surprisingly, it entered popular usage. Erdmann observes that, similarly, hygiene is a worthwhile practice even though complete eradication of disease is beyond our reach. Now, Cohen would surely have objected to this view of ethics and its potential, but the explicit reason he comments upon this text is that Erdmann uses what for Cohen is a mistaken understanding of the biblical injunction to love one's neighbor to support his thesis. Erdmann asks: "Why is it that every fellow human being [*Mitmensch*] is called in the biblical language 'the neighbor' [*der Nächste*; i.e., "the nearest"]? . . . Surely the extremely altruistic thought would be expressed much more purely if it were said: 'Love also the *furthest* [*den Fernsten*: the most distant one] as yourself.'"[34] For Erdmann, this is evidence that what he has dubbed "nosism," and not "altruism," is what the Old Testament tradition preaches. And Erdmann picks up the commonplaces of the biblical criticism of his time in going on to identify the New Testament under-standing of the "fellow human being" as an altruistic expansion of what in the Old Testament means merely, "nosistically," "the countryman [*Volksgenosse*], probably even only the relative."[35]

In his 1914 essay, Cohen of course objects to this line of reasoning because, as he points out, the linguistic phenomenon Erdmann points to does not lead him to wonder about the original term for "neighbor" and its meaning, in which the connotation of nearness is simply not present. Cohen's essay takes the Erdmann piece as a pretext to point to the larger movement of Jewish ethics, in which, as Cohen shows—drawing on both biblical and rabbinic sources, and countering the supersessionist juxtapo-sition of the Old and New Testaments that Erdmann seems to rely on—love of the stranger, the other (*alter*), or the furthest, is indeed what is commanded.[36] This pattern of argument is followed by Cohen through-out his writings on "the neighbor."

To summarize, in the passage I discussed from *Ethics of the Pure Will,* Cohen points out that the term *re'a* has been mired in a history of misun-derstandings according to which love of the neighbor is a matter of de-grees of nearness. He argues that the very fact of this misunderstanding makes the notion corruptible in itself and serves to disqualify it as an ethi-cal category. But in the 1914 essay "The Neighbor," as in other works dedicated to this theme, Cohen provides detailed accounts of why "neigh-bor" is a mistranslation and of the negative consequences and implica-tions of that mistranslation.

Let me return now to Levinas's analyses of "proximity" as a nonspatial confrontation with the other, one that avoids any suggestion that com-monality or the inhabiting of a common space is constitutive of the self-other relation. In *Otherwise than Being* and related writings, in which Le-vinas investigates further, or more radically, what sort of self it is that confronts or correlates with the rupture of alterity, we find extensive and sustained reflections on proximity, and the other that I face is routinely also referred to as the "neighbor [*le prochain*]." These reflections present a sophisticated and extremely complex working-out of the relationship between neighborhood/proximity and distance, between the neighbor and the stranger.

Proximity is one of the headings under which, in *Otherwise than Being* and related writings, Levinas explores and attenuates the paradoxical na-ture of what in *Totality and Infinity* is called the ethical relation or the face to face. Thus, proximity becomes a name for the becoming-ethical of intentionality, conceived as a "reversal," in which subjectivity "enters into contact" with an absolute and unrepresentable singularity.[37] It becomes a name for what in *Totality and Infinity* is described as the circumstance that the face signifies all by itself, its "autosignifyingness [*auto-signifiance*],"[38] and thus for a language that is more originary than the language of representation or communication. The term is used to capture the "immediacy" of the encounter, which is also described in terms of sensibility, sensation (particularly taste and touch) understood as something "coming to pass between the sensing and the sensed."[39] This at once sensible and linguistic immediacy is a rupture in consciousness that at the same time "founds the other" and is thus the event or advent of the ethical: "This is the original language, the foundation of the other [*l'autre*]. The precise point at which this mutation of the intentional into the ethical occurs, and occurs continually, at which the approach *breaks through* [perce] consciousness, is the human skin and face. Contact is tenderness and responsibility."[40] It is important to note that this immediacy of proximity is not a union or a fusion—neither epistemologically nor experientially—but a relation of tension and difference. Levinas defines the "ethical" as follows: "a relationship between terms such as are united neither by a synthesis of understanding nor by a relationship between subject or object, and yet where the one weighs or concerns or is meaningful to the other, where they are bound by an intrigue which knowing can neither exhaust nor unravel."[41] Immediacy, as "contact with the other" is not fusion because "to be in contact is neither to invest the other and annul his alterity, nor to suppress myself in the other." This also holds true if we think of the sensible dimension of contact, in which "the touching and the touched separate, as though the touched, distancing itself [*s'eloignant*], always already other, did not have anything *in common* with me."[42]

As a problem of logic and epistemology, or rather, as a break with traditional logic and with epistemologically based thinking, proximity is distinct from a number of classical logical and epistemological structures: The neighbor is not a member of a genus or species, to the point of not even being singular in the sense of *tode ti*—a uniqueness within a genus; it cannot be captured by what Husserl described as an experiential "horizon of the known and the unknown," nor is it an a priori; rather the neighbor "concerns me outside of" or "before" "any a priori." The concept of the neighbor is thus rigorously distinguished from the meaning of "neighbor" that Levinas wants to avoid in the discussion following "Transcendence and Height": the neighbor has essentially nothing in common with me.[43] As in the interview on Jewish philosophy I cited earlier, one way this neighbor who belongs to no common genus with me is here described is as the *premier venu*, the first-comer or first one to come along: "Absolving himself of all essence, all genus/*genre*, all resemblance, the neighbor, *premier venu*, concerns me for the first time (even if he is an old acquaintance, an old friend, an old lover, long implicated in the fabric of my social relations) in a contingency that excludes the a priori."[44] The noncommonality between the neighbor and myself means that proximity is not coexistence: rather than being a place of rest "with" me, the proximity of the neighbor is a "restlessness," or a trace that is neither simple presence nor absence. In temporal terms, this noncoincidence is expressible as the neighbor's "anachronous presence to consciousness," or as consciousness itself being "always too late for the rendezvous with the neighbor."[45] To "approach the other" is an obsessive condition of "still pursuing what is already present, still seeking what one has found"; it is a unity of approach and proximity.[46]

In quasi-spatial terms, proximity is not to be thought as a relative spatial relationship that tends toward a limit of contiguity or coincidence.[47] Usually (and here we can recall Cohen's frustrations at the connotations of the term *neighbor*) social or intersubjective connection is predicated upon a spatial nearness that is construed as the primary phenomenon. Levinas instead invites us to think "contiguity itself [as] comprehensible [on the basis of] proximity—approach, neighborhood [*voisinage*], contact" and "the homogeneity of [Euclidean-geometric] space"—on the basis of "the human signification of justice against all difference and thus [of] all the motivations of proximity of which justice is the term [or goal; *terme*]": "If in the beginning there were [classical] geometry and physics, [cultural] attributes would never have anything but a subjective existence in the heads of men, and in the customs and writings of peoples."[48] The traditional view of space is a space of absolute coexistence and a priori, homogeneous universality.[49] By contrast, Levinas uses the term *fraternity* to point to the potential that the notion of proximity has for founding a kind of collectivity. But fraternity is not a logical universality; it is "founded," as it were, on a rupture of any genus, species, or quiddity.[50] The signification of proximity is "anarchic," and this means that in proximity "a subject is implicated in a way not reducible to the spatial sense which proximity takes on when the third party troubles it by demanding justice in the 'unity of transcendental consciousness.'" This line occurs in chapter 3 of *Otherwise than Being*, in which "proximity" is analyzed in a general sense—in conjunction with other themes such as sensibility, signification, enjoyment, obsession, and subjectivity. Chapter 3 broaches the theme of the "third party" and thus intimates that proximity has consequences for the analysis of social space—a space that must not be presupposed as a foundation for proximity but that can only be taken to issue from proximity. However, a footnote refers the reader to the place in chapter 5 of *Otherwise than Being* in which these implications are developed more fully.[51]

The sections of chapter 5 in which Levinas charts a course back from the paradoxical proximity of ethics to the sphere of the third, which is that of justice, of community, and of knowing and theorizing, have been much discussed in the scholarship on Levinas. Given Levinas's formal distinction between ethics as the asymmetric and singular confrontation between myself and a transcendent other and politics or justice as the realm in which a "third" interrupts this relation such that I am no longer uniquely bound to the command of the other but must compare and adjudicate between competing demands, readers have been justifiably drawn to this part of *Otherwise than Being*. In it Levinas famously states that we must not think of this interruption by the third as an empirically subsequent moment but that "the others concern me from the first."[52] I would like to propose that the possibility of this way back to politics, which Levinas also describes as a becoming "enigmatic" of the infinite, can be located in the "return" of the neighbor in the phenomenological descriptions that make up the argument of *Otherwise than Being*. Levinas's explorations of the interplay of distance and nearness, presence and absence that paradoxically constitute "contact" or "proximity" lead as if of their own accord to a new posing of the question of social space and community. In chapter 5 of *Otherwise than Being*, the task of specifying what the third is in relation to the singular other arises initially not as a question of politics or of the social sphere but as the quasi-"logical" or quasi-"epistemological" problem that in proximity, which involves a signification that is never fully known or fully present, the idea of a lack of presence or of knowledge is not simply eliminated, and the primacy of the theoretical plane has not been simply overcome.[53] Levinas sounds almost Hegelian here, reminding us that, just as for negation "the sense of which the negation is a negation is [always] conserved," so too the "contestation" or "contradiction" of the claim beyond being has meaning only if this claim is also heard, that is, stated.[54] Contradiction is here understood as taking place "not . . . between two simultaneous statements, but between a statement and its conditions, as though they were in the same time." That is, contradiction occupies an "ambiguous" or "enigmatic" time that corresponds to the "extreme proximity of the neighbor" in all its facets. This also amounts to the idea that the beyond-being or the infinite or transcendence only happens by way of "a subject who confesses or contests it," which is to say that, by virtue of an "inversion of order," revelation "is made by the one who receives it," by a subjectivity marked by "alterity in the same."[55] This is the logical, or quasi-logical, space in which Levinas can speak of the advent of the third, for it is the third that "introduces a contradiction in the saying" that is alterity. It is by virtue of the third, or the question of justice, that we remain not simply in proximity as "an immediacy antecedent to questions" but that, as Levinas puts it, "there is a problem," a troubling of that immediacy. This troubling takes the form of *questions* such as: "What are the other and the third party for one another? What have they done to one another? Which passes before the other?" and "What do I have to do with justice?" Whereas proximity originally pertained to the stranger as *inconnu* (unknown) and as *premier venu*, as no one in particular, as the first-comer, now we have the "latent birth of knowing in proximity." Whereas in proximity "I alone answer, before any question, for my neighbor," by virtue of this knowing I am aware that "the other stands in a relationship with the third party, for whom I cannot entirely answer. The other and the third party, my neighbors, contemporaries of one another, put distance between me and the other and the third party." It is here that Levinas introduces the verse from Isaiah with which I began this essay. In his rendering, it reads: "Peace, peace to the near/neighbor [*prochain*] and to the far [*lointain*]." He understands it as expressing the contradiction that is introduced by the third that is at once "the limit of responsibility and the birth of the question: What do I have to do with justice?" and thus by the fact of consciousness itself. Here, nonspatial proximity gives way to a space of contiguity and of the copresence or synchrony that is the prerequisite for being "on an equal footing as before a court of justice."[56]

For Cohen, too, the category of the "neighbor," properly understood as the "stranger," is a key moment in the origination and pursuit of justice. One way that Cohen guards against the misunderstanding that love of the neighbor as an *affect* is the basis for ethical action and against the associated problem of thinking the neighbor in terms of empirical nearness is by linking the essential equivalence between love of the neighbor and love of the stranger with two important juridical categories:[57] (1) the biblical term *ger*, usually translated as "alien" or "stranger" in Leviticus 19:33–34,[58] which he translates into German as *Beisaß-Fremdling*, meaning "resident-alien"; and (2) its Talmudic transformation into the category of the Noahide, which he calls an "institution of state law [*staatsrechtliche Institution*]." The Noahide, or "son of Noah," is traditionally defined as a non-Jew whose status is equivalent to that of a Jew and who is bound by seven laws that are regarded as binding on all humankind (and have frequently been equated with the modern-day notion of natural law). Cohen underscores the fact that these are legal-political categories (a fact that is also significant in view of Cohen's systematic elaboration of ethics by way of jurisprudence in *Ethics of the Pure Will*): the *ger* or resident-alien is a status that emerges in order to mediate the opposition between the native-born and the foreigner (*nokhri*); and the Noahide, defined as a citizen of the state (*Staatsbürger*), can be understood as mediating the opposition between Israel and the other nations.[59] In this sense, the neighbor or near one, reinterpreted as essentially the stranger or distant one, is for Cohen the key to a messianic peace and justice among the nations. Cohen, commenting in 1914 on the immediate political effects of misunderstanding the biblical "neighbor" in terms of nearness, writes:

> What sort of development and what sort of sincerity would have been gained by political, or historical, culture if instead of the neighbor-love that easily becomes a mere phrase the pregnant command to love the stranger had become the fundamental law of religion? Our current politics would not so hypocritically fly in the face of religion if expressions such as "alien elements" [*fremde Volkselemente*] or even "foreign bodies" [*Fremdkörper*] were impossible in the language of a respectable politics. Politics is not child's play. Massive difficulties constitute its ongoing task. But the basic law of morality and, it is to be hoped, hence also of religion is love to all that bears a human face. And this demand becomes more elevated when from this face shine not the traits of one's own tribe, as the privileged one.

Without wanting to say that Cohen's elaboration of the concept of the "neighbor" is somehow presupposed by, or structurally similar to, Levinas's working out of proximity, I do want to suggest that by looking at the two treatments of neighborhood alongside each other we can read the return of proximity, the analyses of ethical subjectivity in terms of the *prochain*, in Levinas's later writings as perhaps allied with Cohen's thought, perhaps as a "neighboring" thought. What the two have in common at the very least is a sense that neighboring, as an unstable relation that combines contact and difference or distance, far from amounting either to an a priori equivalence or referring to a homogeneous social space that can be taken for granted, names a "problem" both for phenomenological analysis and for a politics based on ethical obligation.

We can go further and say that these two lines of thought also neighbor each other as modern attempts to philosophize in drawing reflectively on Jewish sources. Levinas shares with Cohen some basic views about Judaism: both thinkers engage with Judaism as a living tradition available to thought and reject attempts to present Judaism as a relic. Both call into question commonplaces such as the alignment of Judaism with an empty ritualism versus Christianity as a religion based on conviction or faith. And both attribute to Judaism the idea of love as justice—which Levinas explicitly links to the concept of the neighbor as the third party[60]—and see Jewish law as being oriented toward achieving such justice. But Levinas goes further than Cohen's extremely structured attempts to articulate Judaism and philosophy together in coming up with ever more complex and nuanced ways of capturing a conversation between what I hesitate to call "two traditions," actively weaving two disparate idioms into each other in such a way that they cannot easily be disentangled.

Let us take as an example among so many others a remark from Levinas's essay "Revelation in the Jewish Tradition." This essay is an attempt to express what, philosophically, can be attributed to Judaism, an attempt that I think fully accords with Cohen's attempts to articulate Jewish sources and philosophical reasoning together (and in this case also with Cohen's valorization of obligation to law as an "affinity" between Kantianism and Judaism), but which cannot straightforwardly be read as either a philosophical gloss on a Jewish source or an inner-Jewish discourse:

> I wonder whether the primordial character of the prescriptive in which, in Judaism, the entire Revelation . . . is formed, whether the fact that the mode of receiving what is revealed is obedience [there follows the famous example of Exodus 24:5: "All that the Lord has spoken we will do, and we will hear"] . . . whether all this doesn't indicate the "rationality" of a reason less turned in upon itself than the reason of philosophical tradition. A rationality that would not appear as that of a reason "in decline," but would be precisely understood in its plenitude from out of the irreducible "intrigue" of obedience. An obedience that cannot be traced to a categorical imperative in which a universality is suddenly able to direct a will; [but one that] is traceable to love of the neighbor: to a love without eros, without self-complacency and, in this sense, a love that is obeyed, the responsibility for the neighbor, the taking upon oneself of the destiny of the other, or of fraternity.[61]

To be sure, Levinas is not here polemicizing against a tradition that suppresses the Judaic. But this remark, and many others like it, serve to underscore the striking appearance or idiosyncratic deployment of terms of biblical origin across Levinas's philosophical corpus. We might say that where Cohen, in the late nineteenth and early twentieth centuries, found himself having to militantly assert the contours of a neighborhood in which Judaism would be a particular name for a universal human destiny,

Levinas's works, consciously written in the post-Shoah era, in their mobilization of biblical terms and verses perform a more implicit and thereby more radical, more probing, and more transformative neighboring of Bible and philosophy. In them, what emerges about how philosophy neighbors Judaism is akin to what Levinas says, in "Language and Proximity," of the neighbor in general: that "fraternity with the neighbor [may be seen as] the essence of the original language; it finds universality, or, more precisely, universalization, starting with absolute singularities."[62]

"Love Strong as Death"

Levinas and Heidegger

JEFFREY L. KOSKY

In philosophy and in theology, as in all else, the question we pose and how we pose it can make all the difference. In the case that concerns us (Emmanuel Levinas and his relation to two particular religious traditions: Judaism and Christianity), recognizing this basic fact about our investigations seems as pressing as ever.

My own approach to the issue assumes that we are led astray when we put the question in such a way as to ask whether or not Levinas is a Jewish philosopher, whether or not he offers a Jewish conception of God, or whether or not such and such a Levinasian concept comes from Judaism, the Judaism he learned and to which he never abandoned his commitment. On one hand, the answer to all these questions is "yes": Levinas practiced Judaism, and he was indeed a philosopher; therefore, since a philosophy cannot suspend the position of the philosopher, he must be a Jewish philosopher and we can find the marks of this Judaism throughout his philosophy such that his thought becomes an exemplary instance of an alteration of philosophy by its encounter with alterity, its Jewish other. But sometimes the obvious blocks a questioning that might get closer to things at issue. Perhaps these ways of posing the question, having already been of great service and undeniably useful to our understanding of Levinas, now shift a reader's attention from other questions. Do they entail a normative investigation of what Judaism is, or what makes one a Jew? And would this question mean losing sight of what Levinas might offer for Jewish *and Christian* theologians, not to mention the noncommitted?

One could instead try to read Levinas's text in an effort to think with him so that we can better approach the things at hand, things that he saw and tried to put into words. Along these lines, a better question might be: What can Jews, Christians, and the noncommitted learn from Levinas about matters at issue for them? Levinas's significance for religious and/or theological thought is seen not by asking whether he is theological or not, not by asking whether he belongs to Judaism or not, but by discussing the things that he lets us see.

The issue I propose in this essay is "love strong as death," an issue of concern to members of both Jewish and Christian traditions, and perhaps equally to those committed to neither. Whether or not his account of this love strong as death is Jewish, Christian, or neither is, for this essay, beside the point. We, as readers, confront Levinas's text from our own positions as a Jew, a Christian, a resolutely secular, or some confused commitment to them all. We can learn much about ourselves and our own positions from our response to the challenge his text poses: To what extent do our commitments to these traditions admit alteration by confrontation with Levinas? To what extent do our commitments to these traditions refuse to budge and not let us accept anything from Levinas beyond a certain point? What do our responses to both these questions tell us about ourselves and the world we inhabit?

At the outset of an essay on love strong as death in Levinas, I have to admit that his thoughts on love are very incomplete. After a decade-long protest against using the term, chiefly because he thought it compromised the asymmetry of ethics and responsibility, he comes very late in his career to adopt it in a positive sense. Why? Perhaps that is all we can ask. Perhaps we are looking for too much if we look to Levinas for a developed concept of love, yet we can surely indicate the motivations for and the effects of his adopting the term. Does Levinas's hesitancy before and eventual motivation for adopting love strong as death into his thought provide any resource for Jews, Christians, and the noncommitted concerned to think about love and death . . . perhaps even to think together?

I

I propose a starting point that might seem inappropriate to the concerns of this volume: namely the philosophy of subjectivity. This is to approach love strong as death as neither Jew nor Christian. Adopting this manner of approach to Levinas, we might find him truly "*between* Jews and Christians," so that both Jews and Christians might find something to think about together. I take such a starting point to be warranted by Levinas's own insistence that responsibility "is prior to all civilization" and "is not any sort of cultural gesture,"[1] and by his claims that "I am not for all that an especially Jewish thinker; I am a thinker *tout court*" and "Is all this phenomenology inspired by the Bible? I believe it free of it."[2] And I take such a starting point to imply that the primary sources for my essay will be the philosophical essays, not the Talmudic lectures or the pieces published for a particularly Jewish audience. However interesting I might find the latter pieces (and they are indeed of increasing interest to me as I begin to think about what, for want of a better term, might be called historical actualities), they are not sources for an inquiry into Levinas *between* Jews and Christians.

The notion of love in Levinas is tied to his own search for an interpretation of human subjectivity that does not rest on the "I think." However much Levinas maintains the terms *subject* and *subjectivity*, it is clear that he offers a powerful redefinition of the terms. This redefinition addresses at least two of the dilemmas confronted by the inherited tradition of the philosophy of the subject. We can only understand a love strong as death if we first understand the aporias of traditional theories of human subjectivity, aporias to which love might eventually respond.

In the first place, for a philosophy of subjectivity that takes the subject as the "I think" of knowledge, the I itself can never appear as the subject it claims to be; it can never be a subject of the philosophy it makes possible. When the I is taken as knowledge that represents objects, the living human subjectivity can never appear, precisely because appearance is always the appearance of objects and for the subjectivity of an I to appear, it must not appear as an object but as subject. The knowledge produced by the thinking I is always objective knowledge—that is, knowledge of what is past or has just passed, but subjectivity is lived in the present, where we don't know but live. Levinas acknowledges that Husserl's reduction to the subjective acts or intentions animating the objective world should have marked a breakthrough for this dilemma, one by which the philosophy of subjectivity might explore the lived experience of human subjectivity as such. And yet Husserl, according to Levinas, falls short of making good on this breakthrough when he again loses the life of subjectivity in his fascination with the constitution of objects—among which the I can never, by definition, be counted. Objectivity having been achieved, or even aimed at, subjectivity once again slumbers in its objects, whereas it should be awake and alive.

A second and not unrelated shortcoming of the inherited philosophy of the subject is that it fails to accomplish the ipseity or selfhood that would singularize the I. Received philosophies of the subject determine the subject as an "I think" or intentionality that affirms itself in relation to objects. But the knowledge or constitution of objects never reaches singularity precisely because objects are objective and therefore should be known or constituted in acts common to all. The I of this subject has no unique self of its own since it becomes I only in the constitution or knowledge of objects that any I could achieve. These philosophies thus prove unable to reach what is uniquely my own, what is most intimate to me, and what makes me the self that only I am. This failure to accomplish a self or ipseity that would singularize the I is seen in Levinas's never repudiated charge that received philosophies of the subject are philosophies of the neutral in which the I (as much as the other) is absorbed in the impersonal or anonymous.

Levinas's phenomenology of human subjectivity overcomes these shortcomings in a single gesture by reducing them to a fundamental oversight: namely, the failure to describe the originary event in which, before I am I, the other summons me to appear as myself in responsibility. "Responsibility [Levinas writes] is an individuation, a principle of individuation. On the famous problem 'Is man individuated by matter, or by form,' I support individuation by responsibility for the other."[3] In this bold move, Levinas resolves the two dilemmas of the philosophy of the subject by also resolving a third: the problem of solipsism, a subject closed to alterity. In sum, for Levinas, the failure to describe the singularity of the subject and therefore to present the I itself rests on the failure to describe the prior event in which the other appears first in responsibility and with this appearing summons the self to itself as that self which it alone is. In a formulation that should perhaps be canonical in readings of Levinas, he writes, "The way I appear is a summons. I am placed in the passivity of an undeclinable assignation, in the accusative, a self."[4]

This solution is as simple as it is profound, for it calls for nothing less than "an inversion of consciousness" or "an inversion of intentionality,"[5] in which it is no longer the case that others appear for me through representing or intentional acts, as if I were the unshakeable source or origin of all objects and signification—a solution that for Levinas leads to the solipsism of reducing the other to the same. Rather, it is me who appears or is constituted in response to the summons of the other. For the received philosophies of the subject, the subject *either* appears before itself by means of the I's powers of representation, in which case it at once immediately betrays itself in an objectivity made by the I, *or* it cannot be known or intended and so does not appear at all, remaining abstract and estranged from itself. Put this way, this dilemma rests on the assumption that I am the ultimate, the first and the only source of appearance. When the I is taken as the spontaneous and originary I of I think or I intend, the philosophy of the subject cannot see the birth, creation, or origin of the I itself—what Levinas calls "the latent birth of the subject" or "the self as a creature . . . answering to a call that could not have reached it since, brought out of nothingness, it obeyed before hearing the order."[6] The subject appears not spontaneously but in response to the summons of the other, whose originary call renders me secondary even if the first to respond. If, as Levinas claims, "knowing of oneself by oneself, is not all there is to the notion of subjectivity," but rather subjectivity "already rests on a subjective condition,"[7] then the philosophy that takes this subjective condition into account by thinking the other whose summons subjects me can point toward a way through the impasse.

For Levinas, then, the subject attains ipseity in submitting to its subjection to the summons that demands responsibility. I am thus myself in an original inappropriateness without being the source or master of that self; for I receive myself from a relation to the other, who is there before I am. "It assigns *me* before *I* show myself, before I set myself up" as operator of evidence or representation.[8] This involves a complete reversal in the naming of the subject. "To this command continually put forth only a 'here I am' [*me voici*] can answer, where the pronoun I is in the accusative . . . possessed by the other."[9] *Me voici* or "here I am" does not, therefore, claim the place where I stand as my own possession, as "my place in the sun." Rather, as the first words by which the self would appear, it testifies to the first experience of myself as reception of a me possessed or claimed by the other—a me that, as Levinas writes, "is already constituted when the first act of constitution originates."[10] To capture this sense in which my self (me) is something already constituted when the I comes on the scene and can answer for it, one could perhaps risk translating Levinas's *me voici* with the uncustomary formulation "it's me" or even "this is me," where such a declaration would signify both the acceptance of a selfhood assigned as a duty given by another ("Yes, it's me over whom that claim is exerted. I accept.") and the shock or surprise of coming upon oneself as upon something not originally one's own ("This is me!? I did not know or make this self.").

As "already constituted when the first act of constitution originates," my self appears and appears in an undeniable, indubitable certainty—the certainty of the already done that is done without and before I (think or *cogito*) arrive on the scene. Levinas characterizes this undeclinable certainty of *me voici* by speaking of it as a testimony to "the always already," and at least once he even describes the certainty of *me voici* as a "fact." He writes: "Neither a vision of oneself by oneself, nor a manifestation of oneself to oneself . . . ipseity is a point already identified from the outside . . . an identity already realized, the 'fact' or 'already done' that the oneself contributes to consciousness and knowing."[11] As a fact, my self, *me voici*, must be distinguished from an effect in that the latter would be coordinate with a cause that guarantees the total visibility or intelligibility of the effect by securing an origin and therefore the potential of full presence to itself from the ground up. A fact, however, as always already done, is without cause or origin. It is therefore, to draw on Levinas's own frequently employed lexicon, "an-archic," coming from an "immemorial" past. Submitted to this fact of my self (*me voici*), I am myself, indubitably and undeniably, without my knowing or seeing fully who I am in objective self-presence.

The certainty of myself as *me voici* is therefore not realized by apprehending it and then becoming it or not, but by exposure to it. I do not come to myself in knowledge but in the vulnerability of exposure. "The subject is inseparable from exposure to this appeal or election which cannot be declined."[12] This exposure to the election of the other is so radical that I cannot evade or slip away from it without losing the me that I am. That the ipseity of the I should be given as a fact already done emphasizes that subjectivity does not appear by making itself so much as the subject discovers itself already done without the I knowing or having anything to do with it. This is clearly the sense in which Levinas speaks of responsibility as exposure prior to any commitment. That is, prior to any choice on my part and without regard for any thought or action I may have committed, the other summons me as responsible. My responsibility thus testifies to "an extremely urgent assignation—an obligation anachronously prior to any commitment. This anteriority is 'older' than the a priori [which] expresses a way of being affected which can in no way be invested by spontaneity."[13] It is also why Levinas will invoke an irreducible belatedness in the subjectivity of the subject: summoned to myself in responsibility before I am there to answer, I am separated from myself by an irrecuperable delay or lag. The self is "delayed behind its present moment and unable to recuperate this delay."[14]

One might make the following objection: when the self appears as *me voici*, it does not appear with the objective certainty that it would have were it made present by an "I think" and so it can hardly qualify as subject for philosophy. Such an objection might object that this self is not given with sufficient evidence precisely because it appears as a fact to which I am exposed, not as an object whose experience I can make in vision or knowledge. When Levinas claims that responsibility or *me voici* is "neither a vision of oneself by oneself, nor a manifestation of oneself to oneself," when he continues to claim that "ipseity is a point already identified from the outside,"[15] isn't he confirming this objection? In short, Levinas speaks about a self for which philosophy lacks sufficient evidence and about which it can never be certain.

The objection can be countered by a more strict analysis of its presuppositions. Following leads suggested by his own reading of §§6 and 9 of Husserl's *Cartesian Meditations*, Levinas suggests that apodicticity and adequacy of evidence need not go hand-in-hand, and indeed they do not go hand-in-hand when it is a question of "the living presence of the I to itself."[16] Here, according to Levinas, "the adequation between what is 'intended' [*visé*] and what is "seen" [*vu*] is not the essential thing. 'Apodicticity may, in some cases, belong to inadequate evidence. It possesses an absolute indubitability of a special and well-determined order.'"[17] Whereas Husserl does not venture to offer a positive determination of this apodicticity without adequate evidence, Levinas mobilizes it in the account of the birth of the self in responsibility. In other words, I reach a certainty of my self in exposure to the summons by which the other claims me, even though this certainty does not benefit from an intuition that would be adequate to constituting clear and distinct knowledge. "The indubitable apodictic does not come from any new piece of evidence,"[18] according to Levinas, but rather from the undeniability and irrefutability of the originary summons, which has always already occurred without and prior to me. Appearing in response, the self in responsibility testified to by *me voici* appears with an evidence that is apodictic even if it lacks the definitiveness that would come from the presentation of adequate evidence. In fact, the summons that calls me to myself strikes me with a certainty that is even more apodictic than that produced by adequate evidence—in that, according to Levinas, even when intuition is adequate to the intention the evidence so produced can be rejected or denied, whereas one can never deny the fact of a summons that has always already happened. That one does not fully know the cause of this fact, that the other who summons me remains inconceivable and not presentable to the I (think), does not, for all that, make the fact of the summons any less irrefutable, apodictic, or certain.[19]

Not only does responsibility give certainty of the self to the philosophy of subjectivity, it also gives the singularity of the self. According to Levinas, "The word I means 'Here I am' answering for everything and for everyone."[20] Such an I, responsible for everything and everybody, would be radically incommensurate with others; for if "Here I am" answers for everything and everybody, then no other would be like the one who says "Here I am." "Here I am" thus admits an immeasurable, incomparable difference between the self and others, between what responsibility admits is demanded of me (everything) and what I would demand of others (nothing at all). Responsibility, precisely in what distinguishes it from a universalizable morality, gives the uniqueness or singularity of the I, for no one can take responsibility for me. As Levinas puts it, "no one can substitute himself for me who substitutes for all."[21] In other words, *me voici* is unique in that only it is subjected to or substituted for others. "Its exceptional uniqueness . . . is the incessant event of subjection to everything, of substitution. It is a being divesting itself, emptying itself."[22] Thus, the very uniqueness of the self, in responsibility for everything and everyone, is also its renunciation of self-possession.

To summarize: Levinas's phenomenology addresses two of the main aporias in the philosophy of subjectivity (first, certainty of its nonobjective appearance and, second, its singularity) by reducing them to a third (the failure to constitute the other). It does so by reducing the subject beyond the I to an anterior instance that awakens it, one over which it exercises no mastery but to which it is instead exposed so radically as not to be able to decline it. Levinas calls this anterior instance or subjection of the subject to itself me or *me voici*. These terms name the undeclinable singularity of the subject, a singular self that appears with indubitable certainty even if I do not know it or its cause from the ground up. This singularity consists, or rather con-sists, precisely in its de-sisting, paradoxically, in renouncing self-possession by devoting myself to the other in responsibility.

II

Coming to this conclusion, I am led to a surprising observation: the problem in the philosophy of the subject that Levinas confronts puts him in continuity with his great teacher Martin Heidegger, at least the Heidegger who wrote *Being and Time*. This is not so surprising. What is surprising, however, is that his answer to the dilemmas of such philosophy recalls the pattern or schema of Heidegger's own answers. Only by noting these similarities can we begin to measure or account for the differences between the two. Out of this confrontation between opposing phenomenologies of the human, a meaning for the otherwise intuitively empty phrase "love strong as death" might emerge more clearly. In fact, a quick glance at the texts shows that Levinas employs the phrase most often precisely when he is discussing the limits of Heideggerian ontology and its understanding of human being. What is at stake in the confrontation between Heidegger and Levinas, then, is an understanding of human subjectivity that might be formulated in terms of Levinas's search for a love strong as death. Is the human to be understood within the horizon opened by death or that given by love? Levinas will choose the latter, and in thus opening the human to a "horizon" of signification beyond the world that opens with ecstatic projection toward death, he might show something of significance to religious traditions that also see the human within an otherworldly, or at the very least nonworldly, horizon.

But before this Levinas's choice must first be seen as part of the same problematic as Heidegger's thanatological ontology or ontological thanatology. What I would like to suggest, contrary to an often hasty reading, is that the "mineness" that characterizes Dasein, like the "Here I am" appearing in responsibility, names a "subject" who is absolutely unique and unsurpassable yet not originarily sufficient to itself. Like Levinas, but before him, Heidegger aims to go back behind the I secure in possession of itself to a prior moment in which the I is given to the unique or singular self it has to be, without the possibility of evasion. This anterior instance from which the I receives itself is called Dasein, whose definition Heidegger offers with the term *mineness*. Mineness is the burden of selfhood: "The Being of any such entity is *in each case mine*. . . . Being is that which is an issue [or is at stake] for every such entity." This definition echoes others—for instance, "in each case Dasein has its Being to be, and has it as its own."[23] To say that being is in each case mine is to give ipseity by saying that I can never not be the being that I am. Far from stating an originary property or possession of the subject, mineness—at least at first—is a radical deposition of the sovereign, originary I, rendering its primacy secondary and dependent on the Dasein into which it is thrown or delivered over, passively, to be the unique self it did not make but *that it is obliged to be, indeclinably.*

That I am not the origin of what makes me myself is what Heidegger starts to think under the names *Befindlichkeit* and *Geworfenheit*. These terms characterize the subjective condition in which Dasein finds itself (*Befindlichkeit*) always already in the throes (*Geworfenheit*) of a Being that it is responsible for bearing as its own. As Heidegger puts it, "An entity of the character of Dasein . . . finds itself [*sich befindet*] in its thrownness. In this [*Befindlichkeit*] Dasein is always brought before itself, and has always found itself. . . . As an entity which has been delivered over to its Being, it remains also delivered over to the fact that it must always have found itself."[24] From this perspective, Levinas's effort to work through the impasses of the philosophy of subjectivity by suggesting that the self does not constitute its own appearance appears perfectly in line with Heideggerian thought. The similarities appear even more striking. "Dasein is always disclosed as that entity to which it has been delivered over in its Being; and in this way it has been delivered over to the Being which, in existing, it has to be."[25] This Being that I am obliged to be is received in a condition to which I must originally surrender or be exposed. In other words, I am not master or origin of my own, since mineness, as found or received in affectedness (*Befindlichkeit*), is foreign to the I, even if it is what makes me me.

This character of radical exposure or being delivered over is what Heidegger means by *Geworfenheit* or thrownness: "Dasein is something that has been thrown. It has been brought into its there, but not of its own accord."[26] Thrown into the Being I am obliged to bear as my own burden, Dasein arrives after the fact of its own being has been given and therefore "constantly lags behind its possibilities."[27] Too late to posit my own Being and its possibilities, too late to be the origin of my self, I come into my own without knowing or mastering my self fully. The event in which this "self" or mineness is "found" or appears originarily is subjection to the fact, always already thrown or delivered over to what precedes all that I have known or chosen.

The question then arises: To what is Dasein exposed or delivered over when it is thrown into the instance that makes itself (mineness) appear and appear as the unique, singular self that Dasein alone has to be? The answer is well known: death. If mineness names the uncommon burden of selfhood, the impossibility of being able to evade the "self" into which I alone am thrown or to which I am exposed undeclinably, then I am delivered over to my Dasein in resolute anticipation of death. This death, according to Heidegger's analysis, can be approached, but never grasped conceptually or realized in an intuition that would be adequate to it, only as a possibility that is impossible to realize. Death is the one possibility that is always only possible since actualizing it confiscates all possibility. What makes Dasein itself is therefore something that remains opaque, foreign, and irreducibly other to this Dasein—the possibility of its own death into which it is thrown. However certain and undeclinable death might be, for Heidegger, such certainty does not result in complete or adequate knowledge of who or what Dasein might be, since Dasein is disclosed to itself not by apprehending itself or making itself an object of the I, but by holding itself resolutely open to what Heidegger calls this indefinite certainty.

According to Heidegger's well-known analysis, death brings Dasein before the indefinite certainty of its ownmost, nonrelational, not-to-be-outstripped possibility. In denying, first, that another might represent or substitute himself for me and, inversely, that I might know death by taking the death of others as a substitute theme, Heidegger asserts that death singularizes me radically—distinguishing me from all others by designating what is uniquely and irreplaceably my own: "*No one can take the other's dying from him,*" and "dying is something that every Dasein itself must take upon itself," such that I cannot take the death of others to give the experience of death to me. This leads to Heidegger's strict rejection of the claim that "any Dasein may be substituted for another at random, so that what cannot be experienced in one's own Dasein is accessible in that of a stranger."[28] We should not let the rejection of the notion of substitution here block us from noting the similarity to what Levinas in fact thinks under the name *substitution*. Like Levinas, Heidegger here rejects the idea that what is my own should be comparable to what others also call their own. Death names what is so radically my own as to make me incommensurate with others—what I alone am responsible for and can ask no other to take on as his own.

For Heidegger, then, death subjects me precisely by exposing me to the mineness of my Being: as the always looming (certain) possibility that threatens to arrive at any and every (indefinite) moment, without my being able to prevent or evade it, the indefinite certainty of death is what undoes the security of self-possession by putting my Being at stake or at issue in each moment. Resolute anticipation of death thus frees the I from what it knows it is by exposing it to the Dasein that it has to be or not in each moment. Though death is the possibility of impossibility, the possibility that would put an end to all possibility of existence, it also gives possibility to existence in that some possibility always remains (death might come and change things entirely) so long as existence is not yet dead. It is therefore death, the possibility of impossibility, that possibilizes each moment, making it one to win or to lose, one that is not secure but at issue for me as my own.

And yet, to die is not another possibility that I have the power to accomplish like all the other possibilities making up my existence. Dasein's "death is the possibility of no-longer-being-able-to-be-there."[29] Exposure to the possibility of death thus gives me to the possibility of my ownmost Dasein as one that paralyzes my ability, as one that means "no-longer-being-able-to-be," and so it gives me to my ownmost Being as to a self that I can never fully appropriate or be appropriate to. For Dasein to be itself, it must expose itself to the loss of itself. My ownmost possibility is the one that dispossesses me of my own, of ever seizing myself with definiteness such I could be a sufficient foundation for the security of self-possession. Dasein's "uttermost possibility [Heidegger writes] lies in giving itself up."[30]

III

My reading of Heidegger and Levinas has suggested that their critical revision of the philosophy of subjectivity has led them each to a similar point. These similarities could be summarized as follows: (1) Both mineness and responsibility think the appearance of the I in response to an anterior instance to which (2) the subject must be exposed or thrown such that subjectivity is not first in itself but subjected to. . . . (3) This subjection to an anterior instance that gives the I to itself summons the singularity or uniqueness of the subject that was lost for the transcendental I, but it summons me as unique by (4) dispossessing me of the security of possessing myself in full self-sufficiency. In short, in both cases, I am NOT what makes me me, but I come after the instance that gives me myself as something I can never fully possess or secure from start to finish. Levinas's text itself seems, at least once, to acknowledge a translatability of *me voici* and *Dasein* when he writes, "*My* substitution. It is as *my own* [mienne] that substitution for the neighbor is produced."³¹ Responsibility, as substitution, here appears as the event in which I am reduced to what Levinas, echoing a certain Heidegger, here says is mine or my own.

Levinas's distinction from Heidegger must therefore be found elsewhere than where Levinas often, but not exclusively, asserts it. In the first place, Heidegger's notion of mineness is not reducible to perseverance in being, as Levinas often understands it. When Heidegger says that Dasein's being is at issue in each moment, that in each moment of existence Dasein must put itself at stake in order to achieve its being, he denies that Dasein is a substantial or subsisting I maintaining itself. Whereas Levinas tends to read Dasein as the substantiality or originarity of an I, mineness in Heidegger decenters the I, renders its primacy secondary and dependent on the being to which Dasein is delivered over, passively. Mineness does not mean that Dasein's Being subsists in itself, but that Dasein receives its being only by surrendering or exposing itself to an instance that precedes it and gives it to itself.

Similarly, there is a certain line of argument in Levinas that insists on seeing being toward death as securing the possession indicated by mineness, a way of coming into one's own or being appropriate to oneself. This lies at the heart of Levinas's criticism of Dasein as unjust. Secure in its possession of itself, according to Levinas, Dasein perseveres unquestioned in a place that it claims as its own, appropriate property. This, for Levinas, following Pascal, is the beginning of injustice: "'that is my place in the sun.' That is how the usurpation of the whole world began." But Levinas's reading underestimates, I believe, the extent to which death gives me the certainty of my Dasein precisely by dispossessing me of Dasein. My own-most possibility, my mineness, comes upon me, according to Heidegger, as an inappropriable possibility that ruins my self-sufficiency. Dasein can never be fully appropriate to itself precisely because, though finite, it cannot reach its end. If, according to Heidegger, for Dasein to be is to be possible, Levinas tends to treat this possibility as wholly exhausted in potentiality or power, as the power or potential to be where all its possibilities are within its reach and fall under its power to appropriate. This fails to give enough credit to the important sense in which Dasein does not have power over its most fundamental possibility, death, a possibility that, indeed, appears only ever as an indefinite possibility that no power can make actual.

In short, Levinas seems to accept the Heideggerian notions of *Befindlichkeit* and *Geworfenheit*, but to accuse Heidegger of abandoning their unsettling, destabilizing, decentering effects—arguing that the passivity of thrownness is assumed in the projection of existence ahead of itself. I would suggest, however, that the lacking origin, the lack of self-sufficiency in Dasein, returns as the impossible future of death. The impossibility of death is the ruin of the project of assuming one's own origin, that is, of making thrownness into a basis for a secure and self-possessed life. If the project of existence is the way to appropriate the Dasein into which I am thrown, this project of appropriation is ruined by death. If thrownness means that Dasein finds itself in an originary inappropriateness to itself, death marks the ineradicability of this inappropriateness.

IV

I have aimed to establish the similarities that a philosophy of subjectivity might find between Heidegger and Levinas, and I have suggested that for a philosophy of subjectivity, some of the sharpest differences between them might rest on misrepresentations. But I have not established this rapprochement merely for its own sake. Rather, I have tried to draw the common front that brings them together so that it might become all the more obvious what battle sets them apart. Ultimately this will rest on Levinas's discovering the significance of a love strong as death, a discovery that introduces human being within a horizon (or nonhorizon) of signification that exceeds the world.

To approach the significance of these words in this way—that is, by comparing and contrasting Levinas with Heidegger's alternative phenomenology of human subjectivity—is to do so without reference to particular religious traditions in order to situate Levinas *between* Jews and Christians. If indeed Heidegger represents one of the biggest challenges to the Levinasian conception of human subject (precisely because Heideggerian Dasein is so similar to Levinasian subjectivity), in what can we establish the difference between Dasein and *me voici?* The answer is not hard to divine: in responsibility, I am given to myself in response to the summons of the other who appears in the face. In existing, Dasein is given to itself in responding to death. The question that sets apart what it brings together is therefore something like this: Is the event that gives the uniqueness or singularity of the subject the event of giving myself to another (Levinas) or simply giving myself up (Heidegger)?

Now on what basis does Levinas, coming after Heidegger, decide that the subject of phenomenology is named *me voici* and not Dasein? I'd like to suggest two options. The first is to say that this is where prephilosophical experiences exercise a decisive influence. Here is where we might find justification for invoking the Jewish Levinas, but of course we would have to have decided already who a Jew is. The second is to say that Levinas challenges the philosophical or phenomenological methods and insights on which Heidegger's analysis rests.

Consider the first option: if Levinas decides that the subject is given to itself in responsibility, when it could very well be described similarly in terms of death, this decision comes not from philosophical necessities but from—where? From the other. Levinas's decision to treat the subject as responsibility would indicate the point at which philosophy yields to the prephilosophical experience of ethical summons. This is perhaps why Levinas chooses to conclude the introduction of *Otherwise than Being* with the rather frank and frankly surprising admission, "No doubt [this book] is not completely disengaged from prephilosophical experience."[32]

These prephilosophical experiences would include the inheritance of a Jewish tradition (which one of the several?) that teaches holiness as a social relation and, perhaps more importantly, the prephilosophical experience of the Nazi genocide. On this reading, the effect of Judaism could be seen in the naming of the unknowable other as "the widow, the orphan, the poor" and in the response of the responsible self prior to language stated with the words *me voici*. This response, Levinas insists, is prior to language in that it is the opening of language, the face-to-face within which language is born. And yet, more than once this prelinguistic or wordless response is stated in words bearing quotation marks and a reference to the Hebrew scriptures, Isaiah 6:8. The same can be said for the words that bespeak the wordless expression of the face before language: "Thou shalt not kill!" These references, precisely as citations, might indicate recourse to what would no longer be given in phenomenological description but by literature or historical tradition. Without inheriting the literature of a Jewish tradition, Levinas would have no words to say the ineffable, the ineffable expression of the face and the ineffable response of the subject. When it is a matter of saying the unsayable, one can only use borrowed words or cite a received language. Philosophy would yield to literature—in particular the literature of Jewish tradition. When it comes time to decide between existence and responsibility as the ultimate subjection of subjectivity, Levinas's philosophy would yield to a prephilosophical (literary) experience of Jewish tradition (the scriptures that give the words to speak the ineffable) and Jewish experience (the Holocaust and, more broadly, anti-Semitism, whose victims' appeal is heard as that to which *Otherwise than Being* dedicates its response).

V

But I don't think this would be Levinas's last word. In the final stage of his remarkable career, there is a philosophical challenge to the key methodological gestures and phenomenological interpretations of *Being and Time*. Most notably, Levinas offers a sustained phenomenological account of the central phenomenon in Heidegger's Dasein analytic—namely, death. Rather than having recourse to tradition, Levinas appeals to an understanding of human subjectivity that ultimately discovers in the human a love strong as death. The appeal is not to a particular literature but to an alternative phenomenology of the human subject.

Claiming that death signifies first in my responsibility for the death of the other, not in my remaining resolutely open to my own in anxiety, Levinas seeks—in and through phenomenology, that is to say, without recourse to historical tradition or literary inheritance—to loosen the hold that Heidegger's phenomenology of death exercises in the determination of the subjectivity of man. Human subjectivity, for Levinas, appears not as fundamentally anxious but as determined by what Levinas calls "a love as irrefragable as death."[33] The death of the other gives an irreducible meaning only when human subjectivity is liberated from the fundamental determination of anxiety, and this liberation is accomplished by its subjection to a love strong as death.

Levinas's considerations of this love strong as death start from a renewed phenomenology of the face. From as early as *Totality and Infinity* and even before, the face always signifies the nakedness, vulnerability, or destitution of the other and in this way his weakness, passivity, and powerlessness against suffering—the face appears in "the widow, the orphan, and the poor." This weakness nevertheless expresses an irresistible command that orders me to my responsibility: "Thou shalt not kill!" When Levinas resumes the phenomenology of the face later in his career, he still emphasizes the paradoxical combination of poverty/weakness with command. But now he suggests that the destitution, abandon, and weakness of the face signifies the fact that the other "is alone and can undergo the supreme isolation we call death—there is consequently, in the Face of the Other always the death of the Other."[34] In short, he treats the "Face as the very *mortality* of the other human being."[35] The other is weak and powerless—he has a face—seeing as he is abandoned (thrown) into the destitution of his own mortality. This destitution appears to me in the face, which now signifies exposure to the possibility of impossibility confronted by the mortal other powerless to prevent the indefinite certainty of his own death. By presenting me with the other isolated before what Levinas calls his own "death-bound solitude,"[36] the face thus signifies the singularity of the other. Death, seen in his face, reduces the other to his uniqueness by the very means that Heidegger claims would singularize my own Dasein.

This interpretation of the face has the unexpected consequence that, in responsibility, death does indeed assign me to myself as unique or singular. But the death that assigns me to my ownmost is not itself my own, but the death of the other: "This facing of the face [Levinas writes] in its expression—that is, in its mortality—summons me, demands me, claims me: as if the invisible death faced by the face of the Other . . . were 'my business.'"[37] Furthermore: "The *self* as hostage to the other human being is precisely called to answer for this death. . . . The condition (or noncondition) of the hostage is accentuated in the approach of the neighbor. But so too is his *election*, the uniqueness of he who does not allow himself to be replaced."[38] That is, my subjection to the face summons me to what nobody else can do in my place: namely, take responsibility for the death that concerns me when it appears as a possibility in the face of the other who faces his own. This concern for the death of the other, Levinas claims, means that death affects me "as if, even before being doomed to it myself I had to answer for the death of the Other."[39]

Death, as the death of the other, for Levinas thus summons me to myself in responsibility but leaves me powerless before the inexorability of death—which will surely befall the other despite me and all my best efforts. "Fear and responsibility for the death of the Other [he writes], even if the ultimate meaning of that responsibility for the death of the Other is responsibility before the inexorable."[40] As "responsibility before the inexorable," my response cannot save the other from death. Death is an inevitable, always certain possibility, but I can do nothing against it—not first because I will die but first because it will befall the other. In the responsibility that makes his death my concern, I am, without a doubt, therefore, me brought up against the inexorable. Responsibility therefore delivers me to what Heidegger called the possibility of impossibility—a possibility that it is not possible for me to actualize (sparing the other from death) but that makes me me, the inappropriate and inappropriable self in concern for the death of the other.

Agreeing with Heidegger, then, Levinas *does* claim that death delivers me to myself as the unique self that I cannot decline. And he also follows Heidegger in claiming that this summons to be myself brings me before the impossible, which paralyzes my powers; it is not one I can fully assume, but I am forever guilty of being late to assume or failing to achieve it, accused without accuser. But, departing from Heidegger, Levinas claims that death does not signify this subjection first in anxious anticipation of my own but rather in my concerned fear for the death of the other as that death is expressed in the face.

VI

If we are to credit Levinas's analysis of death and not see it as a dream or the effusiveness of sentimentality, we must establish its possibility in an irreducible subjective experience. Such a project would sit "between Jews and Christians" in that it starts from the tradition and authority of neither Judaism nor Christianity in order to discover something they might think together. This brings us to what I think is the crucial point of departure from Heidegger, one that Levinas believes is established by a phenomenology, not by reference to the demands of history or tradition. This phenomenological "argument" requires questioning Heidegger's account of human subjectivity as fundamentally Dasein insofar as, for Dasein, anxiety is the fundamental mode of subjection, the primordial affect underlying all others. When human subjectivity finds itself primarily in anxiety, fear for the other appears only as a mood that has not yet brought to light its more fundamental anxiety for itself; such a mood seems deluded about itself or mere wishful thinking.

"Fear for the death of the neighbor, is my fear [Levinas claims], but it is in no wise fear *for* me."[41] Here fear is given to me as mine ("my fear") without my being at issue for myself (it is not a fear *for* me). With this analysis of fear, Levinas rejects the Heideggerian interpretation of fear (and every *Befindlichkeit* or affection by an other) according to a sort of double intentionality, which rests ultimately on anxiety. According to

Heidegger's account of fear as a mode of *Befindlichkeit*, fear discloses both *"that in the face of which* we fear, the fearsome" and *"that about which* fear fears . . . [namely:] Dasein." On Heidegger's reading, the former (directed toward objects or beings or others within the world) is possible only on the basis of the latter (the care Dasein shows for itself). "Only an entity for which in its Being this very Being is an issue can be afraid."[42] Without being at issue (*um . . . geht*) for itself in fear, without having beings matter to it (*angegangen*) in fear, in short, without caring (which constitutes Dasein itself), Dasein would not feel its own fear, in which the fearsome being is disclosed.

However much the analysis of thrownness and even being toward death might have wanted to reject interpreting mineness in terms of the completed circle of reflexivity, an underlying reflexive relation thus returns at the base of the Heideggerian analysis of *Befindlichkeit*—in this case, fear. This fundamental reflexivity is revealed in anxiety in distinction from fear. Unlike fear, according to Heidegger, anxiety is undergone when the beings or objects that concern Dasein slip into nothingness: "that in the face of which one has anxiety is not a being within-the-world. . . . Nothing which is ready-to-hand or present-at-hand within the world functions as that in the face of which anxiety is anxious."[43] This loss of all beings reveals, immediately, the fact that I care, that beings matter or are at issue to me. Furthermore, according to Heidegger, in anxiety there is a coincidence of that which inspires anxiety (my ownmost being-at-issue) and that about which anxiety is anxious (as always, my ownmost being-at-issue). By bringing Dasein before nothing, this loss of all beings leaves Dasein with only its own Being-in-the-world, which is revealed to it in anxiety, anxious care about its own being-at-issue.

Anxiety thus serves two central methodological functions for Heidegger. First, it isolates Dasein—suspending the others and the beings that constantly tempt it to fall into an inauthentic and average understanding of its being-at-issue for itself. Only in the isolation of anxiety can Dasein offer authentic testimony of itself by holding itself open to the possibility of impossibility (death), which gives it its ownmost Being to be. Second, anxiety thereby serves to disclose Dasein's ownmost Being, its mineness or being-at-issue. As Jean Greisch has aptly put it, "I do not undergo or understand mineness truly except in and through anxiety. We could equally say that anxiety is mineness undergone as affection."[44] Anxiety thus names and reveals, now as a reflexive self-relation, the being-at-issue for myself (mineness) on which rests the possibility of my experiencing any concern relating to beings or others in the world: "Only because anxiety is always latent in Being-in-the-world can such Being-in-the-world ever be afraid."[45]

When Levinas, by contrast, claims that the event that makes me me is fear for the other's death, which is not fear for me, he therefore does away with the primacy of anxious caring about my own (for me). Levinas is claiming that I am already myself in the everydayness of concerned life with others. That is, Levinas finds, as he puts it, "the signification of subjectivity in the extraordinary everydayness of my responsibility for other men, the extraordinary forgetting of death."[46] Whereas Heidegger saw the everyday as a leveling mediocrity or inauthenticity in which Dasein had fled its ownmost Being for the comfort of being-with-others like it, for Levinas, the everyday being-with-others is by no means average, tranquilizing, or just ordinary. It is, he claims extra-ordinary—"an ignorance of being and death which would not be an evasion, a cowardice, or a fall into the everyday."[47] This interpretation of the everyday as extraordinary would do away with the privilege of anxiety in the search for authentic Dasein. If the everyday of concerned being-with-others is indeed a fall from our ownmost Dasein, then we need an upheaval from everyday existence in order to discover ourselves in our original givenness to ourself; we need the courage of anxiety in opposition to the fears and evasions that make up the everyday in order to reveal ourselves as caring about or mattering to ourselves. When, however, the everydayness of being-with-others is seen as the extra-ordinary responsibility for the death of the neighbor above and beyond mere publicness, as it is in Levinas, what makes me the unique and irreplaceable me that I am is found without the isolation of the heroic, lonely bout with anxiety.

VIII

Therefore, according to Levinas, "Fear for the other man does not turn back into anxiety for *my* death. It overflows the ontology of Heideggerian Dasein,"[48] demanding instead that we think a human subjectivity that is not reducible to *Befindlichkeit*. The interpretation of this human subject would not refer it ultimately to the horizon of the world and worldly significations. Such a nonworldly subjectivity might resonate in important ways with the otherworldly orientation of religious models of subjectivity.[49] It will certainly be connected with Levinas's own thoughts of a love strong as death. Very late in his career, and perhaps more suggestively than completely, Levinas attaches a noticeable importance to thinking the responsible subject subjected to love. Love signifies beyond the horizon of the world opened in anxiety. That is to say, the death of the other finds meaning in the passion of love where the fear for him appears undeniable and irreducible. In short, if human subjectivity is constituted in and by love, not anxiety, one cannot doubt my responsibility for the death of the other.

Two texts might guide us to understanding what is at stake in this late and only barely thematized adoption of love .

The first is: "Responsibility for the other—the face signifying to me 'thou shalt not kill' and consequently also 'you are responsible for the life of this absolutely other other'—is responsibility for the one and only. The 'one and only' means the *loved one*, love being the condition of the very possibility of uniqueness."[50] Clearly, then, adopting the term *love* is tied to the effort to think the singularity of the other, which Levinas comes to realize is the only way to access the otherness of the other: "When I speak of uniqueness, I am also expressing the otherness of the other; the unique is the other in an eminent way."[51] This means that Levinas only comes to accept the term *love* when he no longer sees it as he previously did—as the unity or reciprocity of an amorous couple denying alterity and as the constitution of an inwardness or home withdrawn from the fears and concerns, the responsibilities, of everyday being-with-others. When, by contrast, love and command, love and the asymmetry of obligation, are no longer contradictory (as, for instance, in the command "You *shall* love your neighbor"), Levinas will accept love as access to the other, since it is in obliging or commanding me that the other appears.[52] This overcoming of the contradiction between love and command happens when, late in his career, Levinas sees the face as uniting the singularity of the other given to me in love with the summons to responsibility for the death appearing in that face. As Levinas writes, "the obligation not to leave the other alone in the face of death . . . is . . . love of my neighbor."[53]

The second text reads: "Only the unique is absolutely other. But the uniqueness of the unique *signifies* in love. . . . It is the subjective as such . . . that is precisely the condition of the possibility of the unique. Through the subjective—which is not only knowledge but which makes itself love—there is . . . access to the unique."[54] The text is as difficult as it is significant. Again Levinas adopts the term *love* in an effort to guarantee the appearance of the singularity of the other, a singularity that is given in the face by which the other is exposed to his own death. Here, however, it is also clear that Levinas accepts love insofar as it names the "subjective as such," the first point overlooked by a philosophy of subjectivity that takes the I as "I think." Levinas accepts love as the basic determination of the subject subjected to responsibility. Love is therefore not the deliberately willed activity of aiding the other, which would revert to the primacy of the I and its representations and intentions, but a passion—pure subjection of subjectivity, the "subjective as such."[55] Unlike Heideggerian *Befindlichkeit*, which gives me the Being I am obliged to be as possibility, ultimately the possibility of my own death, love is a passion where, Levinas claims, I find my own in the impossibility of any other possibility: "Death signifies in the concreteness of what for me is the impossibility of abandoning the other to his aloneness, in the prohibition addressed to me of that abandonment."[56] Here subjectivity emerges in subjection to the passion of not being able to do otherwise—the impossibility of abandoning the other to his death. Only love feels (or is impassioned by) the obligation to respond for the death of the other and therefore admits the experience of an irreducible fear for the death of the other.

Against reducing the subject to the anxious anticipation of its own death, fear for the death of the other therefore witnesses a love strong as death, a love that would rival death in determining the subjectivity of the subject. Love would be as strong as death or, as Levinas puts it, "as irrefrangible as death" in that, as Levinas reminds us again and again, my own death does not relieve me of responsibility for the death of the other. He will still die even after my death, even if I give my life for him. The love in which I feel fear for the death of the other therefore opens a meaning that, like death, surely extends beyond the meanings the I bestows (*Sinngebung*), but it also opens a meaning that extends beyond my finite me and the possibilities that might ever befall me as my own. "Thus [Levinas writes] we have not gone to the end of thought and meaningfulness in dying! The meaningful continues beyond my death."[57] As subject to love, I have responsibilities that reach beyond my ownmost, supposedly not to be outstripped, possibility of impossibility. As subject to love, neither my own death nor that of the other is the ultimate, even if an undeniable, end.

This can be seen in the contrast Levinas draws between his own interest in the Father of Faith, Abraham, and Kierkegaard's interest in Abraham's story. Whereas Kierkegaard's favorite story of Abraham is the Akedah narrative, Levinas prefers the story of Abraham intervening on behalf of Sodom and Gomorrah. He uses this story to illustrate this love strong as death. Emphasizing that the Father of Faith prefaces his plea with the words "I am but dust and ashes," Levinas claims that here we find love and responsibility (the plea that arises out of concern for the death of Sodom and Gomorrah) triumphing over death ("I am but dust and ashes"): "In Abraham, the precondition of any possible triumph of life over death is formulated."[58] Whereas Kierkegaard was fascinated with the suspension of the ethical, Levinas is fascinated with the discovery of a meaning of life that rests not on death but on responsibility.

Love would also be as strong as death in that I cannot deny or refute it but find myself by finding myself undeniably in its throes. Love, like death, gives a certain constancy of self to my subjectivity. In exposing me to "the impossibility of abandoning the other to his aloneness"[59] in death, love delivers me to the condition of responsibility in which there is nothing else for me to do. Love for the other gives me to myself without the possibility of doing otherwise. I thus find a certain constancy of self in the passion of not-being-able—the impossibility of being in any other way besides by his side as he dies.[60] And even after the other has died, there remains—unchanged, perhaps—the me who still loves him in spite of everything I know and tell myself or hear from the wisdom of the world about the foolishness or self-defeat of remaining constant in this love. Of course, I often abandon this responsibility and leave the other to die alone; but in this case, it is most often *I* who have done so precisely by restraining the passion that moves *me* irresistibly, undeniably, and constantly—in a love strong as death.

On Levinas's Gifts to Christian Theology

ROBYN HORNER

The name Emmanuel Levinas looms large in contemporary philosophical and religious discourse. His work marks an attempt to think in the wake of Edmund Husserl and Martin Heidegger; beginning with phenomenology, and in the shadow of the Heideggerian question of Being, he tries to create an opening for the interruption of thought by alterity. More specifically, he tries to show that the ethical relation with the other person is prior to, even the condition for, thought.[1] Levinas is of interest philosophically because he traces a path where not being but being's other has the first word.[2] And he is of interest in terms of ethics because of the radical nature of his claim that "all men are responsible for one another, and 'I more than anyone else,'"[3] all the more so because for most of his life Levinas wrote in the wake of the Shoah. But Levinas is also of interest to those fascinated by the name of God. That will be the focus of the present essay, especially insofar as this has ramifications for Christian theology: to what extent is it possible for theologians to adopt Levinas as a dialogue partner?

To engage with this question we will need to consider the parameters of Levinas's thought, particularly his use of the word *God*. Levinas's project might seem to be not only philosophical but theological, since the name of God permeates his writings and in later years even becomes a point of focus.[4] We might be tempted to read in this light the final words of the note prefacing *Otherwise than Being, or Beyond Essence*: "to hear a God not contaminated by Being is a human possibility no less important and no less precarious than to bring Being out of the oblivion in which it is said to have fallen in metaphysics and onto-theology."[5] Yet straightaway it is necessary to point out that Levinas distinguishes what he does from theology, at least in the sense that he apparently rejects not only rational but also revealed theology.[6] Nevertheless, by this he does not preclude the relevance of a consideration of "the God of the Bible," which raises questions about what he understands theology to mean. Levinas's separation of his confessional from his philosophical texts may serve as a marker of his intentions, but only to the extent that with this separation he recognizes the different methodological considerations involved in each discourse.[7] He is still able to speak of the relationship between his philosophy and his Jewish background in a way that acknowledges the sources of the one in the other: "one could say that biblical thought has, to some extent, influenced my ethical reading of the inter-human, whereas Greek thought has largely determined its philosophical expression in language," although elsewhere he maintains that "I am not guided by that [i.e. Jewish] theology explicitly."[8] If we accept the view of Edith Wyschogrod, Levinas is not doing theology, but this is largely because of a Jewish preference for orthopraxy over orthodoxy and because his chief concern is with the ethical rather than the ontological.[9] Jill Robbins nevertheless writes of "the risk that Levinas's *theology* is willing to run."[10] Given that opinions about whether or not Levinas is doing theology are divided, is it more appropriate to consider him a "Jewish philosopher"? Jeffrey Kosky suggests: "Levinas's analysis of responsibility can be seen as a discourse on religion that, at least in its intentions, holds forth without recourse to the authority of any faith or religious tradition. I argue, against readings that identify Levinas as a Jewish philosopher, that the religiosity met in Levinas's phenomenology of responsibility is not an actual religion but the possibility or nonnoematic meaning of religion."[11] This comment will serve as a useful prism through which to view the reflections on Levinas, God, and theology that I will undertake.

We will need to examine what Christian theology involves before turning to consider some of the ways in which Levinas's thought has been adopted by Christian theologians. The discussion will largely be driven by questions concerning the appropriateness of that adoption rather than its content, for it is conceivable that to incorporate Levinas's work into Christian theological projects at all may be to do it violence. But we will also need to determine the implications of applying Levinas's thought to theology. I will argue that borrowing from Levinas ultimately brings theology to the point of having to recognize not only its conditions of possibility but also its conditions of *im*possibility, and that this may be more than many theologians have bargained for. In addressing these matters, I am aware that this study could easily expand into a book. It will quickly become apparent that there are large areas that would benefit from more extended treatment: Levinas's engagement with Jewish theology, the influence on him of Franz Rosenzweig, the contents of his Talmudic commentaries, Levinas and religious philosophy, the monographs relating Levinas to particular Christian theologians, the many shorter works applying Levinasian themes to Christian theology, and broader perspectives on the nature of Christian theology itself. I can do no more than note these necessary limitations in advance and beg the reader's forgiveness for being able to do no more than sketch out some of the territory here.

Levinas and God

When Levinas refers to God, what does he mean? In *Totality and Infinity*, God plays a limited role as the idea of the Infinite.[12] Drawn from the work of Descartes, the idea of the Infinite exceeds the capacity of thought to think it, does not originate in the I, is produced in the finite as desire that cannot be satisfied, and—for Levinas—arises in the face of the other: "the dimension of the divine opens forth from the human face."[13] However, it is unclear whether or not the other and God are to be understood as one and the same. Levinas observes, on the one hand: "there can be no 'knowledge' of God separated from the relationship with men."[14] Yet, on the other hand, he goes on to add that "the Other is not the Incarnation of God, but precisely by his face, in which he is disincarnate, is the manifestation of the height in which God is revealed."[15] Even if we distinguish between the divine and the human other, what Levinas means by "God" in *Totality and Infinity* does not seem to coincide with any God known to the world religions. For a start, relationship with this God assumes a stance Levinas describes as "atheism."[16] It is a connection "with the noumenon which is not a numen," a noumenon that he distinguishes "from the concept of God possessed by the believers of positive religions ill disengaged from the bonds of participation, who accept being immersed in a myth unbeknown to themselves."[17] Since the appearance of God occurs precisely "in soliciting us by his destitution in the face of the Stranger," Levinas is able to describe the relationship with God as "an ethical behaviour and not theology, not a thematization, be it a knowledge by analogy, of the attributes of God."[18] It seems that God names a transcendence to which we are referred in the face of the other, but a transcendence that not only is not an object as such but has no "content," or perhaps no content other than the corresponding activity of justice on the part of the subject. The name *God* appears to serve a function, which is to interrupt consciousness as the Infinite or as excessiveness.[19] And yet God is somehow also personal, soliciting us in the stranger's face.

"The Trace of the Other" (1963) and "Enigma and Phenomenon" (1965) contain three important ideas affecting the development of Levinas's thought of God: those of the trace, illeity, and immemoriality.[20] In *Totality and Infinity*, the idea of Infinity is more or less directly imposed with the face. Levinas apparently does not thereby mean that we are able to conceptualize the Infinite. Since it overflows the thought that thinks it, the manner of its signification is perhaps unclear, particularly when he claims that it "presents itself in the Other."[21] By contrast, in "The Trace of the Other" Infinity is not presented in the face but signifies "as the ever bygone transcendence of the transcendent" (transcendence already in the immemorial past).[22] Here "the beyond from which a face comes signifies as a trace" (a sign that signifies while breaking the knot of reference, as it were) or "in the third person" (that is, as illeity, which we might translate as "he-ness" and which Levinas will later describe as "the *he* in the depth of the you").[23] In the final paragraph, Levinas links God explicitly with three ideas. "The God who passed" and "shows himself only by his trace" is approached only by "go[ing] toward the others who stand in the trace of illeity."[24] Then he underlines that the trace presents nothing of God. The face does not serve as God's icon but only to show God's absence, or having passed (and here Levinas refers us to Exodus 33).[25]

"Enigma and Phenomenon" goes further than "The Trace of the Other" in Levinas's clearer insistence that the immemorial past is not only not present but *has never been* present; it is "a *past* that was never a *now*."[26] The passing of God is in this way absolved from all relation. The trace signifies as an enigma, where "the exorbitant meaning is already effaced in its apparition. The God who spoke said nothing, passed incognito."[27] At the end of the essay, Levinas describes the way in which the face itself almost forces this effacement, coming between the subject and God.[28] He finally declares: "it is then vain to posit an absolute You." While this suggests that we can have no relationship with God as such, it does not imply that God has no meaning. Instead, God has a meaning beyond being:

> He who has passed beyond has never been a presence. He preceded all presence and exceeded every contemporaneity in a time which is not human duration . . . but the original antecedence of God relative to a world which cannot accommodate him, the immemorial past which has never presented itself, which cannot be said with the categories of Being and structure, but is the One, which every philosophy would like to express, beyond being.[29]

In considering *Otherwise than Being*, we might have some sympathy with John Llewelyn when he asks: "After endorsing Nietzsche's proclamation of the death of the God of onto-theology, why is Levinas either unable or unwilling to eliminate the word 'God' from the lexicon in which he expounds what he himself describes as a humanism of the other man?"[30] Llewelyn observes that this text is framed by affirmations of the Nietzschean death "of a certain God inhabiting a world behind the scenes," and yet the word *God* remains in it.[31] Levinas claims, nonetheless, that his references to God have nothing to do with belief or disbelief: "the word God is still absent from the phrase in which God is for the first time involved in words. It does not at all state 'I believe in God.' To bear witness to God is precisely not to state this extraordinary word, as though glory would be lodged in a theme and be posited as a thesis, or become being's essence."[32] In this work, the Infinite signifies as an ambiguous, self-effacing, and immemorial trace, and it signifies in two ways that are evidently connected. It first signifies in the face of the other, as illeity, or in the third person.[33] "Illeity overflows both cognition and the enigma through which the Infinite leaves a trace in cognition."[34] Yet illeity is not a theological device and does not refer us to a God somehow behind or beyond the other: "a face does not function in proximity as a sign of a hidden God who would impose the neighbor on me. It is a trace of itself, a trace in the trace of an abandon, where the equivocation is never dissipated."[35] The second way that the Infinite signifies is in responsibility, that is, by way of substitution. The Infinite "leaves a trace of its impossible incarnation and its inordinateness in my proximity with the neighbor, where I state, in the autonomy of the voice of conscience, a responsibility, which could not have begun in me, for freedom, which is not my freedom."[36]

Perhaps one of the most important texts to consider is "God and Philosophy" (1975), in which Levinas makes clear that, once philosophers or theologians bring God to thought, they have brought God into the realm of being, which is an instant betrayal. Instead, Levinas maintains, "the God of the Bible signifies without analogy to an idea subject to *criteria*, without analogy to an idea exposed to the summons to show itself true or false."[37] The focus of "God and Philosophy" is the working out of this signification prior to being. Once again, Levinas begins with the idea of the Infinite, which breaks up consciousness in a trauma that is "not thought but undergone."[38] As in *Otherwise than Being*, the Infinite is then understood to signify in two interrelated ways. It signifies as Desire (in me), but as a Desire (for a desirable) that must remain disinterested. Hence, as the desirable it orders Desire not to itself but to the undesirable other. The signification of the Infinite is then correspondingly described as a trace in that other, in terms otherwise used of illeity: "intangible, the Desirable separates itself from the relationship with the Desire that calls it forth and, by this separation or holiness, remains a third person: He at the root of You [*Tu*]."[39] By way of this separation, Levinas is able to emphasize that the other and God are not to be identified. "God is not simply the 'first other,' or the 'other *par excellence*,' or the 'absolutely other,' but other than the other, other otherwise."[40] Returning to the first mode of signification, the response of the subject to the neighbor bears witness to the glory of the Infinite. While Levinas insists that the responding subject is "neither the experience nor the proof of the Infinite," he also insists that this glory "is not an abstract quintessence."[41] He describes it instead as "the hyperbolic exigency that immediately overflows the response."[42] It happens or takes place ("*comes to pass*") in a Saying or witnessing of the subject ("the Infinite is not 'in front of' me; it is I who express it") that is anarchic, prior to religious experience, belief, or discourse.[43] In this way, while not intelligible in terms of ontology, God, Levinas claims, nevertheless has a meaning.[44]

Levinas later observes, in a fertile passage from "Philosophy, Justice, and Love" (1982):

> I cannot describe the relation to God without speaking of my concern for the other. When I speak to a Christian, I always quote Matthew 25; the relation to God is presented there as a relation to another person. It is not a metaphor: in the other, there is a real presence of God. In my relation to the other, I hear the Word of God. It is not a metaphor; it is not only extremely important, it is literally true. I'm not saying that the other is God, but that in his or her Face I hear the Word of God.[45]

We find here not only that the difference between the human other and the divine other is reinforced, but that the "reality" of God is underlined. "Reality" is cautiously used, since, while it is intended to reflect Levinas's references to the "real presence of God" that "is not a metaphor" but is "literally true," such a word may overplay what he intends by it. We need to read these references, in other words, in light of his repeated commitments elsewhere not to speak of God ontologically. Certainly, any "metaphysics of presence" could readily be destabilized by Levinas's preference for the language of hearing over the language of sight (I do not see God, I hear God's word). Since we have already noted above that God's word is articulated only by way of the responding subject ("the Infinite is not 'in front of' me; it is I who express it"), there is no guarantee that God's "presence" here has hardened into the sort of ontological presence that

Levinas elsewhere apparently rejects. In the same text, the interviewer suggests to Levinas that the other (or the other's face—the text is ambiguous) "is a mediator between God and us." Levinas's further response is strong: "Oh, no, not at all, it is not mediation—it is the way the word of God reverberates."[46] While maintaining the link between the other and the signification of God, Levinas nevertheless resists an instrumental view of the other as leading to God.[47]

In my brief survey of Levinas's references to God, I have not taken into account his Talmudic texts. To discuss them would far exceed the limits of the present context. However, we might simply observe here Annette Aronowicz's claim that in these texts Levinas translates the word *God* into secular terms:

> but this secularisation, this bringing into the world, into the times, is by no means intended as an elimination of transcendence. Rather, it aims at its *relocation* in the midst of interpersonal exchange. "God" disappears as a reality one can have access to outside human activity. . . . What the text teaches, according to Levinas, is that it is through *action*, not through the fixing of the idea of God in our mind, that the wholly other, transcendent dimension is made accessible.[48]

Supporting this view, Aronowicz quotes from Levinas's 1984 interview with Richard Kearney, where he maintains:

> I do not wish to talk in terms of belief or unbelief. *Believe* is not a verb to be employed in the first person singular. Nobody can really say *I believe*—or *I do not believe* for that matter—that God exists. The existence of God is not a question of an individual soul's uttering logical syllogisms. It cannot be proved. The existence of God . . . is sacred history itself, the sacredness of man's relation to man through which God may pass.[49]

Given how Levinas uses the word *God* in his texts, what might he mean? He apparently intends to exclude from his work any idea of God as a transcendent being.[50] However, to read "God" in Levinas solely in terms of a negation of the transcendent being of (traditional) metaphysics and religion is to limit another, richly suggestive side of his work.[51] It is clear that Levinas distances himself from the God of religions (although not, evidently, from the God of the Bible). God has a meaning: "the rupture between philosophical intelligibility and what is beyond being, or the contradiction there would be in com-prehending the infinite, does not exclude God from the significance that, although not ontological, does not amount to simple thoughts bearing on a being in decline, nor to views without necessity, nor to words that play."[52] At the same time, however, any God considered *in se* or apart from ethical engagement remains ambiguous. God is thought as the Infinite by Levinas, but precisely insofar as the Infinite cannot be thought as such. This leaves open many possibilities, including the possibility that the Infinite might even be confused with the *il y a*.[53] What is not left open any longer, however, is "the question of the existence or the non-existence of God," since this orients God in an ontological framework, when it is only the ethical that is relevant.[54]

Levinas and Theology

Levinas distances himself from theology, even if his work is full of references to God. For him, theology betrays God by attempting to bring God to thematization.[55] This betrayal includes both rational and revealed theology, for, despite the latter's oft-protested independence from its more explicitly philosophical cousin—a protest to which Levinas only obliquely refers—it depends inevitably on philosophical language for its expression. In other words, in Levinas's view revealed theology brings with it the assumptions of ontology.[56] Revealed theology is also a problem for him because on his reading it evokes enthusiasm and promotes the idea of participation in the divine, which is essentially also how he understands (particularly Christian) mysticism.[57] It involves the acceptance of mythology and is the realm of "faith and opinion."[58] The problem with rational theology is not only that thematization brings about the betrayal of transcendence but that the existence of God can never be a question of proof.[59] Finally, in pursuing God in this way, we risk forgetting the priority of the other in our midst.[60]

At the same time, in considering what theology means for Levinas we also need to take into account comments such as: the idea of the Infinite is "an exception indicating human thought coalescing precisely as theology!"; "the *logos* of this theology would differ from theoretical intentionality and the adequacy of thought to that which is thought"; it is "the humanness of man understood as theology."[61] Further, we need to consider what Levinas is doing in his Talmudic texts. While he insists that he does not pursue "Jewish theology," his Talmudic commentaries embody a Jewish form of theologizing that is underpinned by parameters quite different from the essentially Christian style that seems to be the focus of his critique.[62] In fine, much Jewish theology seems not only to be oriented by orthopraxis rather than orthodoxy, but to be deliberately subversive of the very idea of orthodoxy as such. As Levinas writes: "the religious act of listening to the revealed word is thus identified with the discussion whose open-endedness is desired with all the audacity of its problematic."[63] Levinas's Jewish writings are part of an on-going hermeneutics that resists being resolved into dogma. That his considerations of the Talmud (and the Bible) might be understood as theological in this way is reinforced by a (throwaway?) line preceding some biblical reflections: "Shall we do a bit of theology?"[64] To sum up, while theology as a thematization of transcendence as such is definitely not on Levinas's agenda, theology as the practice of ethics is meaningful, and theology as a biblical or Talmudic hermeneutics is evidently possible.

Christian Theology

Given that my focus is how Levinas's thought might be used to enrich Christian theology, it is important to sketch at least a preliminary understanding of what this theology seeks to accomplish. To assume that there is one Christian theology is, of course, erroneous, but one can still paint in broad strokes a picture of what many theologians might agree constitutes their central task. While the word *theology* is frequently translated "the divine science" and literally means "God-talk," Anselm famously defines it in the twelfth century as "faith seeking understanding." Though this definition has been further specified by many, the description provided by the Anglican theologian John Macquarrie is now classic: "theology may be defined as the study which, through participation in and reflection upon a religious faith, seeks to express the content of this faith [that is, beliefs] in the clearest and most coherent language available."[65] This view of theology situates it within the life of practice of the religious faith concerned and requires the believer not only to reflect upon faith but also to attempt to express the content of that faith clearly and coherently. In terms of that content, Christian theology has as its principal object (beliefs about) God, who is primarily revealed in and through the person and work of Jesus Christ. Revelation is, evidently, key to the elucidation of beliefs, and it is understood to occur in time and history and through relationship rather than in the abstractions of any philosophical system. While this dependence on the real flesh and blood of Christ—in more than one sense—has often been central to the appeal of Christianity, Christian theology has still had to deal with broader conceptual questions that have inevitably been articulated using the available language(s) of philosophy. The language that has best suited Christian thinkers historically in their attempts to bring enhanced meaning to the content of faith is the language of being.

Immediately, we can see one of the main difficulties that the adoption of the thought of Levinas would entail. To the extent that Christian theology is articulated within a horizon of being, it would fall under Levinas's critique of being as totalizing. This leads us to raise the question of exactly how wedded that theology is to the thought of being, especially as it has been understood philosophically. The main focus of recent debate has been on the thinking of being within metaphysics and whether theology is inherently metaphysical, thus falling under Heidegger's critique of metaphysics as onto-theo-logy. Specifically, in Christian theology, since God is frequently identified as *esse* ("sheer being"), is God thought as the highest being and ground, or reason? Since he is determinative for much subsequent theologizing, Thomas Aquinas is frequently used as the paradigmatic case in this debate. Given the limitations of space, I will do no more here than note the present truce between Jean-Luc Marion, seen as the chief prosecutor of Thomas on this point, and contemporary Thomistic theologians, who constitute the defense. Thomas, it is argued, thinks divine being quite differently from common being, and certainly not as cause.[66]

A second issue, however, arises from a more deconstructive impulse. This is the question of whether Christian attempts to think the possibility of God remain trapped in the dead-end of language that simply cannot go beyond itself, save through the illusory positioning of a transcendental signifier. In other words, while Christian theologians vigorously argue that their use of language is aware of its limits (being that can be known is only analogous to the being that Thomas ascribes to God), are those limits actually respected? The most sensitive point of any theology lies in its thinking of how God (transcendent and irreducible to experience, in spite of the incarnation) enters into the realm of human discourse and therefore becomes the subject of meaningful reference at all. Sometimes it appears that theology is in fact characterized by a commitment to ontological realism in talk about God that is not diminished by fewer or analogous references to being, since being remains the horizon of possibility. God is thought either according to this horizon (as always receding beyond it, which is essentially a recuperative move) or even *as* this horizon (Karl Rahner). The possible exception here is not negative theology, which potentially remains within the either/or structure of the economy, but mystical theology, as least insofar as it puts in doubt the capacity of any of its words to refer to God at all. Here it differs from dialectical theology, which may doubt the capacity of human words to speak of God but remains convinced of God's capacity to speak transparently through them. And here arises a further difficulty. In spite of a genuine profession of humility in many respects, Christian theology is ultimately undertaken in the belief that not only is it possible to speak of God, but it is possible (and desirable) to speak *rightly* of God. It is thus largely driven by dogmatic creedal formulations, even where their subsequent doctrinal interpretations may vary widely.[67] On the basis of this characterization, it would seem that Levinas would make an unlikely partner for dialogue. He is not interested in questions concerning the existence or nonexistence of God; his "thought" of God situates itself prior to ontology; and he comes from a religious tradition that favors the nondogmatic. Whether or not theology can be characterized *otherwise* is a question to which we will return in the conclusion. In the meantime, however, let us consider how Levinas's work has been utilized by Christian theologians and the extent to which it might place their theologies in question.

Theological Uses of Levinas's Work

There are three main ways in which Levinas's thought has been adopted by Christian theologians. Some thinkers have attempted to bring his work explicitly into dialogue with great twentieth-century theologians such as Karl Rahner, Hans Urs von Balthasar, Karl Barth, Eberhard Jüngel, and Bernard Lonergan.[68] Others attempt to rethink theological themes integrating Levinasian perspectives.[69] Finally, some use Levinas's work to develop a new structure for theology or to reconceive the theological task.[70] It seems to me that the most difficult of all the theological applications of Levinas's work to sustain is the one in which he is to be brought into dialogue with a great theologian. While there is in many senses a natural relationship between philosophy and theology, since there is much (philosophical) common ground between them, it is no longer presumed that philosophers will share the faith commitments of theologians. Philosophical ideas are more readily applicable to theology than are theological ideas to philosophy, because in the latter case an entirely different set of assumptions is being brought to bear on the argument. That is not to say that philosophers are without their own belief systems or ideologies, which are, of course, subject to elucidation and critique. It is likely, however, that there will not be a dialogue between the parties so much as a fertilization or critique of the philosophical dimensions of the thought of one by the philosophical ideas of the other. A further problem with bringing the philosopher and the theologian together is the potential difference between their conceptual worlds. In the case of Levinas and most of the theologians chosen as his dialogue partners, this difference is marked. For many of the sustained studies undertaken, the theologian in question is arguably situated in a metaphysical framework (where metaphysics is onto-theo-logy) that is opposed to Levinas's attempts to go beyond ontology or to do metaphysics *otherwise*.[71] The extent to which Levinas's work places that of any such thinker completely in question demands a radical renegotiation of any basis for discussion. A final and related difficulty emerges because Levinas actually has plenty to say about God, and theology (while we will not examine this aspect of his work, he also uses a "religious" vocabulary in very distinctive ways). It is actually quite difficult to adopt some aspects of his thought without also taking on their theological implications.

In the present context it is impracticable to try to evaluate all the work available. Instead, I will consider representative examples to illustrate the possibilities and the problems. With regard to Levinas and the great theologians, I will focus on Michael Purcell and Richard J. Beauschesne in relation to the work of Rahner, and Michelle Saracino in relation to Lonergan. Purcell is one of the Christian theologians writing most prolifically on Levinas, and he is also one of those most sensitive to Levinas's thought. While Purcell has a book-length study of Levinas and Rahner, for thematic reasons (as well as the need to be brief), I will examine only the earlier article "Gloria Dei, Homo Vigilans: Waking up to Grace in Rahner and Levinas."[72] In this article, he seeks to enhance Rahner's explication of the relationship between grace and nature in terms of the supernatural existential (or its counterpart in the obediential potency) by means of Levinas's understanding of wakefulness and awakening. Purcell clearly appreciates that Rahner's work will be opened up by that of Levinas. Significantly, he is also very aware of the ways in which the thought worlds of the two apparently collide:

> Rahner would seem to be firmly within that ontotheological tradition which Levinas criticizes, seemingly grounding his theology in a rigorous interrogation of Being. . . . Levinas, on the other hand, seeks a transcendence which is also an excendence from Being. Yet the difference between the two would seem to stem primarily from the fact that the transcendental reduction which Rahner undertakes, like that of Husserl, halts too soon, and so remains within Being.[73]

At the same time, he is able to find in Rahner "the possibility of a way beyond ontology" that is not, nevertheless, ultimately achieved.[74] By way of a careful analysis of Rahner, the intersubjective reduction in Husserl, and Levinas, Purcell argues: "one can develop the awakening to grace *as* grace in terms of the relationship with the other person which, for Levinas, has, as its condition of possibility, the relationship with God."[75] In the final part of the article, Purcell gives a thorough exposition of Levinas's thought of God as the trace and illeity. He is cautious to signal, however, that Levinas is not thereby talking about a God somehow hidden behind the other.[76] His conclusion clearly states that, for Levinas, God cannot be known except in the social relation. What is striking is that in reaching this conclusion, Purcell seems to accept Levinas's characterization of God.[77] He has apparently done Levinas complete justice—but what does this mean for theology?

Also writing on the supernatural existential in Rahner, Beauschesne seeks to reappraise it "in light of Emmanuel Levinas's ethical category of 'Desire.'"[78] He argues that the supernatural existential is like the idea of the Infinite, giving rise to desire for the desirable par excellence. In Beauschesne's work it is again clear that Levinas is being used to open up a category in Rahner's thought. However, the means of relating the two thinkers is open to question. Beauschesne is cognizant of their differences, although he categorizes Rahner's thought as a "metaphysics of Being" and that of Levinas as a "metaphysics of Ethics" without clarifying the different senses of metaphysics involved. He then tries to relate them in terms of a common ethical metaphysics. Nevertheless, Beauschesne is aware of the potential methodological problem thus raised: "Since Rahner's thought primarily originates from a metaphysics of being, and Levinas's from a metaphysics of ethics, how does one arrive—without comparing apples to oranges—at a reconsideration of Rahner in light of Levinas?"[79] His means of solving this problem, while drawing from small apertures in the works of each thinker, is unconvincing: "If Levinas, Rahner and Rilke are correct in suggesting (in their diverse ways) the existence of kinds of 'meta-metaphysical' ways of being, thinking, listening, feeling, acting and expressing, then in the reconsideration of Rahner in light of Levinas one might therefore be allowed to by-pass the disparity of diverse influences—be they logical, psychological, or metaphysical."[80] A further difficulty with Beauschesne's work is that while he is apparently appreciative of the link between the face of the other and God, he does not draw into his consideration the conversion of desire from the desirable (God) to the nondesirable (the other person) that forms the crucial part of Levinas's discussion in *Otherwise than Being* and "God and Philosophy."[81] While we are led to an understanding of the supernatural existential as the object of Levinasian desire, and while Beauschesne seems to be aware that for Levinas we are referred to an Infinite without content, the way in which he then dwells on the Infinite rather than the nondesirable other suggests that he may not have fully appreciated either the ethical significance or, in fact, the theological implications of Levinas's thought. With regard to the latter, Beauschesne, like Purcell, appears to accept Levinas's characterization of God, but it is not clear that this is deliberate or that the consequences are fully intended.

Turning to Michelle Saracino, I will again examine aspects of a shorter piece, "Subject for the other: Lonergan and Levinas on Being Human in Postmodernity," rather than her book-length study of Lonergan and Levinas.[82] Again, it is important to consider less the content that is related (that is, subjectivity) than the method of relating the two thinkers. Saracino casts her essay in terms of the contrast between contemporary Continental theory and Christian theology. The former, she claims, is "attentive to suffering and decline," "apprehend[s] the subject . . . as fragmented and decentered," is unable or refuses "to make accurate judgments about what is good and true," and while "valuable in pinpointing the problems in society . . . can be problematic in not attempting to remedy these problems through decision and action."[83] Her assessment is reinforced by the further comment that Continental thought is characterized by "an insidious relativism."[84] Theology, by contrast, sees the subject as being able to act responsibly in spite of contingent experiences and perceives that "such contingencies need not lead to fragmentation, for fragmentation is not normative, but the result of sin and alienation, a consequence of the fall of humanity."[85] Saracino's description of Continental theory apparently overlays her understanding of what she denotes as "postmodernity."[86] While she resists the comparison of Lonergan to Levinas as "modern" to "postmodern," she does so on the basis of a view that Lonergan is not typically modern and Levinas not typically postmodern.[87] Saracino argues, rather, that the basis for comparing the thinkers is their engagement with "similar problems of modernity," which include "how to engage others without perpetuating bias and causing violence."[88] At the same time, one of her negative evaluations of Levinas is based on his rejection of the primacy of being. "I think theologians, before they blindly embrace Levinas's thought, need to think about his rejection of being. In other words, after reading Lonergan one wonders whether Levinas's emotive reaction against the primacy of being actually needed to be so dramatic."[89]

The difficulty with Saracino's method of engagement seems to be that she ignores one of the crucial points of comparison to be made between Lonergan and Levinas—the question of the primacy of being, which is critical to debates about the modern culmination of metaphysics and its potential overcoming.[90] It is not that Saracino tries to conflate the two thinkers. She notes: "the distinct worldviews of Lonergan and Levinas should never be confused. The alterity between their individual histories and personalities must be respected." Nevertheless, they are brought into dialogue on the same plane: "from the perspective of Catholic theology, an encounter with Levinas's contemporary Continental thought is advantageous in a number of ways. Alternatively, Levinas's argument could be strengthened by the foresight of a broad thinker such as Lonergan."[91] After observing Levinas's potential enrichment of theology, Saracino suggests that Levinas could have learned from Lonergan. First she imagines Lonergan to ask Levinas—in a passage redolent with the commitment to ontological realism that is a particular mark of Lonerganian theology— "*Why are you so illusive on the questions of reason and being?*"[92] While it is intellectually defensible to propose a critical stance with respect to critiques of metaphysics as onto-theo-logy—and theologians such as John Milbank proceed along the lines that it makes no sense to attempt to speak other than ontologically—what is unusual here is that such a critique (not developed in this context) is not seen to put in question the very possibility of bringing Lonergan and Levinas into dialogue. The philosophical approaches of the two thinkers are potentially so incompatible as to prevent meaningful exchange. Saracino's second suggestion is essentially "that Levinas's ethics would be improved by Lonergan's method."[93] Again, it is reasonable to critique a thinker on these grounds, but it seems to me that Levinas's method is actually so bound up with what he is trying to achieve that its critique demands an engagement with his questions on his terms, which are quite opposed to those of a thinker like Lonergan.

The three attempts to appropriate Levinas to enrich the work of a theologian that we have examined show varying degrees of success. Purcell has perhaps the most refined reading of Levinas and the most realistic expectations of the encounter, and he uses Levinas's work to think what he (Purcell) sees as nascent but unthought in Rahner. Beauchesne seems less able to relate Levinas to Rahner because of disparities in their respective methods, and his reading of Levinas may emphasize God at the expense of the other person. Yet in taking on Levinas's thought of God, both Purcell and Beauschesne take on a thought of God that is empty of content or unthinkable other than in terms of conditions of possibility and *im*possibility. We might ask whether this takes them further than they wish to go theologically. Saracino's attempt to bring Levinas and Lonergan into dialogue seems unlikely to bring about this compromise and apparently does not address the heart of what would be their essential disagreement.

Of the theologians who have utilized Levinas's work to enhance particular theological themes (rather than to engage with a specific theologian),

Roger Burggraeve stands out for the breadth and depth of his appreciation of that work. I will examine his "Responsibility Precedes Freedom . . .," a festschrift essay from 1988. Burggraeve's aim is "to honor [Louis Janssens's] synthesis of theology and philosophy by searching out a biblical-philosophical foundation for a personalist love ethic."[94] He goes on to describe Levinas as "the inspiration in this project . . . since we find a concept of responsibility in his writings which is kindred to the biblical concept of responsibility."[95] The essay is set out in two sections. In the first, Burggraeve uses biblical and Talmudic texts, often by way of Levinas's commentary, to elucidate a biblical notion of creation. This is followed by an examination of the New Testament in relation to the reign of God. He concludes: "when we synthesize these reflections concerning Jesus' proclamation of the Kingdom of God and concerning the Old Testament beginning with the creation narrative, we can posit that human beings are not merely neutral, ontological beings, one kind of being among others. Rather, human beings are made responsible."[96] From this conclusion he moves into the second part of the essay, where he seeks to develop "the philosophical implications of the above-described 'creatural' responsibility."[97] Here he draws upon features of a Levinasian understanding of subjectivity to argue that "love . . . is not an accidental nor arbitrary invention of a particular religious revelation. On the contrary, love is rooted in the 'nature' or createdness of humanity itself. The ethical task is our very essence."[98] Apart from the careful way in which Burggraeve uses Levinas's texts, what is most significant about the essay for our purposes is the last paragraph, where Burggraeve distinguishes the study he has just completed from the theological task it anticipates for him: "the notion of 'creatural' solidarity cannot be the last word concerning being-human. Precisely because of its radicality, because of its unconditional and unending challenge, 'creatural' solidarity demands that one pass over into the transethical field of mercy and completion. This is the characteristic domain of religion, in our case Judeo-Christianity."[99] Burggraeve has adopted Levinas's philosophical understanding of subjectivity to frame an exegesis of scripture without requiring that Levinas enter into theology.[100] The integrity of Levinas's work is thus preserved, but it is also clear that Burggraeve is not forced to accept the more disturbing theological implications of Levinas's philosophy, since his analysis does not rely on these aspects of Levinas's thought. Burggraeve's work also illustrates the potential for fruitful dialogue between Levinas and liberation theology.

We turn, then, to consider the use of Levinas's work in the development of new fundamental structures for theology. I take as my example here the thought of Jean-Luc Marion, and to some extent, in claiming that he is developing such an approach, I am taking Marion further than he would wish to go. This is primarily because he would insist that his phenomenological work is not a starting point for theology but a means of taking seriously within philosophy phenomena that theology already considers perfectly legitimate—phenomena of revelation.[101] Both Marion and Levinas can be situated within one of the trajectories of phenomenology extending from Husserl through Heidegger and beyond. Whether or not we call this phenomenology or a type of "post-phenomenology" is a matter for conjecture; it is sufficient to note that each thinker locates himself in critical relation to phenomenology, as well as in particular relation to the Heideggerian critique of metaphysics as onto-theo-logy.[102] Within this trajectory, three facets of Levinas's thought emerge as crucial for Marion. First, Levinas's attempts to think "otherwise than being" (here we can only refer in shorthand to the rehabilitation and extension of Husserl and the critiques of Heidegger) help to structure Marion's phenomenological approach and to provide the opening for the possibility of meaning without being. Second, Levinas's thinking of the signification of the other person is especially important for Marion's development of a phenomenology (and theology) of the icon, the face, and, ultimately, of love.[103] Finally, and related to this second point, Levinas's use of the ethical injunction ("Thou shalt not kill") arising from the other is adopted and extended by Marion as the "call" (or "appeal") whose precise origin cannot be known as such but only interpreted.[104] A further similarity between Levinas's and Marion's work is their use of the Cartesian idea of the Infinite as excessive to thought.[105] Without pretending to minimize the differences between him and Levinas, in broad strokes, it is these areas of commonality that allow Marion to arrive at a phenomenology within which there is a place for God.

While Marion is not only a philosopher but a theologian, and while his theological perspectives are clearly beyond Levinas's sphere of interest, it is not a question of trying to compare—to recall Beauschesne's language—apples and oranges. Marion and Levinas are largely working within the same philosophical trajectory. The critical point at which Marion extends Levinas is where Marion maintains that what he understands as excessive or "saturated" phenomena (the event, the idol, flesh, and the icon—which includes the Levinasian "face" and the idea of the Infinite) can be interpreted to allow for the possibility of revelation. In phenomenological terms, revelation can therefore have a content, although such (excessive) content is essentially relimited by the inevitable supplement of a hermeneutics. For Marion, apart from affirming that revelation remains one interpretative possibility for such phenomena, phenomenology can, strictly speaking, go no further, and we enter the domain of theology. Nevertheless, there is an unacknowledged tension within Marion's work concerning the extent to which theology functions as a positive discipline without the need for such a philosophical prolegomenon. On the one hand, Marion accepts without question the authority of the Church to determine phenomena as revelatory, and it might be suggested that he thus sees such phenomena as revelatory in an absolute sense.[106] On the other hand, in recognizing at all the need for a hermeneutics of revelatory phenomena, he effectively grounds his theological works in the phenomenological.[107] Therefore I would argue that Marion develops a new fundamental theology. While it may appear that he goes well beyond Levinas in actually doing theology, it is not clear that he does go beyond Levinas in the sense that saturated phenomena are any more determinable in terms of content than the idea of the Infinite. Unlike Levinas, Marion chooses to go on to discuss revealed theology, but the conditions under which he effectively does so mean that what is revealed is constantly thrown into question and is shown to be based on faith as a hermeneutical risk. And while it seems that entering into a discussion of phenomena as revealed may be entering into the realm of the Levinasian "Said," it is clear from Marion's engagement with mystical theology that his Said is repeatedly being undone by a "Saying," that is, by an unsaying.[108]

It seems to me that Marion's use of Levinas's work does no discernible violence to Levinas.[109] The implications of Marion's phenomenology are certainly different from those arising from Levinas's thought: for Levinas, the orientation to the Infinite has no other point than unending responsibility for the other person, whereas for Marion one has the sense that the orientation to the Infinite is also for its own sake.[110] Nevertheless, with Marion it is not a question of simply adopting Levinasian perspectives but of doing phenomenology from within the same framework. When it comes to the theological extensions of that phenomenology, Marion never implies that he is taking Levinas with him. The violence, if there is any, will instead be extended toward theology, at least as it is traditionally understood. We find ourselves again at the point—although here we have reached it by means of a more explicit philosophical foundation—where the God whose infinitude interrupts our finite capacities does so only to withdraw completely from knowledge.[111] Is this not a violence to faith as it seeks understanding?

Christian Theology Bifurcates

Levinas would indeed make an unlikely dialogue partner for Christian theology as I outlined it earlier. While brief examination of some of the theological adoptions of Levinas's work shows that they have been accomplished with varying degrees of appropriateness, in several instances the incorporation of his ideas effectively puts in question the theological ends for which they were pressed into service. I have suggested that his work may lead us to question the nature of theology, and in this last section my consideration will draw on another unlikely dialogue partner, Jacques Derrida.

In its search for understanding, theology is always already divided, making use of a double sense of faith: while it is said to examine the content of faith (*fides quae*), this is generally undertaken from the perspective of the commitment or relationship of faith (*fides qua*). The examination of the content of faith is understood to yield knowledge and understanding, but what is actually meant by faith as a commitment is precisely not a question of knowledge in a conceptual sense. As Derrida (in quite a different context) observes: "If we refer to faith, it is to the extent that we *don't see*. Faith is needed when perception is lacking; when I see something I don't need to have faith in it. For example, I don't see the other, I don't see what he or she has in mind. . . . So I have to trust the other, that is faith. Faith is blind."[112] In fact, the type of knowledge yielded by theology as the examination of the content of faith is grounded in faith as a trust that is risked without the benefit of sight. ("Blessed are those who have not seen and yet have come to believe"; John 20:29b.) One of the conditions of possibility for theology is faith in the sense of an ungrounded leap: theology is grounded in an *Abgrund*. Nevertheless, the double sense of faith could raise questions about which sense of faith comes first. Does faith lead to the acceptance of specific beliefs, or do beliefs lead to faith? One could argue that, since faith as a commitment or relationship is said to come about as a response to revelation, and since revelation has a double sense (it is understood to be not only God's personal self-communication but also a body of truths unknowable by other means), faith as commitment is in fact secondary to faith as beliefs.[113] That this is not the case is supported by several arguments.

Throughout Christian tradition, reason is typically held to strengthen faith but not to lead to it in its specifically Christian form.[114] The beliefs that might warrant coming to faith—that is, faith's "reasons"—can never be justified as anything more than beliefs and must be risked, which places them squarely in the context of faith as a relationship of trust. Furthermore, the entire momentum of Catholic theology, at least, over the last fifty years or more has been toward an emphasis on the relational rather than the instrumental in understandings of grace, sacraments, and revelation. The implications of the view that faith as commitment or relationship precedes faith as beliefs are, however, enormous. If revelation leads to the commitment of faith as a response, then we must ask about the content of that revelation, and if it is not what forms the substance of beliefs about God but God "in Godself," as it were, then its content by definition must exceed our capacity to contain it. What, then, does revelation reveal? Turning to Derrida again, we find him reflecting: "I'm trying to think something that removes the event that one calls revelation from the scheme of veil, revelation, revealability. I'm trying to think the event as something other than an unveiling of a truth or the revelation of a truth, as something that has effects but makes no reference to light, no reference to vision, no reference to unveiling."[115] On this account, revelation would take place as an event with effects but without determinable content. The immediate theological response to this difficulty is obvious: since Christian revelation is centered on the person of Jesus Christ, the content of God's self-expression is knowable in Christ's personhood. But in what manner is this possible? Apparently not in the sense that God is presented in Christ as such—the Gospels themselves are testimony to the need for inspired discernment. More likely it is in the effects of Christ's life and teaching, effects that are understood to be confirmed in his death and resurrection, that any potential revelation of God is to be glimpsed:

> When John heard in prison what the Messiah was doing, he sent word by his disciples and said to him, "Are you the one who is to come, or are we to wait for another?" Jesus answered them, "Go and tell John what you hear and see: the blind receive their sight, the lame walk, the lepers are cleansed, the deaf hear, the dead are raised, and the poor have good news brought to them."(Matt. 11:2–5)

The effects of revelation are the bringing about of the reign of God. Strangely enough, and in spite of Levinas's clearly contrary views on the question of divine incarnation, the notion that God signifies in Jesus' response to the (undesirable) other replicates in some measure the structure of the excessive idea of the Infinite, signifying as a trace in the other and as responsibility in the subject.[116] Levinas is not a theologian, and Christians must be careful not to turn him into one. But perhaps he offers this gift to a theology brought to recognize its conditions of impossibility: a way to think God as desirable beyond all knowledge and to know God in learning to desire the other person.

The Prevenience and Phenomenality of Grace; or, The Anteriority of the Posterior

Michael Purcell

Tout est grâce. All is grace; grace is everywhere. These words mark the closure of the diary of a country priest (*Journal d'un curé de campagne*), fictional or otherwise, by Georges Bernanos. Perhaps, as Levinas might say: "True as only fiction can be,"[1] like Yosel Rakover's address to God from the Warsaw Ghetto, a God who has not left a forwarding address. Perhaps *Journal d'un curé de campagne* is as "true as only fiction can be." Dying, and in death, the Curé d'Ambricourt, whose life and ministry of service for others can be read as desolation and isolation, finds himself lodged in an attic and, in the face of all that has gone before, utters to the friend who has sought him out his last words: *Tout est grâce.* Grace is everywhere, and all is grace. In this essay, I intend to set out a phenomenological approach to a theology of grace on the basis of response. At the forefront will be the notion of divine initiative and human response, but also the key notion that response to the divine is always by way of the human. First and foremost, theology is ethics, and this is no less true of a theology of grace, however it may be articulated.

Being between Jews and Christians, between Jew and Greek, puts Levinas in a difficult position, but perhaps the "between" comes to our aid in a reflection on grace and its prevenience. Levinas, in dialogue with Buber, drew attention to the lack of reciprocity in the relation between the subject and the other: the other always comes first, and the distance between the self-same and the other person is not the same as the distance between the other person and the self-same.[2] Levinas is a bridge between theology and ethics, and can make it possible to interpret the one ethical covenant both in Jewish and Christian terms and in the language of response and responsibility. The commanding and demanding priority of the other person is at the fore in Levinas. Theologically, this prevenient advance of the other on the same and the provocation of the same toward the other can be articulated in terms of grace. Grace is always prevenient. The other always comes first.

In the Preface to the second edition of *Of God Who Comes to Mind*, Levinas remarks: "We have been reproached for ignoring theology; and we do not contest the necessity of a recovery, at least, the necessity of choosing an opportunity for a recovery of these themes. We think, however, that theological recuperation comes after the glimpse of holiness, which is primary."[3]

Now, the theology of grace is an all-embracing theological doctrine, which, it could be argued, guides all other particular theologies. It is the acknowledgement of an initial sheer gift that guides and provokes all other giving as responsive giving outside any economy of exchange or return. It traverses without transgression the original covenant with Abraham and the renewed covenant in Christ: divine beneficence and the bending or inclination toward those whom God has called to be his own, and the provocation of human response to divine initiative and invitation. It negotiates original goodness and human failing and falling in view of reconciliation and restoration. It finds its theological culmination in an incarnation in which the reconciliation of the divine and the human is achieved, sin is overcome, and there is a responsive obedience and submission to the will of another, even though this leads to a cross. Grace may be termed exorbitant, for, as *ex orbita*, it exceeds any limits the world might impose. It maintains the transcendence of the God of Abraham, Isaac, and Jacob, while recognizing the strange proximity of the remote in the incarnate. To give an adequate account of grace is the very provocation of theology.

The theology of grace, however, is not only a spur for theological reflection. It is also phenomenologically problematical. From the perspective of Christian theology, grace becomes actual, and definitively so, in incarnation. Yet from the perspective of a strict phenomenology, grace, seemingly lacking phenomenality, is a phenomenological transgression for, strictly speaking, there can be no phenomenology of the exorbitant. And yet, grace is not experienced *as such* but always *as*.

As is such a small word, but it is not without phenomenological and theological significance. In terms of phenomenology, it reminds us that an object appearing in consciousness is always intended *as*—that is, it already bears a particular meaning that is given by a meaning-bestowing consciousness. But this is no less true of the theology of grace, a point to which Karl Rahner draws attention when he writes that "the possibility of experiencing grace and the possibility of experiencing grace *as* grace are not the same thing."[4] Grace, which certainly comes first theologically, is only experienced in terms of its effects. Grace, which is certainly prevenient, is only appreciated "after the event." It is anterior to its effects but is known only late, in and through its effects. In short, grace is experienced in the phenomenality of its appearing.

Rahner makes the similar point when, considering the theology of symbol and sacrament, he notes that the causality involved in the sacraments is the causality of the sign: "the sacrament is precisely a 'cause' of grace, *in so far* as it is its "sign" and . . . the grace—seen as coming from God—is the cause of the sign bringing it about and making it so present. . . . *sacramenta gratiam efficiunt, quatenus eam significant*—where this *significatio* is to be understood in the strict sense of symbolic reality."[5]

Again, "*Sacramenta, significando efficiunt gratiam*. . . . The sacraments, precisely as signs, are causes of grace."[6] In other words, grace is experienced *sacramentally* where sacrament is to be understood in its widest symbolic and most pregnant sense.

A further point needs to be made, which is perhaps more evident in such thinkers as Jean-Luc Marion, Michel Henry, and Jean-Louis Chrétien. Although Rahner distinguishes between the experience of grace and the experience of grace *as grace*, he also stresses that what makes its appearance necessarily in the phenomenality of signs is nothing other than grace *as such*. What God offers in grace is nothing other than God's very self; grace is God's self-communication. Marion will speak of this in terms of the *saturated* or *excessive* phenomenon and of the need to consider further the arresting force of excess in any phenomenal appearing. The phenomenon is that which gives itself *as such*, and in its own terms.[7]

Now, taking a cue from Levinas, the striking phenomenon that gives itself from itself and gives itself excessively is the *face* of the other person. The *face* bears the *trace* of what cannot be commanded but which arrests and commands. "Do we not respond in the presence of the other person to an 'order' whose significance remains irreversible derangement, absolutely completed past?" And where this order is not simply command but an ethical reordering of human reality? "The face is precisely the unique opening where the significance of the trans-cendent does not cancel out transcendence to make it enter into an immanent order; on the contrary it is where trans-cendence refuses immanence precisely as ever *completed* transcendence of the transcendent."[8] The phenomenon of the face is not reducible to its appearance, an appearance which can be clothed and cloaked in the world; it bears within itself a trace which consciousness can neither recuperate nor reduce. Levinas uses the term illeity, a "neologism formed with *il* and *ille*,"[9] for the self-signifying exorbitance of the other person. Illeity escapes the world in its very appearing in the world. Indeed, it is the appearing of the face and the unidentifiable trace sketched in its contours which disturbs time and history, for the face speaks from itself, a locution before ever there is inter-locution, ordering before ever it is ordered, ethics before ontology. The face interrupts phenomenology (as also theology). Levinas writes:

> If the significance of the trace consists in signifying without making appear, if it establishes a relation with illeity—a relation, personal and ethical, a relation, obligation, that does not unveil—if, consequently, the trace does not belong to phenomenology, to comprehension of *appearance* and *dissimulation*, it could at least be approached by another path, by situating that significance from the phenomenology it interrupts.[10]

The disturbing fact of illeity and its possible confusion with the *il y a*, both of which interrupt thought, invites an approach to the theology of grace, which is always experienced *as . . .*, and rarely if ever *as such*.

Phenomena are disturbing. Disturbing phenomena—the facts—are always a challenge to theology and phenomenology. Edith Wyschogrod gives helpful comment regarding a phenomenology of excess:

> Nowhere in Levinas' work does the problem of avoiding a world behind the scenes appear more pressing. In the attempt to bypass Kantian noumenality on the one hand, and the Hegelian reduction of being to reason on the other, Levinas seeks to solve the dilemma by reading a double meaning into the already present instantiations, into what already exists phenomenally. What is present is all that *is*. What lies beyond being intrudes into the world of phenomena but its meaning wells up from the phenomenon itself and eliminates the need for intermediate idealization. Meanings lie hidden yet are available to immediate moral awareness rather than to thematising consciousness. It is not difficult to see that Levinas has given ethical weight and import to Heidegger's notion of forest trails. To those who understand forest lore, these trails are meaningful. Similarly there are signs for those who seek a retrieve of being.[11]

Following these ethical tracks, trails, and traces will be important for a theology of grace.

Approaching a Theology of Grace

A theology of grace might be articulated in the language of waking and awakening;[12] through a gradual and careful reduction one could make the move from subjectivity to intersubjectivity, which might bring us to the verge of something which might be termed "religion."[13] Assuming that one might say *gloria Dei, homo vigilans*,[14] such a move would be a move from the vigil and dawning of subjectivity to the glory of an ethical and religious subjectivity: from vigilance to consciousness to conscience (or moral consciousness), and then to religious consciousness as an openness to the possibility of a beyond. One might equally chart such a move as a move from bare, anonymous existence, through "pagan" existence understood as being devoid of any transcendent reference, to an existence which, open to alterity, is properly ethical and religious. Such an approach would obey the rigor which phenomenological analysis demands through a careful reduction of subjectivity as response and responsibility. This, in turn, requires acknowledgment that that which gives itself to consciousness, although latterly or lately discovered by way of a gradual reduction, is actually anterior or prevenient.

One might also begin to speak of grace in terms of desire, pursuing the notion in Aquinas of the subject as *desiderium naturale beatificae visionis* ("a natural desire for the beatific vision").[15] Such an approach would involve a careful analysis of the structure and the dynamic of a desire which does not find its origin in the self but which is rather provoked, excited, or elicited by something other than the self, a desire which does not quite know what it intends or how it might be satisfied, a desire which is not so much a function of subjectivity but which, in fact, is constitutive of subjectivity. The subject exists *as* desire. Such an approach also has phenomenological merit. It begins with the experience of desire and then proceeds by careful analysis to reduce the conditions of that desire, locating its origin elsewhere than the subject.

Both these approaches—the awakening of the ethical or religious subject and the subject constituted as desire—share some features. First, intentionality does not fully know what it intends: *noesis* in its most pregnant sense does not completely coincide with its corresponding *noema*, nor is there always perfect adequation of intuitive fulfillment and intentionality. Both in awakening and in desiring, an object toward which an intention can be directed is yet to make its appearance. Strictly speaking, there can be no phenomenology of awakening or of desire: in the first case, there is as yet no subject; in the second case, the object is excessive to its appearing.

On Distinguishing the Nonphenomenal on the Basis of Response

In attempting a theology (or even a phenomenology) of grace, the difficulty of the nonphenomenal arises. Can an experience of the nonphenomenal be indicated, and if so, how? One possible way of giving an account of the appearing of the nonphenomenal (strictly speaking, a seemingly phenomenological contradiction) is to chart its appearing in terms of the response which is effected in the subject. This will be important for a theology of grace where the tendency toward the good and its achievement are always dependent on the initial and continuing free bestowal of grace, but where the tendency toward evil and the effects which come in its wake result from human failing. Grace is known in its effects.

Take, for example, the seemingly phenomenological impossibility of distinguishing between the notions of the *il y a* and illeity in Levinas. The *il y a* is anonymous, murmuring, bare being, which gives no thing and is not to be confused with the implicit generosity of Heidegger's *es gibt*. Without form or shape, the *il y a* occupies that interval between dusk and dawn, in the hesitation between disappearing and appearing. It hesitates between nonphenomenality and phenomenality, and the ambiguity of each. Illeity is also without form or shape; it escapes phenomenality because it is an opening onto infinity and phenomenal excess. The *il y a* terrorizes; illeity summons toward responsibility. Yet any phenomenological distinction between a lack of appearing and an excess of appearing is difficult to differentiate.

Some illustrations may be helpful.

On walking home through the woods at dusk alone, there is a moment when things disappear and there are no longer any *Holzwegen*. At this moment, there is the withdrawal of the familiar; silence asserts itself; birds suddenly stop singing; the sound of each leaf crumpled underfoot magnifies; trees becomes shapes; shapes become darkness. The world as phenomenon disappears. As form disappears, each fading shape becomes a threat. Behind that object that may have been a tree there lurks no thing. There is no thing looking at me other than the *there is* (*il y a*). And so I quicken my pace, nonetheless, for fear of the anonymous *there is* (*il y a*) which encompasses me. The horror and terror of the night enfolds me. Of course, this is irrational: trees and bushes do not change shape and form, and I am silly not to have walked confidently through the wood, despite the fear that the darkness provokes in me.

On returning home to the darkened city, there is a moment when, leaving the company of friends in the darkness of the night, I make my way home through streets I knew but now have no name and shadowy, unhabited alleyways with subdued amber lights. No one is there (perhaps), but my footsteps quicken, and the echo behind me tells me that something else and unidentifiable is there, and perhaps following. This too is irrational. How could one possibly fear the nonphenomenal phantom which does not appear?

On keeping vigil by the bedside, a time comes when, after years of companionship and intimacy, the one closest and dearest escapes into anonymity, through old age or disease, and I cannot identify what I loved or cared for, but which I still love and care for. "Even beauty must perish [*Auch das Schöne muß sterben!*] . . . it must fade and the perfect must die [*daß Schöne vergeht, daß Volkommene stirbt*]" (Schiller). But it was not what I could command and identify that attracted me; it was something I could not lay hold of but which, rather, attracted, beckoned, commanded. And so I maintain vigil, moistening lips which are dry from breathing, despite threatening darkness and cold. And when flesh becomes parchment, a trace of the indecipherable remains, where illeity competes with the *il y a*, and I call to mind the words of the poet R. S. Thomas:

> It was not the dark filling my eyes
> And mouth appalled me; not even the drip
> Of rain like blood from the one tree
> Weather-tortured. It was the dark
> Silting the veins of that sick man
> I left stranded upon the vast
> And lonely shore of his bleak bed.[16]

And yet not without indifference . . .

And yet, these experiences—whether of the *il y a* or of illeity—do not leave me indifferent. The *il y a* and the illeity of the other person may either not yet have entered or may have escaped the phenomenal clearing in which a phenomenology might be possible, but both *il y a* and illeity are known in the response which they effect in me, whether the terror of the night or the compassion for the other who takes his or her leave of me. Both terror and compassion bring the nonphenomenal into the realm of phenomenology (and theology) by way of the distinct affective response which each provokes in me, even though these may be confused. Does horror not arise at the point where terror and compassion compete and are in conflict? The phenomenological point is that both the lack of being and the excess of being, which are in themselves seemingly indistinguishable, can be distinguished in terms of the response which they provoke. Such a response—whether fear or responsibility—is within the realm of the phenomenal and, as such, phenomenologically accessible. The access to excess finds its point of departure in the phenomenality of response, of which both phenomenology and theology must give some account.[17] The language of grace is both theological and phenomenological, and the distance between the two is less than one might think. Simply put, phenomenology attempts an account of access to phenomena in terms of *the possibility of revelation*, while theology attempts to speak of phenomenal excess in terms of *the actuality and historicity of Revelation*. Both access and excess remain phenomenological and theological challenges.

Distinguishing the Il y a *from Illeity*

An individual existent, yet to be or become a subject, straddles existence between the *il y a* and illeity. Of course, being nonphenomenal, both the *il y a* and illeity confound and challenge phenomenology. The *il y a* precedes subectivity; illeity summons me to ethical subjectivity.

The question arises: Should "illeity" be used only of God, the one who cannot be named? It seems to me that, although Levinas eschews any incarnation or avatar, Judaism is almost the most incarnate of religions. While refusing a particular incarnation, the encounter with God is, for Levinas, always by way of an encounter with others. The divine withdrawal leaves a trace that, insofar as it is encountered in the excess of the phenomenal, can be ascribed to the human, although its inscription is difficult to decipher. The human is a cipher of the divine, and the God who is remote and removes himself remains in the midst of human relations, albeit at a distance that can be negotiated only in terms of intersubjectivity and, for Levinas, by way of the justice that the anonymous and nameless third demands. Illeity is inscribed in the human, perhaps to the point of the knife that cuts and wounds. Illeity is the persistent and insistent remainder of the human that can be neither described nor erased. But what worries or concerns us is the fragile and confused transition between *il y a* and illeity.[18]

However, let us turn to the notion of prevenience and a theology of grace in terms of the anteriority of the posterior.

Prevenience, or the Anteriority of the Posterior

Now, the notions of awakening, desire, and excess are approaches to a theology of grace, both phenomenologically and theologically, on the basis of provoked response. I would like, nonetheless, to suggest a more fundamental consideration of grace, in terms of prevenience (theological) or the anteriority of the posterior (phenomenology).[19] Thought, which always begins from here, in an ongoing reduction opens onto its conditions of possibility. Transcendental though these may be, such conditions of possibility can be phenomenologically exposed through a reduction which takes its point of departure from itself. However, beginning from the present *here* of thought, thought discovers itself to have a past that cannot quite be wholly recalled. Although come across lately and after thought, this irrecuperable past, whose presence cannot be wholly commanded, is not so much an *afterthought* but rather is found to be the condition, the possibility, and the provocation of any thought. What is placed in question is at once thought as absolute origin and its dependency on that which, preveniently, comes first. In theological terms, the prevenience of grace is the provenance of subjectivity. The anteriority of the divine initiative enables, actualizes, and sustains the subject. Grace is an absolute necessity, and is the necessity of the absolute. In grace, the self find itself always and already enabled, actualized, and sustained in its orientation toward the good.

Prevenience

Now, the classic (and ongoing) theological problem of grace might be said to be the problem of how the divine and the human might be co-operatively reconciled, or how self and other relate. In terms of the divine, there is the requirement of maintaining the divine initiative in the economy of grace as both absolutely gratuitous on the part of God and as absolutely necessary on the part of humanity, whether in its original state or its spoiled state. In terms of the human, there is a desire to assert the freedom and responsibility which properly belong to the human, on account of which one might be worthy of praise or of blame, while at the same time affirming human dependency. The theological argument is well played out in the controversy between Pelagius and Augustine. The philosophical issues have also been played out in modernity, where individual and enlightened subjectivity is the key player in the human drama. In short, the theological problem of grace is the problem of the self and the other. The Council of Orange is a good starting point.

The Council of Orange

The Council of Orange provides a useful starting point, for it brings into focus the key elements of Augustine's understanding of grace. The Council of Orange was called by Caesarius, bishop of Arles, on July 3, 529, with the object of countering the ongoing semi-Pelagianism current in Narbonensian Gaul. The canons of the Council incorporated a number of propositions, mainly reflecting an Augustinian theology of grace, which responded to the issue of the relation between grace and free will. It concluded by asserting the universal necessity of grace in all things. In short, grace is always and everywhere prevenient, even in respect of those actions directed toward the good which may seem to be subsequent.

The elements of the controversy between Pelagius and Augustine do not need to be rehearsed here. Basically, Pelagius had argued that, while God gives the possibility (*posse*) of working toward the good, the will (*velle*) to do the good and its achievement (*esse*) are properly a human effort and endeavor. Augustine, by contrast, argued that not only the possibility (*posse*) but also the willing (*velle*) and achieving (*esse*) of the good depend absolutely on grace, which always comes first.

Now, semi-Pelagianism, a milder form of Pelagianism, sought to maintain an element of human responsibility in working toward and achieving salvation. Such responsibility was linked to a prior human freedom. To assert the universal anteriority of grace in all things compromised human freedom and the subsequent responsibility which came in its wake, and the corresponding judgment of the praiseworthiness or blameworthiness which might or might not be attributed to human action.

Now, this debate can be articulated phenomenologically in terms of the relation between responsibility and freedom which one finds argued by Levinas. Levinas pushes the subjective reduction further in the direction of the intersubjective reduction to argue that freedom operates in the context of a prior responsibility. In terms of prevenience, it is the recognition that, although subjectivity may be a starting point, subjectivity discovers after the event that it has a history which not only predates it but also enables it, or that its freedom comes in the wake of responsibility. One can also read *Totality and Infinity: An Essay on Exteriority* as an approach to subjective interiority on the basis of the exteriority of the other.[20] The Council of Orange, then, asserts the prevenience of grace.[21] Explicitly against Pelagius, it asserts that the entire person (Canon 1) and the whole of humanity (Canon 2) are in need of grace on account of original sin and the consequent weakening of the human will. Grace precedes and enables prayer (Canon 3), and the working of the Holy Spirit is essential for the will to be moved (Canon 4). Grace not only augments faith but is also its beginning and the very condition of any desire for faith (*etiam initium fidei ipsumque credulitatis affectum*; Canon 5). Apart from grace, there can be no desiring, striving, laboring, praying, watching, seeking, asking, or knocking (*sine gratia Dei [non autem] credentibus, volentibus, conantibus, laborantibus, orantibus, vigilantibus, studentibus, petentibus, quarentibus, pulsantibus*; Canon 6). Grace is necessary for perseverance in good works (*ut ad finem bonum pervenire, vel in bono possint opere perdurare*; Canon 10); it precedes them and enables them to be done (*gratia, quae non debetur, praecedit, ut fiant*; Canon 18). Even the love with which we love God is the result of a prior gift (*De dilectatione, qua diligimus Deum. Prorsus donum Dei est diligere Deum*; Canon 25).

Caesarius concludes, by way of redaction:

We must, under the blessing of God, preach and believe as follows: the sin of the first man has so impaired and weakened free will that no one thereafter can either love God as he ought or believe in God or do good for God's sake, unless the divine mercy has preceded him. . . . We know and also believe that even after the coming of our Lord this grace is not to be found in the free will of all who desire to be baptised, but is bestowed by the kindness of Christ. . . . We also believe that after grace has been received through baptism, all baptised persons have the ability and responsibility, if they desire to labour faithfully, to perform with the aid and cooperation of Christ what is of essential importance in regard to the salvation of their soul. . . . We also believe and confess to our benefit that in every good work it is not we who take the initiative and are then assisted through the mercy of God, but God himself first inspires in us both faith in him and love for him without any previous good works of our own that deserve reward, so that we may both faithfully seek the sacrament of baptism, and after baptism by his help to do what is pleasing to him. [*Ac sic . . . hoc Deo propitiante et praedicare debemus et credere, quod per peccatum primi hominis ita inclinatum et attenuatum fuerit liberum arbitrium, ut nullus postea aut diligere Deum sicut oportuit, aut credere in Deum aut operari propter Deum quod bonum est, possit, nisi eum gratia misericordiae divinae praevenerit . . . . Quam gratiam etiam post adventum Domini omnibus, qui baptizari desiderant, non in libero arbitrio haberi, sed Christi novimus simul et largitate conferri. . . . Hoc etiam . . . quod post acceptam per baptismum gratiam omnes baptizati, Christo auxiliante et cooperante, quae ad salutem animae pertinent, possint et debeant, si fideliter laborare voluerint, adimplere. . . . Hoc etiam salubriter profitemur et credimus, quod in omni opere bono non nos incipimus, et postea per Dei misericordiam adiuvamur, sed ipse nobis nullis praecedentibus bonis meritis et fidem et amorem sui prius inspirat, ut et baptismi sacramenta fideliter requiramus, et post bapstismum cum ipsius adiutorio ea, quae, sibi sunt placita, implere possimus.*][22]

The key points here are the precedence and initiative of divine mercy and the notion of grace as prior and unmerited gift, and the ability and responsibility that grace inspires, enables, and provokes. The initiative always comes from what is other than the self-same.

Aquinas on Grace

The prevenience of grace in all things is considered further by Aquinas, when he asks: "Is grace satisfactorily divided into prevenient and subsequent grace? [*Utrum gratia convenienter dividatur in praevenientiem et subsequentem*]?" (ST, 1a 2ae, q.111, a.3). The objection could be made that grace should not be divided both as prevenient and consequent but is always prevenient. However, Aquinas, recognizing the many ways in which God works to achieve the good and bring things to perfection, responds:

> Just as grace is divided into operative and cooperative grace according to its different effects, so too it is divided into prevenient and subsequent grace. In whatever sense grace is understood. Now, there are five effects of grace in us: firstly, the healing of the soul; secondly, the willing of the good; thirdly, the efficacious performance of the good willed; fourthly, perseverance in the good; fifthly, the attainment of glory.

The acknowledgment of Augustine's teaching on grace, which Aquinas more or less faithfully follows, is evident. Pelagius had understood grace as enabling (*posse*)—here, the prior healing of the soul in order that it might both will and do the good—but the willing (*velle*) and the performance (*esse*) of the good are achieved through human endeavor. For Augustine, grace is not only an enabling, sanative gift but also necessary for both the willing and the performance of the good. Aquinas continues:

> And so, in that it causes the first effect in us, grace is called prevenient with respect to the second effect; and in that it causes the second effect in us, it is called subsequent with respect to the first. And as a single effect is posterior to one effect and prior to another, so grace can be called both prevenient and subsequent in regard to the same effect, under different respects. *"It precedes us to heal us, it follows us to make us strong once healed; it precedes us to call us, it follows us to make us share in glory."* (ST, 1a 2ae, q.111, a.3, quoting Augustine, *De Natura et Gratia*, 31)

In other words, the entire human existential is always and already a graced existential, in which grace enables and sustains all tending toward and accomplishment of the good.

Now, Aquinas's explanation of the relation between the prior and the posterior (*prius et posterius*) involves a methodology which is not without theological or phenomenological significance. Grace is only known by its effects (*per effectus*), and so one must move from the phenomenality of the effect, which is subsequent, to its logically prior and prevenient cause. In other words—and here Rahner puts it quite clearly, as already indicated—grace is never experienced *as such*, but only *in terms of* that which it brings about: "the possibility of experiencing grace and the possibility of experiencing grace *as* grace are not the same thing."

What, then, are the key points in Aquinas's gospel of grace? It will be useful to remain with Aquinas's consideration of grace, since his reflections resonate with a postmodern understanding of the origin of subjectivity as response and responsibility.

First of all, grace is *necessary*. It is the necessary condition for the beginning, the undertaking, and the accomplishment of any human action in its tending toward the good. It is the possibility of all human possibility.

Second, grace is a *habit*, which can be acquired with due and proper preparation by created humanity; however, *habitual* grace requires as its possibility an *actual* grace which is prevenient. Actual grace, freely given, is the possibility of human willing and enactment: "there is need that man's will should be prepared by God through grace" (a.5). Such "a preparation of the human will for good" is twofold. Grace brings about a habitual disposition which is "the principle of meritorious action" (a.6), but, lest there be an infinite regress, there is the presupposition of "some gratuitous assistance of God moving the soul within, or inspiring a good purpose" (a.6). "And so it is clear that man cannot prepare himself to receive the light of grace except by the gratuitous assistance of God moving him within" (a.6).

Third, grace is *gratuitous*. From this follows a threefold logic of giving, gift, and gratitude (q.110, a.1). It refers to "the love of someone [*pro dilectione alicuius*]," and to "a gift given gratis [*pro aliquo dono gratis dato*]," and to "the display of gratitude for benefits given gratis [*pro recompensatione beneficii gratis dati*]." The second sense of "grace" depends on the first, and the third flows from the second by way of response:

> The second of these three senses depends on the first; for out of the love with which someone regards him favourably, it comes that he bestows something on him gratis. The third sense rises from the second, since the expression of gratitude arises in response to benefits bestowed gratis. [*Quorum trium secundum dependet ex primo: ex amore enim quo aliquis habet alium gratum procedit aliquid ei gratis*

impendat; ex secundo autem procedit tertium, quia ex beneficiis gratis exhibitis gratiarum actio consurgit.] (q.110, a.1)

This could be said otherwise: the logic of giving, gift, and gratitude depends on the free and anterior inclining of one whose inclination to give originates and sustains all subsequent giving. The possibility of giving, even by way of response, is always and already the benefit of a gift already having been given, the consequence of a gracious and beneficent divine condescension toward the creature created in grace and for grace. This prior giving, which originates and sustains all giving, does not establish an economy of exchange which would nullify the gratuity of the gift given; rather, it establishes an economy of salvation in which giving is constantly provoked as gratitude for the gift already and excessively given and received. The return does not cancel out the gift, for response is always inadequate to offer. Thus the logic of uncreated grace becomes a logic of created grace as response and responsibility.

Such an insight can be found in Aquinas: "grace sets up something in the one who receives the grace [*gratia aliquid ponit in eo qui gratiam accipit*]"—namely, "the gift itself given gratis [*ipsum donum gratis datum*]" and "the gratitude for this gift [*huius doni recognitionem*]." But he distinguishes God's grace from human grace. Human grace and goodness, as response, are entirely dependent upon the grace and goodness of God, by whom all things are rendered good and elicit response. The logic of grace is the logic of response. Thus the human will "is moved by the goodness already existing in things [*Voluntas autem hominis movetur ex bono praeexistente in rebus*]" (q.110, a.1).

Now, to frame an understanding of grace in terms of response might seem to indicate that grace is more of a movement or a tendency provoked by a good that is given rather than a quality. Grace, as provocative, would therefore be extrinsic to the soul rather than constitutive, and the semi-Pelagian notion of a subject-origin would persist. Aquinas recognizes this. Grace effects a response and so "in this sense that gratuitous effect in man is not a quality but a movement of the soul [*et hoc modo ipse gratuitus effectus in homine non est qualitas, sed motus quidam animae*]" (q.110, a.2). However, Aquinas also acknowledges that "the gift of grace is a kind of quality [*donum gratiae qualitas quaedam est*]," for it "acts on the soul not in the manner of an efficient cause but in the manner of a formal cause [*agere in animam, non per modum causae efficientis, sed per modum causae formalis*]." This line of thought continues when Aquinas considers whether grace is simply a virtue, and responds that it is not simply a virtue but is "a kind of habitual state [*habitudo quaedam*]" which is the possibility of any virtue (q.110, 3, ad 3) and which characterizes the soul, essentially rather than accidentally. Grace is prior to virtue (*prius virtute*); it "is related to the will as mover to moved [*comparatur ad voluntatem ut movens ad motum*]"; it is "the originating principle of meritorious action [*principium meritorii operis*]."

Rahner develops this in terms of "quasi-formal" causality, noting that "God communicates himself to the man to whom grace has been shown in the mode of *formal* causality, so that this communication is not then merely the consequence of an efficient causation of created grace."[23] Further, uncreated grace "is the homogeneous commencement, already given though still to unfold, of that *communication* of the divine Being taking place *by way of formal causality* to the created spirit which is the *ontological presupposition* of the *visio*."[24] The significance of this is further spelled out when Rahner notes that: "This divine self-communication, in which God makes himself a constitutive principle of the created existent without thereby losing his absolute, ontological independence has 'divinising' effects in the finite existent in whom this self-communication takes place,"[25] for "while in the created entity in general its relation to the divine cause does not belong to the inner distinguishing feature of its *essence,* created grace, as *ultima dispositio* to an immediate communication of the divine Being itself in the mode of formal causality—a communication which can only exist in terms of this formal causality—involves a relation to God which belongs to its very essence."[26] In short, the action of grace is analogous to a causality "in which the 'cause' becomes an instrinsic, constitutive principle of the effect itself."[27]

To say this in a more phenomenological language: grace and goodness effect movement in the soul *as* a quality of the soul, enabling and provoking the soul *as* response. It is, as Levinas might say, the anarchic proximity of the "other-in-me."

Prevenient Grace

And so we come to the prevenience of grace in q.111 on "the divisions of grace." Aquinas first considers grace as "sanctifying." Grace is not simply a freely bestowed gift, but it is a gift given freely which effects a change in the recipient. This change is not simply the result of an efficient cause but a formal change. Thus, "Grace is not said to make pleasing or sanctify by an efficient but by a formal 'making,' such that by it man is justified and made worthy to be called pleasing to God [*Gratia non dicitur facere gratum effective, sed formaliter, scilicet quia per hanc homo justificatur et dignus efficitur vocari Deo gratus]*" (q.111, a.1, ad 1). Second, this bestowal of grace as a free gift that sanctifies involves co-operation. (The gift, of course, can be refused, and one can turn away from doing good. Evil remains a possibility. Ethical imperatives are not ontological necessities.) Operative grace (*gratia per operantem*), then, gives the possibility of cooperation (*gratia per cooperantem*). The *relation* of operation and cooperation is important here, and it is worth quoting Aquinas's response. Against those who would argue that grace ought not to be divided into operative and cooperative grace, Aquinas argues the contrary: "On the other hand, Augustine says, *By his cooperation God perfects in us what he initiates by his operation; since by his operation he initiates our willing who, by his cooperation with us who will, perfects us.* Now the operations of God by which he moves us toward the good belong to grace. Therefore grace is satisfactorily divided into operative and cooperative grace" (q.111, a.2).[28] Aquinas continues by distinguishing the senses in which grace can be considered. On the one hand, it can be considered "as the divine assistance by which God moves us to will and do good [*uno modo divinum auxilium, quod nos movet ad bene volendum et agendum*]"; on the other hand, it is "the habitual gift implanted in us by God [*alio modo habituale donum nobis divinitus inditum*]." God is the one by whom our minds are moved toward the good, and thus is grace operative. But God is also the one who sustains that movement of the mind, once begun in us, and this is grace also cooperative. In terms of interiority—that is, the effect of divine grace in us—there are two kinds of response which this prior bestowal of grace elicits. First, "the interior act of the will [*interior voluntatis*]," which is moved by grace; second, the enactment of this internal provocation in exteriority: "Thus . . . *it is by his operation that we will; but once we will, it is by his cooperation with us that we bring our action to completion.* Thus if grace is understood as the gratuitous motion of God by which he moves us to perform a meritorious good, grace is satisfactorily divided into operative and cooperative grace." In the more essential language of grace as habitual gift, two effects are seen: the first effect of grace is being, from which the second—activity—flows: "Thus habitual grace, in as much as it heals or justifies the soul, or makes it pleasing to God, is called operative; but inasmuch as it is the principle of meritorious action, which proceeds from free choice as well, it is called cooperative." Thus, grace operates as a *formal* cause (*ad 1*), which first provokes the soul and in that same moment cooperates in moving the soul to act. "Thus the whole operation belongs to grace" (*ad 2*).

In developing the doctrine of grace from Augustine's conflict with Pelagius, through the Council of Orange, and in Aquinas, I have sought to draw attention to the notion that grace, as the operation of the "other-in-me," is prevenient in all things pertaining to the willing and the doing of the good, and the operation of this grace is not extrinsic to the human person but intrinsic and constitutive, although grace is known only in the phenomenality of its effects. While the effects logically come first in the order of knowing, they depend upon an anteriority which can be reduced. Grace is anterior, or prevenient.

Let us attempt to augment the theological understanding of grace as the "anteriority of the posterior" with the more phenomenological notion of "the posteriority of the anterior" in Levinas.

Levinas and "the Posteriority of the Anterior"

Levinas speaks of the "posteriority of the anteriority" in *Totality and Infinity* when considering the notion of separation and discourse. Separation marks the disengagement and withdrawal of the self from the world which it happily enjoys; at the same time, separation is the moment (out of time) in which the self recollects itself, or gathers itself together, as the *here* of consciousness from which thought proceeds. The nuclear subject emerges as a point of departure, prior to any awareness of the excoriation or *denucleation* of the subject that alterity inflicts on this logic of the self as apparent origin.

Levinas proceeds by drawing attention to Descartes' *Third Meditation*, in which Descartes speaks of an idea which exceeds the *cogito*. This is the idea of Infinity. But the discovery of the idea of Infinity comes only as "a second move" in the chronology of thought. The paring away of evidence establishes the *cogito* as the first and only, but momentary, indubitable. Thus, "The present of the *cogito*, despite the support it discovers for itself *after the fact* in the absolute that transcends it, maintains itself all by itself—be it only for an instant, the space of a *cogito*."[29] For Descartes, thought establishes a *here* which is a beginning and a point of departure. As Levinas notes in *Existence and Existents*, "Thought . . . is . . . *here*."[30] The logical order would then progress from this original starting point. However, in Descartes' *Meditation*, this origin finds itself thinking a thought of which it cannot be the origin, a thought that interrupts the logical order by introducing a chronology of difference. "That there could be a chronological order distinct from the 'logical' order, that there could be several moments in the progression, that there is a progression"[31]— here is the recognition of a precedence by which the present proceeds.

Levinas introduces a strange and complex chronology, in which the notion of a presence which regulates the temporal ecstases of past, present, and future is placed in question. The present as the recollection or gathering of the subject into self-presence might seem to be the logical beginning of temporality, the instant from which time unfolds. The instant might seem to be the instantiation and inception of the subject and the logical beginning of time, which unfolds from the present of self-presence. In such a conception of the existentiality of time, the future, as time that is yet to come, would be the field of possibility yet to be determined from the vantage point of the present, and the past would be an archaeology and genealogy (and possible justification) of the present. In short, time would be a function of the subject.

For Levinas, however, time is not a function of the subject, nor is the present of presence to be conceived as the bestower or arbiter of meaning of either past or future. Time is gift and given. Time is a function of what is other than the subject, and what is other than the subject enables the subject to function. Subjectivity emerges into a time which is not its own and of which it is neither author nor origin. Said otherwise, if, logically, time begins with awakening, awakening finds itself somewhat lately always and already to have been awakened. The "sheer youthfulness" of thought, which is enjoyment and elemental, is yet "heedless of its slipping into the past and of its recovered self-possession in the future."[32] What thought discovers is that: "Even its cause, older than itself, is still to come. The cause of being is thought or known by its effect *as though* it were posterior to its effect."[33] But this "*as though*" is not illusory; neither is it unfounded. Levinas continues, "The posteriority of the anterior—an inversion logically absurd—is produced, one would say, only by memory or by thought. But the 'improbable' phenomenon of memory or of thought must precisely be interpreted as a revolution in being."[34] For Levinas, such "a revolution in being" is an ethical revolution which disturbs ontology and enables a subject that not only is conscious but also has a conscience, and in which both consciousness and moral consciousness are provoked by what is other than the self. The birth or emergence of the subject is the time of the other. Theologically, it is the birth of the subject into a graced creation of which the subject is not the origin. It is the discovery of paternity in the very awareness of filiality. The provocation of thought effects a separation which is self-consciousness but also consciousness of the other person, who, in making consciousness conscious of itself, summons it to ethical response. Inwardness or interiority thus becomes aware of its origin in an other than itself: "Separation is not reflected in thought but produced by it. For in it the *After* or the *Effect* conditions the *Before* or the *Cause*: the Before *appears* and is only welcomed."[35]

Now, this means that subjectivity is not primarily historical or cultural but, beyond this, is primarily ethical. The subject is not so much a victim of history as a hostage to alterity: "Interiority is the very possibility of a birth and death that do not derive their meaning from history. Interiority institutes an order different from historical time in which totality is constituted, and order where everything is *pending*, where what is no longer possible historically remains always possible."[36] In short, the birth of the subject is ethical, and, if this "original ethical event would also be first theology,"[37] then it is also a theological event; it is the work of "the other-in-me." Subjectivity "is not, in the last analysis, the 'I think' (which it is at first) or the unity of 'transcendental apperception' [but] is, as a responsibility for another, a subjection to the other."[38]

The Proximity of the Other-in-Me; or, Proximity and Prevenience

Confronted by another, the self is provoked into consciousness both of self as separated and of other. The subject is constituted as a moral consciousness, or conscience, and is summoned to respond. Subjectivity is constituted *as* response and responsibility. Levinas speak of this in his later major work, *Otherwise than Being, or Beyond Essence*, when he considers the self in terms of substitution. Here, the notions of anarchy, diachrony, and anteriority feature.

The proximity of the other person is experienced as a disturbing and arresting responsibility which places the self as self-consciousness in question but also effects the self as not "for-myself" but rather as "one-for-the-other." This "one-for-the-other has the form of sensibility or vulnerability, pure passivity or susceptibility, passive to the point of becoming an inspiration."[39] To return to the notions of the *il y a* and illeity, for example, which are differentiated in the response which they provoke, consider the experience of being taken by surprise and the intake of breath which accompanies that experience. While the *il y a* provokes the self as horror, the illeity of the other person provokes the self as an exhalation of responsibility. One breathes in the other person and is instantiated as responsibility. The self is identified as responsibility and is at the service of the other. "In the form of responsibility, the psyche in the soul is the other in me, a malady of identity, both accused and *self*, the same for the other, the same by the other." "The soul is the other in me."[40]

Now, this rendering of the self as the one-for-the-other of responsibility is not an operation which has its origin in the self; rather, it is a willing and co-operative response to the other-in-me who calls on me to respond.

Responsibility, though it is experienced by the self, is not a function of the self; it is the other-in-me who establishes me as for-the-other. In terms of the posteriority of the anterior, the proximity of the other is an *anarchy* whose "me-ontological and metalogical structure" is discovered "in a *responsibility that is justified by no prior commitment*, in the responsibility for another—in an ethical situation."[41] Being instantiated as responsible for the other is not the result of any choosing on my part, but "is an assignation of me by another . . . an obligation anachronously prior to any commitment [whose] anteriority is 'older' than the a priori." It is an obsession, where obsession is to be understood as a "relationship with exteriority 'prior' to the act that would effect it."[42] In other words, responsibility is not a matter of efficient but of formal causality, an effecting of the soul as affection for the good of the other. Levinas writes:

> The one is hypostasised in another one. It is bound in a knot that cannot be undone in a responsibility for others. . . . In the exposure to wounds and outrages, in the feeling proper to responsibility, the oneself is provoked as irreplaceable, as devoted to others, without being able to resign, and thus incarnated in order to offer itself, to suffer and to give. It is thus one and unique, in passivity from the start, having nothing at its disposal that would enable it not to yield to provocation.[43]

The origin of the self

> does not begin in the auto-affection of a sovereign ego that would be, after the event, "compassionate" for another. Quite the contrary: the uniqueness of the responsible ego is possible only *in* being obsessed by another, in the trauma suffered prior to any auto-identification, in the unrepresentable *before*. The one affected by the other is an anarchic trauma, or an inspiration of the one by the other, and not a causality striking mechanically a matter subject to its energy.[44]

Conclusion

In this essay, I have sought to argue for a phenomenology and theology of grace on the basis of response, bringing the theological understanding of grace as prevenient into conversation with Levinas's notion of the posteriority of the anterior. Levinas may be seen to be suspended between the Jew and the Christian, but always situated in the ethical decision that needs to be made when faced with the other person, who is always enigmatic and always comes first. There is covenantal continuity. God goes back neither on his promises nor on his call and the election that comes in its wake. But God does not hide behind the other person; rather, God is accessible *by way of* the incarnate other person, who could be—might be—any other person, for the other always approaches in the guise of a stranger, like the visitors to Abraham and Sarah at the Oak of Mamre. Illeity is integral to, but not apart from, the mystery of the human, which mystery, in its irreducibility, is the trace in the face.

Yet, at times illeity and the *il y a*, in their nonphenomenality, can reach the point of confusion, which makes ethics, whether Jewish or Christian, a difficult and uncertain judgment. Illeity summons responsibility; the *il y a* provokes horror and terror. Now, making the theological transition that Levinas indicates is a cautious maneuver. Nonetheless, theology asserts the prevenience of grace in all things which intend the good. In Augustine, the Council of Orange, and Aquinas, we saw how God not only gives the possibility of being directed toward the good but also provokes the willing (*velle*) of the good and its final achievement (*esse*). This tendency toward the good is integral to human subjectivity. Grace establishes and affirms the subject in its very interiority as a tendency toward the good. The understanding of grace as prevenient is an affirmation of its anteriority, though, insofar as grace is known in its effects which are consequent, grace as grace is discovered posterior to its effects. The theological affirmation of the "anteriority of the posterior" becomes the phenomenological affirmation of the "posteriority of the anterior." Starting with the phenomena, which are logically first, the prior conditions are phenomenologically uncovered.

Finally, the responses which grace provokes and sustains in the self are not impositions on the self but truly acts of the subject resulting from the work of "the-other-in-me," by which the subject can truly become, by grace, "for-the-other." The prevenient proximity of the other provokes the subject as response and is the origin of the orientation toward the good.

Profligacy, Parsimony, and the Ethics of Expenditure in the Philosophy of Levinas

EDITH WYSCHOGROD

The ethics of Emmanuel Levinas is one of radical self-giving, of boundless expenditure in the interest of the other. Does not giving without reserve encourage an ethic of prodigality, an unlimited generosity that, in the long run, may exhaust the resources of the self so that future giving is impaired? If the prodigality of Levinasian giving is not to result in the depletion that is likely to follow upon sheer profligacy, must there not also be a turn to a parsimony that would husband the resources needed for further expenditure? What is more, if self-giving in acts of total self-donation are seen as the ultimate good, am I not, in the interest of the other, obliged to bring home to the other the necessity for her or him to engage in the same sacrificial prodigality I impose upon myself? Would the failure to demand of the other what I require of myself not deprive that other of the opportunity for her or him to engage in the ultimate good of generous self-emptying in the interest of another? Can such an ethics enter the world of actual existence nondiscursively and without attention to moral rules?

In addressing these questions, I shall take into account alternative views of the ethical subject in Levinas's thought by turning first to its emergence following the coming into being of an autonomous self, depicted principally in the opening sections of *Totality and Infinity*, and next to its meaning in the context of time and language, as described in his essay "Substitution."[1] This view is further developed in his major work *Otherwise than Being, or Beyond Essence*.[2] I shall then consider the works of

Marcel Mauss and Georges Bataille as they bear upon the relation of the individual subject to an economy of the sacred, a self that will be shown to bear striking affinities with the pre-ethical self of Levinas. Finally, without endorsing the economic theories in which they are embedded, I hope to recast the radical self-giving of Levinas's ethical subject in terms of prodigality and parsimony as they are framed in the conceptual language of classical economics in order to examine some outcomes of unfettered profligacy. I hope to reconfigure Levinas's ethical subject as one who not only gives but who also stores, not in order to keep but in order to bestow. I shall also assume that the question of storing in the interest of practicability is important for both Judaism and Christianity. Differences between the religions adumbrated by Levinas in a number of contexts are significant, but since practicability is the subject of this essay, I shall not consider these differences here. Common to both religions is the textual appeal of Jeremiah 2:16: "He judged the cause of the poor and the needy. . . . Was this not to know me saith the Lord?" From this passage, Levinas concludes that there is a radical shift from Creator to creature.[3]

Although self-interest figures prominently as a motive for action in the work of Adam Smith, I shall not forgo the primary signification of Levinas's ethical subject as a venture of self-giving, the *terminus a quo* and *terminus ad quem* of ethical existence. However, by analyzing the benefits and drawbacks attributed to parsimony and profligacy, to thrift and expenditure, from the perspective of Smith's version of classical economics, I hope not to abandon but to enhance the viability of an ethics of alterity. Far from suggesting that Levinas's thought belongs (even indirectly) within the conspectus of classical economics in its older or revisionist forms, I hold instead that the primacy of self-interest that motivates economic activity ought not to preclude the appropriation of Smith's work in the interest of enhancing the comprehensibility and practicability of a Levinasian ethics.

From Freedom to the Moral Subject

Consider first the account in *Totality and Infinity* of an ethical subject who arises in a world that can be construed as a rudimentary economy.[4] A monadic solitary self, a conscious existent that is not yet a moral self, emerges from what Levinas calls the elemental, undifferentiated being that precedes the being of the existent, being that is simply there in a state of lambency before the appearance of identifiable entities and upon which layers of basic social and economic functions, habitation, and work will later supervene. In an account reminiscent of Hegel's view of being as life, which is to become a field of struggle with the emergence of mastery and servitude, the elemental must be conquered.[5] The self that appears against the ground of the elemental does so as an event, as the coming into being of an individual existent, without whom there would no freedom, no initiation of activity or beginning. The being that persists in the face of the imagined destruction of the world is the *il y a*. As a solitary existent, consciousness can become the subject of the verb *to be* and, in its mastery over the fatality of being, challenge the anonymity of the *il y a* into which beings can be reabsorbed.[6] This self finds a fixed point of world orientation, creates a home, a dwelling from which it emerges to labor and to which it returns.

I shall revisit the self who emerges from the elemental in connection with its affinities to the individual in the sacred economies depicted in the work of Mauss and Bataille. It should be noted that the self in the foregoing description is a self of practices that Pierre Bourdieu designates *habitus*. In opposition to the perspectives of intellectual idealism, "*habitus* are constituted in practice . . . oriented to practical functions" and operate as "a system of structured, structuring dispositions" that organize practices without a conscious aiming at ends.[7] *Habitus* impose constraints and limits on thought that may overcome the dyadic biases of such conceptualizations as freedom/determinism or conditioning/society. What Bourdieu envisions as the governing structure of social transactions is for Levinas a preliminary stage of the self's development, a difference that should not obscure their phenomenological affinities.

For Levinas, the self that emerges from the elemental and experiences a desire for things is an entrepreneurial self, one whose actions result in productivity. It is thus a self of economy. In this context, desire, in contrast to its later role, is satiable and can, when fulfilled, end with the enjoyment of what is produced, the happiness attendant upon the possession or ownership of what had been desired. By contrast, need is understood as a pressure exerted by being itself that is not extinguished with its satisfaction. When pleasure supervenes upon the fulfillment of need, it is concentrated into a moment that loosens the pressure of need but does not prevent lack from rearising. Thus, an insatiability intrinsic to the ethical and theological desire of Levinas's later writings and inherent in need is ineradicable in human existence.[8]

If, for the subject who emerges from the elemental, need and desire are directed to the world as world, is Levinas not compelled to conflate them? And if so, do they generate contradictory standpoints? If need is not demolished with the satisfaction of need, it must be regarded as insatiable. Desire, by contrast, can find satisfaction in what is desirable, so that for desire satiety is possible. When as world relations they are conflated, need and desire are both satiable and insatiable, a tension that I shall maintain is integral to the motives driving the activities depicted in classical economics. What is more, so long as they belong to the world, objects lack mystery, are tied to a form, are stable and finite and can fulfill the intentions of a consciousness aimed at apprehending them. So long as need and desire are conflated "Levinas [is compelled] to affirm either that there are some things that we can think that are totally formless . . . or to claim that there are objects of need and desire that transcend ontology and therefore do not have to meet the requirement for all thought . . . namely that they have form in order to be thinkable."[9]

That need and desire are, in their initial expressions, relations to objects in the world should not obscure significant differences between their affective expressions. Need, for Levinas, belongs to an economy of gratification. The lack intrinsic to need does not prescind the pleasure that supervenes upon its satisfaction or the sense of plenitude this satisfaction grants. Desire, by contrast, bestows the egoistic pleasure of possession, a difference attributable to their points of origin: "Desire is an aspiration that the Desirable animates; it originates from its 'object'; it is revelation—whereas need is a void of the Soul; it proceeds from the subject."[10] When the object of desire is the other, it may be interpreted as a need that does not consume its object. This relation is not one of consumption but of communication, of thought and language. Thus desire as desire for the other has undergone a transformation in that it presupposes need, satiety, and, in addition, inflected cognitive processes. The entrepreneurial subject who basked in the ownership of objects has become a self that possesses its objects as objects of representation.

The subject who thinks anticipates her or his needs and thereby establishes a distance between need and satiety that is experienced as time. The autonomous being who is freed from the elemental and experiences time's passing is one who lives as a body. As both master and slave of what she or he lives on, the corporeal subject is vulnerable, open to the dangers of the world.[11] It is now the task of an embodied self to arrange time so as to ward off the threat to her or his always already imperiled contingency. If time, as understood by this self, is an assessment of the past in anticipation of future needs, is time not comparably expressed in the circulation of goods, as classical economics maintains? The subject for whom freedom is the use of time, an autonomous self, is always already caught up in networks of economic activity, a point to which I shall recur.

Levinas argues further that things are given not only as objects of use but also as forms, as objects seen. In allowing the object to come into view without alteration, vision would seem to constitute the proper arena of ethics. But Levinas maintains that, *per contra*, the absolute alterity of the other cannot be enclosed in a visible form or construed as an inductively derived or rationally intuited essence. In either case, the other is reduced to the same, to the content of consciousness as its possession, thereby vitiating the radical alterity of the other. When given as a face, the other is not apprehended as a form, a visual datum, but as discourse. "The face, still a thing among things, breaks through the form that nevertheless delimits it. . . . The face speaks to me and thereby invites me to a relation incommensurate with a power exercised, be it enjoyment or knowledge."[12] It speaks proscriptively as a command not to commit violence against it: "Neither the destruction of things, nor the hunt, nor the extermination of living beings aims at the face which is not of the world. They still belong to labor, have a finality and answer to a need. . . . Negation by labor and usage . . . [and] representation . . . rest on or aim at affirmation. To kill is not to dominate but to annihilate."[13]

The passivity of Levinas's ethical subject has often been stressed, a passivity that is not the outcome of the cessation of a Hobbesian state of nature, of a primordial struggle that terminates in a social contract.[14] Instead, the other is the one who is always able to say no and, as such, to invite a violent response. When a violent response is proferred, he, in turn, "can oppose to me a struggle . . . [in] the *unforeseeableness* of his reaction." The power of the other, however, lies not in a greater force that he can exert but in "the infinity of his transcendence."[15] Could it not be argued that physical resistance has, as it were, morphed into ethical resistance, that the restraint of force is itself an expression of power as power withheld? Levinas stresses the ethical impossibility of surrendering to what he describes as "the infinity of the temptation" and its "purely ethical impossibility."[16] Can ethical resistance, however, not be read as the power that resists power and, in this context, as providing an entering wedge for exploring the moral self in the perspective of an economy that would both restrain and empower the prodigality of the ethical self?

In the broader context of Levinas's analysis of power, the world of economy is one in which the products of labor are subject to exchange and usurpation. Designated as tyranny, this economy is as such political, and its attempts to sublate the interiority of the self are represented by the state.[17] The network of functional relationships, framed in terms of polity and economy, is the subject of history and constitutes what Levinas designates as totality, a whole that devours individuality and sublates alterity. It is worth noting that in the context of ethics the other is often depicted through metaphors that directly or indirectly express the depradations of economy. The other is the poor, the stranger, the widow, and the orphan, who are rendered destitute through the violence of economic inequities. What is more, the relation with the other thus understood provides a link with transcendence insofar as there can be no relation with God apart from engagement with the other, who is always already given in her or his exigency. Levinas identifies such a direct relationship with the other as justice. "The uprightness of the face to face is necessary in order that the breach that leads to God be produced," a social relation that is enacted as justice, a justice that is the sine qua non of the rupture with totality.[18]

The Self in Place of the Other

The second context in which to explore the moral subject is Levinas's 1968 essay "Substitution" and the elaboration of its claims in *Otherwise than Being*. In an effort to avoid the resonances of violence inherent in the language of ontology deployed in *Totality and Infinity*, Levinas advances a view of the ethical subject as persecuted, as one who is willing to become hostage for the other. From this fresh perspective, he formulates conceptual possibilities that are conceded to lie beyond ontology but are intrinsic to an Ethic of ethics succinctly described as "*substitution of one for another, the immemorial past that has not crossed the present, the positing of the self that has not deposed the ego, less than nothing as uniqueness, difference with respect to the other as non-indifference.*"[19]

The ethical subject emerges as a disruption not only in the plenitude of ontology but also in the life of consciousness understood as the grasp of an ideality that is governed by a "schematism" in Kant's sense of the term, a realm of consciousness in which epistemic certitude is both sought and seen as always possible. No longer is the *Lebenswelt* of the subject described as an arena of struggle for an autonomous individual, as in the earlier work, nor is the relation to the other exclusively a relation to the face apprehended as proscriptive discourse. Now the connection to alterity is principally one of proximity, of touching understood as caress and language understood not as an exchange of information but as contact bypassing the ideality of the logos.[20] Because the ethical signifies in a radically new way, its mode of temporalization differs from what Derrida famously calls "the logic of presence." Beyond both concept and image and thus beyond the power of consciousness to domesticate what is proximate, to confer an archē upon it, the exteriority that cannot be made present is an-archic. Always already past, proximity "troubles the now."[21] As anarchic, proximity is a relation with the near one, the neighbor understood not in terms of spatial contiguity but rather as a relation with one whom

I do not know and to whom I have a responsibility. The anarchy of proximity is deeply troubling to a self that can never recover itself. With the eruption of the other into the same, into the world of consciousness and being, the "Ego is left speechless, anarchic, obsessed by the alterity that has invaded it." Now Levinas declares "Obsession is persecution."[22] Thus understood, persecution is not to be taken for paranoia but is the very modality in which ethics is lived.

Who in this new context is the self into which alterity penetrates? How does one account for its experienced unity, the unity of a multiplicity, of the adumbrations of the given, if not as the unity of an essence? Is this oneness of the self merely a turning back of essence upon itself?[23] In sum, is the identity of the self an ideal unity conferred by the logos, an identity of reidentification in that "the disclosure of being to itself involves a recurrence?"[24] For Levinas, however, this recurrence is not that of essence but a coming to rest in the unity of a lived self. If this were not the case and recurrence alone were assumed to account for the unity of the self, in the absence of a "something" of a "that which" that recurs, the identical moments would merge into an undifferentiated oneness.

Levinas's description of essence, of meaning as recurrence, bears a surprising resemblance to biological accounts of the gene as a replicator that carries and repeats information determining the character of its offspring Some geneticists construe a gene line as able to exist apart from a phenomenological body as an entity whose interest lies in maintaining its continuity, an expression in an economy of living things, a bioeconomy, of the unseparated recurrence of essence as described by Levinas.[25] The self at the biological level, the level of life, does not experience its identity as one of essence but, for Levinas, is "a unity without rest," indistinguishable from the self that he terms "ipseity." This self does not thematize its identity "but is 'in itself' as one is in one's skin, cramped and ill at ease," a corporeal being that contracts and expands in the manner of respiration or the beating of the heart, a dead time intervening between the recurrences of these motions.[26] This account opens the way to characterizing ipseity as pure passivity, as exposed to wounding and outrage, as persecuted and accused. Because it is beyond the logos, this self cannot counter accusations with argument. It is "accused of what it never willed or decreed, accused of what it did not do. . . . Concretely [it is] responsible for what others do, responsible for the very persecution undergone."[27] This preoriginary self in its passivity does not initiate action but is prior to freedom, always already responsible for the other and designated as a substitute for the other, a "hostage" for the other. The I is not one who enters into a reciprocal relation with a thou but rather "the word 'I' means to be answerable for everything and for everyone."[28] Relation does not come about *between* self and other, an I and a thou, but rather arises as an assymetrical distancing in which the other is higher than the self.

In *Otherwise than Being*, the self of responsibility is interpreted in the context of a distinction between the language of ethics, what Levinas calls the Saying, and the predicative language of ordinary discourse, the said, the expression of essence. If, as he avers, alterity cannot be rendered manifest in the language of essence, is there a way of signifying meaning that is prior to the meaning of being yet can nonetheless be brought to light in the language of essence? Consider first the ontological language of the said, which discloses the difference between Being and beings that exist in time, beings that can be made present and thus illuminates the way in which entities are displayed.[29] In a complex analysis, Levinas maintains that the said in its aspect as verb "is the essence of essence" and in that context the being of entities unfolds temporally. The language that would describe the process, what I would refer to as its metalanguage, is not revealed in predicative propositions themselves but must be made thematic through independent theoretical analysis. In sum, predicative language manifests a duality. "The said can be conceived as a system of nouns identifying entities . . . designating substance, events and relations as substantives or other parts of speech derived from substantives, designating identities, in sum *designating*."[30] The said can also express the verb and, as such, "is essence or temporalization."[31] This distinction inheres in the verb *to be* as an ambiguity that oscillates between the noun and the temporalization of the verb. What is crucial for Levinas is the morphing of the verbality of the verb *to be* into nominalization, so that its temporalization becomes denomination.

To evoke temporalization as lurking in the said is not to give primacy to the said but rather to arouse in the said a Saying that signifies prior to essence, a Saying that is absorbed in the said and in the narrative that that it imposes.[32] Saying is the result of an exposure to the other so radical that the identity of one's own responsibility is inverted: I am always already responsible not only for my own acts but for the acts of the other. Time is no longer the time of freedom, of responsibility for one's own acts, but rather a time without beginning that cannot be made present, experienced as a lapse of time, as instanced in the irrecoverable and uncontrollable time of aging and death. But far from introducing a mystical language of silence into the said, Levinas depicts Saying as entering into the said as a disruption produced as a critique of the said, as speaking otherwise than ontologically. Beyond the amphibology of being, Saying can be understood as a response to the neighbor, an acceptance of unlimited responsibility for her or him, a response that begins in proximity.

It is in this context that Saying's relation to justice can fruitfully be explored. Levinas explains: "Thus the description of proximity as a hagiography of the one-for-the-other subtends society which begins with the entry of the third man. . . . If one is not to abandon oneself to violence [what is called for is] comparison, measure, knowing, laws, institutions—justice. But it is important for the very equity of justice that it contain the signification that had dictated it."[33] Even if one is admonished not to forget the origin of justice, Levinas concedes that at the moment justice is born a "measure superimposes itself on the 'extravagant' generosity of the 'for the other' on its infinity."[34] If justice is to enter into everyday life, must one not ask whether a certain corruption of the Saying is unavoidable as it disrupts the world it penetrates? Is a contamination of the subject as radical passivity, its signification as an immeasurable responsibility for the other, not an unavoidable outcome of existence in the said? What is more, how can justice come about if the ethical subject does not renew or clone itself, as it were, recur in the manner of essence, but disseminates itself in eruptions of profligate expenditure?

Sacred Economies: Expenditure as Gift and Sacrifice

That ethnographic study has influenced Levinas's account of the emergence of the individual subject from a primordium of undifferentiated being, a subject who labors and dwells, is attested in his tribute to the work of anthropologist Claude Lévy-Bruhl. The latter demonstrates that rationality, or *mens*, is not the primary mode of existence in the world but already reflects a prior choice. For "primitive" mentality, the world is experienced in participation, the original condition of existence. "To exist is to participate in a mystical reality."[35]

This perspective is evident in Marcel Mauss's influential account of the economy of the gift, an analysis of the act of bestowing something that is valued upon another or others and of relinquishing that which is valued, acts of giving and of giving up.[36] The subtitle of his work—*The Form and Reason of Exchange in Archaic Societies*—proclaims its subject. In explaining how and why people exchange goods, he directs his attention to the potlatch ceremony of the indigenous peoples of the Pacific Northwest, for whom acts of extravagant gift giving point to conspicuous divestiture in the interest of demonstrating the power conferred by wealth. Mauss's depiction of radical acts of prodigality in the interest of maintaining prestige shows remarkable affinities with what can be perceived as their inversion in Levinas's thought as acts of altruism in which, in the interest of the other, nothing is held back.

The practices of the Kwakiutl, Haida, Tlingit, and other peoples indigenous to the Pacific Northwest reflect the obligation of "a clan, a household, a group of people to give and to receive [pointing to] the purely sumptuary destruction of wealth in order to outdo a rival chief as well as his associate."[37] Gifts circulate with the expectation that extravagant giving is reciprocal.[38] Because some gifts presuppose that time is needed for reciprocity, there is built into gift giving a notion of credit, a practice that did not evolve from later modes of trading but was already inherent in the established routines of exchange.[39] Honor too plays a significant role in giving and receiving. "In certain kinds of potlatch one must expend all that one has, keeping nothing back. It is competition in the interest of seeing who is the richest and also the most madly extravagant. Everything is based upon the principles of antagonism and rivalry."[40]

Mauss interprets potlatch as a "total" phenomenon—religious, economic, and social—in which three moments of obligation can be distinguished. First, the quintessence of the potlatch is the obligation to give, so that one of rank can maintain his prestige and demonstrate through his distribution of wealth that he is favored by supernatural powers. The giver must invite all who are eligible, so that each may show his recognition and gratitude.[41] The second obligation, to receive, requires one who is invited to accept the invitation to attend and not refuse a gift, in that refusal bespeaks the recipient's fear that he may be unable to reciprocate. The third, the obligation to reciprocate, demands that the previous recipient in turn disburse his goods to those whom he invites. The giver, on occasion, not only disburses but destroys property, which then becomes a gift to supernatural spirits. Failure to reciprocate entails not only a loss of prestige but possible enslavement for debt. Yet Mauss also contends that things that have been given away "have a personality," which remains a permanent possession of the clan that has bestowed them, so that what has been given is also retained. In what appears to be an even more startling turnabout and an entering wedge for an altruistic reading of the gift, Mauss interprets the object that is given as a gift of self: "Yet it is also because by giving one gives oneself, and if one gives oneself, it is because one owes oneself—one's person and one's goods—to others.[42]

For Levinas, the gift of self bestowed upon the other is ultimately the gift of death, in that I am always already obligated to sacrifice my life for the other. Derrida astutely observes that for Heidegger death remains one's ownmost possibility, whereas for Levinas "I am responsible for the death of the other . . . inasmuch as the other is mortal. It is the other's death that is the foremost death."[43] Although "I give myself death," I cannot die in place of the other. Rather, I die for the other, sacrificing myself for her or him, which no one can do in my place. It is the other's mortality, not mine, that renders my responsibility exclusively mine and inalienable.[44] Levinas writes, "Death, source of all myths, is *present* only in the Other, and only in him does it summon me urgently to my final essence, to my responsibility."[45]

The world of Georges Bataille, like that of Levinas, is one of radical profligacy. In contrast to the generosity of Levinas, its ultimate desideratum is not the relief of economic destitution but rather the pursuit of an erotics of the sacred. For Bataille, the intent of sacrifice is not to eradicate its victim in the interest of sheer annihilation but rather to destroy the thing-character of the victim, generally an animal, and to transform the deadened sensibilities of the one who sacrifices. The sacrificial act draws the victim from the world of utility into one of "unintelligible caprice."[46] Since they are already deprived of their utility, items of luxury cannot be sacrificed.[47] The would-be sacrificer engaged in the world of use in his everyday existence must first separate himself from that world if he is to enter into the realm of the sacred. He must be prepared to declare: "Intimately I belong to the sovereign world of the gods and myths, to the world of violent and uncalculated generosity," a formula that introduces the sacrificial victim into the intimacy of the divine, "the interior of all that is."[48] Like Levinas, Bataille does not renege on the claims of what is generally perceived as real, since to do so would mean denying the reality of what had been sacrificed, thereby rendering sacrifice meaningless. At the same time, entry into the intimacy of the realm of the sacred necessitates a certain clouding over of consciousness.

Although their objectives differ radically, loosening the grip of the rational in order to arrive at a more primordial level of the subject is common to both Levinas and Bataille. It goes without saying that there is an unbridgeable gap between one who immolates another, whether animal or human, in order to lose the self in intimate immersion in the sacred and the subject who offers his or her life on behalf of the other. Thus Derrida writes of Levinas: "What is most ancient here would be the other, the possibility of dying *of* the other or *for* the other. Such a death is not given in the first instance as annihilation. It institutes responsibility, as a *putting-oneself-to-death* or *offering-one's-death*, that is *one's life*, in the ethical dimension of sacrifice." But, far from plunging into the intimacy of an immanent sacred, as Bataille would have it, death for Levinas is an adieu, as depicted by Derrida: "The a-dieu for God or before God and before anything else and any relation to the other. . . . Every relation to the other would be before and after any thing else, an adieu."[49]

For Bataille, immersion in an immanent sacrality in which things vanish exacts a hidden cost. Because meaning is linked to the future and it is things that have a future, by letting go of the world of discernible entities the subject loses meaning. Because signification is derived from the relation of things to what is to come, death would seem to preclude all meaning by cutting off the continuation of the world. But, Bataille contends, death actually unmasks the imposture of the real or thing-world: "What the real world rejects is not death but the affirmation of intimate life whose measureless violence is a danger to the stability of things."[50] In sum, if death or absence restores intimacy, sacrifice can be viewed as removing the sting of death

It is not difficult to discern a similarity between Bataille's notion of the immanent sacred and Levinas's depiction of the elemental, the nonpossessable environment against which things take shape and that contains them without itself being enveloped, as well as his view of the *il y a*, which opens the possibility of sheer nonbeing, the return of all things to nothingness. For Levinas, the fear aroused by the intimate order of the sacred, into which things can vanish, incites a horror of nonbeing, whereas for Bataille fear can be marshaled to generate the ecstasy of losing oneself in the intimacy of the sacred.

In addressing the troubling issue of human sacrifice, Bataille contends that the sacrifice of persons cannot be dissociated from the sacrifice of things, a perspective that opens the way to considering how the commodification of persons comes about. In contrast to the annihilation of an external enemy in war, the enemy who is not killed may be reduced to slavery and, as such, morph into a commodity. As property, the slave enters the economy of the mythical order so that desire on the part of that order for limitless consumption may be sated. Bataille emphatically rejects the notion that human sacrifice was the apogee of sacrificial consumption, insisting instead that it was an excess that had gone beyond what a society could tolerate. However, sacrifice for Bataille remains "the most radical contestation of the primacy of utility."[51]

The sacred, originally framed as an order of good and evil, is, on Bataille's reading, thinned out, as it were, as the world moves in the direction of utility and the order of things. Ideation converts the "malefic elements" of the sacred into the profane, while its beneficent aspect, previously viewed as divine, becomes purity.[52] In consonance with these changes, thought proceeds to define moral rules that prescribe obligatory relations in order to stabilize the order of things, an order opposed to what was valued in the intimate order: its displays of violence, profligacy, the useless consumption of sacrifice. With this shift, the beneficent sacred, the world of spirit, is transformed into the realm of the intellect or the idea, which is outside of time. Rationality cannot eliminate violence but can condemn it as evil.[53] Bataille concludes that affective intensity cannot be recaptured by destroying the order of things or by abandoning the normal activities of consciousness but rather is regained through a reversal that cancels the operations of clear consciousness. In this way intensity is regained at a new level of clarity that "rediscover[s] the night of the animal intimate with the world into which it will enter."[54]

For Levinas, it is essential to avoid confusing the differentiated oneness of what he calls pagan or mythic consciousness with the infinite other, who is bound up with human others. To recapture the intensity of the sacred by experiencing it through an occlusion of consciousness, as a *numinosum*, violates the relation with the Absolute as an ethical relation. Only when purged of violence, when the Absolute does not captivate but is the addressee of a solicitation, when it is an infinite, a "more" that cannot be encompassed in an idea, does a relation with the Absolute become possible. The access route to God is the face-to-face relation with the other, an other whom one is commanded not to kill. This relation is, for Levinas, justice. "The uprightness of the face-to-face [is] necessary in order that the breach that leads to God be produced—and vision here coincides with the work of justice."[55]

Is an Economy of Justice Possible?

The dilemmas raised by the problem of justice in Levinas's thought are, of course, foreign to the context in which social relations are analyzed in the classical economics of Adam Smith, yet the latter can help clarify and perhaps resolve some built-in difficulties raised by Levinas's account. If there is to be justice, it must be asked, should acts committed with the intention of injuring the other not be subject to retributive justice? And if retributive justice is possible, is its implementation, whether as punishment or pardon, not already subject to rules of exchange? To the question "Does the executioner have a face?" the issue of injustice raised by an interlocutor regarding an individual who is unjust, Levinas responds that the one who threatens the neighbor "the executioner, no longer has a face."[56] But if, as he maintains, we are all guilty for everything and to everyone, do we not all belong to the order of violence? The threat to the other opens the order of justice, which requires a measure of violence and the necessity for judges, institutions, and the state. I would argue that, in instantiating justice, one is thus always already imbricated in economy.

To be sure, for Levinas guilt or innocence is ultimately determined through the eyes of God, a God who is a point of fixity outside of society from which justice emanates. It is God who is the ultimate interlocutor of justice. Even if God arises in the world of the interhuman, God is not identical with the conditions of his upsurge in the realm of intersubjective relations but transcends them. There are significant difficulties with this position. For Levinas, an intimate society of two is not yet just; only with the entry of the third is justice born. However, the principle of justice inaugurated by the third is dialectical. On the one hand, justice that requires a third nevertheless remains a relation with transcendence; on the other, in order for totality to exist, there must also be "the third man." What is more, the irreplaceable singularity of the individual is compromised by the third, so that when justice comes into being through the presence of the third, interiority loses its importance. In sum, because the society of two, one of intimacy or love, lacks the requisite third for the inauguration of justice, this society of two is necessarily unjust. But, paradoxically, the appearance of the third who gives birth to justice is also required if there is to be totality, inescapable historical existence. It is crucial, then, to ask whether the notion of an ethical self can accommodate this duality. Can the use of conceptual terms borrowed from the locus classicus of eighteenth-century economic theory, Adam Smith's *An Inquiry into the Nature and Causes of the Wealth of Nations*, be deployed to expand rather than corrupt the ethics of the ethical subject?

Smith's by now familiar perspective takes for granted that economic relations are always self-interested but also that there is an order of nature, an "invisible hand" that guides individual strivings so that they eventuate in the social good.[57] "We address ourselves not to their humanity but to their self-love, and never talk to them of our own necessities but of their advantages."[58] What is more, these needs cannot be supplied by our own labor alone but require the labor of others, a division of labor that involves us in a network of social relations The surplus part of what a laborer produces, what is not needed for his own consumption, is exchanged for the surplus of what is produced by another, a mercantile arrangement in which "every man lives by exchanging."[59] If this arrangement is to succeed, prudence dictates not only that there must be an excess of what is produced for oneself but that this surplus must also be a commodity desired by others so that the surplus earns a profit. What is owned and expected to produce this revenue is designated as capital, which falls into two categories: goods needed by an employer, such as land, machinery, or instruments of trade, that remain in his possession, namely, fixed capital;

and goods that are sold for money or exchanged for other goods, circulating capital.[60]

The deployment of capital must be balanced, so that what the industry of a society produces must not exceed what its capital can employ. If the number of those employed must be in proportion to the capital of a society, it might be thought to follow that commerce should be regulated. Smith's response is the by now familiar apothegm of *laissez faire* economics: "no regulation of commerce can increase the quantity of industry in any society beyond what its capital can maintain."[61] It cannot be established that "artificial direction" is more beneficial to a society than unregulated trade.

Smith argues further that capital must be active, productive, and that capital kept in reserve is "dead stock." As soon as it is turned into money, it can once more become active and productive. If capital is to circulate freely, it would seem that unhampered circulation might encourage a certain prodigality. Yet, Smith insists, the prodigal can see that a refusal to confine his expense within his income eats into his capital.[62] At both an individual and a social level, the sumptuary economy is motivated by the desire for momentary pleasure, a passion for present enjoyment, whereas the principle endorsing saving expresses a desire to improve one's condition, a desire that is "generally calm and dispassionate and comes with us from the womb and never leaves us until we go into the grave."[63] One can only improve one's circumstances through saving and the accumulation of a part of what is acquired. Human beings vacillate between improvident spending and withholding. Even if it is not always possible to compensate for public or private profligacy, Smith insists, frugality generally predominates. In what seems premonitory of a Marxist critique, Smith argues that the high rate of profit of monopoly capitalism encourages an economy of extravagance. Indulgence in luxury by "the owners of the great mercantile capitals" erodes the sober virtue of parsimony.[64] It is parsimony rather than industry that causes the increase of capital. Can the demand to give all that one is and has not be seen as in danger of replicating at the level of ethics the negative outcomes of untamed economic profligacy? If the ethical subject is "a being-torn-up-from-oneself-for-another in the giving-to-the other–of-the-bread-out-of-one's-own mouth . . . [if] the body [is] extirpated from its *conatus essendi* in the possibility of giving," what is left to give for all the other others?[65]

In/conclusions

In support of the claim that the ethical subject may also be reinvigorated by appealing to the accounts of gift and sacrifice in Mauss and Bataille, it is important to notice that gift and sacrifice in the archaic economies they describe are made possible by the constant recommencement of production in the interest of maintaining ongoing rounds of ceremonial giving. Like the self of archaic societies, the moral self of Levinas is one of radical self-divestiture, a self outside totality and beyond production. But when it is understood as a self emptied of itself, one of two outcomes is possible: either the self withholds an aspect of itself, so that self-divestiture remains incomplete or the self succeeds in emptying itself so that no one, no "who," is left to be affected by the other, one who could enter into relation with a transcendent source of justice. In either case, justice issues in a contradiction. Yet another bind is suggested in Derrida's account of Levinas's injunction to give without expectation of return. The injunction is itself presumed to be a gift, the gift that Levinas bestows upon the reader. But if, by heeding his injunction, the reader or addressee accepts the gift, she or he has made a return of the gift (even if inadvertently) and thereby disobeyed the injunction. One can accept the gift only by refusing it.[66] These contradictions are primarily intended not to disclose logical difficulties but to attest to dualities intrinsic to actual life.

Rather than reject prodigality, it can be useful to recast the moral subject in terms of classical economics and to recall Smith's caveat that not all prodigality is to be avoided. What he terms "expenditure prodigality" can, if properly exercised, issue in socially desirable outcomes. "The revenue of an individual may be spent in things which are consumed immediately . . . [that] can neither alleviate or support that of another or it may be spent in things more durable, which can therefore be accumulated" and which may sustain future expenditure.[67] In regard to unfettered prodigality, Smith writes, "Every prodigal appears to be a public enemy, and every frugal man a public benefactor."[68]

In sum, in balancing the intricate relations between expenditure and thrift, Smith's classical economics can provide an entering wedge for expanding the Levinasian conception of the moral self. Alterity can now be reconfigured as primordially social, always already more than the single other. Levinas maintains that the "vision of the Face applies to the first comer," but, because there is always a third party, one must ask whether the relation to the face of the other or justice takes precedence. Levinas awards preference to justice, yet also denies that justice can be primary in that justice requires judgment and theoretical reason, which are not themselves primordial.[69] Must one not ask whether traces of the other others who require our beneficence are not inscribed in the face of any single other, just as in the said there lurks a Saying that is responsible to multiple others? In an exceptional aside, Levinas remarks, "The third party isn't there by accident. In a certain sense all the others are there in the face of the other."[70] Does the indigence of the other not stand in need of reserves that can be acquired only by husbanding resources? Is the failure to do so not a betrayal of ethics? An expanded subject can exist as a tension between prodigality and parsimony, the latter exercised in the interest of ongoing generosity, a subject whose resources are withheld on behalf of the future needs of others. If justice is framed in the context of law and polity, does alterity itself need to become a collective noun? In a novel rejoinder Levinas writes: "As in the glorious abasement common to both Judaism and Christianity the 'collective' can be produced in multiple singularities and not in a being exterior to this number who would count the multiples."[71] While retaining singularity, can we not learn from Smith that Levinasian indigence and reserves withheld can be given together if, as a Levinasian ethic demands, indigence is to speak?

Excess and Desire

A Commentary on Totality and Infinity, *Section I, Part D*

JEFFREY BLOECHL

Levinas could be disarmingly clear about his position regarding Christianity. Explaining himself in a 1983 conversation in Geneva, he observed: "I say of the face of the neighbor what the Christian says of the face of Christ."[1] This, of course, is only a singular expression of what was barely unstated in numerous passages dating at least from the 1950s, wherever Levinas invoked a messianism that is concretized specifically in ethics. But a messianism it truly is, and one that is clearly not without a robust conception of God sustaining it. "It is for man to save man," he wrote, "the divine manner of tending to misery does not consist in God intervening there."[2] As Levinas's readers have had to learn, this God who does not intervene is in fact central to his thinking, which shoulders the task of reinstating God and goodness after the twilight of the idols, the destruction of onto-theology, and, not least, the collapse of classical theodicy. Between Levinas and Christianity, the thesis of certain possibilities present already in any human face and not only in the singular face of Jesus Christ must go hand in hand with the idea that God does not explicitly intervene in our affairs and yet somehow does leave each of us bound to one another in a vocation to justice. Where the Christian invokes the gift of Jesus Christ as the way and the means to justice, Levinas calls us to recognize that this gift is given already in human plurality as such.

This difference in the domain of ethics, furthermore, cannot be considered apart from an accompanying difference between the conceptions of religious transcendence to be found in, respectively, the restricted messianism of a unique Incarnation the general messianism of the other person. This cannot be the occasion to entertain the essential complexities of even a simplified Christology. I therefore propose to address this second but more profound difference from only one side of the discussion: what sort of God abides in mystery not before and beyond a single and unrepeatable Son, but before and beyond the entire community of children?

I

True religion, Levinas often insists, takes place in our relation with the other person.[3] Any attempt to situate his conception of the religious is therefore inseparable from an attempt to situate his conception of the ethical, and indeed the latter must arguably come first. One might begin with some attention to his conception of heteronomy: subjectivity, the individual human being, neither provides itself with its own law nor, however, conducts itself in the absence of any law whatsoever. In the philosophy of Levinas,[4] this is asserted not in order to deny the possibility of living *as if* one were autonomous, but instead to contest the viability of that way of life—and indeed, its desirability. It is giving nothing away to state up front that Levinas challenges the pursuit of individual autonomy first of all with a view to recognizing the rights and well- being of the other person, for whom one is said to be responsible already before any pretense of self-rule. What tends to receive less attention is his accompanying suggestion that the pursuit of autonomy also commits each person to a conception of personal freedom that turns out to be unsustainable. The freedom of someone who is intent on determining his own course of action and way of life *solely under his own powers* is a freedom that must give meaning to everything it meets; this freedom, says Levinas, is in need of constant renewal and, indeed, ceaseless movement, without possibility of ever granting itself rest. The underlying thought could hardly be simpler: generally speaking, one may truly rest only on something that does not depend on oneself. In the terms of Levinas's existential analysis, this must be a presence that comes with its own meaning. Of course, and according to the ethical inflection of the argument, such a *quieting* presence would also be a *commanding* presence, since its approach would signal an end to the assumption that the subject is the center and locus of all meaning. Henceforth, and as the price of lasting peace, the subject must somehow come to terms with the fact that it does not and cannot have emprise over all that it encounters. In the effort to do so, we may recognize a nascent ethics.

None of this yet explains how the free subject who starts out in need of determination by an exterior law actually welcomes such a law, before making it the condition of its proper movement. How, or under what condition, could a subject in whom Levinas sees a natural tendency to comprehend everything in its own terms in fact prove capable of recognizing a law that by definition arrives from wholly beyond all such terms? It is tempting to appeal directly to Levinas's account of the face of the other person, as the self-expression of an otherness that exceeds all meaning I may give to it and that therefore, as the sign of my true condition, stands over me even while I struggle to understand and respect it. Yet this only begs the question of how I am able to make sense of such an otherness at all, let alone with the specifically ethical determination that Levinas famously assigns it.[5] The matter cannot be resolved without assuming in the subject a prior susceptiveness to its approach, whether in an image (as, for instance, my neighbor's face) or in words (as in her call for help). In order for freedom in need of law to become freedom committed to law—in order for the subject to recognize and embrace a law that will ground it and stand over it—one must already have been attuned to its revelation and its command.

Let us not fail to appreciate the difficulty of this notion: the subject who hears a call from beyond all comprehension is a subject who is exposed to the arrival of that call before any possible closure into the identity that becomes the starting point from which it grasps a datum and constitutes its meaning. One's susceptiveness to the call of the other would thus lie deeper than any origin—anterior to the positing of a ground and the setting up of a perspective. One is always already laid bare; one is passive before any question of activity, whether egoistic or altruistic.

It is at this most ancient point, "older than the ego," that ethics would exhibit a religious dimension. Absolute passivity, we are told, is the mark of being a "creature."[6] As a creature, each human being is exposed to the other before and outside any possible mediation, according to what Levinas variously calls a "plot" (une intrigue), a matrix, and an ordering that subtends every system or set. This would mean, for instance, that we creatures are a plurality not yet gathered into a totality before we are members of a totality who sometimes chafe against its limits. In turn, it would also mean that *before* the otherness of the other person is defined—before she is a citizen, a member, or a representative of any group—she is already there, closer to me than any act of discovery or identification. Our relationship is "'anterior' to the act that would effect it."[7]

In *Totality and Infinity*, this vision of human plurality is interpreted as the inverse figure of the Infinite. Our plurality, we are told, is due to the "creative contraction" of the Infinite, in order to leave place for the separated, finite being.[8] As we have known for some time, this proposal has important affinities with Kabbalah and thus bears some resemblance to elements of the Neoplatonic thinking that partly informs it.[9] (One thinks, along a divergent line, of Cusa's *aliud non aliud*.) Regardless of Levinas's particular place in this tradition, one sees immediately that he is intent on anchoring two principles at once: on the one hand, the Infinite reveals itself in and through the plurality in which the subject and the other are related without yet belonging to a totality; on the other hand, the fact—if it is a *fact*—that their relation is anterior to the very possibility of totality requires a thought of the Infinite. Is either of these theses strictly prior to the other? They seem rather to presuppose and confirm one another at the heart of Levinas's thinking: the infinity of the Infinite is said to reveal itself in human plurality, and human plurality is said to be properly grasped only within the (non)horizon of the Infinite.

Let us try to understand this better. We have already taken note of Levinas's conception of the subject, in need of an exterior law to ground its freedom. The subject is not, for all of that, simply fated to endless striving. Because the other person is always already there with the subject as it strives to establish itself, and because that striving is therefore always a turning away from the other that presupposes the proximity of the other, it is always possible for her face to awaken the subject to its proper ground in their relation. If this awakening truly brings an end to the solitary project of self-assertion—if it offers respite and perhaps even the beginning of a conversion to care for the other before all care for oneself—then the face will have been the approach of an otherness that is absolute *and* the subject itself will have been touched in a passivity that is unqualified. This, of course, occurs at the initiative of the other.[10] One thus comes to at least one meaning of Levinas's frequent claim that true peace comes in the face of the stranger: the advent of the other person, as shocking as it may be, promises the subject a freedom no longer consumed with the endless project of self-justification. Atomistic models of the human relation will have failed to recognize this. Agonistic models of human interaction seem to rule it out. Levinas's use of the word *creature* is plainly a response to those accounts of our humanity. Creaturliness, as the subjectivity of the subject, indicates both a positive relation with the other person and, at the same time, a relation with the transcendence by which that positive relation is "situated" (293 / 269). Put otherwise, and now by way of summary, the infinity of the Infinite effects a separation between subject and other that eludes totalization, and according to this separation everything the subject is and does both presupposes and responds to her presence. Levinas does not shrink from the immediate implication: to open oneself to the priority of the other person is at the same time to open oneself to the infinity of the Infinite, which orders our relation.

There is no immediate need to insist on the importance of this distinction between ethical and religious alterity, since in any case Levinas plainly does recognize that there is one. What seems less evident is the manner in which the acting, responsible subject itself might also recognize that distinction, *if indeed Levinas considers that to be necessary*. After all, a direct and unavoidable implication of his close alignment of religion and ethics is the thesis of a consciousness that is open at one and the same time to the Infinite and to the approach of the other person. This thesis of a twofold openness calls for further attention.

II

Levinas's argument that consciousness is always already open to the Infinite is explicitly Cartesian in origin. In *Totality and Infinity*, the move from a critique of ontology as a philosophy of power and totality to a defense of the ethical relation prior to any totality passes through the argument of Descartes's Third *Meditation*:

> The relation of the same [i.e., the subject] with the other, where the transcendence of the relation does not cut the bonds a relation implies, yet where these bonds do not unite the same and the other into a Whole, is in fact fixed in the situation described by Descartes in which the 'I think' maintains with the Infinite it can nowise contains and from which it is separated a relation called "the idea of infinity." (48 / 19)

In what sense does the *idea* of infinity constitute a *relation* with infinity? Levinas places the classical reading in the service of his own position. The *Meditations*, revealing the ego and God as distinct but "mutually founding" moments, presents us with "the very meaning of separation" (48 / 19). Where Descartes first secures thinking being in the certitude of its relation to itself, Levinas finds a means to begin his own analysis with an account of the inner unicity of the subject. And where Descartes later discovers the ground for thinking being and its perceptions in its relation with a supremely perfect being (*ens summe perfectum*),[11] he sees proof that that subject's natural inclination to take itself as its own origin and reference—its spontaneous tendency toward closure into itself—already presupposes a deeper opening that denotes what he has called "plurality."

Now, the order of progression lain down on Descartes's text is not unimportant for a proper understanding, especially of his second principle, the idea of infinity. Already before reading the Third and Fourth *Meditations*, one will have understood that the self-certainty discovered at the heart of consciousness in the Second *Meditation* is still not enough for one to be certain about his own perceptions—even of his very self. This means that, until the achievement of those later passages, or rather, failing that, all perception occurs without possibility of secure judgment. We might understand the general position this way: so long as the *Meditations on First Philosophy* thus isolates the sphere of perception—of presence and meaning giving—from the sphere of judgment, it permits us to speak of ideas only as perceptions of the mind, as opposed to the common understanding of ideas as reflections of things. It is finally the idea of infinity that secures judgment, *first* by overflowing the idea itself, such that it is impossible to think that, in at least this one case, the idea is only a product of the mind, and *second* by yielding an equation between infinity as superabundance and infinity as benevolent God. Yet even here we do not meet with an exception to the preceding definition of idea so much as with its *exemplar*: after all, infinity turns out to be precisely what we perceive it to be—namely, that which exceeds capture in or by any possible idea. The idea of infinity is able to ground judgment about all other ideas not because it is of an entirely different character but because it perfects the character it has in common with them. This must be the essential meaning of the claim that the idea of infinity is *in us* (according to an expression sometimes favored by Levinas). Neither in the world in the manner of finite things that submit to correlation with ideas, nor wholly opposed to that world as if defined by the negation of all finitude and every idea, infinity has always already entered the mind, which, for its part, has only to discover it there.[12]

Is it possible for a finite being concerned with the problems of its own existence to discover this exceptional idea entirely through its own efforts? Can we achieve true recognition of the Infinite without immediately subjecting it to the limits inevitably belonging to the recognizing mind? If the *Meditations on First Philosophy* includes within itself any sort of argument for the existence of God, then Descartes will have considered this to be possible. To be sure, the argument claims only to know the Infinite as transcending every "measurable and ordered object," but an awareness of this very transcendence would have to include within itself, as another sort of knowing, a sense of immeasurable grandeur.[13] Needless to say, the knowing that corresponds to grandeur must have the character of *submission*, as Descartes himself notes—for instance, in a letter to Mersenne cited at least once by Levinas.[14] One does not grasp the immeasurable, as if distinguishing among what is measurable; one endeavors to *receive* it by surrendering the right to grasp it.

If Levinas resists this sort of conclusion, it is no doubt because the appeal to an emotional attitude—submission—appears to shift the definition of our relation with the Infinite toward affectivity, which he considers to be a clouded and diminished form of activity. The affective response has already taken rudimentary possession of its interlocutor, without the stability necessary to avoid collapsing into participation or even fusion. As readers of Levinas will recall, he is certainly willing to apply this critique to any religion judged overly committed to emotion, whether it be a matter of the so-called primitive mentality studied by Lucien Lévi-Bruhl or the mystical experiences of Western monotheism (or, for that matter, popular devotion and ritual practice). Modern thought thus appears to flirt with a return to this problem when it abandons representation in favor of what it claims are the more primordial dimensions of affectivity.[15] Against this, Levinas contends that it is above all representation, with its lucid reassurance of a world of objects present to me, that closes the subject sufficiently into itself for there to be true separation from the wholly other; it is above all our spontaneous trust in representation that accomplishes a relation in which the finite subject is truly a finite subject and in which the infinity of the Infinite must exceed every negation and analogy.

This, of course, means that the finite subject, in its natural attitude, is not as such capable of sustaining an adequate relation to the Infinite. Absorbed in its own concerns and reassured by the successes of representation and comprehension, the finite subject must await the sheer disruption wrought by the face of its neighbor in order perhaps to become conscious of the infinity that positively exceeds it. Yet even then the proper relation with the Infinite cannot be direct, since that would reinstate the pretense of comprehension. There is no arrival at the Infinite, no final satisfaction for the desire that seeks it. Only the face itself can ground free movement toward the Infinite and focus the desire that drives it. If it is only through our encounter with the human face, putting our freedom in question, that we become aware of our relation with the Infinite, then it is also only in our response to that face that our desire for the Infinite finds its proper path and contours. Hence the close association between ethics and religion that is so distinctive of Levinas's thinking is finally a matter of thinking *responsibility* in terms of *desire*: the face of the other person is a trace of the Infinite—it points to the God who has always already withdrawn into an irretrievable past[16]—and the desire to put her concerns before my own is immediately a desire that aims beyond the conditions of finite existence.

III

This desire for "something else entirely," for the "absolutely other," is in fact the first theme of *Totality and Infinity*. The "customary analysis of desire," says Levinas, traces it back to a prior loss or fall. This, however, does not explain what he calls the "singular pretension" of a craving for positive excess, a desire that wants more than the desiring being could ever hold (33–34 / 3). Let us note immediately that unless this desire is secured before and outside our relation to the world, its movement beyond the world must be characterized negatively as flight. That is to say, while its movement evidently takes place in this world, it does so according to a relation and a dynamism that this world cannot account for. On this point, the fact that this desire finds its essential expression in care for the other person changes nothing at all. "Metaphysical desire," expressed in absolute responsibility, is *in* the world but not wholly *of* the world; it is already otherwise than in this world, even as it indeed takes place there.

This point is evidently fundamental, and so one immediately anticipates that it will open the way to any number of other important determinations. Note, to begin with, that Levinas defines the ethical relation, as the essential form of true religion, without original reference to the world. Neither the remarkable solidarity proposed for the infinity of the Infinite and the plurality of the finite nor the drama of a self-absorbed subject awakened by the face of his neighbor seems to require a positive thought of the natural world as such, considered solely in itself—and indeed, when Levinas does apply himself to some such sense of world, he develops it as a source of nourishment, first for the life of the subject but then, in the work of goodness, for the needs of the other person. (One knows the image: responsibility for the other commands that I make a gift of the very bread that sustains me.[17]) It is good, then, that the world sustains ethical beings and even better that it offers itself to ethical acts. But would it also be good before and apart from that? Might the world, too, and in its own way, bespeak the divine? A classical tradition has always thought so, most prominently in the thought of an entire cosmos emanating from or created in divine love. For a long time, Western thought took it for granted that our definition of human nature should be sought within the frame of a wider sense of nature as a whole, and that what is good for human beings is consistent with a more general good for that whole. Levinas's silence on this point and his tendency to reserve the language of goodness for human activity put him at some distance from Aristotle and indeed the Thomism that has come to define much of Catholic Christian thought. Of course, for the latter the natural world is evidently good not only as the work of a Creator God but also insofar as it is capable of welcoming the Word without immediately muting it. From that perspective, and for reasons that evidently run quite deep, Levinas may sometimes appear surprisingly close to the modern perspective from which the natural world is at best "amoral."[18] After all, modern thought, as directly opposed to its classical predecessor, takes for granted that the world is indifferent to our moral endeavors. Still, this is not enough to declare that Levinas is therefore simply a modern thinker. One might better recognize a modern sympathy in his thinking where, or to the degree that, his ethics of the other is defined without any reference to cosmology. If there are difficulties or a certain impoverishment in such a position, this would certainly not be unique to Levinas. It is not yet clear just what it would mean for ethics, let alone religion, for us to have a diminished capacity to think of the world as good in its own right. In this particular context, the least that can be said of the philosophy of Levinas is that it offers us considerable means toward one possible answer.

The absence of a notion that the natural world and perhaps natural things might have a moral goodness properly their own, and thus also a revelatory function properly their own, strengthens the association of religion with the ethical relation already developed with greater force in Levinas's critique of the being of the subject as innately self-centered. In short, after the critique of the subject has required us to think that the Infinite can reveal itself only from beyond the range of our own efforts, the absence of reflection on the natural world now seems to rule out one other possible occasion for that revelation. In Levinas's philosophical works, we may be awakened to the Infinite *only* in and through the human face, and our desire for greater intimacy with the Infinite, with God, *must* be expressed in acts that put the other person before oneself.

All of this returns us to the theme of "metaphysical desire" with a clear and simple question in hand: Why must desire for the Infinite become—exclusively, by all appearances—care for the other person? Allow me to repeat a few prior observations. We already know that (1) the very infinity of the Infinite insures that human plurality is defined by separation and that (2) according to the structure of separation, everything the subject is and does presupposes and in that basic sense *responds to* the presence of the other person. We also know that (3) the face of the other awakens the subject from a natural tendency toward self-centeredness, giving rise to the possibility of a concrete moral response. And finally, we know that (4) the exceptional idea of Infinity, as the openness of consciousness to what no consciousness could ever contain, in fact leaves us susceptible to that awakening by the face of the other. Levinas thus gives us every reason to think that the Infinite is in fact actively engaged in the human drama: it is *due to* my relation with the Infinite, before and outside the cycle of my relation with my world and myself, that the face of the other does not merely obstruct me or contest me in my being, as Sartre thinks, but puts my entire being in question. That said, Levinas nonetheless wishes to distinguish his notion of engagement by the Infinite from the behavior of the anthropomorphic gods. *Otherwise than Being, or Beyond Essence* thus *does* speak of the illeity—the he-ness—of the withdrawal of the Infinite, binding me to the other person, but not without also insisting that it does so *without* "[entering] into a theme like a being" or presenting itself as an "alleged interlocutor."[19] In the essay entitled "God and Philosophy," the noncausal engagement of the Infinite in the finite is defined as "non-indifference" (not to be confused with the nonindifference of the ethical *subject*).[20] It is due to this nonindifference of the Infinite to the finite that the plot of our relation is rooted more deeply than mere spatial contiguity, in the responsibility of creatures.

All of this should dispel once and for all the charge that Levinas's claim that the response to God, to the Infinite, must take the form of a response to the other person is therefore straightforwardly a reduction of religion to ethics. A better understanding of the claim would state rather that the infinity of the Infinite, positively engaged in the finite, *prepares the way* for the awakening that can and must occur only when the other person faces me—and that my response to her face is at the same time, though in a certain sense indirectly, a response to the Infinite. Put otherwise, the infinity of the Infinite, always already present in consciousness, like a hollowing out that goes unrealized until the face of the other person makes it resonate, prepares me for the "trauma" to my self-assurance that is visited upon it by her face. What, then, will be the religious character of my response to the trauma of the human face? Either a return to the sphere of immanence defined by self-interest or a movement toward transcendence defined by what Levinas calls the "dis-interest" of *responsibility* to and for the other—the disinterest of one who no longer approaches the other person according to an interest first and foremost in himself and yet is not for all that simply uninterested. Here at last is the proper context for understanding "metaphysical desire." Evidently, it will be a desire without possession, without fulfillment, and without satisfaction—a "desire outside of concupiscence,"[21] as Levinas himself puts it. (I will return to this notion in a moment.) In the same line, it will also be a desire that aims at what can only be, in the most elevated sense, *undesirable*.[22]

IV

Would this exorbitant desire, too, be rooted in the infinity of the Infinite, which, after all, is always already present in the subject who thus desires? One might reverse the order of the question: Would the Infinite itself somehow prepare the way not only for the ethical trauma but also for the desire that it awakens—would the Infinite somehow stimulate metaphysical desire? My word *stimulate* comes to mind easily when analyzing desire, but it is also commonly invested with a sense of efficient causality and thus, since it is a matter of the Infinite, the crudest sort of onto-theology. Levinas's own language suggests something more like "pre-original inspiration": *preoriginal* because the relation with the Infinite involves conditions antedating any beginning in time, and *inspiration* because we are thus animated by a spirit that seems to endow us with a potential difficult to explain solely in terms of our being in the world. This extraordinary potential comes to light, or perhaps is at last liberated, when the separated subject is traumatized by the face of the other person. Initially, this is, as the word *trauma* indicates, painful; it is an interruption that both shocks and disorients. The pain itself is registered as an assault on the egocentric mode of being, which now appears to have been false, coupled with a correction made virtually inevitable by—let us not forget it—the way the idea of infinity hollows out the subject, rendering it vulnerable. It goes without saying that the subject's response will always consist in one or another search for recovery. And this can take either of two general forms: some of us, or perhaps all of us some of the time, retreat blindly back into a way of being that has just been exposed, if only one might see it, as pretentious; but some move forward, away from that prior way of being, thus away from self-interest and its foibles, to a way that strives to empty itself of all such interest. In the latter instance, we must, no doubt, see the mature expression of metaphysical desire. Touched by the Infinite prior to any possible memory, the subject is a creature who responds to the face of his neighbor with a desire that transcends the conditions of worldly existence, and this desire commands a self-emptying that issues in concrete acts of responsibility.

Emphasizing the close relation of this desire to the infinity of the Infinite, Levinas sometimes refers to it as "infinition." The desire by which I put the other person before myself carries me beyond all prior limits of my being, beyond self-interest toward the positive dis-interest that produces goodness. To transcend myself in responsibility for the other is thus also to correct for the "diminution" entailed in what Levinas has called "the creative contraction of the Infinite." To care for the other person, he thus concludes, is to contribute to the work of redemption.

Even more strongly than the absence of a means to recognize moral goodness for the natural world itself, and thus *a fortiori* the absence of a means to think that nature or natural things might reveal the divine, this analysis of metaphysical desire suggests that our movement toward God occurs only in acts of responsibility to and for the other person. This still does not reduce religion to ethics, but it does seem to ethicize our desire for the Infinite. We have already seen the implications of this proposal for moral reflection in Levinas's own claim that the relation with the other person must be driven by a "desire outside concupiscence": ethics would have to be opposed to, and try to do without, an erotics, in the modern sense of that word. One should endeavor to love the other person beyond every attachment to her, or rather, one must strive for a love that would perfect itself in *doing away with* all attachment—which is not the same thing as a love that simply *includes more than* attachment. It is not for nothing that the most tortured passages of *Totality and Infinity* propose a "Phenomenology of Eros" in which sexual desire is to be given full expression and yet contained within an argument for a relation situated before and beyond its reach: for Levinas, the desire that possesses and attaches is a dangerous possibility contained within the desire that empties and therefore transcends. But at its noblest, when it is directed to the conception of a child, it nonetheless supports and confirms the movement of transcendence. It is the fecundity proper to sexual desire to bring a new other into the world. Needless to say, this marks a point of unexpected agreement between Levinas and the sexual ethic of most Catholic magisterial teaching.

Whatever one makes of that, there is no mistaking the fact that it further secures Levinasian ethics in a distinctive philosophy of religion. I hope to have shown by now that both his assimilation of desire for God to the desire to serve the other person and now his strong insistence on protecting that desire from final dissolution into erotic attachment must be traced to a conception of the Infinite that withdraws it from any possible representation or comprehension. This suggests the following summary of Levinas's position on these matters: *because the infinity of the Infinite is present in consciousness only as the trace of its withdrawal from consciousness, the desire by which the finite subject moves toward the Infinite can only take the form of responsibility for the other.*

From this, there follows at least one final warning, and in its wake the elements of a conclusion: if one hesitates at the severity of Levinas's theses on desire—if, for instance, the notion of a desire without attachment seems to ask too much or else simply proceeds from a wrong description of the things themselves, and if one therefore proposes a more moderate position on the matter of desire, then one should anticipate being led also to ask whether his philosophy does not accord *too much transcendence* to the divine. Such a question strikes most deeply when it is heard in the metaphysical register, where it calls for a more moderate conception of divine transcendence that somehow would not, for all of that, fall immediately into idolatry. At this late moment, a single question will have to suggest more prolonged extensive reflection, best reserved for another occasion: Is it certain that what truly appears is therefore handed over to the grasp of the subject? The question returns us, inevitably, to the God-Man. Perhaps the Christ in whom Christians find the paradigm and possibility of a humility not altogether opposed to Levinas's ethical kenosis offers human understanding an excess of meaning that is not, however, the excess of absolute otherness. The figure of the Christ exceeds understanding by always differing from what it nonetheless gives of itself to be thought. It is God in the world and in that sense accepting the world, but as a paradox that refuses the world. The phenomenality of Christ—and phenomenality there is—is inexhaustible but not therefore unintelligible, *more than* intelligible, absolutely rich. This is attested too well and too long and by too great a tradition for adequate treatment here. Let me, then, simply note one more implication: the divine transcendence does *not* preserve itself according to a withdrawal from any and all presence that would accompany me in this world and in the drama of my existence, but without this being a matter solely of the drama of my responsibility. With one eye on that possibility—that is, from a Christian perspective—it may appear that what Levinas proposes as ethics must in part be understood as the consequence of a specific sort of divine absence. In an important sense, God, as he defines it, leaves us first and finally to one another. It is true, of course, that this is not at all the same thing as leaving each of us entirely to his or her own fate; yet for all of that the burden is indeed as heavy as the future is undefined. We have no way of knowing whether the plurality of ethical subjects will be enough for us to bear, let alone truly solve, the problems of this world.

The Care of the Other and Substitution

JEAN-LUC MARION

I

The striking originality of Emmanuel Levinas can be felt on every page of his work. But it is perhaps nowhere more striking than when he speaks of the notion, introduced between 1968 and 1974, thus late in his career, of substitution.

This notion is astonishing, in fact, since it marks a redoubling of responsibility—in other words, "one degree of responsibility more, the responsibility for the responsibility of the other"—that involves me substituting myself for the other in what is most his own, his own responsibility: "the overemphasis of openness is responsibility for the other to the point of substitution."[1] This does not mean a simple hyperbole of responsibility, where I take upon myself, by sympathy or solidarity, the charge that belongs properly to the other. It means first of all "a responsibility with regard to men we do not even know,"[2] but also and especially "responsibility for the persecutor."[3] A strange and shocking assertion. Strange, for if there is indeed a man whom we know well and whose face we will never forget, wouldn't it be precisely our persecutor, our executioner? Shocking, too, for how could we take upon ourselves responsibility for the wrong done against us? There would already be the enormous difficulty of not seeking revenge, but how are we to qualify the difficulty in taking upon oneself, the victim, the fault of the persecutor? Wouldn't this demand, "in the trauma of persecution . . . to pass from the outrage undergone to the responsibility for the persecutor,"[4] betray something like a perversion of ethics, which would then become a machine for condemning the victims instead of the hangmen? How can this demand not contradict the famous dedication of *Otherwise than Being* "to the memory of the victims of the same hatred of the other man, the same anti-Semitism?"

No doubt there is, *in the final analysis*, no contradiction, and I am going to make an effort to show how and why. Nevertheless, even if in the end I succeed in removing this impediment, my investigation will not become, for all that, merely rhetorical. It may perhaps result from the confrontation of two conceptual lexicons, two modes of questioning, which play against each other like two tectonic plates in the earth's crust, opposing and balancing each other at the same time. I am referring to two authorities that no doubt contest and sustain one another all along Levinas's path of thinking: what belongs to phenomenology and what arises from what is called, for lack of any better term, his Judaism. This tension, felt in "substitution," in effect defines all of *Otherwise than Being*: "The overemphasis of openness is responsibility for the other to the point of substitution, where the for-the-other proper to disclosure, to monstration to the other, turns into the for-the-other proper to responsibility. This is the thesis of the present work." And: "This book interprets the *subject* as a *hostage* and the subjectivity of the subject as a substitution breaking with being's *essence*."[5] It could not be said any more clearly: substitution (which constitutes me as "hostage," a term we still do not understand) does not arise first from ethics (though it stays there absolutely) because it contradicts the determination of subjectivity in terms of essence (therefore in terms of Being). Subjectivity—obviously the term should no longer be understood in its metaphysical signification but should once again become a problem, so as to be redefined precisely in terms of substitution: "Subjectivity as hostage. This notion reverses the position where the presence of the ego to itself appears as the beginning or as the conclusion of philosophy."[6] Thus, with substitution, beyond (or on the hither side of) its at first glance ethical strangeness, what is at issue is quite clearly a challenge to the "essence of Being" as "philosophy" (read: metaphysics) presupposes it when it defines the "subjectivity" of man. How can we understand so radical a "destruction"?

II

But first, a preliminary question: Where does the notion of substitution, for Levinas, come from? Or rather (for its lexicographical provenance matters little, supposing that it could even be traced), what function, what impact, and what prior history can qualify substitution to the point that it assumes such a polemical role in so vast a "destruction"?

Let me suggest a response: the question of substitution is posed to Levinas by Heidegger, in §26 of *Being and Time*. Heidegger, despite all his faults, would not have had, and would not have kept to the end, such prestige in the eyes of Levinas if the question of the other were missing from the existential analytic.[7] Contrary to an opinion too widely shared, *Being and Time* does not pass over in silence the question of the other, even if the other does not occupy the center of the question. The border between Heidegger and Levinas does not run between, on the one hand, Dasein without alterity and, on the other hand, *me* determined by the other. It runs, more precisely, between two opposed ways of describing the relation of *me* (Dasein?) to the other. The difficulty consists in spotting exactly where the line of division runs and in describing it correctly. I will try to show that the opposition is played out over the possibility of a substitution.

The transcendental analytic, after having determined *being in the world* (c. 2), then the worldhood of the world (c. 3), and before reaching *being in as such* (c. 5) and Care (*Sorge*, c. 6), with which it climaxes, specifies *being in the world* as being oneself *(Selbst-sein)* and also as being with (*Mitsein*). Importantly and with absolutely no ambiguity, this being with implies the other—that is to say, the other as an (other) Dasein: "The world of Dasein is a *with-world* [Mitwelt]. Being-in is *Being-with* others. Their Being-in-themselves within-the-world is *Dasein-with* [Mitdasein]."[8] In other words and unambiguously, Dasein, precisely because it opens a world, opens it as *open*, as a co-world. Therefore, to be in this co-world implies being with others, and others being themselves in the mode of Dasein. In short, Dasein implies co-Daseins in its very being. "Das eigene Dasein ist nur, sofern es die Wesensstruktur des Mitseins hat, als für Andre begegnend Mitdasein": no Dasein can be without co-Being, and only in this way can it have encounters with (that is, let itself encounter) the other as co-Dasein. That Dasein implies another Dasein (as it does) does not cause any difficulty. The difficulty begins with what follows, when it becomes a question of determining how one encounters the other. The other (as) Dasein can be encountered only as a Dasein, not as a being within the world, one that would not be in the mode of a Dasein (a being *nichtdaseinmässig*). It should therefore be one to which Dasein relates otherwise than in *Besorgen* ("concern"), which applies only to beings within the world. This mode cannot be called *Sorge* ("care"), because that term will arise legitimately in view of being toward death. It will therefore be necessary that Dasein relate to the other (as) Dasein in a particular mode,

Fürsorge ("assistance" or, according to the Macquarrie and Robinson translation, "solicitude").

I want now to describe this mode of access to the phenomenon of the other (as Dasein). One point must be noted. The German *Fürsorge*, taken first of all as "a factical social arrangement," suggests what the French calls *assistance publique* and the American "Medicare" (or "social care").[9] There inevitably follows a "deficient" acceptance of this term: *assistance* or "social care" will at first and for the most part be concerned with (in the mode of *Besorgen*) beings within the world of which an other (as) Dasein is deprived. It will therefore procure food, clothing, shelter, etc. for this other (as) Dasein. One could be surprised, indeed scandalized, to find that the (biblical) care for "the widow and the orphan" is here reduced to the level of a "deficient" mode of *Fürsorge*, and one would have very good reason for such a response, because this primary care (solicitude in the form of first aid of the first importance), however imperfect it might turn out to be, remains nevertheless the (existential, not merely existentiell) condition for the possibility of other modes of *Fürsorge*. But one should also do justice to Heidegger's reasons for qualifying it as he does: this solicitude, precisely because it is focused on the basic necessities, in fact concerns directly only beings within the world (the ready-to-hand, *Zu-hande*), and not the other (as) Dasein. As a result, the latter becomes un-differentiated, anonymous, such that the same solicitude could also be offered to this or that other without distinction. Paradoxically—a point that, moreover, attests to the pertinence of Heidegger's analyses— solicitude (*Fürsorge* as *Besorgen*, "taking care" that is unaware) does not yet care for the alterity of the other (as) Dasein because it does not yet consider individuated alterity, identified as such and with itself. Solicitude socializes alterity, rendering it indifferent. It does not succeed in individu-ating the other and falls short of *alterity*. Heidegger's analysis therefore remains the terrain that Levinas will occupy.

This is in contrast to the positive mode of *Fürsorge*, or more exactly, the "two extreme possibilities" of this positive mode. One consists in "putting oneself in his position in concern: it can *leap in* for him [*für ihn einspringen*]" so as to disburden him of his care (*Sorge*) by taking his place in managing his needs and concerns (*im Besorgen*). This first mode is not suitable for a (so to speak) Hegelian reason that Heidegger states explic-itly: such a Dasein, disburdened of his care (*Sorge*) by another Dasein, would immediately fall under his domination (*Herrschaft*), however silent or unconscious it might be. Hence we must pass to the second "extreme possibility" of *Fürsorge*: "*leap ahead* of him [*ihm* vorausspringt] in his exis-tentiell potentiality-for-Being, not in order to take away his 'care' but rather to give it back to him [*zurückzugeben*] authentically as such for the first time." Here, for the first time, solicitude (*Fürsorge*) no longer deals with the beings within the world with which the other might be concerned (*Besorgen*) but with his very existence as Dasein. *Fürsorge* thus becomes authentically care (*Sorge*) for the other as such, namely as another Dasein.[10] Care for the other (as) Dasein consists in not having the pretense of taking his place but in letting him assume charge of the burden of his own possibility. Care for the other amounts to not *sich an seine Stelle setzen*, not taking his place, not substituting oneself for him.[11]

III

Why does Heidegger maintain this strange paradox that genuine care for the other consists in *not* substituting for him? Obviously it is not on account of egoism or indifference, which are strictly ontic determination and therefore without relevance here. Rather, responding to a strictly ontological requirement, it is out of a concern to grant the other the originary determination of Dasein: that it is the being in which its own Being is at issue each time, Being as its own—*Jemeinigkeit*. Now this property—that of winning its ownmost self and winning its own by appropriating Being, or rather by letting itself be appropriated by Being as such (and to it)—is one that Heidegger shows Dasein accomplishes only in being toward death. That is, the possibility of my death, at once certain and indeterminate,[12] implies that nobody can take it away from me or take it over from me. No doubt, another can "die in my place," in sacrifice or devotion to me (or to another). But even in this case, (1) the one who sacrifices himself will still die his own death and not mine (which he will have spared me or delayed), and (2) he will have spared me it only for a while, provisionally, for in the end there will always come a moment when I, myself in person, will have to live *my* death. Nobody can ever do that in my place. "Death is a possibility-of-Being which Dasein itself had to take over in every case," or *"No one can take the Other's dying away from him."*[13] If I, Dasein, want to win my own and my ipseity (*das Selbst, die Selbstheit*), I must never let the other substitute for me, particularly not at the instant of my death. This demand is confirmed, *a contrario*, by the fact that substitution always refers to *das Man* (the They), in its ever-repeated attempt to disappropriate Dasein of itself. To be sure, the possibility of substitution belongs essentially to Dasein inasmuch as it is open to others ("the fact that one Dasein *can be represented* by another belongs to its possibilities of Being in Being-with-one-another in the world"),[14] but the substitution that follows therefrom is always a perversion of this Dasein in a public event, accessible to everybody and nobody, in short, to the They: "Dying, which is essentially mine in such a way that no one can be my representative, is perverted into an event of public occurrence which the 'they' encounters."[15] Substitution, either of me for the other or the other for me, blocks the appropriation (in me or in him) of Dasein by itself. Thus it becomes clear that, for Heidegger, substitution contradicts, in all cases (of me for the other or the other for me), the accomplishment of ipseity. I am Dasein only in the first person, and never by an other or for an other.

Consequently, we must conclude from this that *Fürsorge* always belongs through and through to *Sorge*: "Care is always concern and solicitude, even if only privatively."[16] Even here, the *für-* remains a mere prefix, which changes nothing in the gravitational center of *Sorge*. *Sorge* remains, as the meaning of the Being of Dasein,[17] centered around Dasein as mine. In other words, "*Fürsorge* proves to be a state of Dasein's Being."[18] Whereas Husserl hesitates in deciding whether the other offers only "a double of myself"[19] or another center, irrevocably decentered from my own, Heidegger does not hesitate. He concedes to the alterity of the other only that it might repeat the nonsubstitutability of ipseity: "The Other would be a duplicate of the Self."[20]

IV

What is at stake now becomes perfectly clear: for Heidegger, ipseity excludes having the other substitute for me and me for him. It is decided by *my* anticipatory resolution alone, which can bear only on *my* ultimate possibility, that of *my* death. In positing that "subjectivity is from the first substitution,"[21] Levinas tries to overturn Heidegger's thesis entirely, so as to establish that I win my ipseity only in substituting for the other or letting the other substitute for me—for *here* the one amounts to the other, if the one, *me*, amounts to the other and not to itself. But how can this be shown?

The first step involves challenging the claim that ipseity can be won on the basis of the I alone, understood as Dasein—that is to say, of the I as alone, isolated. That is, "consciousness, knowing of oneself by oneself, is not all there is to the notion of subjectivity."[22] This means not that subjectivity sinks into unconsciousness but that the circle of the *cogitatio* never permits reaching what, in the ego, specifies it most radically as itself. The same impossibility is also found in the privileged modality of the *cogitatio*, the will: the self is "this original expiation—involuntary—prior to the will's initiative (prior to the origin)."[23] Here I must emphasize that what Levinas does not hesitate to call "an inversion of intentionality," which "goes against intentionality,"[24] implies nothing less than a whole-sale "inversion of consciousness" that "traverses consciousness counter-currentwise."[25] Thus, Levinas keeps Descartes' idea of the Infinite as readily as he rejects his *cogito* (at least in its standard formulation), and this for an important reason: while the ego of the cogito decides for itself in a thought that is centrifugal but always returns to itself, the ego of the idea of the Infinite finds itself preceded by what will always remain other, the Infinite itself, and will always define the ego more originally than the ego can define itself. If subjectivity there must still be, it will no more name itself than think itself. Subjectivity without I, without a name in the nominative, it no longer bears any name other than the one that is attributed to it as a nickname, *me*. Me, or the name that comes from elsewhere, which names me as the other sees me and as I will never see myself or say myself. As a result, at the origin I am named in "the accusa-tive form—which is a modification of no nominative."[26] I have no proper name because even my I is "not I Myself, but me under assignation"[27]—which assignation and by what? Obviously, my assignation by what ac-cuses me, me who has a "self, from the first in the accusative form (or under accusation!)."[28]

Here the second step must be taken: identifying or at least designating who or what accuses. Or more exactly, that by relation to which (or to whom) I discover myself in a situation where someone or something names me in the accusative. One could stick with a simple explanation: I am named in the accusative, me, because an other, playing the part of the Other in general, accuses me. This explanation does not, however, suffice—not because it arbitrarily presupposes my guilt, as if this were always self-evident, but because it admits that I *would be* myself first so as next to receive the charge of the accusation. On this reading, my existence as I would still precede my nomination as me, if only in order to render the latter possible. But the challenge is to think a me prior to the I, a me that has dispensed entirely with the I and never passed thorough it. "Not strictly speaking an I set up in the nominative in its identity, but *from the outset* constrained to . . . as it were in the accusative"[29]—"from the outset" because the accusation is not grounded on something (a being) that would precede it and, resting on itself, would resist it or ex-cuse itself. It is there-fore not enough that one accuse me for me to discover myself originally as a me in the accusative. To the contrary, the position of the accused, when limited solely to the moral horizon, presupposes still and always my *ontic* sufficiency, precedence, and independence. It accords me still and always a being, which appropriates me to myself as subject—be this only so as to then be able to accuse me inasmuch as moral or juridical subject. Paradoxically, the moral interpretation of the accusative weakens it, to the benefit of an implicit ontic nominative.

Whence the third step: the accusative must constitute me without presupposing any subject prior to the accusation. How? How can the accusative be thus radicalized? We just saw how: by not making the accusative depend on any fault committed by a prior I. No doubt. But am I not, in one way or another, always already guilty of a fault that I have committed, therefore, am I not always already a being in existence before it, by being an I in the nominative? Is it therefore necessary to abandon naming me "from the outset" in the accusative, that is to say, before every accusation? Not at all, for a path remains open: the accusative is exerted in a nonmoral way, which in no way implies that I am responsible in the mode of something that ontically precedes it. For this path to open, I must let myself be named responsible not for what I have committed (for what I am in fact to blame) as an I (prior being) but for what I *have not* committed and by definition cannot have done—namely, what the other did. And what is it that I can know with certainty that the other did? What he committed against me, his persecution of me, "the unlimited accusative of persecution."[30] Paradoxically but necessarily, responsibility in the extra-moral sense will be a responsibility of the second order, for what *the other and not I* committed, one that is imposed on me because he committed it *against me*. "The self's responsibility for what it never willed," or "responsibility for the responsibility of the other,"[31] constitutes it as a *me*, precisely because it is set forth without its will,[32] without any prior being.[33] Only this second-order responsibility, which is therefore *in a sense extra-moral*, invests me definitively in the accusative, as an originary self: "under accusation by everyone, the responsibility for everyone goes to the point of substitution. The subject is a hostage."[34]

Here we must be very careful. "Subjectivity as hostage"[35] does not mean merely that my exposure to the other does not depend on me since it precedes me. It signifies above all that it does not depend on the other either, at least not first according to a relation with him as with another being: "Through substitution for others, the oneself escapes *relations*."[36] Between him and me, there is no common ground, no third, no mediator, not even a relation, but the pure "possibility of putting oneself in the place of the other," which precedes sympathy and respect because it alone renders them possible: "the unconditionality of being hostage is not the limit case of solidarity, but the condition for all solidarity."[37] The hostage who finds himself responsible for everyone and everything that has been done by every other has not, however, committed any fault. He is phenomenalized in the accusative without anybody accusing him of anything. Hostage in the extra-moral sense, he finds no fault in himself, receives no sentence, but wins the only ipseity possible for him: "Ipseity, in its passivity without archē characteristic of identity, is a hostage. The word *I* means *here I am* [me voici] answering for everything and for everyone."[38] Substitution therefore does not belong within morality or ethics because it accomplishes ipseity, in a nonmetaphysical and nonontological mode. One makes it un-intelligible so long as one does not approach it as an extramoral concept. And only this extra-moral sense, as determination of ipseity, lets us understand that it makes ethics and morality possible.

V

In this way, substitution is set up as the fulfillment of individuation and of ipseity. The question of the self and its mode of being (or nonbeing), the question that occupied Levinas from the very beginning, is one he never abandoned. In the end, his answer is put as plainly as possible: the individuation of the self does not pass through the I—in particular, not through my possibility, as Dasein, of being toward death—but comes from my responsibility to the other, before all accusation and all response. The other accuses me (*Autrui m'accuse*) in the sense in which by highlighting (*en accusant*) the features of a face, one makes it appear better: the other accuses me in the accusative, and thereby brings me to light and manifests me (even to myself) as myself, "accused as unique."[39] What makes me myself does not coincide with what I think, or even with what I am, but with that for which I respond and that to which I respond. "I am 'in myself' through the others."[40] This exteriority, this deportation of me outside the self, in fact operates as a sort of phenomenological reduction. Since it concerns reaching an "ipseity *reduced* to the irreplaceable,"[41] one must ask: What in me cannot be substituted for anything else that would efface it? Not my thought, which can always be replaced by another; not my resolution to be or not to be according to my ultimate possibility, which can always be disowned; but only my responsibility. Not in the sense of that for which I become responsible by a (moral) decision, coming after the (ontic) I, but of that for which I find myself responsible without having wanted or thought it because it is others who made me, in advance, hostage to their own responsibilities. I discover myself the "*non-interchangeable* par excellence,"[42] because "nothing is unique, that is, *refractory* to concepts, except the *I* involved in responsibility."[43] That is, I become irreducibly me—in other words, I identify myself with what resists all reduction of *me*—when I win this perfect *residuum*: assuming not the variations and irregularities of the I (even as Dasein), but the fait accompli of my responsibility for what *does* not depend on me, *has never* depended on me, and *will never* depend on me: namely, the responsibilities that others have assumed without me but for me.

We can now better glimpse the power of Levinas's revival and reversal of the doctrine of selfhood elaborated in *Being and Time*. There where Dasein reigns in the first person, arises me in the accusative. There where resolution decides and wills, the hostage submits to a decision that he never made. There where Dasein anticipates its own possibility, the substituted knows himself fixed in what is no longer possible for him to avoid. But above all, there where Dasein is individualized by itself, therefore in standing constantly by itself (*Selbst-ständigkeit*) precisely because "Existentially, *'Self-constancy'* signifies nothing other than anticipatory resoluteness,"[44] the hostage wins the "superindividuation of the Me" only by leaving it up to the other, for the "uniqueness of the self is the very fact of bearing the fault of another."[45]

In fact, Levinas did once comment on *Being and Time* §26. He concluded his challenge with these words: "Myself is the one who is elected to respond for the neighbor and *thus* is identical to itself, and *thus* for itself. Uniqueness of election!"[46] There is nothing more I could add.

Translated by Jeffrey L. Kosky

Should Jews and Christians Fear the Gifts of the Greeks?

Reflections on Levinas, Translation, and Atheistic Theology

PAUL FRANKS

I

What in Levinas's thinking is Jewish, and what is Christian? There is no good reason to think that these questions will be easier to answer than the question What is Jewish, and what is Christian?

Here is a familiar dialectic. You are tempted to say of some idea or doctrine: *that* is essentially Jewish and not at all Christian, or *that* is essentially Christian and not at all Jewish. Perhaps you succumb to the temptation. Then you find—depending on your predilections, either to your despair or to your delight—that something excruciatingly hard to distinguish from that very idea or doctrine is found in the other religion after all. You may stand your ground, of course, by expelling the uncooperative idea or doctrine from *authentic* Judaism or Christianity. But then you had better be prepared to show your basis for what is now clearly a *prescriptive* claim. Nor is this the only alternative.

Surely—to enter the dialectic—nothing could be more Christian and less Jewish than the idea of divine incarnation. So Levinas is thinking in Jewish terms when he says, in a passage expounded by Robert Gibbs: "The other person is not the incarnation of God, but precisely by his face, in which he is disincarnate, the manifestation of the height in which God is revealed."[1] Yet, as Elliot Wolfson points out, an idea of divine incarnation—or something excruciatingly close to it—in the Torah is central to kabbalah, including the Lithuanian, antiecstatic tradition that Levinas valorizes.[2] To be sure, poetic incarnation is not personal incarnation. But both seem to involve what Levinas would regard as an illicit ontologizing of what is properly ethical. Is Levinas endorsing—perhaps constructing—a particular brand of Judaism? Or is his philosophy just as non-Jewish as it is non-Christian?

Again: surely the affirmation of a creed and its articulation in theology are quintessentially Christian, as Richard Cohen argues, while the practice and consideration of law and ethics are Jewish, as Leo Strauss says in a passage quoted by Leora Batnitzky.[3] But could any version of Christianity really be *exhausted* by the affirmation of dogma? Moreover, even if the history of Judaism involves nothing *exactly* like patristic controversies over creedal formulations, attended by denunciations of heresy, it does involve an early controversy over belief in resurrection, said to be central to the disputes between Pharisees and Sadducees, while disagreements over practice have often turned on more or less explicit differences in doctrine. Could any version of Judaism be *exhausted* by law-based ritual, ethics, and study, without *any* beliefs or presuppositions about being? If Levinas is prescribing an exclusively ethical Judaism, what is the basis of his proposal, and what is the cost of its acceptance?

Could the peculiar intimacy of Judaism and Christianity consist in a dance in which they repeatedly trade positions, without ever ceasing to insist on their differences?

II

Levinas himself is not immune to the temptation to announce the exclusive essences of Christianity and Judaism. Yet something in his thinking can help us to resist the temptation.

In his reading of TB Sotah 37a-b, Levinas says, "We have still not finished translating the Bible. The Septuagint is incomplete."[4] On one reading—hardly supported by scholarly study of the formation of the Hebrew and Greek Bibles, but sometimes suggested by Levinas—Judaism is the unchanging Urtext from which proceed many translations, including the New Testament and, more generally, the various Christianities. On another reading—more sensitive to the practice of translation and to the history of religions—there is no Urtext. Just as much as Christianity, the various Judaisms—Hellenistic, Rabbinic, Geonic, Neo-Platonic, Aristotelian, kabbalistic, hasidic, mitnaggedic, etc.—are moments in an ongoing process of translation, a process within which the aforementioned dialectical dance takes place.

What divides dancing from fighting? Sometimes no more than the edge of a knife. So we should thank Levinas for his contributions to peace between Judaism and Christianity. In particular, he has given Christians a conception of Judaism, and he has given Jews a conception of Christianity, that each can not only tolerate but also acknowledge.

Levinas's gift to Christians is more evident. There are longstanding tendencies within Christianity to create dualisms—between spirit and letter, faith and law, and so on—whose negative pole is occupied by Judaism or by some phantasm that bears its name. In the last two centuries, one of the most challenging has been the Kantian distinction between autonomy and heteronomy. The distinction has roots in Paul's Epistle to the Romans.[5] In Kant's hands, it becomes the contrast between "the sole principle of all moral laws and of duties in keeping with them" and a hodgepodge of putative principles that "not only [do] not ground any obligation at all but [are] instead opposed to the principle of obligation and to the morality of the will."[6] Since "The *Jewish faith*, as originally established, was only a collection of merely statutory laws [*statuarische Gesetze*] supporting a political state," and since the authority of these laws is based on their origin not in reason but in the revelation of a transcendent God, it follows that Judaism is irremediably heteronomous.[7] Moreover, since "The one and true religion contains nothing but laws, i.e., practical principles, of whose unconditional necessity we can become conscious and which we therefore recognize as revealed through pure reason," it follows that Judaism is not even religion, but rather "a *delusion of religion* [*ein* Religionswahn], and acting upon it constitutes counterfeit service [*ein Afterdienst*], i.e., a pretension of honoring God through which we act directly contrary to the true service required by him."[8] Only "The euthanasia of Judaism is pure moral religion, freed from all the ancient statutory teachings."[9]

Of the many responses offered on Judaism's behalf, perhaps the most daring is the one that may be found in Levinas. He does not argue that Judaism is—in virtue of its content, or of the choice to will it—autonomous after all. Instead, taking the battle to the enemy's heartland, Levinas may be said to argue that ethics—indeed, *reason itself*—consists in a higher heteronomy: responsiveness to the law that is given through and in the other. Is this what Jews have meant in their emphasis on the *mitzvah*? In regarding Israel as chosen for the yoke of *mitzvoth*, have they meant that the subject is individuated by election for ethical responsiveness? This would be a Judaism that Christians—if not Kantians—can appreciate and even acknowledge as something that is, or should be, their own.

Less evident is Levinas's gift to Jews. This is not least because Jews have felt less bound to reconsider their relationship to Christianity than Christians to re-evaluate their relationship to Judaism. In my experience, however, Levinas's later accentuation of responsibility to the point of substitution is apt, on first hearing, to strike Jews as Christian. When Jews hear that I am supposed to be responsible not only *to* but also *for* the other, that I am subject to "an indebtedness before any loan,"[10] they are likely to hear this as some version of the Christian doctrine of original sin. When they hear that my responsibility includes "expiation for another,"[11] they are likely to hear it as a version of the Christian doctrine of vicarious atonement. Does Judaism not insist, by contrast, on the individuality of responsibility and repentance? That "the ego [is] accused by the other to the point of persecution, and responsible for its persecutor" is especially hard for Jews to hear.[12] In the dispute between Levinas and Heidegger discussed in this volume by Jeffrey Kosky and Jean-Luc Marion, it is, ironically, Heidegger who is apt to seem more consonant with Judaism.[13]

However, on closer reflection, Levinas's concept of substitution can be seen as based on a Talmudic dictum: that all Israel are guarantors (*arevim*) for one another—where this is understood to mean not only that each is responsible for the deeds of the other but also that each is responsible for the responsibility of the other.[14] This is not specifically Christian, since it is not one particular individual who is responsible for all others.[15] Is this a version of vicarious atonement that Jews can appreciate and even acknowledge as their own?

Perhaps, but Levinas's talmudically based concept of responsibility is not specifically Jewish, either. As he notes:

> I have it from an eminent master: each time Israel is mentioned in the Talmud, one is certainly free to understand by it a particular ethnic group which is probably fulfilling an incomparable destiny. But to interpret in this manner would be to reduce the general principle in the idea enunciated in the Talmudic passage, to forget that Israel means a people who has received the law and, as a result, a human nature which has reached the fullness of its responsibilities and its self-consciousness.[16]

On this view, it is each human being in the ethically full sense—regardless of ethnicity—who is responsible for the responsibility of the other. But what is the status of the freedom granted to the interpreter who construes Israel as . . . the Jewish people? Does Levinas regard such an interpreter as proceeding responsibly, provided that the universal significance of Israel is not forgotten? Or does he view the particularistic interpreter as exercising the freedom to be irresponsible? In short, what room is there in Levinas's thought for the particular people of Israel? Does Levinas's way of insisting on the ethical significance of Judaism come at the price of what most Jews would regard as Judaism's essentially particular aspect?[17]

Has the Judaism that has become available to Christians ceased thereby to be a Judaism that Jews can regard as their own? The analogous question arises for the Christianity that Levinas has made available to Jews. Should Jews and Christians thank Levinas for these translations, or should they fear Levinas as a Greek who bears dangerous gifts?

There is, I think, a genuine danger of reducing Judaism and Christianity to ethics. Although the ethics may not be Kantian, the effect would still be destructive. Even if Levinas intends no such reduction, he may suggest it to others. Yet there are other possibilities. Could Levinasian ethics be regarded as a "natural religion" that anticipates the revealed religions in both structure and content, while necessarily refraining from their particularities? Could it be, in Rosenzweig's terms, an "atheistic theology"—in particular, a theology regarded by atheists as sufficient, but by Jews and Christians as preparing the way for their own theisms? Could Levinas have staked out a common ground between Jews and Christians that can function as common only insofar as it is also shared by atheists?

Thinking about God and God-Talk with Levinas

MEROLD WESTPHAL

Emmanuel Levinas is a Jewish thinker. This claim has at least three meanings, two of them quite unproblematic, while the third is more than a little. First, in his confessional writings (Jerusalem, Talmud) he is overtly a Jewish thinker. Second, in these writings he is with equal clarity not a Christian. Third, in his philosophical writings (Athens, phenomenology) the matter becomes a bit muddy. He appeals to phenomenological evidence or, perhaps better, postphenomenological nonevidence, in a manner addressed to philosophers who need not be Jewish or share his reverence for the Talmud. We are all supposed to see what he is trying to show and to do so without appeal to scriptural texts or religious traditions as authoritative. On the other hand, his employment of such religious terms as *God, creation, revelation, glory, height, expiation, substitution*, and so forth suggests that he is operating within a monotheistic hermeneutical circle, while his designation of the neighbor or other person as the widow, orphan, and stranger evokes the specifically Hebrew scriptures. So it is hard to say with precision and without ambiguity whether and, if so, in what sense Levinas is a Jewish *philosopher*.

I make these points not because I propose to try to settle this third issue but in order to clarify my goals in these reflections. The formula is "Levinas between Jews and Christians," and I take it to signify a conversation among those who love and learn from Levinas and who bring their Jewish or Christian faith with them to the conversation rather than bracketing it. The first two points mentioned above can be taken for granted, and from my perspective the third is way down the list of topics calling for discussion. Other issues arise,[1] not all of which turn out to be debates between Jews and Christians but, as I shall argue, are sometimes debates among Jews and among Christians.

But first an issue whose bearing on Levinas may be indirect, though I think it is of crucial importance for any conversation between Jews and Christians. In many contexts it has become politically correct for Christians either to abandon supersessionist interpretations of Judaism or at least not to mention them in public. In its contemporary usage, as I understand it, *supercessionism* has become a four-letter word that places a taboo on the Christian claim that Jesus is the Christ, the Messiah promised to biblical Israel and, accordingly, that any Judaism that fails to acknowledge this is importantly incomplete. In other words, it needs to be superceded by incorporating the Christian claim about who Jesus is, along with the other changes entailed by such a confession.[2]

It is in this context that we find the suggestion that for Levinas Christianity is "a monotheistic religion for the Gentiles." I am not clear whether Levinas ever used this phrase or even how accurately it may capture the implication of what he does say. What interests me is an ironical implication of this phrase and of the (sometimes self-imposed) requirement that Christians abandon anything that hints of supersessionism. To appreciate this irony we need to remind ourselves of two facts, one historical and one textual.

The historical fact is that Jesus and his earliest followers were Jews, not Gentiles, and that the conflict between those who confessed that Jesus was the awaited Messiah and those who denied this was an intra-Jewish debate. Moreover, the question for the earliest Christian communities was never whether Jesus was both Lord and Christ (Messiah) but whether the gospel was for Gentiles as well as (obviously) for Jews. This process by which this question was emphatically decided in the affirmative is narrated in the book of Acts and echoed in the epistles. The good news brought to the Jews is to be shared with the Gentiles. Christianity certainly didn't start out as monotheism for the Gentiles.

In the narrative time of the gospels and Acts, this universal claim textually precedes the question and answer among the early churches. Thus John the Baptist points to Jesus as "the Lamb of God who takes away the sin of the *world*" (John 1:29).[3] Simeon, who had been promised that he would see "the Lord's Messiah," takes the infant Jesus in his arms and gives thanks that he has seen "a light for revelation to the Gentiles, and for glory to your people Israel" (Luke 2:26, 32). Jesus tells Nicodemus that "God so loved the *world* that he gave his only Son" (John 3:16), and the resurrected Jesus commissions his disciples, "Go therefore and make disciples of *all nations*. . . . and you will be my witnesses in Jerusalem, in all Judea and Samaria, and to the ends of the earth" (Matt. 28:19, Acts 1:8).

Echoing this memory from the life of Jesus and the earliest Christian communities, Paul writes that "in Christ, God was reconciling the *world* to himself" (2 Cor. 5:19). He is convinced that the gospel is "the power of God for everyone who has faith, to the Jew first and also to the Greek" (Rom. 1:16). He, or perhaps one of his followers, writes to Gentiles, who were once "without Christ, being aliens from the commonwealth of Israel, and strangers to the covenants of promise, having no hope and without God in the world" to celebrate the fact that

> now in Christ Jesus you who once were far off have been brought near by the blood of Christ. For he is our peace; in his flesh he has made both groups into one and has broken down the dividing wall, that is, the hostility between us . . . that he might create in himself one new humanity in place of the two, thus making peace, and might reconcile both groups to God in one body through the cross. . . . So he came and proclaimed peace to you who were far off and peace to those who were near; for through him both of us have access in one Spirit to the Father. (Eph. 2:12–18)

In short, Christianity was a missionary religion from the very outset because of the conviction that Jesus was not just the Messiah of the Jews but as such the Lord and Savior of the whole world.[4]

Now we can see the irony involved in the phrase "a monotheistic religion for the Gentiles" and the general expectation that Christians abandon, or at least not mention, anything that smacks of supersessionism. It is simply this: in requiring that Christians not ask them to convert to a religion not their own, Jews are requiring Christians to convert to a religion not their own, to abandon the normative source of their own identity. Just how much this is the case can be seen by rewriting the New Testament in tune with this demand.

"Behold the Lamb of God, who takes away the sins of the Gentiles."

"God so loved the Gentiles that he gave his only Son"

"In Christ, God was reconciling the Gentiles to himself."

This glaring textual violence is not Christianity.

It seems to me inescapable that there is a fundamental disagreement between Judaism and Christianity. Each side thinks the other side to be deeply mistaken about the significance of Jesus, and I see no reason why this fact should be whisked (or perhaps wished) away as a precondition of dialogue. In this context I think it important to see what the Christian proclamation of Christ as the Lord and Savior of the whole world does *not* mean.

First, it provides no cover or comfort for "Christian" anti-Semitism, past or present. In order for the universal claims of Christ to provide justification for crusades or inquisitions or pogroms or final solutions or Klannish "patriotism," additional premises would be needed that are both dubious and detestable. Of course, the universalism of Christianity can be (and has been) used as an excuse for such attitudes and practices. Evil can always find an excuse, and religious excuses are almost always popular.[5] But self-serving excuses are one thing, justifications quite another.

Second, it does not follow that two parties who disagree deeply cannot converse in an atmosphere of respect and tolerance, which means that neither is willing to resort to violence or manipulation (which is a rhetorical form of violence). That so much of what passes for political and religious discourse in contemporary America fails to embody the civility of which I speak here only shows how deeply we are sinners, not that disagreement necessarily results in disrespect and intolerance.[6]

Third, one of the main reasons for the previous point is that deep disagreement is no necessary barrier to the hope and even the expectation that one may learn from the other. I differ sharply from Levinas on various points, most of which do not fall along the Jew/Christian axis. But I love him and have learned a great deal from him, and I fully hope and expect to continue to do so.

Fourth, deep divergence is not incompatible with substantive convergence. One can think here of the common ground found by the (often secular) Jews and Christians who risked life and limb together in the civil rights struggles that significantly (if not sufficiently) changed America in the mid-twentieth century. Even the phrase "monotheistic religion for the Gentiles" reminds us of monotheistic common ground between Judaism and Christianity,[7] and it seems to me that there is a deep agreement between Levinas and Christian teaching that we are not the condition of the possibility of the moral and religious life but receive the call to responsibility from a voice not our own. Exploring convergence is just as important and perhaps more fruitful than defining difference. But honest dialogue requires both.

Finally, in biblical context, distinctive election is no basis for the arrogant presumption of superiority. Through its particularity Israel was called to a universal mission, to be a light to the nations (Isa. 42, 49, 60).

But Moses reminds Israel: "It was not because you were more numerous than any other people that the LORD set his heart on you and chose you—for you were the fewest of all peoples. It was because the LORD loved you and kept the oath that he swore to your ancestors" (Deut. 7:7–8).[8] And Amos will later remind the covenant people of God that their election is not a matter of privilege, as if they were teacher's pet:

> You only have I known
> of all the families of the earth;
> therefore I will punish you
> for all your iniquities. (Amos 3:2)

Similarly, if the particularity of the Christian community is embedded in a universal responsibility, this is not a recipe for a Christendom of privilege and power. So Jesus teaches his disciples:

> You know that among the Gentiles those whom they recognize as their rulers lord it over them, and their great ones are tyrants over them. But it is not so among you; but whoever wishes to become great among you must be your servant, and whoever wishes to be first among you must be slave of all. For the Son of Man came not to be served but to serve, and to give his life a ransom for many. (Mark 10:42–45)[9]

Surely this applies as much to Christians collectively (the church) as to individual Christians.

Especially since Constantine, Christians have all too often confused election and mission with privilege, power, and intolerance. Perhaps the demise of Christendom in Europe and the degeneration of "Christian America" here at home into partisan presumption and pride stem in large part from Christians being too unchristian, proclaiming Jesus as the Christ but refusing to walk in his ways. The Jewish protest against supersessionism, while deeply problematic in its own right, can and should be heard as a prophetic call to repentance.

࿏

I turn now to four important issues raised by these essays. I hope it will be clear in each case that they do not fall along the fault line that divides Jews and Christians from each other but rather represent issues each community must face both internally and in dialogue with each other.

What about theology? First there is the question of the religious implications of Levinas's critique of ontology. Like Heidegger's critique of ontotheology, it is not directed against every account of how things are but at a quite specific mode of discourse.[10] For the mainstream of the tradition, being is what gives itself to human understanding to be thought *and thought in a quite specific way.*[11] This is why the critique of ontology so frequently seems like epistemology, for, as Levinas reads the tradition, being is that which gives itself to human thought in terms of Plato's doctrine of recollection, Descartes' *cogito,*[12] Kant's transcendental unity of apperception, Husserl's account of intentionality as the origin and source of meaning, and Heidegger's account of disclosure.[13] On this account, the subject is itself before encountering its other and contains within itself, or better, simply is the condition for the possibility of comprehension. Adequation is the legitimate goal of this knowing, which has the form of struggle, command, and eventually mastery and possession. Knowing is a form of enjoyment whose mirroring analogy is but cover for a deeper analogy: alimentation. The knowing subject is "for itself as the 'famished stomach that has no ears.'"[14]

This kind of structure is what Levinas understands by intentionality, representation, and disclosure. It is clear enough why he considers it to be the reduction of the other to the same,[15] a mode of discourse and an interpretation of being that must be transcended if the transcendent other is not to be either evicted or domesticated. This is why, when talking about obsession and persecution in relation to the other, Levinas can write, "The approach is not the thematization of any relationship, but is this very relationship, which resists thematization as anarchic. *To thematize this relation is already to lose it,*"[16] and why he can speak of thematization as the traitorous and idolatrous betrayal of the immediacy it loses.[17] What concerns Levinas is "proximity and not truth about proximity."[18] One is reminded of Thomas à Kempis, supposed author of *The Imitation of Christ,* who writes, "I had rather feel contrition, than know the definition thereof."[19]

But just as theologians, Jewish or Christian, may well reflect on the nature of true contrition, so Levinas's writings might well be summarized as the attempt to tell us "the truth about proximity." It is not reflection as such that he repudiates, but reflection in a certain mode or posture, designated by such technical terms as thematization, representation, recollection, intentionality, and disclosure. We must not confuse the renunciation of thematization and representation with the refusal to speak at all about that which transcends their grasping grasp. Levinas talks a great deal not only about the neighbor (the widow, the orphan, and the stranger) but also about God. As such a speaker he is himself a theologian.

So there must be a legitimate place for theology both as theory and as performative act, confession of one's faith. The first and most obvious condition is that one must abandon for this mode of reflective discourse the epistemic model of the sovereign subject, disinterested and disengaged in relation to the "object" it seeks to master and possess. As if King Midas were the model and the task were to amass huge piles of justified true propositions to admire. But that is not enough. The primacy of the ethical, of acknowledged responsibility before the other, means "that theological recuperation comes *after* the glimpse of holiness, which is primary."[20] This is not merely a formal statement about the relation of immediacy to reflection. The precondition for theological recuperation is a certain conversion, the abandonment of the posture of the sovereign and disengaged spectator and an openness, a vulnerability to being invaded and called into question by the other whom one has always already welcomed. It is only in a posture of "obedience and submission to the will of another" that one may be a theologian.

This is what is meant, I believe, by the description of theology as faith seeking understanding. Levinas is a welcome reminder that this formula betrays its deepest intentions when it reduces faith to mere propositional assent and thereby reduces theology to mere theory, giving aide and comfort to the primacy of orthodoxy over orthopraxy.[21] But biblical faith is never mere creedal assent. "You believe that God is one; you do well. Even the demons believe—and shudder" (James 2:19). The orthodoxy of the demons does not place them among the faithful. Biblical faith always involves an element of belief, to be sure, but always in the context of trust, obedience, and gratitude—in Levinas's language, the welcoming of the always already intruding and interrupting God. Thus Levinas writes, "The sentence in which God comes to be involved in words is not 'I believe in God.' . . . It is the 'here I am' [*me voici*]."[22]

But this is not the either/or it is sometimes made out to be. It concerns priority. Theology betrays itself and its relation to God whenever its cuts itself off from its proper starting point, seeking to articulate "I believe in God" apart from the "here I am." Levinas's argument doesn't abolish theological reflection but serves as the powerful reminder that "theological recuperation comes *after* the glimpse of holiness, which is primary." First conversion, then reflection.

What does "God" signify? There seems, then, to emerge from Levinas's thought no barrier to reflective God-talk as such, whether we call it theology (Jerusalem) or philosophy (Athens). So the question becomes all the more pressing: What does Levinas mean by "God"? I find myself sympathetic when John Llewelyn asks, "After enduring Nietzsche's proclamation of the death of the God of onto-theology, why is Levinas either unable to unwilling to eliminate the word 'God' from the lexicon in which he expounds what he himself describes as a humanism of the other man?"[23] In other words, it seems to me that, for all his God-talk, Levinas is in the final analysis an atheist. But he has an answer to Llewelyn's question, and to understand it we need to distinguish two kinds of atheism. One kind, to which Llewelyn refers, denies the reality of God as held by the Abrahamic monotheisms and thinks we would all be better off if we simply stopped using the word *God*. The other kind denies or refuses to affirm the theistic God, a personal Creator, Lawgiver, Judge, and Redeemer, but thinks the word *God* still has some valuable uses. They offer what Charles Stevenson has called a " 'persuasive' [re]definition, one which gives a new conceptual meaning to a familiar word without substantially changing its emotive meaning, and which is used with the conscious or unconscious purpose of changing, by this means, the direction of people's interests."[24]

Spinoza and Hegel are examples of this kind of atheism.[25] Neither has any place for a God who knows us, who speaks to us, and who loves us. In their systems the only knowers, speakers, and lovers are human. In this elimination of a personal God from their thinking, they are atheists, but each retains the word *God*, for which they find other uses. For Spinoza, nature, as he understands it, shares such traditional divine attributes as infinity and causal ultimacy. Thus *Deus sive natura*. Similarly, for Hegel, spirit, as he understands it, shares such traditional divine attributes as freedom and absolute knowing, though the sites of these attributes are human subjects and societies.[26] Thus the Holy Spirit is the human spirit at its highest levels of freedom and rationality.

It seems to me for several reasons that Levinas is this kind of atheist.

1. To speak of creation is simply to refer to the passivity of the human subject in its proximity to the other human person and to the anarchic time in which this proximity has always already occurred.

2. Correspondingly, there is no "world behind the scenes" as there would have to be if the biblical, theistic notion of God as Creator and Redeemer were to be affirmed.[27] With this denial Levinas seems to me to eliminate God and immortality in one fell swoop.

3. As if to make sure we don't miss the point, Levinas insists, "It is then vain to posit an absolute You."[28] God is not a perfect knower, speaker, and lover distinct from the widow, the orphan, and the stranger.

4. Such attributes as infinity, revelation, glory, height, expiation, and substitution are transferred to human persons. This is "by no means intended as an elimination of transcendence. Rather, it aims at its *relocation* in the midst of interpersonal exchange."[29]

5. Accordingly, Levinas assigns a double significance to the human face. On the one hand, it is merely empirical, and its nakedness is that of literal hunger and cold. On the other hand, its nakedness is that it stands "beyond every attribute," transcending every sensible or intelligible form as in apophatic theology (for which in its theistic sense Levinas has no use).[30] If Derrida can say that "every other is wholly other [*tout autre est tout autre*],"[31] Levinas can say, in effect, "Every other is the union of the human and the divine." Thus the face is not a sign that points beyond itself to God but rather a "trace of *itself*."[32]

6. Finally, there is Levinas's habit of labeling any discourse that hints at a personal God distinct from human persons as idolatrous mythology unfit for a religion for adults.

I draw several conclusions from these features of Levinas's thought. First, his God is not the god of the Bible but a radical redefinition of the God of Abraham, Isaac, and Jacob. Second, it may be that Levinas's God is best understood as the depth dimension of each human person by virtue of which a categorical, infinite, asymmetrical call to responsibility emanates. Thus God is "the *he* in the depth of the you."[33] Third, Levinas's motivation throughout his work is crystal clear: he seeks to rescue ethical responsibility from its eclipse in dominant ways of thinking in the west. The result, it seems to me, is a reduction of religion to ethics. Thus he writes, "It is our relations with men . . . that give to theological concepts the *sole signification* they admit of. . . . Everything that cannot be *reduced* to an interhuman relation represents not the superior form but the forever primitive form of religion."[34] He seeks "to prohibit the metaphysical relation with God from being accomplished in the ignorance of men and things. . . . There can be no 'knowledge' of God separated from the relationship with men."[35]

That the prior claim about reduction does not follow from this latter claim about ignorance and separation, which surely belongs to the Bible in both its Jewish and its Christian forms, can be seen by thinking about the following text, which may be thought of as a commentary on Jesus' summary of the law, according to which the first commandment is to "love the Lord your God with all your heart, and with all your soul, and with all your mind, and with all your strength," while the second commandment is to "love your neighbor as yourself" (Mark 12:28–34): "Those who say, 'I love God,' and hate their brothers or sisters, are liars; for those who do not love a brother or sister whom they have seen, cannot love God whom they have not seen. The commandment we have from him is this: those who love God must love their brothers and sisters also" (1 John 4:20–21). As I read this text, the "also" with which it ends is important. Love of God and love of neighbor are *inseparable*; one cannot have the former without the latter. But they are nevertheless *distinct*. God is not reducible to the depth dimension of my neighbor, and religion is not reducible to ethics. As Levinas would read this text, if we allow love of God and of neighbor to be *distinct*, we will inevitably make them *separable*. This temptation is a very real one, and all too often concern for orthodoxy and even ritual forms of orthopraxy have *separated* themselves from love of neighbor and concern for justice in human society. But to me it is a strange either/or logic that responds by seeking to eliminate any form of love for God that is *distinct* from love of neighbor and reducible thereto. Of course, if God is not one who loves us, then perhaps God cannot be one whom we love above (but not apart from) all others.

The issue here is not one between Jews and Christians. A robust theism that understands God as distinct from but immanent within the worlds of nature and history and fully personal, in the sense of being a knower, a speaker, and a lover, can be found, both at present and historically, in both Judaism and Christianity. Yet both redefinitional atheism and the reduction of religion to ethics can be found in both traditions, though this seems to me a betrayal of their biblical roots, an unnecessary capitulation to secular modernity.[36] Levinas reminds us how significant is the question What does "God" mean?

Does Levinas give us a theology of law without grace? I have sometimes thought so, but perhaps there is reason to say both Yes and No. Perhaps his theology give us as much grace as his God allows. The "law without grace" formula stems, of course, from an either/or, Kantlike logic that seeks to preserve duty and responsibility by excluding any concern for happiness. Levinas's allergy to salvation themes is well known, and it is hard to know just how he would read the Exodus narrative, the psalms of individual and community thanksgiving, or the message of second Isaiah. His God is not a Savior.

But the grace motif in the Hebrew scriptures is not limited to themes of deliverance and redemption. The law itself is a gift and not just a task. Thus the psalmist exults:

Oh, how I love your law!
It is my meditation all day long . . .
Your word is a lamp to my feet
and a light to my path. (Ps. 119:97, 105)

Thus the face that speaks and commands "You shall not commit murder" interrupts my intentionality, my *conatus essendi*, not just as a task but also as a gift that can be and at some level always has been welcomed.[37]

But Levinas's teaching about the face and the voice of the other person belongs not just to a theology of grace but to a theology of prevenient grace. It comes before, is always first. It occurs in that anarchic, immemorial, preontological past that was never present and thus can never be recuperated or re-presented. As command it evokes responsibility, but as gift it provokes desire, metaphysical desire that cannot be satisfied because it desires the Transcendent, the Infinite. A Christian writer about prayer invokes the same structure:

> But does the desire for God originate within ourselves as a spontaneous reaching out of the human spirit? A breakthrough of faith occurs when we recognize that our desire for God originates not in ourselves but in God. It is God who gives, kindles and fuels the desire for God. What we feel as our desire is the effect of God desiring to be desired, knowing that our responsive desiring will bring us to life.[38]

We must take this last phrase about the response that brings us to life quite seriously. For Levinas the call is not addressed to the subject, for the latter does not yet exist. The response is not something done by the subject, for it is in the response that the subject is born and comes into being.[39] This means that the self is not a substance in the classical sense, for, to use the language that is here undermined, the relation to the infinite other belongs to the very essence of the subject.[40]

Thus we find in Levinas a twofold theology of grace: a presentation of the law as gift, though this theme is rather muted,[41] and a presentation of the structure of grace as prevenient. What we don't find is a theology of grace as promise and fulfillment, as deliverance, redemption, salvation. While this kind of grace is intrinsic to the God of the Bible, it is not really a possibility for Levinas's God. Given Levinas's allergy to anything supernatural, his God seems not to be a speaker and an agent distinct from human speakers and agents, and it is not clear that even in their deepest depths the widow, the orphan, and the stranger can play the role of Savior or Redeemer. It is the absence of this dimension of grace that has evoked the "law without grace" formula, which we now see to have a point but to be insufficiently precise.

Once again, this is not a Jewish/Christian issue. Consider grace as promise. In Genesis 12 the command to Abram to migrate comes with a promise of blessing. Or again, in Exodus 33, the command to leave Sinai for "a land flowing with milk and honey" is preceded by a reminder of the promise to Abraham, Isaac, and Jacob and with a new promise, "My presence will go with you, and I will give you rest." Then in 2 Samuel 7 there is the covenant promise to David, "Your house and your kingdom shall be made sure forever before me; your throne shall be established forever." And in Jeremiah 31 there is the promise of a new covenant: "I will put my law within them and I will write it on their hearts; and I will be their God, and they shall be my people . . . for I will forgive their iniquity and remember their sin no more."

But grace is fulfillment as well as promise. The God of the Bible does not just talk the talk but also walks the walk. We see this nowhere more clearly than in Exodus 20. "I am the L ORD your God, who brought you out of the land of Egypt, out of the house of slavery; you shall have no other gods before me." This last clause is, of course, the beginning of the Ten Commandments. But before God commands, God delivers, and as God commands, God reminds of that redemption. We might say that in the Bible, *Heilsgeschichte* is first philosophy. Not only is ontology as the comprehension of reality by human understanding not primary, ethics isn't either. Prior to ethics and as its presupposition is not merely the promise of salvation but deliverance itself. Obedience is not a matter of fear but of gratitude. "There is no fear in love, but perfect love casts out fear; for fear has to do with punishment, and whoever fears has not reached perfection in love. We love because he first loved us."[42] But this can only occur where God is the God of the Bible and religion is not reduced to ethics. For Jews and Christians alike, the question posed by these reflections is not whether there is prevenient grace but whether the God of grace is a speaker who makes promises as well as commands and is an agent who keeps those promises.[43]

Inverse Intentionality. If one were to ask what Levinas's most fundamental contribution is, one would doubtless be buried under many well-formed and well-founded formulas. But for my money the answer would be: inverted intentionality, the idea that the most fundamental consciousness of . . . does not have the form of "I think",[44] in which the arrows of intentionality emanate from me in an act of *Sinngebung*[45] but rather that they emanate from another in an act whose target I am. The subject-object relation is reversed; the other is the subject and I am the object, and I come to awareness of myself and my world as always already defined by the gaze or the voice of another. I am not the one who names myself or defines the situation in which I find myself.

The subject cannot be described on the basis of intentionality, representational activity, objectification, freedom and will; it has to be described on the basis of the passivity of time. The temporalization of time, the lapse irrecuperable and outside of all will, is quite the contrary of intentionality. . . . Responsibility for the other, going against intentionality and the will, which intentionality does not succeed in dissimulating, signifies not the disclosure of a given and its reception, but the exposure of me to the other, prior to every decision . . . a traumatic hold of the other on the same . . . a fission in the mysterious nucleus of inwardness of the subject by this assignation to respond.[46]

Several brief observations about the structure of inverted intentionality are in order. First, there is a strong tendency for the voice to take priority over vision, the dominant metaphor for thought in the West since at least Plato. To be sure, I lose the ring of Gyges and, instead of being the sovereign subject who sees without being seen, I am the one seen without being able to see (thematize, represent) the one who sees me.[47] But especially in the context of Levinas's emphasis on language, conversation, and saying, both early and late, I become even more basically the one addressed.

Second, whether the voice by which I am called into being is exhausted by command and accusation or also expresses love by promising forgiveness, reconciliation, and even everlasting life becomes a fundamental theological question, both for Jews and for Christians.

Third, in either case, I am confronted by the alternative of fleeing the gaze and the voice of the other, like Adam and Eve in the garden of Eden, or responding, with Abraham, Jacob, Moses,[48] Samuel, Isaiah, and Mary, "Here am I [me voici]." The temptation to flee, or, philosophically speaking, to reassert the primacy of intentionality,[49] stems from the fact that the trauma of inverted intentionality is a decentering in which I lose the autonomy I otherwise cherish.[50] This will be as true when the voice speaks a promise as when it speaks in command and accusation. As the biblical characters just mentioned illustrate, the gracious promise of God gives me an identity I did not choose and an agenda I cannot carry out with my own resources. In the biblical world of divine promises, "ought" implies not "can" but rather "I cannot, but with God all things are possible."

Finally, it becomes clear that inverted intentionality signifies a distinctive structure for theology, both philosophical and confessional. Philosophically speaking, it points to phenomena that burst the boundaries of classical phenomenology and the evidences on which it seeks to found itself. To call them nevertheless "phenomena" is not to say that we must somehow make them fit the Husserlian or Heideggerian molds but rather to suggest that they bear witness to a "beyond" that "is reflected *within* the totality and history, *within* experience."[51] This will be true even if we do not name the other who sees and addresses us in keeping with any confessional tradition.

For confessional theology, inverted intentionality signifies the replacement of metaphysics in its onto-theological constitution with a theology of revelation, one whose foundation is the voice of another and whose telos can never be mere propositional propriety but must be obedience (love, justice, peace) and gratitude as the deepest motivation for obedience.

This may almost be a new structure for philosophical theology. But it is surely not a new structure for confessional theology, at least in Christian terms.[52] The combination of phenomenology and theology that makes up the work of Jean-Luc Marion is perhaps the most conspicuous current example.[53] But the theologies of Augustine, Aquinas, Luther, Calvin, Kierkegaard, and Karl Barth, to name only a few major figures, are surely theologies of revelation in which the believing soul is dramatically decentered both as knower and as agent.[54] Those who would theologize in any of these traditions can find in Levinas not only a kindred spirit but one from whom they can learn much about how and how not to speak about God.[55] And those who, in order to keep a place for religion in the university, would subsume theology under religious studies in such a way that God-talk neither presupposes conversion on the part of the author nor calls to conversion on the part of the reader—such scholars, from whatever tradition, might well consider more seriously the provocation to be found in Levinas.

Words of Peace and Truth

A-Dieu, Levinas

MICHAEL A. SIGNER

I take my subtitle from the eulogy delivered by Jacques Derrida upon the death of his friend and mentor Emmanuel Levinas.[1] It is true, as Kevin Hart states in the Introduction to this volume, that Levinas breaks the easy elision of the supernatural and the natural by transferring the burden of responsibility to human beings in their interaction with one another. It would seem that, while Levinas presses for the truth, his exorbitant description of the asymmetry between human beings dislodges the individual from any form of solipsism. To be responsive to the other who makes demands upon me would seem to create a permanent state of imbalance in human interaction. Egocentrism has no place in the Levinasian universe because the "I" is always subordinated to the Other. To stand under the judgment of Levinas's orbit is always to totter, waiting for the next demand. Does Levinas, then, lead us to an ethics that promotes Shalom or peace while demanding that we speak the truth to one another? The essays by Jews and Christians in this volume provide traces of an answer.

These closing remarks bid *adieu* to these essays, which Kevin Hart has called a "snapshot" of the dialogue between Christians and Jews in the forty years since the Second Vatican Council and *Nostra Aetate* (1965). I want to link some of the issues presented by these philosophers to the writings that have been central to theologians engaged in the same enterprise. I shall first examine some of the most explicit statements Levinas made about the post–*Nostra Aetate* relationship between Christianity and Judaism, followed by echoes of his work in two prominent Christian theologians, the writings of Pope John Paul II and Johann Baptist Metz, as well as two outstanding Jewish theologians, Rabbi Joseph B. Soloveitchik and Rabbi Abraham Joshua Heschel. I hope to demonstrate that there is a mutual attraction between the thought of Levinas and the theologians who have engaged in the renewed relationship between Jews and Christians after the Second Vatican Council.

Before turning to those who have contributed to what has been called the "literature of Jewish-Christian dialogue," it is significant to highlight at least two contributions that Levinas himself made to that literature. In a roundtable discussion, "Judaism and Christianity after Franz Rosenzweig," which included Bishop Klaus Hemmerle of Aachen and the Catholic theologian Bernhard Caspar, among others, Levinas made his most direct statements about his involvement with Catholicism.[2] He began in a rather ironic manner, claiming that he had discussed the theme of the conference with his friend the poet Claude Vigée in the form of a "confession," and quickly explained that he wanted to use the word in a "Jewish sense," because the Jew is free to state what is clear to him because "we have no synagogue giving an official line." In order to move from subtle allusions to specifically Christian ideas and their relationship to Judaism, Levinas utilized a word that might appear to be common to Christians and Jews but immediately provided the Jewish context. He then proceeded to explain that, in his childhood, Christianity was a "closed off world." It was "a world from which one could, as a Jew, expect nothing good."[3] His first knowledge of Christianity was gained from reading about the Inquisition. He claimed that his early years provided him with very little experience with Christians "because there was no contact between these two groups." When he read the gospels, he discovered a paradox: those passages that did not attack Judaism (Levinas said "me") taught things that were very familiar to him. Still later, Levinas discovered the concept of the Eucharist and explained "that the authentic Eucharist is actually in the moment when the other comes to face me." However, Levinas argues that people are also taught the very same lesson in Isaiah 58, where people are said to seek to know God's ways but God approaches only when people help the poor and feed the hungry. He concludes that "what remains unintelligible is not the man, but rather the entire Mystery. The whole theological theme—that remains closed off." In other words, Levinas's experience of the Eucharistic liturgy moved him to reconsider the theme of the nearness and approachability of God through his own understanding of Hebrew scripture. God approaches people when they move toward acts that engage the poor and the lost. Moreover, and perhaps most importantly for Levinas, Christianity did not deter people from doing what they did in the Holocaust. In that sense, "The message of the Gospels has been forever compromised for us by history."

The Shoah, or Holocaust, revealed two aspects of Christianity for Levinas. On the one hand, the power of baptism did not prevent Christians from engaging in atrocity. On the other hand, another aspect of Christianity appeared to him—*caritas, charité, misericordia*. He narrates an experience that occurred during a funeral in a church where he saw a picture of Hannah at prayer, who "speaks the prayer of the heart, the prayer of the soul. It is the concrete relation, the *mise-en-scène* of the soul." It was the proximity—the nearness of genuine prayer in the midst of the sadness of the funeral taking place within the church—that remained with him. As a result of that moment, Levinas felt "obligated to this *charité*." He would experience *charité* even more directly when his wife and daughter were saved in a cloister.

Levinas, then, stood outside the inner discourse of Christianity. The Mystery remains closed to him except insofar as he recognized links to his own scripture (which also is part of Christian scripture) and his experience of love, or *charité*. The paradox was revealed during the bleak period when he and his family experienced Nazi persecution. The Christian tradition did not prevent people from perpetrating acts of cruelty. However, the very same tradition provided his family with love and compassion in the cloister. From his perspective, it is in the lived relationships between human beings who are Jews and Christians that the opportunity arises to demonstrate their capacity to engage in acts of love and kindness toward others.

A decisive moment arrived when the Second Vatican Council opened the door for Christians to examine their past. By thoroughly examining the teachings that led to the long and sorry history of Christian persecution of Jews, the possibility for the important theme of love for others to assume its centrality might be realized. He pointed to the parallel between Judaism and the Christian teaching of *kenosis*: the universality of the common element in all human beings and the universality of what is *for* human beings. This led him to describe Christianity as "to live and die for everyone." However, he turns this notion back toward his own understanding of Judaism, claiming, "what is genuinely human is that part of being which being-a-Jew, an echo is in particular."[4] Ultimately, Levinas claims that: "What is important with us is not belief but doing (*Tun*). Doing certainly means behaving morally, but it also means doing ritual. As if that were two different things! What does it mean to believe? As the Psalms say—with your whole body (Ps. 35:9–10). Doing is an act of faith."[5]

It seems that Levinas is repeating Jewish claims about Christianity that had been part of the standard German-Jewish apologetic since Moses Mendelssohn and that remain popular in contemporary encounters between the communities: "Christianity is a religion of creed, and Judaism is a religion of deed." However, Levinas is more subtle when he defines "doing" as both ethics and ritual performance. In taking that position, he may appear to be redefining Christianity in terms of Judaism. Yet he is recalling a central claim of Christianity, where Jesus demands that his followers "Love one another as I have loved you" (John 15:12).

Levinas describes a dialogue between Jews and Christians that is grounded in their common humanity. On that basis each community engages in a search for profound echoes of that humanity in its respective tradition. He begins with his own rabbinic tradition, which is built upon the Hebrew scriptures, a text shared by Jews and Christians. The lens is always Judaism. In the course of the discussion, he responds to Bishop Hemmerle:

> I think everything you have said occurs to the Jew without Christ. That is the Jew's stubbornness: "For Thou art our Father, though Abraham does not know us and Israel does not acknowledge us" (Isaiah 63:16). Not all Jews get to this spiritual height, just as very few Christians imitate Christ. But it comes absolutely to the fore in Jewish spirituality. I mean Jesus without incarnation, without the drama of the cross. Yet there is still a moment in which what we share is still quite different. I mean that you begin with "God is love." The Jew begins with obligation. And the *happy end* is uncertain.[6]

In addition to these explicit comments about an ameliorated relationship between Judaism and Christianity, Levinas also participated, together with the chief rabbi of France, Renée Samuel Sirat, Rabbi Charles Touati, and Professor Georges Vajda, in a 1973 "Commission of Experts" that drafted a statement entitled "Christianity in Jewish Theology."[7] The report of the commission makes two major points. It indicates that the rejection of Christianity "might have been avoided." In a lengthy parenthesis, the report cites passages from the Babylonian Talmud that indicate a response to Jesus that revealed "a certain regret." The second point proclaims: "The Christians are not idolaters. They adore God who created the world and they have a certain number of beliefs in common with the Jews." This statement is followed by a lengthy citation of Jewish legal sources, ranging from antiquity through the medieval period, that provide a warrant for this statement. By his participation in this commission, Levinas appears to promote a foundational argument for Jews to open themselves to Christians and their religious faith, which appear as "transformations of Judaism and who help to prepare the way for the messiah." This statement is consistent with the views that he expressed about Christianity in "Judaism and Christianity after Rosenzweig." The report of the commission reflects the texts of the rabbinic tradition that do not describe Christianity as an idolatry that would constitute a threat to Judaism.[8] This approach reflects Levinas's consistently generous approach toward post–Second Vatican Council Christianity, where the dimension of *charité* toward Judaism was opened.

The reality of a more positive relationship between Jews and Christians was central to the papacy of John Paul II, who acknowledged Levinas as a significant influence on his work.[9] From the early years of his papacy, when he visited the concentration camp at Auschwitz, to his visit to the synagogue of Rome in 1985 and the climactic visit to Jerusalem in the jubilee year 2000, John Paul demonstrated that a profoundly mystical theology could also have a profound anthropological and experiential dimension that was open to Jews and Judaism. During his travels, Pope John Paul made a special point of visiting with members of the Jewish community.[10] After he moved from Krakow to Rome, he restored his childhood friendship with Jerzy Kluger—a Jew from Wadowice.[11]

The experience of the other human being in all its totality discloses itself consistently in his writings and, at the same time, in his prodigious capacity for friendship. John Paul acknowledges his debt to the "philosophers of dialogue," such as Martin Buber and Levinas, claiming: "The path passes not so much through being and existence as through people and their meeting with each other, through the 'I' and the 'Thou.' *This is the fundamental dimension of man's existence, which is always coexistence.*"[12]

The foundation of this "coexistence" links philosophical anthropology with biblical studies. There is a dual level of "I" and "Thou": first is the human level and everyday life, but there is also the level of the absolute and definitive, where "I" and "THOU" is "first the God of Abraham, Isaac, and Jacob, the God of the fathers, and then the God of Jesus Christ and the Apostles, the God of our faith." In the end, the Bible provides a paradigm of the community of God's people in communion with the Eternal "Thou."[13] As a warrant for this description, he singles out Levinas, "who represents a particular school of contemporary personalism and the philosophy of dialogue."

John Paul acknowledges the debt Levinas owes to Rosenzweig, who emphasizes the relationship between the human "I" and the divine, absolutely sovereign. In the same passage, John Paul makes explicit reference to God as the supreme legislator at Sinai, who made "Thou shalt not kill" a moral imperative. John Paul did not link the Sinai prohibition against murder to the teachings of Jesus in the New Testament. Rather, his reference to Levinas and his co-religionists who "deeply experienced the tragedy of the Holocaust" offers a remarkable formulation of this fundamental commandment of the Decalogue. "The human face and the commandment are ingeniously joined by Levinas and thus become a testimony for our age, in which governments; even democratically elected governments, sanction executions with such ease."[14]

The influence of Levinas among theologians of Jewish-Christian dialogue also had a strong influence in Germany. Johann Baptist Metz has been identified with coining the phrase *nach Auschwitz*, "after Auschwitz," to describe the period of the Nazi campaign to annihilate the Jews. In his brief but engaging essay "Facing the Jews," Metz refracts the ideas of Levinas about the necessity for Christians and Jews to take responsibility for one another after Auschwitz.[15] In the first thesis Metz proposes, "Christian theology after Auschwitz must—at long last—be guided by the insight that Christians can form and sufficiently understand their identity only in the face of Jews." He clarified the notion of "in the face of Jews" as directly addressing the human face of Jews. Metz was eager to avoid the Christian theological propensity for abstraction, emphasizing that "Judaism has no face and no eyes that can be remembered . . . it can be objectified as an outdated precursor of the history of Christianity . . . it can be objectified so that contemporary Jews need not be seen either as partners or (even) only as opponents."

Metz utilizes the reality of the Jewish face as an axial point to pry Christian systematic theology away from the use of "system concepts" and move it toward "subject concepts." The concrete historical memory of atrocities committed by baptized German Christians at Auschwitz must bring the concrete political and praxis reality of Christianity into question. The focus then is on a new orientation of the Christian "I" that opens itself to the reality of the Jewish human being, who has eyes, ears, and a face. Christian identity is thus formed through memory and narration or retelling. As they cease to erase or block the Jewish heritage of their religious tradition, Christians will discover a "being on the road, a being underway, even a being homeless, in brief: a discipleship." While Metz does not acknowledge the influence of Levinas in this essay, clearly there are intersections with the latter's ideas of the face and the power of the other to evoke a change in the orientation of the self.

In contrast to the direct influence of Levinas on Christians who promoted a rapprochement with Judaism, Rabbi Joseph B. Soloveitchik formulates an assessment of the boundaries that have to be maintained with respect to interreligious dialogue. On some level it is clear that Levinas and Soloveitchik concur about these boundaries. As we noted above, Levinas himself insists on maintaining a distance from the use of Christian theological formulations and reorienting explicitly Christian notions back to the Hebrew Bible. Soloveitchik's essay "Confrontation" appeared in 1964, before the final session of the Second Vatican Council.[16] However, the news that the Catholic Church was considering a reassessment of its relationship to Judaism was already public knowledge. Soloveitchik was the scion of a line of Talmudic scholars steeped in traditional Jewish learning, but he also had studied philosophy at the University of Berlin prior to World War I.[17]

Although it is unlikely that Soloveitchik knew or read the writings of Levinas, his essay offers some resonances with the notion of the face to face encounter between two religious communities. Drawing upon the two stories of creation in the book of Genesis, he develops two unique typologies of Adam: the first Adam is "irresponsive to the pressure of both the imperative from without and the 'ought' from within." The Adam of nature is hedonistic, desires pleasure, and is a beauty worshipper. However, Soloveitchik describes the Adam of the second creation narrative as coming suddenly to a stop, turning around, and "casting a contemplative gaze upon his environment." In that moment, the human being becomes aware of something beyond, "an outside that defines and challenges him." This new consciousness creates a distinction between what Soloveitchik calls "I awareness" and "non-I awareness."

At that point, the first human being receives the first divine command. Henceforth humanity lives with the continual choice between the freedom to exercise dominion and the profound commitment to live with the consciousness of the divine commandment. In the second narrative of Genesis, the human creature is described as "Confronted." Because of the new consciousness of the other, the "confronted human" experiences loneliness. This sense of isolation comes to an end with the gift of another human being, the woman. From that point onward, Adam lives in a double confrontation on both metaphysical and physical levels. The two human beings must communicate through language. However, language serves the dual purpose of joining humans and distancing them from one another. Soloveitchik utilizes the typology of individual human–divine and human-human communication at the level of communities. This notion leads him to conclude that "a confrontation of two faith communities is possible only if it is accompanied by a clear assurance that both parties will enjoy equal rights and full religious freedom." Jews experience a "double confrontation" vis-à-vis the larger culture in which they live. Their faith utilizes a unique covenantal language, which can be understood only by those who live within the realm of the covenant of the divine commandment. Jews are also co-citizens in a greater society and contribute to its productivity. This means that Jews discern "no contradiction between coordinating our cultural activities with all men and at the same time confronting them as members of another faith community." Within non-Jewish society, each individual sees himself under a double aspect: first, as a member of a creative cultural community in which all are committed to a common goal and, at the same time, as an individual living in seclusion and loneliness.

Central to the confrontation between Christians and Jews for Soloveitchik, then, is the distinction between culture and faith. At the level of culture, he is prepared to assert that "it is quite legitimate to speak of a cultural Judeo-Christian tradition." Within the sphere of culture, one can point to a continuing interchange between Jews and non-Jews in the shaping of Western culture. However, with respect to faith, the Jewish community is unique. No interreligious encounter of Jews with the majority community ought to demand changes or discussion of this unique covenantal language. He summarizes this argument in the following way:

> Hence, it is important that the religious or theological logos should not be employed as a medium of communication between two faith communities whose modes of expression are as unique as their apocalyptic experiences. The confrontation should occur not at a theological, but at a mundane level. There, all of us speak the universal language of modern man. As a matter of fact, our common interests lie not in the realm of faith but in that of the secular orders. The relationship between the two communities must be outer-directed and related to the secular orders with which men of faith come face to face.[18]

Soloveitchik and generations of his students have followed this culture/faith distinction with respect to encounters between Christians and Jews in the wake of the Second Vatican Council. These Jewish scholars insist upon an exclusion of topics that relate to matters where any theological theme might impinge upon the conversation. However, they have been very active in pursuing matters that relate to the improvement of social and moral conditions. There surely are echoes of images and language utilized by Levinas in his engagement with Christian theologians. He maintains a distance from describing "mystery," and he translates Christian concepts and terms into the framework of the Hebrew scriptures through his use of Isaiah to understand the message of Jesus in the Gospels. We can discover no element of apologetic for an accommodation of Judaism in its belief and praxis to Christianity. However, Levinas impresses upon both Jews and Christians their mutual responsibility for one another. While Soloveitchik insists upon the loneliness that is part of the double confrontation, Levinas would argue that the gaze upon the other is precisely what evokes the power that another human being exercises over the individual, irrespective of the intimacies of faith language. Rather than insist upon a simultaneous confrontation of isolation and community, Levinas presses his readers consistently to overcome their loneliness through an overwhelming sense of empathy with and responsibility for human suffering.

On the point of empathy and responsibility as integral to the encounter between Judaism and Christianity, we can turn to Rabbi Abraham Joshua Heschel. Heschel was actively engaged in interreligious dialogue and developed a significant relationship with Augustine Cardinal Bea, the promoter of Nostra Aetate, during the Second Vatican Council.[19] Two essays written by Heschel have become part of the standard bibliographies for Jewish-Christian dialogue: "No Religion is an Island" (1965) and "The God of Israel and Christian Renewal" (1967).[20] Heschel's writings and activities remain a significant resource and inspiration for those who study and teach interreligious dialogue.

There Heschel emphasizes that the moment is one of broader horizons and greater danger. "Religious isolationism is a myth. We must choose between interfaith and internihilism." In contrast to Soloveitchik, Heschel does not distinguish between issues of faith and issues in the world.

The refusal to create this dichotomy between religious communities is amplified in the essay by an anthropological approach, where the encounter with another human precedes religious commitment. Heschel proposes that a commonality among humans can be found in their physical presence: the face, the heart, the voice. This physical presence, in Heschel's view, is concurrent with the presence of a soul, which is disclosed in fears, hope, the ability to trust, and a capacity for compassion and understanding. Heschel insists on the concrete nature of the human being. He or she is not a specimen of the species called *Homo sapiens*. This human being who stands before me is a "disclosure of the divine." Human beings are the "holy of holies."

Therefore, "to meet a human being is to sense the image of God, the presence of God."

The human encounter takes place in a mixture of the physical and the spiritual. To put it in Heschel's terms, "fear and trembling, humility and contrition, where our individual moments of faith are mere waves in the endless ocean of humankind's reaching out for God, where all formulations and articulations appear as understatements."

Lest we think that Heschel proposes flattening differences between humans of different religious communities, he assures the reader that "We disagree in law and creed, in commitments which lie at the very heart of religious existence. We say 'no' to one another in some doctrines essential to us." Therefore, "interfaith must come out of the depth, not out of a void or the absence of faith."

Heschel proposes a taxonomy of levels for the interfaith encounter that allow humans to "reach out across the abyss." He describes four dimensions of religious existence, four necessary components of man's relationship to God:

1. Teaching, whose essentials are summarized in the form of a creed and serve as guiding principles in our thinking about matters temporal or eternal, the dimension of doctrine;
2. Faith, inwardness, the direction of one's heart, the intimacy of religion, the dimension of privacy;
3. The law, or the sacred act to be carried out in the sanctuary in society or at home, the dimension of the deed;
4. The context in which creed, faith, and ritual come to pass, such as the community of the covenant, history, tradition, the dimension of transcendence.

When Heschel analyzes each of these categories, he inserts a fifth analytic term into the list, "the deed," already foreshadowed in (3). It might be suggested that Heschel considers "the deed" to be prior to these categories because, first, it is preverbal and allows for humans to act in solidarity upon a problem "particularly as it relate[s] to social action." Rhetorical structure then allows him to indicate that actions in the world, taken in solidarity with one another, may precede the deed. However, they may also be the result of the shared teaching or sacred act that takes place within any single community. Action is possible before sharing across communal lines but may be strengthened precisely because the disclosure of how human beings embody their religious commitments takes place.

Again in contrast to Soloveitchik, Heschel addresses the question of "mutual esteem," and he therefore makes demands upon the Jewish community. He insists that Jews acknowledge the eminent role of Christianity in God's design for the redemption of humanity. Heschel cites Maimonides, who describes both Christianity and Islam as the divine disclosure of Israel's God to the nations of the world. However, his interpretation is more generous than Maimonides, because he specifically calls upon Jews to acknowledge that the Church made the Hebrew scriptures available to mankind. "This [contribution] we Jews must acknowledge with a grateful heart."

Heschel insists that mutual esteem between Jews and Christians becomes possible only with humility and contrition, because "There is no truth without humility, no certainty without contrition." Yet, while he urges Jews and Christians to reach out to one another in mutual esteem and respect, Heschel—like Soloveitchik—argues that holiness and piety grow in privacy.

At the conclusion of his essay, Heschel echoes a profound theme of Levinas. Dialogue between Jews and Christians serves to remind both communities of the presence of God in the world. In other words, it is precisely when Jews and Christians engage in dialogue with one another that they are presented with the interruption that allows "God to come to mind." It is not in the encounter between equals that God "enters" but in a profound asymmetry. The other has an absolute demand upon my behavior, but when a third party comes along, then what constitutes my "I" is compelled to enter into judgment. In that process of triangulation, a temporal duration, God enters the arena. Heschel's call for Jews and Christians to bring the presence of God into the world echoes the process that Levinas describes as possibility for both communities to "act" and bring the Infinite into the finite.[21]

The writings of Levinas make exorbitant demands on both Jews and Christians in the very sense that Kevin Hart has described. He seizes the lived moment of encounter between both communities to reiterate his long-developed phenomenological examination of the relationship between human beings to indicate that the post-Holocaust moment must become the moment of turning to one another—of recognizing the face of the other. He reverses the asymmetry of power implicit in the assumption that Western civilization speaks only Greek and its tradents are exclusively Christians. By translating the kenotic Christian moment into the demands of the prophetic books of the Hebrew Bible, Levinas also calls upon Jews to recognize that traces of their most intimate religious demands are at the heart of the Christian message. This demand upon Jews then replaces the asymmetry of power with an imbalance of the overwhelming humanity of the face of the Christian.

When we read Levinas expound passages from Isaiah we can discern that his message disorients Christians and Jews. Tugging them out of the comfort of their clear boundaries and self-definition, he pulls them into a third orbit: a shared message of responsibility and love for those who suffer. Insofar as each community risks this new asymmetry it moves into a broader capacity for understanding the compelling need for action (*Tun*) that emerges out of the self-orientation in each community. Levinas rejects the notion that particularity in religious language lacks compelling power. Rather, he reorients those who read and think and do toward the demand/command "Thou shalt not kill." The correlation between theologians writing after the Second Vatican Council and the literary legacy of Levinas will, together with the essays in this volume, move Jews and Christians to what he called a "question, prayer"—"a question-prayer that . . . would be anterior to all dialogue."[22]

Notes

Introduction: Levinas the Exorbitant, by Kevin Hart

1. Friedrich Nietzsche, *Thus Spake Zarathustra*, trans. Thomas Common (New York: Modern Library, 1917), 32.

2. See Emmanuel Levinas, *Of God Who Comes to Mind*, trans. Bettina Bergo (Stanford: Stanford University Press, 1998). On problems with international humanitarianism, see a book that appeared years after Levinas's death, although one that would have intrigued him, David Kennedy, *The Dark Sides of Virtue: Reassessing International Humanitarianism* (Princeton: Princeton University Press, 2004).

3. On several occasions Levinas refers to Vasily Grossman's *Life and Fate* (1959), in which small acts of goodness are lauded above systems of the Good. See, for example, "Interview with François Poirié," *Is It Righteous to Be? Interviews with Emmanuel Levinas*, ed. Jill Robbins (Stanford: Stanford University Press, 2001), 80–81.

4. Emmanuel Levinas, "From the Carefree Deficiency," *Of God Who Comes to Mind*, 50. Levinas quotes from Blanchot's "Discours sur la patience (en marge des livres d'Emmanuel Levinas)," *Le Nouveau Commerce* 30–31 (1975): 21. The passage is reprinted in Maurice Blanchot, *The Writing of the Disaster*, trans. Ann Smock (Lincoln: University of Nebraska Press, 1986), 1. Blanchot's sentence runs: "Penser le désastre (si c'est possible, et ce n'est pas possible dans la mesure où nous pressentons que le désastre est la pensée), c'est n'avoir plus d'avenir pour le penser." Levinas writes *dis-astre* for emphasis. Also see his *Ethics and Infinity: Conversations with Philippe Nemo*, trans. Richard A. Cohen (Pittsburgh: Duquesne University Press, 1985), 50. Levinas also quotes the same line

from Blanchot in "The Thinking of Being and the Question of the Other," *Of God Who Comes to Mind*, 120.

5. See, e.g., Bernard Carr, ed., *Universe or Multiverse?* (Cambridge: Cambridge University Press, 2007).

6. Levinas, "From the Carefree Deficiency," *Of God Who Comes to Mind*, 50.

7. See Franz Rosenzweig, *The Star of Redemption*, trans. Barbara E. Galli (Madison: University of Wisconsin Press, 2005), 18.

8. Emmanuel Levinas, *Totality and Infinity: An Essay on Exteriority*, trans. Alphonso Lingis (The Hague: Martinus Nijhoff, 1979), 28.

9. Alan Udoff and Barbara E. Galli, ed. and trans., "The New Thinking," in *Franz Rosenzweig's "The New Thinking"* (Syracuse: Syracuse University Press, 1999), 82.

10. See Husserl, *The Paris Lectures*, trans. and introd. Peter Koestenbaum (Dordrecht: Kluwer, 1998), and *Cartesian Meditations: An Introduction to Phenomenology*, trans. Dorion Cairns (The Hague: Martinus Nijhoff, 1977).

11. See Augustine, Sermon 88, in *Sermons* III, 51–94, *Sermons on the New Testament*, trans. Edmund Hill, ed. John E. Rotelle (Brooklyn: New City Press, 1991), 429; Gregory of Nyssa, *The Life of Moses*, trans. and introd. Abraham J. Malherbe and Everett Ferguson, pref. John Meyendorff (New York: Paulist Press, 1978), 59; John Chrysostom, "Homily III," *On the Incomprehensible Nature of God*, trans. Paul W. Harkins (Washington: Catholic University of America Press, 1984), 100. Pseudo-Dionysius Areopagite observes, "the manifesting image of the divine goodness—our great, completely radiant, and always lit sun which is the least echo of the good—illuminates all of those which are capable of sharing its light," *The Divine Names*, 697 C-D. See *The Divine Names and Mystical Theology*, trans. and introd. John D. Jones (Milwaukee: Marquette University Press, 1980).

12. See Bonaventure, *On the Reduction of the Arts to Theology*, trans. and introd. Zachery Hayes, vol. 1 of *Works of St Bonaventure* (St Bonaventure: Franciscan Institute, 1996).

13. Emmanuel Levinas, *Existence and Existents*, trans. A. Lingis (Dordrecht: Kluwer, 1988), 22. Levinas also notes that art is thought by way of light. He takes Heidegger to be exemplary here, and Blanchot to have departed from the tradition. See his "The Poet's Vision," *Proper Names*, trans. Michael B. Smith (Stanford: Stanford University Press, 1996), 137.

14. Jacques Derrida, "White Mythology: Metaphor in the Text of Philosophy," *Margins of Philosophy*, trans. Alan Bass (Chicago: University of Chicago Press, 1982), 251.

15. Emmanuel Levinas, "The Ruin of Representation," *Discovering Existence with Husserl*, trans. Richard A. Cohen and Michael B. Smith (Evanston, Ill.: Northwestern University Press, 1998), 118.

16. Levinas will, of course, argue against Buber that the relation between myself and the other person is asymmetric and not reciprocal. See his three essays

on Buber in *Outside the Subject*, trans. Michael B. Smith (Stanford: Stanford University Press, 1994).

17. Levinas, "Interview with Myriam Anissimov," *Is It Righteous to Be?*, 84.

18. See Christophe Bident, *Maurice Blanchot, partenaire invisible: Essai biographique* (Seyssel: Champ Vallon, 1998), 38–42.

19. Levinas, "Freiburg, Husserl, and Phenomenology," *Discovering Existence with Husserl*, 32.

20. Quoted by Jean-François Lavigne, "Lévinas avant Lévinas: L'introducteur et le traducteur de Husserl," in Emmanuel Levinas, *Positivité et transcendance, suivi de Lévinas et la phénoménologie*, ed. Jean-Luc Marion (Paris: Presses Universitaires de France, 2000), 53.

21. See, e.g., Levinas, "Interview with François Poirié," 32.

22. Maurice Blanchot, "Our Clandestine Companion," in Richard A. Cohen, ed., *Face to Face with Levinas* (Albany: State University of New York Press, 1986), 41.

23. See Edmund Husserl, *Logical Investigations*, trans. J. N. Findlay, 2 vols. (London: Routledge and Kegan Paul, 1970), vol. 2, chap. 2, "Consciousness as Intentional Experience."

24. See Levinas, "The Ruin of Representation."

25. See ibid., 121, and "Peace and Proximity," *Alterity and Transcendence*, trans. Michael B. Smith (London: Athlone, 1999), 139.

26. See Husserl, *Ideas Pertaining to a Pure Phenomenology and to a Phenomenological Philosophy, I: General Introduction to a Pure Phenomenology*, trans. F. Kersten (Dordrecht: Kluwer, 1983), § 58.

27. See Jean Wahl, *Existence humaine et transcendance* (Neuchatel: Éditions de la Bacconière, 1944), 129.

28. At first, in his early study *Time and the Other* (1947), Levinas figured the feminine as marking the otherness of the other person. This position is modified in *Totality and Infinity* and the texts that follow it. See his *Time and the Other*, trans. Richard A. Cohen (Pittsburgh: Duquesne University Press, 1987), 84–90.

29. Elizabeth S. Haldane and G. R. T. Ross, ed. and trans., *The Philosophical Works of Descartes*, 2 vols. (Cambridge: Cambridge University Press, 1931), 1:166.

30. Levinas appears to have adapted the notion from Maurice Merleau-Ponty. See Merleau-Ponty, *Phenomenology of Perception*, trans. Colin Smith (London: Routledge and Kegan Paul, 1962), 242.

31. See Emmanuel Levinas, *Otherwise than Being, or Beyond Essence*, trans. Alphonso Lingis (The Hague: Martinus Nijhoff, 1981), 45–47.

32. Paul Celan, *Breathturn*, trans. Pierre Joris (Los Angeles: Sun and Moon Press, 1995), 232–33.

33. See Wahl, *Existence humaine et transcendance*, 35. Also see in this regard Levinas's notion of *excendance*. See Levinas, *On Escape*, trans. Bettina Bergo (Stanford: Stanford University Press, 2003), 54.

34. *Otherwise than Being* differs from *Totality and Infinity* in several of its emphases. The later work makes no mention of "metaphysical desire," for instance, and develops instead a theory of subjectivity in which the other person is always and already within my subjectivity, behind my intentional consciousness, as it were.

35. Levinas, *Totality and Infinity*, 90. In this work "justice" means "ethics" rather than the distribution of resources called for by the advent of the third person.

36. Emmanuel Levinas, "Phenomenon and Enigma," *Collected Philosophical Papers*, trans. Alphonso Lingis (The Hague: Martinis Nijhoff, 1987), 73.

37. Levinas, *Totality and Infinity*, 80.

38. Levinas, *Otherwise than Being*, 183.

39. Quoted by Salomon Malka, *Emmanuel Levinas: His Life and Legacy*, foreword by Philippe Nemo, trans. Michael Kigel and Sonja M. Embree (Pittsburgh: Dusquesne University Press, 2006), 265.

40. Emmanuel Levinas, "Ethics of the Infinite," in Richard Kearney, *Dialogues with Contemporary Continental Thinkers: The Phenomenological Heritage* (Manchester: Manchester University Press, 1984), 68.

41. See Emmanuel Levinas, *The Theory of Intuition in Husserl's Phenomenology*, trans. André Orianne (Evanston, Ill.: Northwestern University Press, 1973), 142–51.

42. See Levinas, *Otherwise than Being*, 112, 101.

43. Ibid., 187n5. It is worth noting that Derrida titles an important section of his *Of Grammatology* "The Exorbitant: Question of Method." Whether Levinas influenced Derrida in this choice of word is uncertain. See *Of Grammatology*, trans. Gayatri Chakravorty Spivak (Baltimore: Johns Hopkins University Press, 1974), 157–65.

44. Levinas, *Of God Who Comes to Mind*, 89. Paul Ricoeur notes that hyperbole in Levinas is always Dosteyevskian. Malka quotes the remark in his *Emmanuel Levinas*, 194.

45. Levinas, "Dialogue: Self-Consciousness and Proximity of the Neighbor," *Of God Who Comes to Mind*, 148.

46. It needs to be kept in mind, however, that Levinas did not claim to be a deep reader of the New Testament. As he said in 1984, "I have never experienced the reading of the New Testament, since I live the reading of the Old Testament, in which I am not missing anything," "Discussion Following 'Transcendence and Intelligibility,'" *Is It Righteous to Be?*, 277.

47. See Levinas, "Foreword," *Of God Who Comes to Mind*, xi.

48. Levinas, "Interview with Saloman Malka," *Is It Righteous to Be?*, 97.

49. See Levinas, "Being-Toward-Death," *Is It Righteous to Be?*, 137.

50. See Augustine, Sermon 52 in *Sermons* III, 56–57, and Aquinas, *Summa Theologiae*, 1a. 3. 1. Also see Robert Sokolowski, *The God of Faith and Understanding: Foundations of Christian Theology* (Washington: Catholic University of America Press, 1995), 23–29.

51. Levinas, "The Vocation of the Other," *Is It Righteous to Be?*, 109.

52. Levinas, "Interview with François Poiré," 40–41.

53. Ibid., 69. See, in particular, Levinas, "'Between Two Words' (The Way of Franz Rosenzweig)," *Difficult Freedom: Essays on Judaism*, trans. Seán Hand (Baltimore: Johns Hopkins University Press, 1990). Also see Kevin Hart, "From *The Star* to *The Disaster*," *Paragraph* 30.3 (2007): 84–103.

54. See Levinas, "Judaism and Christianity after Rosenzweig," *Is It Righteous to Be?*, 157. Earlier drafts of the document had impressed Levinas even more.

55. Levinas, "Beyond Dialogue," *Alterity and Transcendence*, 87.

56. Emmanuel Levinas, "On Jewish Philosophy," *In the Time of the Nations*, trans. Michael B. Smith (Bloomington: Indiana University Press, 1994), 171–72.

57. See Levinas, *Ethics and Infinity*, 23.

Levinas Between German Metaphysics and Christian Theology, by Leora Batnitzky

NOTE: Parts of this essay appear in a somewhat different form in Leora Batnitzky, *Leo Strauss and Emmanuel Levinas: Philosophy and the Politics of Revelation* (Cambridge: Cambridge University Press, 2006).

1. Emmanuel Levinas, *Totality and Infinity: An Essay on Exteriority*, trans. Alphonso Lingis (Pittsburgh: Duquesne University Press, 1969), 28; *Totalité et Infini: Essai sur l'extériorité* (The Hague: Martinus Nijhoff, 1961), 14. Hereafter page numbers from both editions are cited, with the French following the English.

2. Robert Gibbs, *Correlations in Rosenzweig and Levinas* (Princeton: Princeton University Press, 1992); Richard Cohen, *Elevations: The Height of the Good in Rosenzweig and Levinas* (Chicago: University of Chicago Press, 1994).

3. Emmanuel Levinas, "'Between Two Worlds' (the Way of Franz Rosenzweig)," in *Difficult Freedom: Essays on Judaism*, trans. Seán Hand (Baltimore: Johns Hopkins University Press, 1990), 183; "Entre deux mondes: Biographie spirituelle de Franz Rosenzweig, suivi de Débats sur la conference de M. Levinas," in *La conscience juive: Données et débats*, ed. Eliane Amane, Amado Levy-Valensis, and Jean Halpérin (Paris: Presses Universitaires de France, 1963), 121–49. Page numbers hereafter refer only to the English translation.

4. Ibid., 194–95.

5. Ibid., 14.

6. Ibid., 13.

7. Ibid., 100.

8. Stéphane Mosès, *System and Revelation: Philosophy of Franz Rosenzweig*, trans. Catherine Tihanyi (Detroit: Wayne State University Press, 1992); *Système et révélation: La philosophie de Franz Rosenzweig* (Paris: Seuil, 1982).

9. Levinas, *Difficult Freedom*, 185.

10. Levinas, *Totality and Infinity*, 43 / 33.

11. Franz Rosenzweig, *The Star of Redemption*, trans. William W. Hallo (New York: University of Notre Dame Press, 1985), 156; *Der Stern der Erlösung*

(The Hague: Martinus Nijhoff, 1976), 174. Hereafter page numbers to both editions are give, with the German following the English.

12. Ibid., 183 / 204.

13. Ibid.

14. Emmanuel Levinas, *Otherwise than Being or Beyond Essence*, trans. Alphonso Lingis (The Hague: Martinus Nijhoff, 1981), 122; *Autrement qu'etre ou au-delà de l'essence* (The Hague Martinus Nijhoff, 1974), 195. Hereafter cited in both languages, with the French following the English.

15. Ibid., 109 / 172–73.

16. Samuel Moyn, "Judaism Against Paganism: Emmanuel Levinas's Response to Heidegger and Nazism in the 1930s," *History and Memory* 10, no. 1 (Spring/Summer 1998): 25–58.

17. Franz Rosenzweig, *Der Mensch und sein Werk: Gesammelte Schriften* (The Hague: Martinus Nijhoff, 1974–84), 3:690.

18. Ibid., 694.

19. Immanuel Kant, *The Critique of Pure Reason*, trans. Norman Kemp Smith, (New York: St. Martin's Press, 1965), A314/B370, p. 310.

20. Ian Hunter, *Rival Enlightenments: Civil and Metaphysical Philosophy in Early Modern Germany* (Cambridge: Cambridge University Press, 2001).

21. Leo Strauss, *Persecution and the Art of Writing* (Chicago: University of Chicago Press, 1988), 18–19.

22. See, e.g., J. B. Schneewind's *The Invention of Autonomy: A History of Modern Moral Philosophy* (Cambridge: Cambridge University Press, 1998). In many ways, Schneewind's study captures what Hunter's seeks to criticize, namely, the simultaneously ahistorical and teleological claim that moral philosophy culminates in Kant.

23. Martin Luther, *Disputation Against Scholastic Theology*, in *Martin Luther's Basic Theological Writings*, ed. T. F. Lull (Minneapolis: Fortress Press, 1989), 16, as quoted in Hunter, *Rival Enlightenments*, 34.

24. See, e.g., Lewis White Beck, *Early German Philosophy: Kant and His Predecessors* (Cambridge: Harvard University Press, 1969), citing Heido Oberman, *The Harvest of Mediaeval Theology* (Cambridge: Harvard University Press, 1963). Schneewind also describes Luther as an irrationalist; see *The Invention of Autonomy*, esp. 31.

25. Hunter, *Rival Enlightenments*, 35.

26. Ibid., 40–51.

27. Thomasius, *Summarischer Entwurf der Grundlehren, die einem Studioso Iuris zu wissen und auf Universitäten zu Lernen nötig sind* (Aalen: Scientia Verlag, 1979), 47–48, as quoted in Hunter, *Rival Enlightenments*, 52.

28. Ibid.

29. Ibid., 47–48, as cited in Hunter, *Rival Enlightenments*, 9.

30. Emmanuel Levinas, "Reflections on the Philosophy of Hitlerism," *Critical Inquiry* 17 (1990): 62–71.

31. Levinas, *Totality and Infinity*, 87 / 86.

32. Emmanuel Levinas, "Freedom and Commandment," in *Collected Philosophical Papers*, trans. Alphonso Lingis (Dordrecht: Martinus Nijhoff, 1988), 17.

33. Levinas, *Otherwise than Being*, 159 / 248.

34. Walter Sparn, *Wiederkehr der Metaphysik: Die ontologische Frage in der lutherischen Theologie des fruehen 17. Jahrhunderts* (Stuttgart: Calwer, 1976).

35. Hunter, *Rival Enlightenments*, 26.

36. Ibid., 56.

37. Ibid., 57.

38. Levinas, *Totality and Infinity*, 34–35, 23.

39. Walter Sparn, "Das Bekenntnis des Philosophen: Gottfried Wilhelm Leibniz als Philosoph und Theologe," *Neue Zeitschrift für Systematische Theologie* 28 (1986): 139–78.

40. Hunter, *Rival Enlightenments*, 47.

41. Emmanuel Levinas, *Du Sacré au Sainte* (Paris: Minuit, 1977), 156.

42. Emmanuel Levinas, *Ethics and Infinity: Conversations with Philippe Nemo*, trans. Richard A. Cohen (Pittsburgh: Duquesne University Press, 1985), 117.

43. See esp. Rosenzweig's discussion of "miracle" in *The Star of Redemption*, 97 / 107.

44. The necessity of recognizing our distance from the past is at the heart of Rosenzweig's hermeneutic approach to the translation of the Bible that he worked on with Martin Buber. See esp. Rosenzweig's and Buber's essays in *Scripture and Translation*, trans. Lawrence Rosenwald (Bloomington: Indiana University Press, 1994); *Die Schrift und ihre Verdeutschung* (Berlin: Schocken, 1936).

The Disincarnation of the Word: The Trace of God in Reading Scripture, by Robert Gibbs

1. Emmanuel Levinas, *Totality and Infinity*, trans. Alphonso Lingis (Pittsburgh: Duquesne University Press, 1969), 78; *Totalité et Infini* (The Hague: Martinus Nijhoff, 1961), 51.

2. Ibid., 197 / 171.

3. Ibid.

4. Ibid.

5. Ibid.

6. Ibid.

7. Emmanuel Levinas, *Beyond the Verse*, trans. Gary D. Mole (Bloomington: Indiana University Press, 1994), 109; *L'Au-delà du Verset* (Paris: Minuit, 1982), 135.

8. Ibid.

9. Emmanuel Levinas, *In the Time of the Nations*, trans. Michael B. Smith (Bloomington: Indiana University Press, 1994) 159; *A L'Heure des Nations* (Paris: Minuit, 1988), 71.

10. Emmanuel Levinas, "Meaning and Sense," trans. Alphonso Lingis, in *Collected Philosophical Papers* (The Hague: Martinus Nijhoff, 1987), 106; "La

signification et le sens," in "*L'Humanisme de l'autre homme* (Montpelier: Fata Morgana, 1973), 69.

11. Ibid., 106–7 / 69–70.
12. Ibid., 107 / 70.
13. Ibid.
14. Levinas, *Beyond the Verse*, 121 / 150.
15. Ibid., 122 / 150.
16. Ibid.
17. Ibid.
18. Ibid.
19. Ibid., 200 / 233.
20. Ibid.
21. Ibid.
22. Ibid.200–201 / 233–34.
23. Ibid., 201 / 234.

Secrecy, Modesty, and the Feminine: Kabbalistic Traces in the Thought of Levinas, by Elliot R. Wolfson

1. Charles Mopsik, "La pensée d'Emmanuel Lévinas et la Cabale," in *Emmanuel Levinas, Cahier de l'Herne*, ed. Catherine Chalier and Miguel Abensour (Paris: L'Herne, 1991), 428–41; Richard A. Cohen, *Elevations: The Height of the Good in Rosenzweig and Levinas* (Chicago: University of Chicago Press, 1994), 241–73; Oona Ajzenstat, *Driven Back to the Text: The Premodern Sources of Levinas's Postmodernism* (Pittsburgh: Duquesne University Press, 2001), 139–99; Catherine Chalier, *La trace de l'infini: Emmanuel Levinas et la source hébraïque* (Paris: Cerf, 2002), 77–106, 156–58, 189–201, 208–31. For a categorical rejection of the influence of kabbalah on Levinas, see the passing remark of Susan A. Handelman, *Fragments of Redemption: Jewish Thought and Literary Theory in Benjamin, Scholem, and Levinas* (Bloomington: Indiana University Press, 1991), 178.

2. I borrow this locution from Samuel Moyn, *Origins of the Other: Emmanuel Levinas Between Revelation and Ethics* (Ithaca: Cornell University Press, 2005), 182–86. See also François Raffoul, "Being and the Other: Ethics and Ontology in Levinas and Heidegger," in *Addressing Levinas*, ed. Eric Sean Nelson, Ante Kapust, and Kent Still (Evanston, Ill.: Northwestern University Press, 2005), 138–51.

3. Emmanuel Levinas, *Totality and Infinity: An Essay on Exteriority*, trans. Alphonso Lingis (Pittsburgh: Duquesne University Press, 1969), 77.

4. Ajzenstat, *Driven Back*, 146.

5. Catherine Chalier, "L'âme de la vie: Lévinas, lecteur de R. Haïm de Volozin," in *Emmanuel Levinas, Cahier de l'Herne*, ed. Catherine Chalier and Miguel Abensour (Paris: L'Herne, 1991), 387–98. For an extensive discussion of the religious philosophy of Ḥayyim of Volozhyn, see Norman Lamm, *Torah Lishmah: Torah for Torah's Sake in the Works of Rabbi Ḥayyim of Volozhin and His Contemporaries* (Hoboken, N.J.: Ktav Publishing House, 1989).

6. Emmanuel Levinas, *Beyond the Verse: Talmudic Readings and Lectures*, trans. Gary D. Mole (Bloomington: Indiana University Press, 1994), 154. See ibid., 157, where Levinas similarly asserts that Ḥayyim of Volozhyn was "suspicious of Hasidic mysticism."

7. Ibid., 155.

8. The decidedly nonmystical framing of the thought of Ḥayyim of Volozhyn is also evident in the way that Levinas philosophically reinterprets the treatment of prayer in the *Nefesh ha-Ḥayyim*. On this matter, see Emmanuel Levinas, "Prayer Without Demand," in *The Levinas Reader*, ed. Seán Hand (Oxford: Blackwell, 1989), 227–34, and the analysis in Tamra Wright, *The Twilight of Jewish Philosophy: Emmanuel Levinas' Ethical Hermeneutics* (Amsterdam: Harwood Academic Publishers, 1999), 128–33.

9. As suggested by Moyn, *Origins*, 190.

10. On the compatibility of philosophy and the Jewish hermeneutical tradition, see Jacob Meskin, "The Other in Levinas and Derrida: Society, Philosophy, Judaism," in *The Other in Jewish Thought and History: Constructions of Jewish Culture and Identity*, ed. Laurence J. Silberstein and Robert L. Cohn (New York: New York University Press, 1994), 402–23, esp. 417–19. Needless to say, many other scholars have weighed in on this topic. For a recent discussion with reference to several other key works, see James Hatley, "Levinas in the Jewish Context," *Philosophy and Rhetoric* 38 (2005): 173–89.

11. Emmanuel Levinas, *Nine Talmudic Readings*, trans. and introd. Annette Aronowicz (Bloomington: Indiana University Press, 1990), 4.

12. Jacques Derrida, *Writing and Difference*, trans. and introd. Alan Bass (Chicago: University of Chicago Press, 1978), 152–53. See also John Llewelyn, *Appositions of Jacques Derrida and Emmanuel Levinas* (Bloomington: Indiana University Press, 2002), 143–55; "Translator's Introduction" to *Nine Talmudic Readings*, x–xv; Michael J. MacDonald, " 'Jewgreek and Greekjew': The Concept of the Trace in Derrida and Levinas," *Philosophy Today* 35 (1991): 215–27.

13. Emmanuel Levinas, *Difficult Freedom: Essays on Judaism*, trans. Seán Hand (Baltimore: Johns Hopkins University Press, 1990), 15. See also idem, "L'actualité de Maïmonide," *Paix et Droit* 15, no. 4 (1935): 6–7; idem, *In the Time of the Nations*, trans. Michael B. Smith (London: Athlone Press, 1994), 170 and 172.

14. Levinas, *Difficult Freedom*, 21.

15. Ibid., 136.

16. Ibid., 175.

17. Levinas, *In the Time*, 144.

18. Levinas, *Difficult Freedom*, 176.

19. Moyn, *Origins*, 186–94.

20. Levinas, *Beyond the Verse*, xvi. In *Difficult Freedom*, 26, Levinas remarks that the notion of being chosen "can degenerate into that of pride but originally expresses the awareness of an indisputable assignation from which an ethics springs and through which the universality of the end being pursued involves the

solitude and isolation of the individual responsible." On the defense against the charge that the characterization of the Jews as the chosen people is an affront to Judaism's universalism, see *Difficult Freedom*, 176–77. For discussion of the paradoxical implication of Levinas's "universalization of Jewish particularity," see Moyn, *Origins*, 232–33.

21. Levinas, *Difficult Freedom*, 22.

22. Ibid., 109.

23. Ibid., 174.

24. On Levinas's attitude toward Christianity, see Georges Hansel, "Emmanuel Levinas et le christianisme," *Cahiers du Judaïsme* 13 (2003): 96–114.

25. Moyn, *Origins*, 117–18, 129–32, 141–51, 158–63, 167–68, 227–30, 256–57.

26. Emmanuel Levinas, "On the Jewish Reading of Scriptures," in *Levinas and Biblical Studies*, ed. Tamara Cohn Eskenazi, Gary A. Phillips, and David Jobling (Atlanta: Society of Biblical Literature, 2003), 26.

27. Elliot R. Wolfson, *Alef, Mem, Tau: Kabbalistic Musings on Time, Truth, and Death* (Berkeley: University of California Press, 2006), 49–54. See also Peter E. Gordon, *Rosenzweig and Heidegger: Between Judaism and German Philosophy* (Berkeley: University of California Press, 2003), 185–205.

28. Levinas, *Difficult Freedom*, 184.

29. Heidrun Friese, "Augen-Blicke," in *The Moment: Time and Rupture in Modern Thought*, ed. Heidrun Friese (Liverpool: Liverpool University Press, 2001), 73–90.

30. Shaun Gallagher, *The Inordinance of Time* (Evanston, Ill.: Northwestern University Press, 1998), 17–52.

31. Moyn, *Origins*, 213–14.

32. Tina Chanter, *Time, Death, and the Feminine: Levinas with Heidegger* (Stanford, Calif.: Stanford University Press, 2001), 140–69; Gallagher, *Inordinance of Time*, 108–26; David Wood, *The Deconstruction of Time* (Evanston, Ill.: Northwestern University Press, 2001), 382–83.

33. My language is indebted to Catherine Malabou, "La compulsion de révélation," in *Judéités: Questions pour Jacques Derrida*, ed. Joseph Cohen and Raphael Zagury-Orly (Paris: Galilée, 2003), 205–17. Many of the themes discussed in that study, which focuses on *le cas Derrida* (inspired by Levinas's interrogation of *le cas Spinoza*), resonate with categories I have independently applied to the study of Jewish esotericism, to wit, textual embodiment and poetic incarnation.

34. Levinas, "On the Jewish Reading," 28.

35. Emmanuel Levinas, *Otherwise than Being or Beyond Essence*, trans. Alphonso Lingis (Dordrecht: Kluwer, 1991), 140.

36. Levinas, *Totality and Infinity*, 79–81.

37. David G. Leahy, "Cuspidal Limits of Infinity: Secret of the Incarnate Self in Levinas," in *Rending the Veil: Concealment and Secrecy in the History of*

Religions, ed. Elliot R. Wolfson (New York: Seven Bridges Press, 1999), 209–48. See also Diane Perpich, "Sensible Subjects: Levinas and Irigaray on Incarnation and Ethics," in *Addressing Levinas*, ed. Eric Sean Nelson, Ante Kapust, and Kent Still (Evanston, Ill.: Northwestern University Press, 2005), 296–309.

38. Levinas, *Otherwise than Being*, 73–74.

39. Levinas, *In the Time*, 164.

40. Ibid., 144.

41. Fabio Ciaramelli, "Levinas's Ethical Discourse Between Individuation and Universality," in *Re-Reading Levinas*, ed. Robert Bernasconi and Simon Critchley (Bloomington: Indiana University Press, 1991), 83–105; Alex Klaushofer, "The Foreignness of the Other: Universalism and Cultural Identity in Levinas' Ethics," *Journal of the British Society for Phenomenology* 31 (2000): 55–73.

42. Levinas, *Nine Talmudic Readings*, 33.

43. Levinas, *In the Time*, 161.

44. Ibid., 162.

45. Ibid., 163. In his piece "The Spinoza Case," in *Difficult Freedom*, 109, Levinas notes that the "homage to Christianity" on the part of Rosenzweig "consists in showing it a different destiny to the one Judaism accomplishes."

46. Levinas, *In the Time*, 61–62. For a representative list of studies dealing with Jewish-Christian dialogue in Levinas, see Glenn Morrison, "Jewish-Christian Relations and the Ethical Philosophy of Emmanuel Levinas; 'At the Very Moment Where All is Lost, Everything is Possible,'" *Journal of Ecumenical Studies* 38 (2001): 316–29; Michael Schulz, "Der Beitrag von Emmanuel Levinas zum jüdisch-christlichen Dialog: Menschwerdung Gottes?" *Münchener Theologische Zeitschrift* 56 (2005): 148–61.

47. Levinas, *In the Time*, 171. For discussion of the implications of this scriptural injunction in Levinas, see Tamara Cohn Eskenazi, "Love Your Neighbor as an Other: Reflections on Levinas's Ethics and the Hebrew Bible," in *Levinas and Biblical Studies*, ed. Tamara Cohn Eskenazi, Gary A. Phillips, and David Jobling (Atlanta: Society of Biblical Literature, 2003), 145–57.

48. Levinas, *In the Time*, 168.

49. Levinas, *Difficult Freedom*, 109.

50. Levinas, *Totality and Infinity*, 256.

51. Levinas, *Otherwise than Being*, 137.

52. Ibid., 140.

53. Levinas, *Totality and Infinity*, 257.

54. Levinas, *Otherwise than Being*, 44, 46 (emphasis in the original).

55. Edith Wyschogrod, "Language and Alterity in the Thought of Levinas," in *The Cambridge Companion to Levinas*, ed. Simon Critchley and Robert Bernasconi (Cambridge: Cambridge University Press, 2002), 195–98.

56. Levinas, *Totality and Infinity*, 254. See Bettina Bergo, "Ontology, Transcendence, and Immanence in Emmanuel Levinas' Philosophy," *Research in Phenomenology* 35 (2005): 141–77.

57. Levinas, *Totality and Infinity*, 256.

58. Chanter, *Time, Death, and the Feminine*, 147–57.

59. Levinas, *Totality and Infinity*, 256–57.

60. This is not to deny the influence of the apophatic dimensions of Neoplatonic metaphysics on Levinas's thought or their resonance with it. For discussion of this topic, see: Theodore de Boer, "Levinas and Negative Theology," in *Théologie négative*, ed. Marco M. Olivetti (Padua: CEDAM, 2002), 849–59; Martin Kavka, *Jewish Messianism and the History of Philosophy* (Cambridge: Cambridge University Press, 2004), 129–92.

61. Levinas, *Totality and Infinity*, 259.

62. See Elliot R. Wolfson, "Facing the Effaced: Mystical Eschatology and the Idealistic Orientation in the Thought of Franz Rosenzweig," *Journal for the History of Modern Theology* 4 (1997): 39–81, esp. 51–55.

63. Levinas, *Totality and Infinity*, 254–55.

64. Ibid., 264.

65. Ibid., 257–58. And see the depiction of the caress in Emmanuel Levinas, *Time and the Other*, trans. Richard A. Cohen (Pittsburgh: Duquesne University Press, 1987), 89.

66. Levinas, *Totality and Infinity*, 260.

67. Ibid., 260–61.

68. Ibid., 261.

69. Ibid., 257.

70. Levinas, *Time and the Other*, 86.

71. Ibid., 85.

72. Levinas, *Nine Talmudic Readings*, 161–77. A host of scholars have written on the theme of the feminine in Levinas, but particularly germane to my own analysis here is the argument proffered by Hanoch Ben Pazi, "Rebuilding the Feminine in Levinas's Talmudic Readings," *Journal of Jewish Thought and Philosophy* 13 (2005): 1–32, esp. 6–10. For other relevant studies on the role of the feminine and Judaism in Levinas, see: Claire Elise Katz, *Levinas, Judaism, and the Feminine: The Silent Footsteps of Rebecca* (Bloomington: Indiana University Press, 2003); idem, "From Eros to Maternity: Love, Death, and 'The Feminine' in the Philosophy of Emmanuel Levinas," in *Women and Gender in Jewish Philosophy*, ed. Hava Tirosh-Samuelson (Bloomington: Indiana University Press, 2004), 153–75; idem, "Reinhabiting the House of Ruth: Exceeding the Limits of the Feminine in Levinas," in *Feminist Interpretations of Emmanuel Levinas*, ed. Tina Chanter (University Park: Pennsylvania State University Press, 2001), 145–70; Susan Shapiro, "'And God Created Woman': Reading the Bible Otherwise," in *Levinas and Biblical Studies*, ed. Tamara Cohn Eskenazi, Gary A. Phillips, and David Jobling (Atlanta: Society of Biblical Literature, 2003), 159–95. For more general discussions on the construction of the feminine in Levinas, see Luce Irigaray, "Questions to Emmanuel Levinas: On the Divinity of Love," in *Re-Reading Levinas*, ed. Robert Bernasconi and Simon Critchley (Bloomington: Indiana University Press, 1991), 109–18; idem, *An Ethics of Sexual Difference*, trans. Carolyn Burke and Gillian C. Gill (Ithaca: Cornell University Press, 1993),

185–217, reprinted in *Feminist Interpretations of Emmanuel Levinas*, ed. Chanter, 119–44; idem, "What Other Are We Talking About?" *Yale French Studies* 104 (2004): 67–81; Catherine Chalier, "Ethics and the Feminine," in *Re-Reading Levinas*, ed. Bernasconi and Critchley, 119–29; Tina Chanter, "Antigone's Dilemma," in *Re-Reading Levinas*, ed. Bernasconi and Critchley, 130–46; idem, "Feminism and the Other," in *Provocation of Levinas: Thinking the Other*, ed. Robert Bernasconi and David Wood (New York: Routledge & Kegan Paul, 1988), 32–56; idem, *Time, Death, and the Feminine*; idem, "Conditions: The Politics of Ontology and the Temporality of the Feminine," in *Addressing Levinas*, ed. Eric Sean Nelson, Ante Kapust, and Kent Still (Evanston, Ill.: Northwestern University Press, 2005), 310–37; Cohen, *Elevations*, 195–219; Alison Ainley, "The Feminine, Otherness, Dwelling: Feminist Perspectives on Levinas," in *Facing the Other: The Ethics of Emmanuel Levinas*, ed. Seán Hand (Surrey: Curzon, 1996), 7–20; Stella Sandford, *The Metaphysics of Love: Gender and Transcendence in Levinas* (London: Continuum, 2000); idem, "Levinas, Feminism, and the Feminine," in *The Cambridge Companion to Levinas*, ed. Simon Critchley and Robert Bernasconi (Cambridge: Cambridge University Press, 2002), 139–60; Paulette Kayser, *Emmanuel Levinas: La trace du féminin* (Paris: Presses Universitaires de France, 2000); Diane Perpich, "From the Caress to the Word: Transcendence and the Feminine in the Philosophy of Emmanuel Levinas," in *Feminist Interpretations of Emmanuel Levinas*, ed. Chanter, 28–52; Donna Brody, "Levinas's Maternal Method from 'Time and the Other' Through *Otherwise Than Being*: No Woman's Land?" in *Feminist Interpretations of Emmanuel Levinas*, ed. Chanter, 53–77.

73. Levinas, *Nine Talmudic Readings*, 165.

74. Ibid., 169.

75. Ibid.

76. Jacques Derrida, "At This Very Moment in This Work Here I Am," in *Re-Reading Levinas*, ed. Robert Bernasconi and Simon Critchley (Bloomington: Indiana University Press, 1991), 40.

77. See, most recently, Elliot R. Wolfson, *Language, Eros, Being: Kabbalistic Hermeneutics and Poetic Imagination* (New York: Fordham University Press, 2005), 46–110.

78. Levinas, *Difficult Freedom*, 35.

79. Levinas, *Totality and Infinity*, 257.

80. Ibid., 258.

81. Ibid., 259.

82. Ibid., 260.

83. Ibid., 262.

84. Ibid., 260.

85. Ibid., 118.

86. Levinas, *Time and the Other*, 87.

87. Levinas, *Totality and Infinity*, 257.

88. Wolfson, *Language, Eros, Being*, 128–35.

89. Restriction of the secret to the humble is implied in the statements in Babylonian Talmud, Qiddushin 71a, regarding either the transmission of the twelve-letter name of God to the modest priests or the transmission of the forty-two-letter name to the modest and humble middle-aged man. On the use of the term *ṣeni'u* to designate the hidden and incomprehensible nature of Ein-Sof, see *Zohar* 3:26b.

90. *Zohar* 1:50a, 122a. It is of interest here to compare the zoharic orientation to the following words of the Persian poet and mystic Rūmī, in *The Mathnawí of Jalálu'ddin Rúmí*, ed. and trans. Reynold A. Nicholson (London: Luzac & Co, Ltd, 1968), 5:3292–93, "Spiritual experience is (like) *the women who look modestly*: it shows no sign but to its possessor. That wine is (like) *the women who look modestly*, while these vessels screening it (from view) are like *the tents*" (emphasis in original). The wine, which is the secret or inner meaning, is compared to women who look in a modest way so that only their lovers can behold the hints, whereas the vessels that contain the wine are the external meaning that hides the secret from the unworthy.

91. See Nicole Loraux, *Tragic Ways of Killing a Woman*, trans. Anthony Forster (Cambridge: Harvard University Press, 1987), ix, 2–3, 21–22; Jocelyn Wogan-Browne, "Chaste Bodies: Frames and Experiences," in *Framing Medieval Bodies*, ed. Sarah Kay and Miri Rubin (Manchester: Manchester University Press, 1994), 24–42; Constant J. Mews, "Virginity, Theology, and Pedagogy in the *Speculum Virginum*," in *Listen, Daughter: The Speculum Virginum and the Formation of Religious Women in the Middle Ages*, ed. Constant J. Mews (New York: Palgrave, 2001), 23–24.

92. Monica H. Green, "From 'Diseases of Women' to 'Secrets of Women': The Transformation of Gynecological Literature in the Later Middle Ages," *Journal of Medieval and Early Modern Studies* 30 (2000): 5–39.

93. Ibid., 12.

94. Ajzenstat, *Driven Back*, 140.

95. *Nefesh ha-Ḥayyim*, 4.27, p. 273.

96. Mopsik, "La pensée d'Emmanuel Lévinas," 379; Ajzenstat, *Driven Back*, 178.

97. Levinas, *Totality and Infinity*, 104.

98. *Nefesh ha-Ḥayyim*, 3.11, pp. 176–78.

99. Levinas, *Beyond the Verse*, 166–67. See also *In the Time of the Nations*, 123, where Levinas explains the positing of myriad worlds according to the kabbalists as "the possibility of being-toward-being, of alterity." For the interpretation of Ḥayyim of Volozhyn's doctrine of *ṣimṣum* on the part of Levinas, see Chalier, "L'âme de la vie," 395–97.

100. *Nefesh ha-Ḥayyim*, 4.28, p. 274.

101. Levinas, *Difficult Freedom*, 66–67.

102. For reference to this seminal kabbalistic conception, see Elliot R. Wolfson, *Through a Speculum That Shines: Vision and Imagination in Medieval Jewish Mysticism* (Princeton: Princeton University Press, 1994), 376n174 and 388n226.

103. Levinas, *Beyond the Verse*, x, see also 154.

104. Levinas, *In the Time of the Nations*, 59.

105. Levinas, *Beyond the Verse*, 122.

106. *Nefesh ha-Ḥayyim*, 1.16, p. 55, and especially the note of the author's son on p. 87.

107. *Zohar* 1:39b; 3:68b, 71b, 75a, 98b.

108. Levinas, *Beyond the Verse*, 122.

109. Ibid.

110. Ibid., 212n6.

111. This is the depiction of Jesus in Colossians 1:15. On Christ's image as the icon of God, see Barbara C. Raw, *Trinity and Incarnation in Anglo-Saxon Art and Thought* (Cambridge: Cambridge University Press, 1997), 120–42. For an illuminating theological discussion of the idol, icon, and visibility of the invisible, see Jean-Luc Marion, *God Without Being: Hors-Texte*, trans. Thomas A. Carlson, with a foreword by David Tracy (Chicago: University of Chicago Press, 1991), 7–24. See also idem, *The Idol and Distance: Five Studies*, trans. and introd. Thomas A. Carlson (New York: Fordham University Press, 2001), 1–9; idem, "The Event, the Phenomenon, and the Revealed," in *Transcendence in Philosophy and Religion*, ed. James E. Faulconer (Bloomington: Indiana University Press, 2003), 87–105. A challenge to the possibility of a "pure" experience, the epistemological condition necessary for the appearance of the other, the giving/showing of the nonphenomenalizable, is presented by Marlène Zarader, "Phenomenality and Transcendence," in *Transcendence in Philosophy and Religion*, 106–19. For an alternative approach to the nexus of the image and idol in the theistic religious imagination, see Paul Mommaers, *The Riddle of Christian Mystical Experience: The Role of the Humanity of Jesus* (Louvain: Peeters Press, 2003), 5–41.

112. See, e.g., *Zohar* 3:170a; Isaiah Tishby, *Wisdom of the Zohar*, trans. David Goldstein (Oxford: Oxford University Press, 1989), 764–65.

113. Bezalel Safran, "Rabbi Azriel and Naḥmanides: Two Views of the Fall of Man," in *Rabbi Moses Naḥmanides (Ramban): Explorations in His Religious and Literary Virtuosity*, ed. Isadore Twersky (Cambridge: Harvard University Press, 1983), 75–106.

114. Moshe Idel, *Kabbalah: New Perspectives* (New Haven: Yale University Press, 1988), 184–85; Elliot R. Wolfson, "Mystical Rationalization of the Commandments in *Sefer ha-Rimmon*," *Hebrew Union College Annual* 59 (1988): 231–35.

115. The kabbalistic representation of Torah as body is supported by the idea that the 248 positive commandments correspond to the 248 limbs and the 365 negative commandments to the 365 sinews. This formulation is a modification of the tradition attributed to R. Simlai (Babylonian Talmud, Makkot 23b), according to which the 248 positive commandments correspond to the limbs and the 365 negative commandments to the days of the year. See Gershom Scholem, *On the Kabbalah and Its Symbolism*, trans. Ralph Manheim (New York: Schocken

Books, 1969), 128. It is worth noting, however, that the 248 limbs and 365 sinews are mentioned in Targum Pseudo-Jonathan to Genesis 1:27 as an explication of the "divine image" with which Adam was created. See Wolfson, "Mystical Rationalization," 231n78. Concerning Simlai's dictum with special reference to its impact on medieval Jewish philosophy, see Arthur Hyman, "Rabbi Simlai's Saying and Belief Concerning God," in *Perspectives on Jewish Thought and Mysticism*, ed. Alfred L. Ivry, Elliot R. Wolfson, and Alan Arkush (Amsterdam: Harwood Academic Publishers, 1998), 49–62.

116. Stephen D. Benin, *The Footprints of God: Divine Accommodation in Jewish and Christian Thought* (Albany: State University of New York Press, 1993), 147–62.

117. It is also possible to explain this matter in terms of the distinction between spiritual and corporeal substance, a Neoplatonic motif that was known by kabbalists in Provence and northern Spain. If we adopt this hermeneutical framework, we could say that for kabbalists the mystery of incarnation entails the transformation of the former into the latter, a transformation facilitated by the mystical conversion of the latter into the former. See discussion of a similar theme in Isma'ili Neoplatonism in Mohamed A. Alibhai, "The Transformation of Spiritual Substance into Bodily Substance in Isma'ili Neoplatonism," in *Neoplatonism and Islamic Thought*, ed. Parviz Morewedge (Albany: State University of New York Press, 1992), 167–77.

118. Wolfson, *Language, Eros, Being*, 190–260, esp. 242–46. On the use of poetry as a literary model to articulate an incarnational language from within a Christological framework, see Kathleen Norris, "A Word Made Flesh: Incarnational Language and the Writer," in *The Incarnation: An Interdisciplinary Symposium on the Incarnation of the Son of God*, ed. Stephen T. Davis, Daniel Kendall, and Gerald O'Collins (New York: Oxford University Press, 2002), 303–12.

119. The point is well grasped in the lecture "The Kabbalah," by Jorge Luis Borges, in his *Seven Nights*, trans. Eliot Weinberger, introd. Alastair Reid (New York: New Directions, 1984), 95–98: "The diverse, and occasionally contradictory, teachings grouped under the name of the Kabbalah derive from a concept alien to the Western mind, that of the sacred book. . . . The idea is this: the Pentateuch, the Torah, is a sacred book. An infinite intelligence has condescended to the human task of producing a book. The Holy Spirit has condescended to literature which is as incredible as imagining that God condescended to become a man." For extended discussion of the kabbalistic influence on Borges, see Saúl Sosnowski, *Borges y la Cabala: La búsqueda del verbo* (Buenos Aires: Pardés Ediciones, 1986).

120. For an exemplary study of this theme, see David Lyle Jeffrey, *People of the Book: Christian Identity and Literary Culture* (Grand Rapids, Mich.: William B. Eerdmans Publishing Company, 1996). On the attempt to forge a nexus between interpretation and incarnation, see Alla Bozarth-Campbell, *The Word's Body: An Incarnational Aesthetic of Interpretation* (University: University of Alabama Press, 1979). See also discussion of the metaphorical conjunction between

corpus and *verba* in Augustine by Jesse M. Gellrich, *The Idea of the Book in the Middle Ages: Language Theory, Mythology, and Fiction* (Ithaca: Cornell University Press, 1985), 116–22. According to this insightful analysis, Augustine draws a parallel between his own writing and the incarnational Word that became flesh so that saving words could be spoken and written. In short, Augustine's *verba* become the *corpus* to explain God's *Verbum*. For further elucidation of these points, see Calvin L. Troup, *Temporality, Eternity, and Wisdom: The Rhetoric of Augustine's Confessions* (Columbia: University of South Carolina Press, 1999), 82–116.

121. Anna Sapir Abulafia, "Jewish Carnality in Twelfth-Century Renaissance Thought," in *Christianity and Judaism: Papers Read at the 1991 Summer Meeting and the 1992 Winter Meeting of the Ecclesiastical History Society*, ed. Diana Wood (Oxford: Blackwell, 1992), 59–75.

Against Theology, or "The Devotion of a Theology Without Theodicy": Levinas on Religion, by Richard A. Cohen

NOTE: The quotation in the title of this essay comes from Emmanuel Levinas, "Diachrony and Representation"(1982), in Emmanuel Levinas, *Time and the Other*, trans. Richard A. Cohen (Pittsburgh: Duquesne University Press, 1987), 120.

1. Because Levinas does not aim to create a technical vocabulary (indeed, he aims at the reverse), there are many isolated exceptions in his use of the term *theology*. For instance, he uses it in such specific forms as "negative theology" and "onto-theology," the former expression referring primarily to its medieval usage by Islamic, Jewish, and Christian religious thinkers, and the latter expression being a neologism of Martin Heidegger, invented in order to speak of and criticize the Western historical forgetfulness of Being—or rather, of the "ontological difference"—by reducing it to an ontic entity, in this case "God," as was especially the case throughout the medieval period, though certainly not exclusively then. In the course of this essay, I will invoke Heidegger's term *onto-theology* and his critique of it in the name of "fundamental ontology."

2. However, one must beware of commentators who mistake Levinas's loose usage of the term *theology* for his strict usage. How does one tell the difference? It is a long story, a matter of integrity. Very simply, one must know how to read, which is to say, to learn.

3. Emmanuel Levinas, *Beyond the Verse: Talmudic Readings and Lectures*, trans. Gary D. Mole (Bloomington: Indiana University Press, 1994), 139. Levinas writes: "The strict formulas which, in the shape of dogmatic principles, would bring the multiple and sometimes disparate traces left in Scripture by the Revelation back to unity, are absent from the spirit of Judaism. . . . In Judaism, the formulations of articles of faith is a late philosophical or theological genre" (138–39).

4. I am using the word *performative* here in the sense J. L. Austin gave to this term in his William James Lectures delivered at Harvard University in 1955; see J. L. Austin, *How to Do Things with Words*, ed. J. O. Urmson (New York:

Oxford University Press, 1962). So, whether one is "sincere" or not (and how does one measure or determine such a thing from the outside?—one cannot, which is the problem, indeed the impossibility of verifying all religious "witnessing"), if at the appropriate moment in a wedding service, say, one pronounces the words "I do," then one *is* married (assuming that the other person in the marriage has also said "I do"). In another context, Levinas refers to Austin as "a master philosopher"; "Interview with Emmanuel Levinas: December 31, 1982," conducted by Edith Wyschogrod, in *Philosophy & Theology* 4, no. 2 (Winter 1989): 116.

5. Monotheism is based on a paradox that is irrational to rationalists but supra-rational to monotheists. See my article "Levinas and the Paradox of Monotheism," *Cahiers d'Études Levinassienes* 1, no. 2 (2003): 61–67; reprinted in *Emmanuel Levinas: Critical Assessments of Leading Philosophers*, ed. Claire Katz (London: Routledge, 2005), 3:59–71.

6. While Levinas opposes the "holy" to the "sacred," in English the term *sacred* is often used to mean precisely what Levinas means by the "holy." Levinas is not instituting an artificial or technical language; the careful reader must attend to what he means—in this case by "sacred" in contrast to "holy"—rather than becoming attached to words, which almost always have several meanings.

7. See Emmanuel Levinas, *Nine Talmudic Readings*, trans. Annette Aronowicz (Bloomington: Indiana University Press, 1990), pt. 2, pp. 91–197.

8. The three letter "root" of this word consists in the Hebrew letters Kof, Dalet, and Shin. See H. Schacter-Haham, *Compound of Hebrew* (Jerusalem: Kiryat-Sefer Ltd., 1989), 595–96, for a variety of related terms derived from the same root.

9. Levinas, *Nine Talmudic Readings*, 141.

10. Ibid., 152. The loss of identity is also Socrates' critique of defining knowledge in terms of perception in the *Theatetus*—"that nothing *is* one thing just by itself, but is always in process of becoming for someone" (157a). Levinas refers to this dialogue and its critique of Protagoras's claim that "man is the measure of all things" in *Totality and Infinity: An Essay on Exteriority*, trans. Alphonso Lingis (Pittsburgh: Duquesne University Press, 1969), 59. "I am surprised," Socrates says in the *Theatetus*, "that he [Protagoras] did not begin his *Truth* with the words, 'The measure of all thing is the pig, or the baboon, or some sentient creature still more uncouth' (161c)."

11. Levinas, *Nine Talmudic Readings*, 152.

12. See, esp., the Preface to Levinas, *Totality and Infinity*, 21–30.

13. Emmanuel Levinas, *The Theory of Intuition in Husserl's Phenomenology*, trans. André Orianne (Evanston, Ill.: Northwestern University Press, 1973), 157.

14. See ibid., 156.

15. Ibid., 157. I have discussed the debate between Husserl and Eugen Fink, and Levinas, regarding the origin of philosophy elsewhere; see Richard A. Cohen, *Ethics, Exegesis and Philosophy: Interpretation after Levinas* (Cambridge: Cambridge University Press, 2001), 91–95.

16. For a more detailed analysis of the intimate relation joining the positive and the negative in Levinas (and Rosenzweig), see my *Elevations: The Height of the Good in Rosenzweig and Levinas* (Chicago: University of Chicago Press, 1994), 162–72.

17. Emmanuel Levinas, *Otherwise than Being or Beyond Essence*, trans. Alphonso Lingis (The Hague: Martinus Nijhoff, 1981),120.

18. Ibid., 121.

19. Ibid.

20. "The Ruin of Representation" is the title of an article by Levinas published in 1959. It appears in English translation in a collection of Levinas's writings on Husserlian phenomenology: Emmanuel Levinas, *Discovering Existence with Husserl*, ed. Richard A. Cohen, trans. Richard A. Cohen and Michael B. Smith (Evanston, Ill.: Northwestern University Press, 1998), 111–21.

21. See Levinas, *Totality and Infinity*, 54 ("the posteriority of the anterior") and 24; see also n. 22 below.

22. This complex structure or movement, linking the universal work of justice and the exceptional exigencies of morality, which I call the "double dialectic" of Levinas's thought, is its most central and characteristic movement. It is a movement at once relative, dealing with the moral issues and options of today, and absolute, moved by what forever transcends today both in moral terms and in terms of justice or truth. To grasp this structure fully, we would have to contrast what Levinas calls the intersubjective time of "diachrony," which is the ultimate structure/movement of time, with the derivative structures of the spatial time of representation and the ecstatic temporality of existence. Such an exposition, however, exceeds the limits of the present paper.

23. Levinas, *Otherwise than Being*, 155.

24. Ibid., 197.

25. Levinas, Totality and Infinity, 40.

26. "Interview with Emmanuel Levinas: December 31, 1982," 107.

27. Emmanuel Levinas, *In the Time of the Nations*, trans. Michael B. Smith (Bloomington: Indiana University Press, 1994), 162. In Matthew 25, Jesus says, referring to the neglect of the needs of the hungry, the thirsty, the stranger, the naked, and the sick: "Truly I say to you, to the extent that you did it to one of these brothers of Mine, even the least of them, you did it to Me" (25:40) and "Truly I say to you, to the extent that you did not do it to one of the least of these, you did not do it to Me" (25:45).

28. In an interview with François Poirié, Levinas humorously comments on Pope John Paul II's historic visit to a synagogue in Rome, at which time he referred to Judaism as the Church's "elder brother." "Of course," Levinas comments, "in the Bible the elder brothers are often those who turn out badly." On a more serious note, in the same answer Levinas notes "that the executioners of Auschwitz must have all done the catechism, and that did not prevent them from committing their crimes" (*Is It Righteous to Be? Interviews with Emmanuel Levinas*, ed. Jill Robbins [Stanford: Stanford University Press, 2001], 70).

29. The first statement of this is by Saint Cyprian of Carthage, in his *Letters*, and reads: *Quia salus extra ecclesiam non est*. The Fourth Lateran Council (1215) declared: "There is but one universal Church of the faithful, outside which no one at all is saved." It is a doctrine repeated by too many popes to enumerate. In 1953, Pope Pius XII declared: "the Church alone is the entrance to salvation." The Dogmatic Constitution *Lumen gentium*, 14, of the Second Vatican Council declared: "They could not be saved who, knowing that the Catholic Church was founded as necessary by God through Christ, would refuse either to enter it, or to remain in it." The Congregation for the Doctrine of Faith in 2000 declared in *Dominus Iesus* that "it must be firmly believed that the Church, a pilgrim now on earth, is necessary for salvation, the one Christ is the mediator and the way of salvation." Protestant churches have also declared their own versions of this doctrine of exclusivity, though of course preferring their own versions of Christianity to that of the Roman Catholic Church.

30. The importance of this point can hardly be overemphasized. No dialogue is possible between a religion that (whatever its surface good manners) must convert its interlocutors and one that need not. One enables speech, respects the unsurpassable conditions of communication that Levinas's entire philosophy strives to articulate, while the other does not. For this reason Judaism (and Levinas) conceives of universality in terms of *shalom*, the peace or harmony of differences, where a plurality of voices and perspectives are necessary for "the truth," and hence where tolerance is a sign of an ever growing conviction and truth. Merold Westphal has put the point nicely: "each of us has good reason to think that we might learn something from the other, and this is the best rational for conversation that is not chatter but a serious meeting of the minds" ("Whose Philosophy? Which Religion?" in *Transcendence in Philosophy and Religion*, ed. James E. Faulconer [Bloomington: Indiana University Press, 2003], 28). The "serious" alternative, however, and unfortunately, is not chatter but the religion that must convert rather than converse. In the hubris of having nothing to learn, it prefers silencing others into submission rather than respecting different voices, each of which has its own contribution to the communal search for salvation. Its spiritual error, as I consider it, derives from a fundamental category mistake: displacing the universality of the religions (properly *shalom*) with the allegedly accomplished ideal truth values of mathematical science. While such universality makes perfect sense in science (but there as an ideal subject to continual intersubjective verification and revision), when imported into religion and frozen in eternality it produces not peace or truth but violence and totalitarianism. Instead of celebrating differences, and in this way celebrating Creation, it would eradicate them. Because he thought Christian theology incapable of genuine conversation, Rabbi Joseph Soloveitchik, perhaps the preeminent "modern orthodox" rabbi of the twentieth century, argued that "inter-faith" dialogue with Christianity was simply not possible (though he continued to endorse joint efforts for social causes). For more on these different forms of universality, see my article "Benamozegh and Levinas on Jewish Universalism," in *Per Elia Benamozegh*, ed. Alessandro Guetta (Milan: Edizioni Thalassa De Paz, 2001), 89–105.

31. Levinas, *In the Time of the Nations*, 162.

32. Levinas, *Nine Talmudic Readings*, 87.

33. Martin Heidegger, "Phenomenology and Theology," in *The Piety of Thinking: Essays by Martin Heidegger*, ed. and trans. James G. Hart and John C. Maraldo (Bloomington: Indiana University Press, 1976), 9, 10, 11.

34. See my *Elevations*, 300–301, esp. n. 12.

35. In 1944 Levinas wrote that onto-theology, in contrast to fundamental ontology, produces merely narratives and myth. Ontic "theology is essentially history and mythology. This is why, in the matter of theology, *authority* guarantees truth" (in Jean Wahl, *Existence humaine et transcendence* [Neuchatel: Editions de la Baconnier, 1944], 136). He adds: "Heidegger therefore breaks with theology to the precise extent that he makes the distinction between the ontic and the ontological" (137; my trans.). Of course, Levinas rejects Heidegger's fundamental ontology for the same reason, ultimately, that he rejects so-called ontic theology: both remain disclosure.

36. Roger Burggraeve, *The Wisdom of Love in the Service of Love: Emmanuel Levinas on Justice, Peace, and Human Rights*, trans. Jeffrey Bloechl (Milwaukee: Marquette University Press, 2002). I cannot recommend this book too highly.

37. Jean-Luc Marion, *God Without Being*, trans. Thomas A. Carlson (Chicago: University of Chicago Press, 1991), 150–51.

38. See, e.g., Martin Heidegger, *The Question of Being*, trans. Jean T. Wilde and William Kluback (1956; rpt. New Haven, Conn.: College and University Press, n.d.).

39. Emmanuel Levinas, *Basic Philosophical Writings*, ed. Adriaan T. Peperzak, Simon Critchley, and Robert Bernasconi (Bloomington: Indiana University Press, 1996), 5.

40. Martin Heidegger, "On the Essence of Truth," trans. R. F. C. Hull and A. Crick, in Martin Heidegger, *Existence and Being*, ed. W. Brock (Chicago: Henry Regnery, 1970), 292–324.

41. The phrase comes from Dante, of course, but it is also the title Levinas uses for subsection four of "God and Philosophy," trans. Richard A. Cohen and Alphonso Lingis, in Emmanuel Levinas, *Collected Philosophical Papers*, ed. and trans. Alphonso Lingis (Dordrecht: Martinus Nijhoff Publishers, 1987), 153–73.

42. Levinas's position is, of course, close to that of the "Social Gospel" vision of Christianity; see, e.g., Walter Rauschenbusch, *A Theology for the Social Gospel* (1917; rpt. Nashville: Abingdon Press, 1978). I will cite only two of the many relevant claims made by Rauschenbusch in this book: "The Church is primarily a fellowship for worship; the Kingdom [of God] is a fellowship of righteousness. When the latter was neglected in theology, the ethical force of Christianity was weakened; when the former was emphasized in theology, the importance of worship was exaggerated" (134); "The establishment of a community of righteousness in mankind is just as much a saving act of God as the salvation of an individual from his natural selfishness and moral inability" (139–40).

43. Levinas, *Basic Philosophical Writings*, 8.

44. Ibid.

45. Ibid., 7.

46. Emmanuel Levinas, "Ideology and Idealism" (1973), trans. Sanford Ames and Arthur Lesley, in *The Levinas Reader*, ed. Seán Hand (Oxford: Basil Blackwell, 1989), 247.

47. Levinas, *In the Time of the Nations*, 171.

Is the Other My Neighbor? Reading Levinas Alongside Hermann Cohen, by Dana Hollander

NOTE: Research assistance on this project by Leo Stan is gratefully acknowledged.

1. Hermann Cohen's earliest work on "the neighbor" is "Love of the Neighbor in the Talmud" ("Die Nächstenliebe im Talmud"), which originated as expert-witness testimony at the so-called Marburg Anti-Semitism Trial of 1888, and his discussions of that topic extend to chaps. 8 ("The Discovery of Man as Fellowman") and 9 ("The Problem of Religious Love") of the posthumously published *Religion of Reason out of the Sources of Judaism*, trans. Simon Kaplan (Atlanta: Scholars Press, 1995); *Religion der Vernunft aus den Quellen des Judentums*, 2d ed. (Frankfurt am Main: J. Kauffmann, 1929; rpt. Wiesbaden: Fourier, 1978).

2. Hermann Cohen, "Gesinnung," *Jüdische Schriften* (Berlin: Schwetschke, 1924), 1:205–6. See the related argument in *Religion of Reason*, chap. 9, according to which love of God begins with love of the neighbor as the stranger.

3. Emmanuel Levinas, *Ethics and Infinity: Conversations with Philippe Nemo*, trans. Richard A. Cohen (Pittsburgh: Duquesne University Press, 1985), 105–6; *Ethique et infini: Dialogues avec Philippe Nemo* (Paris: Fayard / France-Culture, 1982), 111–12.

4. Emmanuel Levinas, "God and Philosophy," in *Of God Who Comes to Mind*, trans. Bettina Bergo (Stanford: Stanford University Press, 1998), 75; "Dieu et la philosophie" (1975), in *De Dieu qui vient à l'idée*, 2d ed. (Paris: Vrin, 1986), 123.

5. Emmanuel Levinas, "On Jewish Philosophy," trans. Michael B. Smith, in *Is It Righteous to Be? Interviews with Emmanuel Levinas*, ed. Jill Robbins (Stanford: Stanford University Press, 2001), 243–44; "Sur la philosophie juive," interview with Françoise Armengaud in *Revue de métaphysique et de morale* (July-September 1985), republished in *À l'heure des nations* (Paris: Minuit, 1988), 202.

6. Ibid. 246 / 204; trans. modified. Placement of the closing quotation mark has been modified from both the French transcription of this interview and the English translation.

7. The next few paragraphs also appear in my "Some Remarks on Love and Law in Hermann Cohen's Ethics of the Neighbor," special issue "The Ethics of the Neighbor," *Journal for Textual Reasoning* 4, no. 1 (November 2005).

8. Hermann Cohen, *Der Nächste: Vier Abhandlungen über das Verhalten von Mensch zu Mensch nach der Lehre des Judentums* (Berlin: Schocken, 1935).

9. Hermann Cohen, *Ethik des reinen Willens* (1904/1907), 5th ed., *Werke*, vol. 7 (Hildesheim: Olms, 1981), 216.

10. Immanuel Kant, *Kritik der praktischen Vernunft*, Akademie-Ausgabe 5:79. I am indebted to David L. Clark for having laid out some of these issues in Kant in his presentation to the Mellon Sawyer Seminar "The Ethics of the Neighbor" at UCLA, January 14, 2004.

11. Ibid., 5:82.

12. For a helpful explanation of Kant's concept of *Gesinnung*, see Henry E. Allison, *Kant's Theory of Freedom* (Cambridge: Cambridge University Press, 1990), 136–45.

13. On the difficulties of translating the Kantian term *Schwärmerei*, apparently also taken over by Cohen, into English, see Peter Fenves, "A Note on the Translation of Kant," in *Raising the Tone of Philosophy: Late Essays by Immanuel Kant, Transformative Critique by Jacques Derrida*, ed. Peter Fenves (Baltimore: Johns Hopkins University Press, 1993), x–xii.

14. Hermann Cohen, *Kants Begründung der Ethik*, 3d ed., *Werke*, vol. 2 (Hildesheim: Olms, 2001), 332–33.

15. In a piece he published to commemorate the centenary of Kant's death, Cohen underscores the "great difficulty" of Kant's notion of autonomy, which strikes a delicate balance between freedom and obedience to law—indeed, "overcomes" their opposition (Hermann Cohen, "Immanuel Kant: Zu seinem hundertjährigen Todestage [12. Februar 1904]," in *Allgemeine Zeitung des Judentums*, February 12, 1904, 76).

16. Hermann Cohen, "Innere Beziehungen der Kantischen Philosophie zum Judentum," in *Jüdische Schriften*, 1:292.

17. Cohen, *Ethik des reinen Willens*, 210–13.

18. Lev. 19:34; cited in ibid., 214.

19. Ibid., 216.

20. Ibid., 213.

21. Ibid., 218–19, 217.

22. Emmanuel Levinas, "Transcendence and Height" (1962), in *Basic Philosophical Writings*, ed. Adriaan T. Peperzak, Simon Critchley, and Robert Bernasconi (Bloomington: Indiana University Press, 1996), 26–27; "Transcendance et hauteur: Séance du 27 janvier 1962," *Bulletin de la Société Française de Philosophie* 56, no. 3 (July–September 1962): 106–7.

23. Ibid., 27 / 107–8, trans. modified.

24. Ibid., 27–28 / 108–9.

25. Emmanuel Levinas, *Totality and Infinity: An Essay on Exteriority*, trans. Alphonso Lingis (Pittsburgh: Duquesne University Press, 1969), 34–35; *Totalité et infini: Essai sur l'extériorité* (The Hague: Martinus Nijhoff, 1961), 4–5.

26. Ibid., 34 / 3, trans. modified.

27. Ibid., 76–77 / 49.

28. See, e.g., ibid., 77 / 49, 78 / 50, 215 / 190.

29. "The gaze that supplicates and demands . . . deprived of everything because entitled to everything, and which one recognizes in giving . . . this gaze is precisely the epiphany of the face as a face. The nakedness [*nudité*] of the face

is destitution [*dénuement*]. To recognize the Other is to recognize a hunger. To recognize the Other is to give" (ibid., 75 / 48).

30. Ibid., 78 / 50.

31. Ibid., 78 / 50–51. Cf.: "It is our relations with human beings . . . that give to theological concepts the sole signification they admit of" (ibid., 79 / 51).

32. Cf. Levinas, "Peace and Proximity" (1984), *Basic Philosophical Writings*, 166.

33. Hermann Cohen, "Der Nächste: Bibelexegese und Literaturgeschichte" (1914), in *Werke*, vol. 16, *Kleinere Schriften V, 1913–1915* (Hildesheim: Olms, 1997), 55–56.

34. K. O. Erdmann, "'Nosismus': Ein terminologischer Vorschlag," *Der Zeitgeist: Beiblatt zum "Berliner Tageblatt,"* no. 51 (December 22, 1913), 2. Cited in Cohen, "Der Nächste," 57.

35. Ibid.

36. Ibid., 57–59.

37. Emmanuel Levinas, "Language and Proximity," *Collected Philosophical Papers*, trans. Alphonso Lingis (Dordrecht: Martinus Nijhoff, 1987), 116; "Langage et proximité" (1967), *En découvrant l'existence avec Husserl et Heidegger*, 3d ed. (1974; Paris: Vrin, 1988), 225; original emphasis removed.

38. Ibid., 120 / 229.

39. Ibid., 117 / 227.

40. Ibid., 116 / 225.

41. Ibid., 116n6 / 225n1.

42. Emmanuel Levinas, *Otherwise than Being, or Beyond Essence*, trans. Alphonso Lingis (The Hague: Martinus Nijhoff, 1981), 86; *Autrement qu'être ou au-delà de l'essence* (The Hague: Martinus Nijhoff, 1974), 108–9.

43. Ibid., 86 / 109; 192n20 / 109n20; Levinas, "Language and Proximity," 120–21 / 230–31.

44. Levinas, *Otherwise than Being*, 86 / 109.

45. Levinas, "Language and Proximity," 119 / 229.

46. Ibid., 120 / 230.

47. Levinas, *Otherwise than Being*, 81 / 102.

48. Ibid., 81 / 102, trans. modified.

49. Ibid.

50. Levinas, "Language and Proximity," 122–23 / 232–33.

51. Levinas, *Otherwise than Being*, 81–82 / 103.

52. Ibid., 159 / 202. Cf. also ibid., 158 / 201: "The other is from the first the brother of all the other men. The neighbor that obsesses me is already a face, both comparable and incomparable, a unique face and in relationship with faces, precisely visible in the concern for justice." Among the insightful analyses of the significance of these pages of *Otherwise than Being* for Levinas's philosophy of ethics and politics—analyses that have helped inform my own understanding of this issue—are Robert Bernasconi, "The Third Party: Levinas on the Intersection of the Ethical and the Political," *Journal of the British Society for Phenomenology*

30, no. 1 (January 1999): 76–87; idem, "Wer ist der Dritte? Überkreuzung von Ethik und Politik bei Levinas," in *Der Anspruch des Anderen*, ed. Bernhard Waldenfels and Iris Därmann (Munich: Wilhelm Fink, 1998), 87–110; and Oona Ajzenstat, *Driven Back to the Text: The Premodern Sources of Levinas's Postmodernism* (Pittsburgh: Duquesne University Press, 2001), chap. 2, "The Bible and Prophecy."

53. Levinas, *Otherwise than Being*, 155 / 197.

54. Ibid., 156 / 198.

55. Ibid., 156 / 199.

56. Ibid., 157–58 / 200–201, trans. modified. Levinas's translation from Isaiah 57:19 thus differs from the one he gives in the passage from "God and Philosophy" quoted above. There it reads "Paix, paix à qui est loin et à qui est proche," whereas in the present passage from *Otherwise than Being* it reads, "Paix, paix au prochain et au lointain."

57. See, e.g., Hermann Cohen, "Die Nächstenliebe im Talmud: Ein Gutachten, dem Königlichen Landgerichte zu Marburg erstattet" (1888), in *Jüdische Schriften*, 1:148–50.

58. In the New Jewish Publication Society translation (2d ed., 1999): "When a stranger resides with you in your land, you shall not wrong him. The stranger who resides with you shall be to you as one of your citizens; you shall love him as yourself, for you were strangers in the land of Egypt." (In the New Revised Standard Version, "stranger" is translated as "alien.")

59. Cohen, "Die Nächstenliebe im Talmud," 158–59, and *Religion of Reason*, chap. 8: 115ff; *Religion der Vernunft aus den Quellen des Judentums*, chap. 8: 133 ff.

60. Emmanuel Levinas, "A Religion for Adults" (1957), *Difficult Freedom: Essays on Judaism*, trans. Seán Hand (Baltimore: Johns Hopkins University Press, 1990), 18; "Une religion d'adultes" (1957), *Difficile liberté: Essais sur le judaïsme*, 3d ed. (1976; Paris: Livre de Poche, 1984), 34.

61. Emmanuel Levinas, "Revelation in the Jewish Tradition," *Beyond the Verse: Talmudic Readings and Lectures*, trans. Gary D. Mole (Bloomington: Indiana University Press, 1994), 146–47, trans. modified; "La révélation dans la tradition juive" (1977), *L'Au-delà du verset: Lectures et discours talmudiques* (Paris: Minuit, 1982), 176–77.

62. Levinas, "Language and Proximity," 122 / 232.

"Love Strong as Death": Levinas and Heidegger, by Jeffrey L. Kosky

1. Emmanuel Levinas, *Otherwise than Being or Beyond Essence*, trans. Alphonso Lingis (Dordrecht: Kluwer Academic Publishers, 1991); 198n6 and 144.

2. Emmanuel Levinas, *Autrement que Savoir, Emmanuel Levinas* (Paris: Editions Osiris, 1988); 83 and 81.

3. Emmanuel Levinas, "Philosophy, Justice, and Love," *Entre Nous: Thinking-of-the-Other*, trans. Michael B. Smith and Barbara Harshav (New York: Columbia University Press, 1998), 108.

4. *Otherwise than Being*, 139.

5. Ibid., 101 and 47.

6. Ibid., 139 and 113.

7. Ibid., 102.

8. Ibid., 103; my emphasis.

9. Ibid., 142.

10. Ibid., 105.

11. Ibid., 106–7.

12. Ibid., 53.

13. Ibid., 101.

14. Ibid.

15. Ibid., 106–7.

16. Husserl, *Cartesian Meditations*, §6, cited in Emmanuel Levinas, " "From Conscience to Wakefulness: Starting from Husserl," in *Of God Who Comes to Mind*, trans. Bettina Bergo (Stanford: Stanford University Press, 1998), 22.

17. Ibid.

18. Ibid., 22, trans. modified.

19. I should note that in this particular essay Levinas separates the terms *apodicticity* and *certainty*. He still reads certainty as equivalent to adequate evidence, while admitting an apodicticity that would not appear in evidence and so would not be certain. I see no reason why we could not claim that apodicticity and certainty belong together in distinction to adequate evidence. My reasons for doing this will become more clear when we confront Heidegger's analysis of death, for Heidegger will speak of death's indefinite certainty as a certainty that does not arise for knowledge in adequate evidence. Levinas would speak of the apodicticity of death where Heidegger still uses the term *certain*.

20. Levinas, *Otherwise than Being*, 114.

21. Ibid., 126.

22. Ibid., 117.

23. Martin Heidegger, *Being and Time*, trans. John Macquarrie and Edward Robinson (San Francisco: Harper & Row, 1962); 32–33.

24. Ibid., 174.

25. Ibid., 173.

26. Ibid., 329.

27. Ibid., 303.

28. Ibid., 284 and 283.

29. Ibid., 294.

30. Ibid., 308.

31. Levinas, *Otherwise than Being*, 126.

32. Ibid., 20.

33. Levinas, *Entre Nous*, 128.

34. Ibid., 104.

35. Ibid., 167.

36. Ibid., 146.

37. Ibid., 145.

38. Ibid., 167–68.

39. Ibid., 146.

40. Ibid., 130.

41. Levinas, "Bad Conscience and the Inexorable," *Of God Who Comes to Mind*, 176.

42. Heidegger, *Being and Time*, 179 and 180.

43. Ibid., 231.

44. Jean Greisch, *Ontologie et temporalité* (Paris: Presses Universitaires de France, 1994), 235.

45. Heidegger, *Being and Time*, 234.

46. Levinas, *Otherwise than Being*, 141.

47. Ibid., 177.

48. Levinas, "Bad Conscience and the Inexorable," *Of God Who Comes to Mind*, 176.

49. On the phenomenology of a nonworldly signification of the religious, one could consult Michel Henry's *Paroles du Christ* (Paris: Seuil, 2002).

50. Levinas, "Diachrony and Representation," *Entre Nous*, 168.

51. Levinas, "Dialogue on Thinking-of-the-Other," ibid., 205.

52. I think of Kierkegaard and Rosenzweig, who both wrote beautifully on the noncontradiction of love and command. Both clearly influence Levinas on this point in ways that merit consideration. Whereas command might contradict ethics (assuming ethics is the realm of freedom and autonomy), it finds its home in love—hence Levinas's eventual adoption of the term *love*, in place of *morals* or *ethics*. Kierkegaard on commanded love that does not despair could clearly be read in opposition to Heideggerian anxiety. Ordinary love despairs when the beloved is gone or does not return it, as in Heidegger, where the loss of the being leads to anxiety. But, according to Kierkegaard, love does not slip into despair when its object is gone because love is commanded.

53. Levinas, "Nonintentional Consciousness," *Entre Nous*, 130–31.

54. Levinas, "Uniqueness," ibid., 194.

55. One might ask, as Merold Westphal did in a conversation about this paper: What is love that does not do something—at the very least, say "I love you"? My response to Westphal's question would be twofold. First, do I decide when and to whom I give love? Does interpreting love to mean, at the least, stating "I love you" mean that I love you and not you, this other and not that other? If so, would love be relativized by attributes or qualities of the other (race, gender, ethnicity) that would determine who is lovable and who is not? Would there be an I independent or separate from "I love," an I who, taking his distance from this passion, would make decisions about who to love based on detached observation and knowledge of others? I would remind this objector of Paul Ramsey's account of the story of the Good Samaritan in his *Basic Christian Ethics* (Louisville, Ky.: Westminster John Knox Press, 1950), 92ff: love does not ask who is my neighbor but turns the question around, directing it to me and

demanding that I go and act neighborly toward the first one on the scene. Second, I would suggest that perhaps "I love you" is a good translation of *me voici* as it is used in Levinas's very late writings. Both utterances can be read as testimonies, witnessing the claim that the other exercises over me. Like *me voici*, "I love you" is a response. I only pronounce these words in response to the passionate movement of love. In other words, I am moved to say "I love you." The words come to me, an inspiration, in love. Love, then, is not exactly or not only something I do; it is e-motion toward the other, in which the distinction between activity and passivity collapses.

56. Levinas, "From the One to the Other: Transcendence and Time," *Entre Nous*, 146.

57. Levinas, "Diachrony and Representation," ibid., 174.

58. Emmanuel Levinas, *Proper Names*, trans. Michael B. Smith (Stanford: Stanford University Press, 1998), 77.

59. Levinas, "From the One to the Other," *Entre Nous*, 146.

60. Here Levinas's thought of love could be compared with that of Kierkegaard, who emphasizes that commanded love does not despair over the loss or absence of its beloved but remains constant.

On Levinas's Gifts to Christian Theology, by Robyn Horner

1. "To me, the Other Person [*Autrui*] is the other human being" (Emmanuel Levinas, "Philosophy, Justice, and Love," *Entre Nous: Thinking-of-the-Other*, trans. Michael B. Smith and Barbara Harshav (New York: Columbia University Press, 1998), 110.

2. "Transcendence is passing over to being's *other*, otherwise than being. Not *to be otherwise*, but *otherwise than being*. And not to not-be" (Emmanuel Levinas, *Otherwise than Being, or Beyond Essence*, trans. Alphonso Lingis [The Hague: Martinus Nijhoff, 1981], 3).

3. In this he echoes a character in Dostoyevsky's novel *The Brothers Karamazov*: "we are all guilty for everything and everyone, and I more than all the others." While this phrase appears many times in his work, here we find it quoted in "Philosophy, Justice, and Love," *Entre-Nous*, 107, 105.

4. Emmanuel Levinas, "God and Philosophy," *Of God Who Comes to Mind*, trans. Bettina Bergo (Stanford: Stanford University Press, 1998), 55–57; *God, Death, and Time*, trans. Bettina Bergo (Stanford: Stanford University Press, 2000).

5. Levinas, *Otherwise than Being*, xlvii.

6. Levinas, "God and Philosophy," *Of God Who Comes to Mind*, 57.

7. "I always make a clear distinction, in what I write, between philosophical and confessional texts. I do not deny that they may ultimately have a common source of inspiration. I simply state that it is necessary to draw a line of demarcation between them as distinct methods of exegesis, as separate languages" (Richard Kearney and Emmanuel Levinas, "Dialogue with Emmanuel Levinas," *Face to Face with Levinas*, ed. Richard A. Cohen [Albany: State University of New

York Press, 1986], 18). See the discussion in Catherine Chalier, "Levinas and the Talmud," *The Cambridge Companion to Levinas*, ed. Simon Critchley and Robert Bernasconi (Cambridge: Cambridge University Press, 2002), 100–101. See also the observations by Jeffrey Kosky on the potential overdetermination of this distinction: Jeffrey L. Kosky, *Levinas and the Philosophy of Religion* (Bloomington: Indiana University Press, 2001), xix.

8. Kearney and Levinas, "Dialogue," 21; Levinas, "Philosophy, Justice, and Love," *Entre Nous*, 108. In *Ethics and Infinity*, Levinas explains further: "I have never aimed explicitly to 'harmonize' or 'conciliate' both traditions [i.e., biblical and philosophical thought]. If they happen to be in harmony it is probably because every philosophical thought rests on pre-philosophical experiences, and because for me reading the Bible has belonged to these founding experiences. It has thus played an essential role—and in large part without my knowing it—in addressing all mankind" (Levinas, *Ethics and Infinity: Conversations with Philippe Nemo*, trans. Richard Cohen [Pittsburgh: Duquesne University Press, 1985], 24).

9. "It is fundamental to Levinas's characterization of himself as thinker to disclaim the role of theologian. Even when asked to comment at a conference of Catholic intellectuals upon so patently theological an issue as the humanity and divinity of Jesus, he takes up the question as a problem from Husserlian phenomenology rather than as a question for theological speculation. His diffidence stems not from lack of familiarity with the ongoing concerns of theologians, but from a more fundamental dissent arising from his view of Jewish religiosity. // For Levinas, authentic Judaism conceptualizes itself in terms of moral interiority; the supernatural is not its primary concern" (Edith Wyschogrod, *Emmanuel Levinas: The Problem of Ethical Metaphysics*, 2d ed. [New York: Fordham University Press, 2000], 176–77).

10. Jill Robbins, "Tracing Responsibility in Levinas's Ethical Thought," in *Ethics as First Philosophy: The Significance of Emmanuel Levinas for Philosophy, Literature and Religion*, ed. Adriaan T. Peperzak (New York: Routledge, 1995), 179.

11. Kosky, *Levinas and the Philosophy of Religion*, xxi. Kosky maintains that scholars such as Robert Gibbs and Richard A. Cohen, in particular, see Levinas as a "Jewish philosopher."

12. Emmanuel Levinas, *Totality and Infinity: An Essay on Exteriority*, trans. Alphonso Lingis (The Hague: Martinus Nijhoff, 1979), 77–78. Levinas also refers to this as the "idea of infinity." On the question of the unthought theological constitution of *Totality and Infinity*, see Jacques Derrida, "Violence and Metaphysics," *Writing and Difference*, trans. Alan Bass (Chicago: University of Chicago Press, 1978), 79–153, and chap. 2 of Kosky, *Levinas and the Philosophy of Religion*.

13. See Levinas, *Totality and Infinity*: "infinity overflows the thought that thinks it" (25); "The idea of infinity hence does not proceed from the I, nor from a need in the I gauging exactly its own voids; here the movement proceeds from what is thought and not from the thinker" (61); "The infinite in the finite,

the more in the less, which is accomplished by the idea of Infinity, is produced as Desire—not a Desire that the possession of the Desirable slakes, but the Desire for the Infinite which the desirable arouses rather than satisfies" (50); "The idea of infinity, the overflowing of finite thought by its content, effectuates the relation of thought with what exceeds its capacity, with what at each moment it learns without suffering shock. This is the situation we call welcome of the face" (197). The quote given in the text is from p. 78.

14. Ibid., 78.

15. Ibid., 79. It is in light of this comment that we might interpret the "and" that Adriaan T. Peperzak suggests perpetuates the possible confusion of divine with human otherness in this work: "It [i.e., "alterity, non-adequate to the idea"] is understood as the alterity of the Other *and* of the Most-High" (ibid., 34, quoted in Adriaan T. Peperzak, *Beyond: The Philosophy of Emmanuel Levinas* [Evanston, Ill.: Northwestern University Press, 1997], 32; emphasis added.)

16. "To relate to the absolute as an atheist is to welcome the absolute purified of the violence of the sacred. . . . Atheism conditions a veritable relationship with a true God" (Levinas, *Totality and Infinity*, 77). Yet compare the comment "and there is no atheism in this way of not taking God for a term," made in the 1975 discussion that appears as "Questions and Answers" in Emmanuel Levinas, *Of God Who Comes to Mind*, 95. Compare the mention of atheism made in Emmanuel Levinas, "The Trace of the Other," in *Deconstruction in Context*, ed. Mark C. Taylor (Chicago: University of Chicago Press, 1986), 346. See also the discussion in Michael Purcell, "Gloria Dei, Homo Vigilans: Waking Up to Grace in Rahner and Levinas," *Louvain Studies* 21 (1996): 242–43. With regard to the violence of the sacred, we note that Levinas distinguishes between the sacred and the holy in very strong terms; see Emmanuel Levinas, *Nine Talmudic Readings*, trans. Annette Aronowicz (Bloomington: Indiana University Press, 1990) 141.

17. Levinas, *Totality and Infinity*, 77.

18. Ibid., 78.

19. See Marc Faessler, "L'intrigue du Tout-Autre: Dieu dans la penseé de Levinas," *Les Cahiers de La Nuit Surveillée: Emmanuel Levinas*, ed. Jacques Rolland, vol. 3 [LaGrasse: Éditions Verdier, 1984], 125).

20. On the pivotal role these texts play between *Totality and Infinity* and *Otherwise than Being*, see Roger Burggraeve, *The Wisdom of Love in the Service of Love: Emmanuel Levinas on Justice, Peace, and Human Rights*, trans. Jeffrey Bloechl (Milwaukee: Marquette University Press, 2003) 37; Peperzak, *Beyond*, 32.

21. "Signification is the Infinite, but infinity does not present itself to a transcendental thought, nor even to meaningful activity, but presents itself in the Other" (Levinas, *Totality and Infinity*, 207). See also Derrida's analysis of Levinas's writing on the face in *Totality and Infinity*, esp. "Violence and Metaphysics," 108ff.

22. Levinas, "The Trace of the Other," 355. The immemorial past is here characterized as "an irreversible past," something the traces of which "no

memory could follow," "perhaps eternity." Later he adds: "a trace is a presence of that which properly speaking has never been there, of what is always past" (358).

23. Ibid., 355–56. In my shorthand definition of the trace as a sign that signifies while breaking the knot of reference, I am not unaware that Levinas also says that the trace is "not a sign like any other." See the discussion in Wyschogrod, *Emmanuel Levinas*, 160–63. Levinas goes on to define the trace as follows: "a trace in the strict sense disturbs the order of the world. It occurs by overprinting. Its original signifyingness is sketched out in, for example, the fingerprints left by someone who wanted to wipe away his traces and commit a perfect crime. He who left traces in wiping out his traces did not mean to say or do anything by the traces he left. He disturbed the order in an irreparable way. He has passed absolutely. *To be* qua *leaving a trace* is to pass, to depart, to absolve oneself" ("The Trace of the Other," 357). With regard to illeity, he notes: "Through a trace the irreversible past takes on the profile of a 'He.' The *beyond* from which a face comes is in the third person. The pronoun *He* expresses exactly its inexpressible irreversibility, already escaping every relation as well as every dissimulation, and in this sense absolutely unencompassable or absolute, a transcendence in an ab-solute past. The *illeity* of the third person is the condition for the irreversibility" (ibid., 356). The description of "the he in the depth of the you"—illustrative but anachronistic here—is from the Lingis translation of "God and Philosophy," in Emmanuel Levinas, *Collected Philosophical Papers*, trans. Alphonso Lingis (Dordrecht: Martinus Nijhoff Publishers, 1987), 165.

24. Levinas, "The Trace of the Other," 359.

25. See the helpful commentary on this passage (undertaken in relation to its citation in "Enigma and Phenomenon") in Robbins, "Tracing Responsibility," 179ff, particularly in terms of its juxtaposition of the rabbinic commentary only noted by Levinas here but cited by him in "Revelation and the Jewish Tradition," which can be found in Emmanuel Levinas, *Beyond the Verse: Talmudic Readings and Lectures*, trans. Gary D. Mole (Bloomington: Indiana University Press, 1994), 44. See also Derrida, "Violence and Metaphysics," 108ff.

26. Emmanuel Levinas, "Enigma and Phenomenon," in *Emmanuel Levinas: Basic Philosophical Writings*, ed. Adriaan T. Peperzak, Simon Critchley, and Robert Bernasconi (Bloomington: Indiana University Press, 1996), 77.

27. Ibid., 71.

28. "A You is inserted between the I and the absolute He" (ibid., Levinas 77).

29. Ibid.

30. John Llewelyn, *The Genealogy of Ethics* (London: Routledge, 1995), 150.

31. Ibid., 149. Llewellyn reads Levinas through the prism of his relationship with Franz Rosenzweig. He suggests that Levinas retains the name of God "lest the silent return of the God of a reality behind the scenes be facilitated by the obliteration of His name" (160). See also the discussion in John D. Caputo, "Adieu-sans Dieu: Derrida and Levinas," in *The Face of the Other and the Trace*

of God: Essays on the Philosophy of Emmanuel Levinas, ed. Jeffrey Bloechl (New York: Fordham University Press, 2000), 300ff.

32. Levinas, *Otherwise than Being*, 149.

33. This is almost the grammatical third person and can be distinguished from the "third" of which Levinas speaks with regard to justice. See ibid., 150. In *Otherwise than Being, or Beyond Essence*, illeity is described in the following ways. "Illeity lies outside the 'thou' and the thematization of objects. A neologism formed with *il* (he) or *ille*, it indicates a way of concerning me without entering into conjunction with me." "The detachment of the Infinite from the thought that seeks to thematize it and the language that tries to hold it in the said is what we have called *illeity*." "The subject is inspired by the Infinite, which, as *illeity*, does not appear, is not present, has always already past, is neither a theme, telos nor interlocutor" (ibid., 12, 147, 148).

34. Ibid., 162.

35. Ibid., 94. Buried in the footnotes of this text (195–96n) is the important comment: "All the descriptions of the face in the three final studies of the second edition of our book *En découvrant l'existence avec Husserl et Heidegger*, which describe the very ambiguity or enigma of anarchy—the illeity of infinity in the face as the trace of the withdrawal which the infinite qua infinite effects before coming, and which addresses the other to my responsibility—remain descriptions of the non-thematizable, the anarchical, and, consequently, *do not lead to any theological thesis*" (my emphasis).

36. Ibid., 161: Lingis observes of this signification in response: "God, the Infinite, is properly neither designated by words nor even indicated or named, but borne witness to in the peculiar character of the 'Here I am,' a pure saying unconvertible into something put forth, said." Further: "Thus there is really not anything like evidence, or a certainty, of God. Not only is God invisible, not manifest in the cosmic order, but his command is inaudible, or audible only in my words. The force of God, the proximity of infinity, has all its inscription in my own voice. There is not even really a belief in God, which would supply for the inadequate evidence. Thus the proximity of God can be completely repudiated" (Alphonso Lingis, Translator's Introduction, in ibid., xl, xli).

37. Levinas, "God and Philosophy," 56.

38. Ibid., 64.

39. Ibid., 69.

40. Ibid.; *God, Death, and Time*, 224.

41. Levinas, "God and Philosophy," 73.

42. Ibid.

43. Ibid., 74–75, 75.

44. Ibid., 76–77. On questions of the order of relationship between the Infinite and ethics, see Kosky, *Levinas and the Philosophy of Religion* 172ff., esp. 182–83.

45. Levinas, "Philosophy, Justice, and Love," *Entre Nous*, 109–10.

46. Ibid., 110.

47. This point is reinforced in a different way in Kosky's discussion of the priority of the ethical over the theological (Kosky, *Levinas and the Philosophy of Religion*, 181ff).

48. Aronowicz, Translator's Introduction, *Nine Talmudic Readings*, xxiii.

49. Kearney and Levinas, "Dialogue," 18.

50. Nevertheless, note the ambiguity of the following: "Superiority does not reside in a presence in the world, but in an irreversible transcendence. It is not a modulation of the being of entities. As He and third person it is somehow outside the distinction between being and entities. Only a being that transcends the world can leave a trace" (Levinas, "The Trace of the Other," 358).

51. Cf. John Llewelyn's reading of *Otherwise than Being*, in *The Genealogy of Ethics*.

52. Levinas, "God and Philosophy," 77. "Transcendence as signification, and signification as the signification of an order given to subjectivity before any statement: a pure one-for-the-other. Poor ethical subjectivity, deprived of freedom! Unless this would be but the trauma of a fission of oneself come to pass in a venture risked with God or through God. But in fact even this ambiguity is necessary to transcendence. Transcendence owes it to itself to interrupt its own demonstration and monstration, its phenomenality" (ibid., 78). See also Levinas, *Otherwise than Being*, 12: "The trace left by the infinite is not the residue of a presence; its very glow is ambiguous."

53. Levinas, "God and Philosophy," 69; *God, Death, and Time*, 224. See Richard Kearney's, "Desire of God," where he develops this idea in terms of Derrida and the "monstrous," and the ensuing discussion between Caputo, Kearney, and Derrida in *God, the Gift, and Postmodernism*, ed. John D. Caputo and Michael Scanlon (Bloomington: Indiana University Press, 1999), 112–45. Kearney includes much of this material in Richard Kearney, *The God Who May Be: A Hermeneutics of Religion* (Bloomington: Indiana University Press, 2001), 73ff.

54. Kosky, *Levinas and the Philosophy of Religion*, 183.

55. "The impossibility of manifesting itself in an experience can be due not to the finite or sensible essence of this experience but to the structure of all thought, which is correlation. Once come into a correlation, the divinity of God dissipates, like the clouds that served to describe his presence. All that could have attested to his holiness, that is, to his transcendence, in the light of experience would immediately belie its own witness already by its very presence and intelligibility, by its chain of significations, which constitute the world" (Levinas, "Enigma and Phenomenon," 67).

56. "The *narrative* of religious experience, inasmuch as it is a narrative, does not shake what philosophy will say in purifying the narrative; therefore it could not disrupt the present whose fulfillment is philosophy. It is possible that the word 'God' could have come to philosophy from the religious. But philosophy understands the religious discourse in which the word 'God' is inscribed as composed of propositions concerning a theme, as invested by a meaning resting upon

unveiling or disclosure. The messages of the religious experience conceive no other significance or meaning. The religious revelation is already assimilated to the disclosure effectuated by philosophy. . . . It follows that the religious human being interprets what he has lived as experience, and as a consequence, he interprets God, whom he claims to experience, in terms of being" (Levinas, *God, Death, and Time*, 214–15). See also a similar passage in "God and Philosophy," 62. This includes the following: "The religious 'revelation' is henceforth assimilated in philosophical disclosure—*an assimilation that even dialectical theology maintains*" (my emphasis).

57. "He [the Infinite] is not numinous: the I who approaches him is neither annihilated on contact nor transported outside of itself, but remains separated and keeps its as-for-me. . . . Transcendence is to be distinguished from a union with the transcendent by participation" (Levinas, *Totality and Infinity*, 77). "What is the relationship which, while remaining one of the *more in the less*, is not transformed into the relationship in which, according to the mystics, the moth drawn by the fire is consumed in the fire? How can separate beings be maintained, and not sink into participation, against which the philosophy of the same will have the immortal merit to have protested?" (Levinas, "Philosophy and the Idea of Infinity," in *Collected Philosophical Papers*, 54, trans. modified). "The numinous or the Sacred envelops and transports man beyond his powers and wishes, but a true liberty takes offence at this uncontrollable surplus. The numinous annuls the links between persons by making beings participate, albeit ecstatically, in a drama not brought about willingly by them, an order in which they founder. This somehow sacramental power of the Divine seems to Judaism to offend human freedom. . . . The Sacred that envelops and transports me is a form of violence" (Emmanuel Levinas, *Difficult Freedom: Essays on Judaism*, trans. Seán Hand [Baltimore: Johns Hopkins University Press, 1990], 14). A number of writers react to Levinas's understanding of mysticism as dissolution in God. Note, e.g., David Tracy's comment: "Until Levinas shows phenomenologically (instead of simply asserting) that 'mysticism,' 'the sacred,' and 'paganism' are synonymous with idolatry, I shall remain unconvinced by his curiously undialectical analysis of these complex religious phenomena" ("Response to Adriaan Peperzak," in *Ethics as First Philosophy: The Significance of Emmanuel Levinas for Philosophy, Literature and Religion*, ed. Adriaan T. Peperzak [New York: Routledge, 1995], 197). On the background in *mitnagged* Judaism to Levinas's dislike of religious enthusiasm, see Burggraeve, *The Wisdom of Love*, 22–23. On a distinction we might draw in Levinas's thought between Christian and Jewish mysticism, note the comment: "in Jewish mysticism the faithful, in his approach to God, is like the moth that circles around the fire; it comes very close, but it never enters the fire. . . . All of Jewish mysticism is like this moth that does not burn its wings" (Levinas, "Questions and Answers," *Of God Who Comes to Mind*, 94).

58. Levinas, *Totality and Infinity*, 77. We may well ask what this implies for Levinas's use of the Bible—see the helpful discussion in Chalier, "Levinas and the Talmud," 104–5. On "faith and opinion," see Levinas, "God and Philosophy," 57.

59. Kearney and Levinas, "Dialogue," 18; Levinas, "God and Philosophy," 56.

60. Levinas, *Nine Talmudic Readings*; Merold Westphal, "Levinas's Teleological Suspension of the Religious," in *Ethics as First Philosophy: The Significance of Emmanuel Levinas for Philosophy, Literature and Religion*, ed. Adriaan T. Peperzak (New York: Routledge, 1995), 151–60.

61. Emmanuel Levinas, "The Idea of the Infinite in Us," *Entre Nous*, 220, 222.

62. Levinas, "Philosophy, Justice, and Love," 108. Levinas does not explicitly limit himself to criticizing Christian theology and refers more broadly to positive religions in general (thus introducing another question about whether or not "religion" and "theology" can be collapsed into the same thing; note the further complication of Levinas's use in other contexts of a quite specialized understanding of religion as relationship with the other). Nevertheless, it seems to me that his readings of theology are undertaken within a Judeo-Christian trajectory that is overlaid by the history of Western philosophy.

63. Levinas, *Beyond the Verse*, 138.

64. Levinas, "Philosophy, Justice, and Love," 110.

65. John Macquarrie, *Principles of Christian Theology*, rev. ed. (London: SCM, 1977), 1. Macquarrie's reflections on Levinas's philosophy and thought of God are largely negative: "Postmodernism in Philosophy of Religion and Theology," *International Journal for Philosophy of Religion* 50, nos. 1–3 (2001): 18.

66. See: Anthony J. Godzieba, "Ontotheology to Excess: Imagining God Without Being," *Theological Studies* 56 (1995): 3–20; Wayne J. Hankey, "Why Philosophy Abides for Aquinas," *Heythrop Journal* 42, no. 3 (2001): 329–48; John van den Hengel, "God With/out Being," *Method: Journal of Lonergan Studies* 12, no. 2 (1994): 251–79; G. Kalinowski, "Discours de louange et discours métaphysique: Denys l'areopagite et Thomas D'Aquin," *Rivista di Filosofia Neo Scolastica* 73 (1981): 399–404; Tony Kelly, "The 'Horrible Wrappers' of Aquinas' God," *Pacifica: Journal of the Melbourne College of Divinity* 9, no. 2 (1996): 185–203; John Macquarrie, review of Jean Luc Marion. *God Without Being*, in *The Journal of Religion* 73, no. 1 (1992): 99–101; Jean-Luc Marion, *God Without Being*, trans. Thomas A. Carlson (Chicago: University of Chicago Press, 1991); Jean-Luc Marion, *Dieu sans l'être*, 2d ed. (Paris: Presses Universitaires de France/Quadrige, 2002); John Martis, "Thomistic *Esse*—Idol or Icon? Jean-Luc Marion's God Without Being," *Pacifica: Journal of the Melbourne College of Divinity* 9, no.1 (1996): 55–68; Brian J. Shanley, "Saint Thomas, Ontotheology, and Marion," *The Thomist* 60, no. 4 (1996): 617–25. See also John D. Caputo, *Heidegger and Aquinas: An Essay on Overcoming Metaphysics* (New York: Fordham University Press, 1982). Caputo ultimately argues that Acquinas does not have a metaphysical conception of God. Acquinas understands metaphysics as the divine science based on a thinking of *ousia*, supplemented by ontology and by the knowledge of causes. See the Prologue to Thomas Aquinas, *Commentary on the Metaphysics of Aristotle*, trans. John P. Rowan, 2 vols. (Chicago: Henry

Regnery Company, 1961). Nevertheless, theologians argue that the being studied by metaphysics is *ens* (the being that beings have in common, or common being) rather than *esse* (the act of being, sheer being, what it means to be), which is Acquinas's primary name for God, except where *esse* provides the context for *ens*. Thus Marion quotes from Aquinas: "divine things do not belong to metaphysics as one of its objects; rather, they only intervene in metaphysics indirectly in the capacity of principles for its objects" (Marion, *God Without Being*, xxiii). Marion further argues that the Thomistic understanding of divine causality does not allow for any simple metaphysical retrieval of God: "after having reached God following the guiding thread of causality, he vigorously refused to conceive God according and subject to cause, in rejecting the pertinence of any *causa sui* and in leaving the divine *esse incausatum*" (Jean-Luc Marion, *In Excess: Studies of Saturated Phenomena*, trans. Robyn Horner and Vincent Berraud [New York: Fordham University Press, 2002], 8). In the same manner, one could argue that theologians like Rahner, Lonergan, and Macquarrie, while they think God in terms of Being, do not thereby simply think God as the highest being or cause. For Rahner, for example, God is infinite Being known as unthematized horizon. See, e.g., Karl Rahner, *Foundations of Christian Faith: An Introduction to the Idea of Christianity*, trans. William V. Dych (New York: Crossroad, 1992), 73. Macquarrie's understanding of God as Being is as follows: "Strictly speaking, however, one cannot say that God 'exists' in this way either, for if God is being and not *a* being, then one can no more say that God *is* than that being *is*. God (or being) *is* not, but rather *lets be*. But to let be is more primordial than to be, so that, as has already been said, being 'is' more 'beingful' than any possible being which it lets be; and this justifies us using such expressions as 'being is,' provided we remain aware of their logically 'stretched' character" (Macquarrie, *Principles*, 118). For all these writers, the relationship between divine being and the world could be summed up in Caputo's words: "We must find in God's relationship to the world not causality but presencing. For if God is in all things inasmuch as all things have *esse*, then God, from whom their *esse* is shared, is present to them. We must learn to think of God not as the cause of the world but as that fullness of presence which is intimately present to the Being of things" (Caputo, *Heidegger and Aquinas*, 283). The key to this whole argument seems to be, however, the nature of the relationship between *ens* and *esse*, and how this is known. John Martis argues: "*Esse* is the giver of Being; this Being in turn gives *esse* meaning *as* Being, but in a way that also gives *esse* meaning as other than Being. This last giving has in one sense, of course, only the 'shape' of a giving of *esse* as Being; nevertheless, within this shape, the meaning of *esse* as God is successfully indicated as non-identical with is meaning as Being." He continues: "the meaning of Being *generates the indication, as pre-apprehended, of a meaning which cannot in principle be expressed*—namely the meaning of uncreated *esse*" (Martis, "Thomistic *Esse*," 63–64). *Esse* is known, therefore, by an analogical predication that never reduces it to the univocal meaning evoked by Suárez and that is actually the focus of Heidegger's critique.

67. I include here claims about God that are made on the basis of a reading of the Bible.

68. See, e.g., work by Richard J. Beauchesne, Yves Bizeul, M.-T. Desouche, David F. Ford, Glenn Morrison, Michael Purcell, Michele Saracino, Steven G. Smith, and Graham Ward.

69. See, e.g., work by Marie Baird, Michael Barnes, J. F. Bernier, Roger Burggraeve, David F. Ford, J. F. Lavigne, David J Livingston, Anselm Kyongsuk Min, Glenn Morrison, F. Poche, Michael Purcell, Michele Saracino, Derek Simonn, J. P. Strandjord, Andrew Tallon, Gabriel Vahanian, Guy Vanderveldem M. Vannin Terry A. Veling, Stephen Webb, Krzystof Ziarek, Enrique Dussell, Juan Carlos Scannone, Lamberto Schuurman, J. F. Goud, and Josef Wohlmuth.

70. See, e.g., the work of Jean-Louis Chrétien, Stephen Curkpatrick, and Jean-Luc Marion.

71. Some would suggest that Eberhard Jüngel is the exception here. We also bear in mind the extent to which Levinas himself is criticized for his onto-theology. See chap. 2 of Kosky, *Levinas and the Philosophy of Religion*.

72. In *Mystery and Method: The Other in Rahner and Levinas* (Milwaukee: Marquette University Press, 1998), Michael Purcell reflects at length on the propriety of placing the two thinkers in dialogue.

73. Ibid., 239.

74. Ibid., 241.

75. Purcell, "Gloria Dei, Homo Vigilans," 255. This raises the question of whether or not theology is a precondition for ethics, which troubles Kosky and others.

76. "This absolute withdrawal of the Other, however, is not to be interpreted in terms of some theological *via negativa* in which one might seek a *Deus absconditus* whose very hiddenness is signalled in the face of the Other who thereby becomes a means on the way to some theological end" (ibid., 257).

77. In the penultimate sentence Purcell notes: "Levinas's deeper transcendental reflection on subjectivity reveals the subject to be constituted intersubjectively, that is, in a relationship of responsibility-*for*-the Other, a relationship sustained by the illeity of the Other which opens not only on to the whole of humanity, but ultimately to God" (ibid.). This seems to indicate an acceptance of the implications of Levinas's thought for theology. It might be argued that the sentence that follows, which brings the text back to its focus on subjectivity, deflects the reader from this conclusion, but it seems to me that Purcell has no issue with what Levinas implies.

78. Richard J. Beauschesne, "The Supernatural Existential as Desire: Karl Rahner and Emmanuel Levinas Revisited," *Église et théologie* 23, no.2 (1992): 221.

79. Ibid., 234.

80. Ibid., 236.

81. Chap. 9 of Kosky, *Levinas and the Philosophy of Religion*, argues that ethics is primary here.

82. Michele Saracino, *On Being Human: A Conversation with Lonergan and Levinas* (Milwaukee: Marquette University Press, 2003).

83. Michele Saracino, "Subject for the Other: Lonergan and Levinas on Being Human in Postmodernity," in *In Deference to the Other: Lonergan and Contemporary Continental Thought*, ed. Jim Kanaris and Mark J. Doorley (Albany: State University of New York Press, 2004), 66.

84. Ibid., 72.

85. Ibid., 66.

86. For an analysis of the problems associated with the terms *postmodernity*, *postmodernism*, and *the postmodern*, see Robyn Horner, *Jean-Luc Marion: A Theo- Logical Introduction* (Aldershot: Ashgate, 2005), 13–17. It appears that Saracino conceives of an era as well as a mood, and hence uses the word *postmodernity*.

87. Saracino, "Subject for the Other," 66–67. We find in a footnote: "Argu- ably it is unfair and inaccurate to label Lonergan as blatantly modern. For Lon- ergan is not modern in the sense that he blindly embraces rationalism; rather, he is modern in that his work is grounded in a concrete struggle to adequately engage human reason in order to achieve the common good," and further: "labeling Levinas as postmodern is somewhat unhelpful, for even as he seems to perform many postmodern theoretical moves, his intention is that of achieving justice, not of wavering in an abyss of relativism" (ibid., 85n6).

88. Ibid., 66, 67. Saracino explains, in the footnote cited immediately above, how she sees each thinker to be related to modernity. This analysis does not extend to their respective relationships to metaphysics as onto-theo-logy. The thinkers are to be compared in terms of their "orientation for the Other."

89. Ibid., 82.

90. In saying this I am not thereby arguing that "modern" to "postmodern" is the best basis for comparison. Given the limitations of the uses of "post- modern," I would prefer to locate the comparison in more complex terms of the modern, metaphysics, phenomenology, hermeneutics, and post-structuralism.

91. Ibid., 80.

92. Ibid., 82; emphasis in original.

93. Ibid. Here I am reducing what Saracino sets out as two points to one, but it seems to me that they both come down to the question of method.

94. Roger Burggraeve, "Responsibility Precedes Freedom: In Search of a Biblical-Philosophical Foundation of a Personalistic Love Ethic," trans. Vincent Sansone, in *Personalist Morals*, ed. Joseph A. Selling et al. (Louvain: Leuven Uni- versity Press, 1988), 109.

95. Ibid., 109–10.

96. Ibid., 120.

97. Ibid., 121.

98. Ibid., 121–28, 123, 131.

99. Ibid., 132.

100. We could say, without entering into theology to any extent other than it might be implied by a biblical or Talmudic hermeneutics.

101. See Jean-Luc Marion, *Being Given: Toward a Phenomenology of Givenness*, trans. Jeffrey L. Kosky (Stanford: Stanford University Press, 2002), 234–37. On the problems of referring to "revelation," see Robyn Horner, "Aporia or Excess: Two Strategies for Thinking r/Revelation," in *Derrida and Religion: Other Testaments*, ed. Kevin Hart and Yvonne Sherwood (London: Routledge, 2004), 325–36. It could also be argued that what Marion does fits better within the second application of Levinas's work, that is, that he uses various themes within Levinas's thought to open up certain theological ideas. Nevertheless, I would maintain that Marion's use of Levinasian perspectives is so fundamental to both his phenomenology and his theology that a structural consideration—even if here it can be undertaken as no more than a sketch—is warranted.

102. See his phenomenological trilogy: *Reduction and Givenness: Investigations of Husserl, Heidegger and Phenomenology*, trans. Thomas A. Carlson (Evanston, Ill.: Northwestern University Press, 1998), 1–3; *Being Given*; and *In Excess*. See also his *God Without Being*, esp. chaps. 2 and 3. On Levinas's relationship to phenomenology and Heidegger, see, e.g., Kearney and Levinas, "Dialogue," 13–15.

103. See Jean-Luc Marion, "From the Other to the Individual," trans. Robyn Horner, in *Transcendence: Philosophy, Literature, and Theology Approach the Beyond*, ed. Regina Schwartz (New York: Routledge, 2004), 43–59; *In Excess*, chap. 5; "The Face: An Endless Hermeneutics," *Harvard Divinity Bulletin* 28, no. 2–3 (1999): 9–10; *Prolegomena to Charity*, trans. Stephen E. Lewis (New York: Fordham University Press, 2002), chap. 4; *The Erotic Phenomenon*, trans. Stephen E. Lewis (Chicago: University of Chicago Press, 2007), §§20 and 24. For both similarities and differences between Marion and Levinas in this area, see Robyn Horner, "The Face as Icon: A Phenomenology of the Invisible," *Australasian Catholic Record* 82, no. 1 (January 2005): 19–28; idem, *Jean-Luc Marion*; and idem, "The Weight of Love," in *Counter-Experiences: Reading Jean-Luc Marion*, ed. Kevin Hart (South Bend, Ind.: University of Notre Dame Press, 2006), 235–51.

104. See esp. Jean-Luc Marion, "The Final Appeal of the Subject," trans. Simon Critchley, in *The Religious*, ed. John D. Caputo (Oxford: Blackwell, 2002) 131–44, and *The Erotic Phenomenon*.

105. This has already been extensively noted in Levinas; with regard to Marion, see esp. *On Descartes's Metaphysical Prism: The Constitution and the Limits of Onto-theo-logy in Cartesian Thought*, trans. Jeffrey L. Kosky (Chicago: University of Chicago Press, 1999).

106. See, e.g., the discussion in Jean-Luc Marion, "Christian Philosophy and Charity," *Communio* 17 (1992): 468–69, and Marion, *God Without Being*, 153ff. See also the incisive critique of Jean-Luc Marion, "They Recognized Him; and He Became Invisible to Them," *Modern Theology* 18, no. 2 (2002): 145–52, in Shane Mackinlay, "Eyes Wide Shut: A Response to Jean-Luc Marion's Account of the Journey to Emmaus," *Modern Theology* 20, no. 3 (2004): 447–56.

107. Cf. the comment in Marion's Preface to the American Edition of *Being Given*, ix.

108. See the final chapter, e.g., of Marion, *In Excess*.

109. Not all are in agreement on this point. See Christina M. Gschwandtner, "Ethics, Eros, or Caritas? Levinas and Marion on Individuation of the Other," *Philosophy Today* 49, no. 1 (2005): 70–87.

110. It could be argued that Levinas and Rahner are in some agreement on this point. See Karl Rahner, "Reflections on the Unity of the Love of Neighbor and the Love of God," *Theological Investigations* (London: Darton, Longman and Todd, 1969) 6:231–49. Purcell makes this observation in "Gloria Dei, Homo Vigilans," 259–60n180, and in *Mystery and Method*, 290. Marion does not ignore this dimension (see, e.g., "Amour de Dieu, amour des hommes," *Résurrection* 34 (1970): 89–96; *Prolegomena to Charity*; and chap. 6 of *The Erotic Phenomenon*), although he is often interested in love as it makes the other specific to me rather than in charity as such. For a discussion of love that took place between Levinas and Marion, see Guy Petitdemange and Jacques Rolland, eds., *Emmanuel Levinas: Autrement que Savoir* (Paris: Éditions Osiris, 1988).

111. On the question of Marion and knowing as loving, however, see Horner, *Jean-Luc Marion*, 66–71,135–34.

112. Jacques Derrida, in "Hospitality, Justice and Responsibility: A Dialogue with Jacques Derrida," in *Questioning Ethics: Contemporary Debates in Philosophy*, ed. Richard Kearney and Mark Dooley (London: Routledge, 1999), 80.

113. In terms of faith being a response to revelation, see Dermot Lane, *The Experience of God: An Invitation to Do Theology* (New York: Paulist, 1981), 38. On the double sense of revelation, see Gerald O'Collins and Mario Farrugia, *Catholicism: The Story of Catholic Christianity* (Oxford: Oxford University Press, 2004), 97.

114. Supporters of this position are as diverse as Thomas Aquinas and Blaise Pascal, but for anecdotal evidence on the role of reason in coming to faith, see the conversion story in C. S. Lewis, *Surprised by Joy* (London: Fount, 1998).

115. John D. Caputo, Kevin Hart, and Yvonne Sherwood, "Epoché and Faith: An Interview with Jacques Derrida," in *Derrida and Religion: Other Testaments*, ed. Kevin Hart and Yvonne Sherwood (London: Routledge, 2004), 44.

116. Levinas, "A Man-God?" *Entre Nous*, 53–60. The significant difference is, of course, that for Levinas God signifies in every act of responsibility, whereas Christians claim that God signifies uniquely in Christ. This is the very point about which Levinas complains: "How can I expect another to sacrifice himself for me without requiring the sacrifice of others? How can I admit his responsibility for me without immediately finding myself, through my condition as hostage, responsible for his responsibility itself?" (60).

The Prevenience and Phenomenality of Grace; or, The Anteriority of the Posterior, by Michael Purcell

1. See Emmanuel Levinas, "Loving the Torah More than God," in Z. Kolitz, *Yosl Rakover Talks to God* (London: Jonathan Cape, 1999), 80.

2. See Emmanuel Levinas, "Martin Buber and the Theory of Knowledge," in *Proper Names*, trans. Michael B. Smith (Stanford: Stanford University Press, 1996), 17–39.

3. Emmanuel Levinas, *Of God Who Comes to Mind*, trans. Bettina Bergo (Stanford: Stanford University Press, 1998), ix.

4. Karl Rahner, "Concerning the Relationship Between Nature and Grace," in *Theological Investigations* (London: Darton, Longman and Todd, 1961), 1:300.

5. Karl Rahner, "The Theology of the Symbol," in *Theological Investigations* (London: Darton, Longman and Todd, 1966), 4:242.

6. Karl Rahner, *The Church and the Sacraments* (London: Burns & Oates, 1964), 37.

7. See Jean-Luc Marion, *The Visible and the Revealed*, trans. Christina M. Gschwandtner and others (New York: Fordham University Press, 2008). Marion, reflecting on the relation between intention and intuition in Husserl (*Logical Investigations*, VII, §§ 40 and 63), notes "In other words, intention and signification surpass intuition and fulfillment. 'A surplus in signification [*ein Überschuss in der Bedeutung*] remains, a form that finds nothing in the phenomenon itself to confirm it,' because in principle 'the realm of signification is much wider than that of intuition.' Intuition remains essentially lacking, poor, needy, indigent" (27). , " Again, "Phenomenality is indexed according to intuition" (29); "intuition, which alone gives, is essentially lacking" (29); and "Phenomena suffer from a deficit of intuition, and thus from a shortage of givenness" (31).

8. Emmanuel Levinas, *Humanism of the Other*, trans. Nidra Poller (Urbana: University of Illinois Press, 2003), 40. I have deliberately used "other person" rather than "Other" as a translation of *Autrui*.

9. Emmanuel Levinas, *Otherwise than Being, or Beyond Essence* (The Hague: Martinus Nijhoff, 1981), 12–13.

10. Levinas, *Humanism of the Other*, 41.

11. Edith Wyschogrod, *The Ethical Metaphysics of Emmanuel Lévinas* (The Hague: Martinus Nijhoff, 1974), 147. Wyschogrod also refers to Heidegger's *Holzwege*: "Heidegger's idea becomes *religio* in Levinas's thought since there is no interrogation of being guided by traces but an instant upsurge of transcendence in the field of the other's presence" (ibid.).

12. Michael Purcell, "Gloria Dei, Homo Vigilans: Waking Up to Grace in Rahner and Levinas's," *Louvain Studies* 21 (1996): 229–60.

13. For more on the reduction to religion, see Jeffrey L. Kosky, *Levinas and Philosophy of Religion* (Bloomington: Indiana University Press, 2001).

14. The original quote from Irenaeus is *gloria Dei autem homo vivens*.

15. Michael Purcell, "The Natural Desire for the Beatific Vision: Desiring the Other in Levinas and 'La Nouvelle Théologie,'" *Philosophy and Theology* 9, no. 1–2 (1995): 29–48.

16. From R. S. Thomas's poem "Evans," in *Collected Poems: 1945–1990* (London: Phoenix Press, 2000), 74.

17. I place to the side a consideration of the theology of grace in terms of the saturated or excessive phenomenon, though this is important. It seems to me that Jean-Luc Marion has already made phenomenological and theological advances into this area that would contribute to a theology of grace.

18. Distinguishing illeity and the *il y a* is complex, since both are at the fringes of phenomenality, being characterized by nonappearance. It seems to me interesting that much of the reflection on illeity and the *il y a* in Levinas arises in relation to literature and its exploration of the human. William Young, for example, in "Otherwise than *Being John Malkovitch*: Incarnating the Name of God," *Literature and Theology* 18, no. 1 (March 2004): 95–108, draws attention to the question of identity and relates it to the idea of illeity in Levinas. In *Being John Malkovitch* one can get into another's head—the head of John Malkovitch—but in terms of illeity, the incarnate other person endlessly escapes me, and "Corporeality thus becomes a *surplus* of intentionality" (99). Existence as incarnate and intersubjective is key. Confronted by the other person, whose illeity defies denomination, my existence is not so much a "having-to-be" as a "having-to-say." The name of God, evacuated of all content, can be spoken only in terms of the enigmatic human, and incarnate justice toward the other person, who remains persistently and insistently "an uncertain epiphany." Thus is speech always a risk, hesitant and unsure of itself.

Similarly, Dan Mellamphy, in *A Look Anew at Beckett's Other Peg Modern Drama* 49, no. 4 (Winter 2006): 491–99, draws attention to Mother Pegg in Beckett's *Endgame*. Mother Peg is a "dramatis *non*-persona" who "*figurelessly functions*" (491) and who is the "the *non*-persona obscured by the persona" (491). Mother Pegg is the "ill-seen" and "ill-heard" illeity who is displaced and replaced by the other personae present in the play. She exists "by proxy" as an absent other, as a being lost to the play (*être manqué*). But such an existence remains "when everything knowable and sayable is eliminated" (492).

19. See Fabio Ciaramelli, "The Posteriority of the Anterior," *Graduate Philosophy Journal* 20, no. 2–21, no. 1 (1997): 409–25. Ciaramelli notes: "The paradoxical temporality by which the originary bursts open and turns out to be already constituted, in a movement consisting in itself preceding itself, thus lays out the structure and advent of subjectivity" (411).

20. Emmanuel Levinas, *Totality and Infinity: An Essay on Exteriority* (Pittsburgh: Duquesne University Press, 1969).

21. See Heinrich Denzinger and Adolf Schönmetzer, *Enchiridion Symbolorum et Definitionum et Declarationum de rebus fidei et morum* (Freiburg: Herder, 1965), 370–79.

22. Ibid., 396–97. English translation at: http://www.iclnet.org/pub/resources/text/history/council.orange.txt.

23. Karl Rahner, "Some Implications of the Scholastic Concept of Created Grace," *Theological Investigations* (London: Darton, Longman and Todd, 1961), 1:334.

24. Ibid., 1:335.

25. Karl Rahner, *Foundations of Christian Faith* (London: Darton, Longman and Todd, 1978), 120. This is, of course, akin to the metaphysics of desire that one finds in Levinas. While the Desirable is not fully grasped and remains exorbitant, it is not merely an external attraction but is constitutive of the subject *as* desire. (See *Totality and Infinity*, 33–35.)

26. Rahner, "Some Implications," 333–34n3.

27. Rahner, *Foundations*, 120.

28. Augustine, *De gratia et libero arbitrio,* xvii.

29. Levinas, *Totality and Infinity*, 54.

30. Emmanuel Levinas, *Existence and Existents, trans. Alphonso Lingis* (The Hague: Martinus Nijhoff, 1978), 68.

31. Levinas, *Totality and Infinity*, 54.

32. Ibid.

33. Ibid.

34. Ibid.

35. Ibid.

36. Ibid., 55.

37. Emmanuel Levinas, *Is It Righteous to Be? Interviews with Emmanuel Levinas*, ed. Jill Robbins (Stanford: Stanford University Press, 2001). The interview was given in 1992, 182.

38. Emmanuel Levinas, "God and Philosophy," *Collected Philosophical Papers*, trans. Alphonso Lingis (The Hague: Martinus Nijhoff, 1987), 165.

39. Levinas, *Otherwise than Being*, 67.

40. Ibid., 69, 191n3.

41. Ibid., 102.

42. Ibid., 101.

43. Ibid., 105.

44. Ibid., 123.

Profligacy, Parsimony, and the Ethics of Expenditure in the Philosophy of Levinas, by Edith Wyschogrod

1. Emmanuel Levinas, *Totality and Infinity: An Essay on Exteriority*, trans. Alphonso Lingis (Pittsburgh: Duquesne University Press, 1969); Emmanuel Levinas, "Substitution," in *Basic Philosophical Writings*, ed. Adriaan T. Peperzak, Simon Critchley, and Robert Bernasconi (Bloomington: Indiana University Press, 1996),79–95.

2. Emmanuel Levinas, *Otherwise than Being, or Beyond Essence*, trans. Alphonso Lingis (The Hague: Martinus Nijhoff, 1981).

3. Emmanuel Levinas, "A Man-God," in *Entre Nous: Thinking-of-the-Other*, trans. Michael B. Smith and Barbara Harshav (New York: Columbia University Press, 1998), 58. For a compact formulation of Judaism's reading of the Bible, see Emmanuel Levinas, "The Strings and the Wood: On the Jewish Reading of the Bible," in *Outside the Subject*, trans. Michael B. Smith (Stanford: Stanford University Press, 1987), 126–34. His "Franz Rosenzweig: A Modern

Jewish Thinker," *Outside the Subject*, 49–66, analyzing Rosenzweig's work, is suggestive of his own view of the affinities between Judaism and Christianity.

4. A detailed account of separation from the elemental and its outcomes can be found in Levinas, "Interiority and Economy," *Totality and Infinity*, 109–86. I shall not enter into the question of the feminine that emerges in this context, an issue that has received excellent extensive elaboration in the works of Catherine Chalier, Jill Robbins, Tina Chanter, and Claire Katz, to name a few. I retain masculine pronouns when they reflect Levinas's usage.

5. G. W. F. Hegel, *The Phenomenology of Mind*, trans. A. V. Miller (Oxford: Oxford University Press, 1977), 104–11.

6. Levinas, *Totality and Infinity*, 18.

7. See Pierre Bourdieu, *The Logic of Presence*, trans. Richard Nice (Stanford: Stanford University Press, 1990), 52.

8. Emmanuel Levinas, *On Escape*, introd. Jacques Rolland, trans. Bettina Bergo (Stanford: Stanford University Press, 2003), 69–71.

9. This is the position I take in *Emmanuel Levinas: The Problem of Ethical Metaphysics*, 2d ed. (New York: Fordham University Press, 2000), 22.

10. Levinas, *Totality and Infinity*, 62.

11. Ibid., 65.

12. Ibid., 198.

13. Ibid.

14. Robert Bernasconi, in "What Is the Question to Which Substitution Is the Answer?" in *The Cambridge Companion to Levinas*, ed. Simon Critchley and Robert Bernasconi (Cambridge: Cambridge University Press, 2002), writes: "Levinas is engaged in an ongoing polemic against Hobbes although Levinas never engages with Hobbes textually" (234).

15. Levinas, *Totality and Infinity*, 199.

16. Ibid.

17. Levinas, *Entre Nous*, 101–2.

18. Levinas, *Totality and Infinity*, 78ff; see Wyschogrod, *Emmanuel Levinas*, 106.

19. Levinas, *Otherwise than Being*, 58. In a 1982 conversation with Levinas, I asked whether there was a turning in his work from the perspective of *Totality and Infinity* to that of *Otherwise than Being*. To this he responded, "Je ne suis pas Heidegger."

20. Levinas, "Substitution," *Basic Philosophical Writings*, 80.

21. Ibid., 82.

22. Ibid.

23. Ibid., 83–84.

24. Ibid., 83.

25. See Edith Wyschogrod, "Levinas's Other and the Culture of the Copy," *Yale French Studies*, no. 104 (2004): 126–43; rpt. in Edith Wyschogrod, *Crossover Queries: Dwelling with Negatives, Embodying Philosophy's Others* (New York: Fordham University Press, 2006), 173–88.

26. Levinas, "Substitution," *Basic Philosophical Writings*, 84–86.

27. Ibid., 88.

28. Ibid., 90. The ethical relation cannot be limited to the intimacy of two, a difficulty Levinas finds in Martin Buber's account of the I– thou. He also sees Buber as failing to posit a requisite asymmetery in the relation between self and other, so that the other is higher than the self. See Levinas, "Philosophy, Justice, and Love," *Entre Nous*, 105. I consider their relation in *Emmanuel Levinas*, 142–45.

29. On the relation between Levinas and Heidegger in regard to the amphibology of being, see Jacques, Derrida's seminal reading of the links between Levinas and Heidegger concerning the *Seinsfrage*, the question of being, in "Violence and Metaphysics: An Essay on the Thought of Emmanuel Levinas," *Writing and Difference*, trans. Alan Bass (Chicago: University of Chicago Press, 1978), 79–154. John Llewellyn comments on this question in his "Levinas and Language," in *The Cambridge Companion to Levinas*, ed. Simon Critchley and Robert Bernasconi (Cambridge: Cambridge University Press, 2002), 125–27.

30. Levinas, *Otherwise than Being*, 40.

31. Ibid., 42.

32. Ibid., 43.

33. Ibid., 193n33.

34. Levinas, "Uniqueness," *Entre Nous*, 195.

35. Levinas, "Levy-Bruhl and Contemporary Philosophy," *Entre Nous*, 39–52. The influence of early-twentieth-century ethnographers upon Ernst Cassirer, Heidegger, and Levinas is extensive and has largely been unnoticed. See my "Fear of Primitives, Primitive Fears: Anthropology in the Philosophies of Heidegger and Levinas," in *Emotion and Postmodernism*, ed. Gerhard Hoffman and Alfred Hornung (Heidelberg: Universitatsverlag C. Winter, 1997), 401–42; rpt. in Wyschogrod, *Crossover Queries*, 488–503. The ascription of the problematic term *primitive* to peoples and cultures has received warranted criticism. I retain the word in the interest of reflecting the sources cited.

36. I invoke Marcel Mauss's *The Gift: The Form and Reason for Exchange in Archaic Societies*, trans. W. D. Halls (New York: W. W. Norton, 1990), to demonstrate conceptual affinities between his thought and that of Levinas rather than to follow out its subsequent influence on literary criticism and anthropology. The continuing importance of Mauss can be measured by the ongoing positive and negative responses it has garnered. Remaining within Mauss's framework, anthropologist Maurice Godelier writes that, in order for there to be society, "There must be certain things that are given, others that are sold or bartered, and still others that must be kept for good," and that the task of anthropology is to bring these functions into reflective awareness in present-day contexts. See Maurice Godelier, "Some Things You Give, Some Things You Sell, but Some Things You Must Keep for Yourselves: What Mauss Did Not Say about Sacred Objects," in *The Enigma of Gift and Sacrifice*, ed. Edith Wyschogrod and Jean-Joseph Goux (New York: Fordham University Press, 2002), 34–35. In the same volume,

George Marcus, in "The Gift and Globalization: A Prolegomenon to the Anthropological Study of Contemporary Finance Capital and Its Mentalities," tracks revisions of Mauss in Bourdieu's work, where "meaning is produced as the management of time [opening the way] for considering exchange or circulation itself as a regime of culture" (41).

37. Mauss, *The Gift*, 6.

38. Ibid., 35.

39. Ibid., 36.

40. Ibid., 37.

41. Ibid., 41–42.

42. Ibid., 46.

43. Emmanuel Levinas, "La mort et le temps," cited in Jacques Derrida, *The Gift of Death*, trans. David Wills (Chicago: University of Chicago Press, 1995), 46.

44. Ibid., 43–44.

45. Levinas, *Totality and Infinity*, 179. See Edith Wyschogrod, "Language and Alterity," in *The Cambridge Companion to Levinas*, ed. Simon Critchley and Robert Bernasconi (Cambridge: Cambridge University Press, 2002), 188–205.

46. Georges Bataille, *Theory of Religion*, trans. Robert Hurley (New York: Zone Books, 1989), 43.

47. Ibid., 50.

48. Ibid., 44.

49. Derrida, *The Gift of Death*, 47–48.

50. Bataille, *Theory of Religion*, 46–47.

51. Ibid., 60–61.

52. Ibid., 69.

53. Ibid., 76.

54. Ibid., 100.

55. Levinas, *Totality and Infinity*, 78–79.

56. Levinas, "Philosophy, Justice, and Love," *Entre Nous*, 105.

57. Adam Smith, *An Inquiry into the Nature and Causes of the Wealth of Nations*, ed. Edwin Cannan (New York: Random House 1967), 423. Mark. C. Taylor, in *Confidence Games: Money and Markets in a Wold Without Redemption* (Chicago: University of Chicago Press, 2004), notes that Calvin, for whom God's providence sustains the world, first used the image of the invisible hand later appropriated by Adam Smith (4). Taylor's original and perceptive reading of the uncertainties of economy tracks its historical changes and subsequent postmodern manifestations, in which the real is seen as having morphed into the virtual and social and economic relations are seen as networks.

58. Smith, *Wealth of Nations*, 14.

59. Ibid., 42.

60. Ibid., 262–63.

61. Ibid., 421.

62. Ibid., 322.

63. Ibid., 324.

64. Ibid., 578. The parsimony endorsed by Smith should not be seen as premonitory of John Maynard Keynes's advocacy of the control of trade. For Smith, parsimony is a system of internal moral regulation not mandated by external agents, so he need not renege on his support of unregulated free trade. By contrast, in considering inflation and deflation, Keynes writes, "For these grave causes we must free ourselves of the deep distrust which exists against allowing the regulation of the standard of value to be the subject of deliberate decision" (*Monetary Reform* [New York: Harcourt Brace, 1924], 45).

65. Levinas, *Otherwise than Being*, 141–42. Derrida views this text in the context of Levinas's view of ethics as the radical self-exposure of the subject; see Jacques Derrida, "At This Moment in This Very Work Here I Am," trans. Ruben Berezdivin, in *A Derrida Reader: Between the Blinds*, ed. and introd. Peggy Kamuf (New York: Columbia University Press, 1991), 413–14.

66. Ibid., 409–10.

67. Smith, *Wealth of Nations*, 329.

68. Ibid., 324.

69. Levinas, "Philosophy, Justice, and Love," *Entre Nous*, 103.

70. Ibid., 106.

71. Levinas, *Totality and Infinity*, 251.

Excess and Desire: A Commentary on *Totality and Infinity*, Section I, Part D, by Jeffrey Bloechl

1. Emmanuel Levinas, *Transcendance et intelligibilité* (Geneva: Labor et Fides, 1984), 51. He made the remark during a conversation that, unfortunately, does not accompany the English translation of Levinas's lecture given the previous day. That translation appears in Adriaan T. Peperzak, Simon Critchley, and Robert Bernasconi, eds., *Emmanuel Levinas: Basic Philosophical Writings* (Bloomington: Indiana University Press, 1996), 150–59.

2. Emmanuel Levinas, *Les imprévus de l'histoire* (Montpellior: Fata Morgana, 1994), 186.

3. See, e.g., Emmanuel Levinas, "God and Philosophy, trans. Alphonso Lingis, in Levinas, *Collected Philosophical Papers* (Pittsburgh: Duquesne University Press, 1998), 168; *De Dieu qui vient à l'idée* (Paris: Vrin, 1982), 118. I have slightly modified some translations.

4. The present reflections are self-consciously restricted to Levinas's *philosophical* works and say nothing at all about his commentaries on the Talmud or his so-called Jewish denominational writings. Rather than pleading incompetence with those latter genres and beyond the matter of fidelity to a distinction Levinas himself often seems to preserve, my reason for this choice is strictly phenomenological: scriptural verses or letters do not have the same objectivity, or, if one prefers, do not have the same phenomenality as does the human face. In other words, it seems unlikely to me that any sort of written text could ever *traumatize* in the sense that Levinas reserves for the face of the stranger.

5. Other with respect to what? In what context? Against what background sameness? Analytic philosophy would not be wrong to ask for qualifiers to define what is other than me and mine but nonetheless a meaningful datum of experience. Classical phenomenology prepares a corresponding move with its insistence on horizons for meaning. The thought of an otherness that enters experience from beyond the horizon of a subject's world (*Umwelt*) is perilously close to the subjectivist illusion of an otherness that is wholly devoid of any intelligible content. Perhaps an advance can be made if the question is applied to the subjectivity of the subject. Could it be shown that a single subject is adequately responsive both to its world and everything in it, and to an otherness that does not belong there? A general theory of "responsivity" as a key to subjectivity has been developed in much of the work of Bernhard Waldenfels, including, most recently, his *The Question of the Other* (Hong Kong: Chinese University Press, 2007), esp. 21–35. A similar notion is developed, inspired partly by Levinas, in Adriaan T. Peperzak, *Elements of Ethics* (Palo Alto: Stanford University Press, 2003), 98ff.

6. Emmanuel Levinas, *Otherwise than Being, or Beyond Essence*, trans. Alphonso Lingis (The Hague: Martinus Nijhoff, 1981), 121; *Autrement qu'être ou au-delà de l'essence* (The Hague: Martinus Nijhoff, 1974), 155.

7. Ibid., 101 / 127.

8. Emmanuel Levinas, *Totality and Infinity: An Essay on Exteriority*, trans. Alphonso Lingis (Pittsburgh: Duquesne University Press, 1969), 104; *Totalité et infini* (The Hague: Martinus Nijhoff, 1961), 77. Future page references to this work will appear parenthetically in the text.

9. Levinas's possible relation with Kabbalah is the subject of increasing interest. Early investigations include C. Mopsik, "La pensée d'Emmanuel Lévinas et la cabale," in *Emmanuel Lévinas*, ed. M. Abensour and C. Chalier (Paris: L'Herne, 1991), 378–86; and M.-A. Ouaknin, *Méditations érotiques* (Paris: Belland, 1992). A comprehensive account can be found in J. Meskin, "The Role of Lurianic Kabbalah in the Early Philosophy of Emmanuel Levinas," in *Levinas Studies: An Annual Review*, ed. Jeffrey Bloechl, vol. 2 (Pittsburgh: Duquesne University Press, 2007), 4–77. One should also consult the penetrating analyses in Elliot R. Wolfson's contribution to this volume.

Levinas's complex relation to Neoplatonic thought—where the differences finally matter more than the affinities—receives careful treatment by Jean-Marc Narbonne in his portion of the dual publication *Lévinas et l'héritage grec*, by Jean-Marc Narbonne, with *Cent ans de Néoplatonisme en france*, by W. Hankey (Paris: J. Vrin / Québec: Les Presses de l'Université Laval, 2004), esp. 96ff.

10. Levinas, *Otherwise than Being*, 50 / 64.

11. The *Meditations* contain numerous instances of this expression for the Infinite, understood as God: "most perfect being, that is, God," "God, or a being who is supremely perfect," etc. (René Descartes, *Meditations on First Philosophy* [Cambridge: Cambridge University Press, 1996], 51, 54). For instructive commentary, see Jean-Luc Marion, *On Descartes' Metaphysical Prism* (Chicago: University of Chicago Press, 1999), 240–44.

12. Hence the remark in the Third Meditation: "my perception of the infinite, that is God, is in some way prior to my perception of the finite, that is, myself" (Descartes, *Meditations on First Philosophy*, 31).

13. Here again, Marion's analysis is illuminating. See Marion, *On Descartes' Metaphysical Prism*, 249ff.

14. Descartes to Mersenne (January 28, 1641): "I have never treated Infinity except to submit to it." Levinas cites this letter in his encyclopedia article "Infinity," reprinted in Emmanuel Levinas, *Alterity and Transcendence*, trans. Michael B. Smith (New York: Columbia University Press, 1999), 75–76.

15. This worry is suspended over modern reflection on religion in Levinas's essay "Lévi-Bruhl and Contemporary Philosophy," in *Entre Nous: Thinking-of-the-Other*, trans. Michael B. Smith and Barbara Harshav (New York: Columbia University Press, 2000), 39–52.

16. Levinas, *Otherwise than Being*, 96–101 / 123–27.

17. See, e.g., ibid., 79 / 99.

18. The word *amoral* and my characterization of the modern conception of the world are taken from R. Brague, *The Wisdom of the World: The Human Experience of the World in Western Thought* (Chicago: University of Chicago Press, 2003), 185–98 and *passim*.

19. Levinas, *Otherwise than Being*, 156, 158 / 199, 201–2.

20. On this use of the word *nonindifference*, see Levinas, "God and Philosophy," 162 / 111.

21. Levinas, *Otherwise than Being*, 123 / 158.

22. As Levinas acknowledges in several places, this strand of his thinking plainly draws on the Platonic notion of a divine desire (*Phaedrus* 244a ff) for the Good that is by definition beyond being and appearing (*Republic*, bk. 6). This is not the occasion to examine Levinas's adaptation of Plato or the occasional rumors of his Platonism, but it can fairly be said that the ethical inflection he gives to his own conception of a desire without self-interest is difficult to find in the dialogues that are his sources. These matters are pursued much further in J.-F. Mattéi, "Lévinas et Platon," in the collective edition *Emmanuel Lévinas: Positivité et transcendence* (Paris: Presses Universitaires de France, 2000), 73–87.

The Care of the Other and Substitution, by Jean-Luc Marion

1. Emmanuel Levinas, *Otherwise than Being, or Beyond Essence*, trans. Alphonso Lingis (The Hague: Martinus Nijhoff, 19u81), 117, 119; *Autrement qu'être ou au-delà de l'essence* (The Hague: Martinus Nijhoff, 1974), 150 and 152.

2. Ibid., 100 / 127.

3. Ibid., 111 / 141.

4. Ibid.

5. Ibid., 119, 184 / 152, 232.

6. Ibid., 127 / 163.

7. "This is why Heidegger seems to us to dominate from on high the philosophy of existence, whatever the breakthroughs or the modifications one must

add to the content of his analyses. One can be in relation to him only what Male-branche or Spinoza was in relation to Descartes. This is not so bad, but it is not Descartes' fate" (Emmanuel Levinas, *En découvrant l'existence avec Husserl et Heidegger* [Paris: Vrin, 1967], 101).

8. Martin Heidegger, *Being and Time*, trans. John Macquarrie and Edward Robinson (New York: Harper and Row, 1962), 155.

9. I confess not to understand why the Stambaugh translation in English chooses to render *Fürsorge* (p. 121, l. 26) as *welfare work* (p. 115, l. 14), thereby losing every connection with *Sorge/care*. The Macquarrie Robinson translation, from which the citations in this essay have been taken, renders it as *solicitude*, which also hides the connection with *Sorge/care*.

10. Heidegger, *Being and Time*, 158–59.

11. Ibid., 158.

12. "Thus death reveals itself as that *possibility which is one's ownmost, which is non-relational, and which is not to be outstripped*" (Ibid., 294).

13. Ibid., 294, 284.

14. Ibid., 283.

15. Ibid., 297.

16. Ibid., 238.

17. Ibid., 358ff.

18. Ibid., 159.

19. Edmund Husserl, *Cartesianische Meditationen* §43, Hua. I, p. 146.

20. Heidegger, *Being and Time*, 162.

21. Levinas, *Otherwise than Being*, 145 / 185.

22. Ibid., 102 / 130.

23. Ibid., 118, trans. modified / 151.

24. Ibid., 47, 111 / 61, 142. See also ibid., 141 / 180.

25. Ibid., 101 / 128.

26. Ibid., 124 / 159.

27. Ibid., 142, trans. modified / 180.

28. Ibid., 53 / 69.

29. Ibid., 85, trans. modified / 107; my emphasis.

30. Ibid., 118 / 151.

31. Ibid., 114, trans. modified, 117 / 146, 150.

32. Ibid., 116 / 148 ("without a choice"); ibid., 118 [correcting a significant typographical error, reading "voluntary" where it should say "involuntary"] / 151 ("involuntary . . . prior to the will's initiative"); ibid., 146 / 186 ("before all freedom").

33. Ibid., 110 / 140 ("in the accusative, without recourse in being"); ibid., 141 / 180 ("Responsibility for the Other is extraordinary, and it is not prevented from floating over the waters of ontology").

34. Ibid., 112 / 142.

35. Ibid., 127, trans. modified / 163. (Cf. "This book interprets the subject as a *hostage*," ibid., 184 / 232.)

36. Ibid., 115 / 146. Cf. "absolved from every relationship, every game, literally without a situation, without a dwelling place, expelled from everywhere and from itself" (ibid., 146 / 186).

37. Ibid., 117 / 150.

38. Ibid., 114 / 145.

39. Ibid., 135 / 173.

40. Ibid., 112 / 143.

41. Ibid., 152, trans. modified / 196; my emphasis.

42. Ibid., 117 / 149, my emphasis.

43. Ibid., 139 / 177, my emphasis.

44. Heidegger, *Being and Time*, 369.

45. Levinas, *Otherwise than Being*, 118 / 151,112 / 143.

46. Emmanuel Levinas, "Dying for . . .," in *Entre Nous: Thinking-of-the-Other*, trans. Michael B. Smith and Barbara Harshav (New York: Columbia University Press, 1998), 217.

Should Jews and Christians Fear the Gifts of the Greeks? Reflections on Levinas, Translation, and Atheistic Theology, by Paul Franks

1. See Gibbs's contribution to this volume, p. 36.

2. See Wolfson's contribution to this volume.

3. See Cohen's contribution to this volume, and Batnitzky's contribution, p. 24.

4. Levinas, "The Pact," in *The Levinas Reader*, trans. Seán Hand (Oxford: Blackwell, 1989), 217.

5. See Immanuel Kant, *Werke* (Berlin: Akademie, 1900–), 2:14 and 7:23.

6. Ibid., 5:33.

7. Ibid., 6:126.

8. Ibid., 6:168.

9. Ibid., 7:53.

10. Emmanuel Levinas, *Otherwise than Being, or Beyond Essence*, trans. Alphonso Lingis (The Hague: Martinus Nijhoff, 1981), 111. See Jacques Derrida, *The Gift of Death*, trans, David Wills (Chicago: University of Chicago Press, 1996), 51: "This guilt is originary, like original sin."

11. Levinas, *Otherwise than Being*, 125.

12. Ibid., 126.

13. See the contributions to this volume by Jeffrey Kosky and Jean-Luc Marion.

14. See Levinas, "The Pact,," on TB Sotah 37a-b.

15. See Levinas, *Otherwise than Being*, 126: "One must not think of it as the state of original sin; it is, on the contrary, the original goodness of creation."

16. Emmanuel Levinas, *Nine Talmudic Readings*, trans. Annette Aronowicz (Bloomington: Indiana University Press, 1990), 98. The eminent master is presumably Levinas's mysterious teacher, Shoushani. In the passage cited, Levinas is discussing TB Baba Metsia 83a-b, but he perhaps also has in mind TB Baba Metsia 114b: "You are called man [*adam*] and idolaters are not called man."

17. To say that Judaism has an essentially particular aspect is not, of course, to deny that it also has an essentially universal aspect. But this universal aspect could be identified with some specific content, such as the seven Noahide commandments. This is a traditional approach. It is one of Levinas's great innovations to depart from this tradition, to see Judaism *as a whole* as possessing both aspects.

Thinking about God and God-Talk with Levinas, by Merold Westphal

1. At the conference that gave rise to this volume, my assignment was to comment on each paper from a Christian perspective. But now it is to reflect, not on each paper but on the issues (possibly raised by one or more of them) that are especially pertinent to conversation among Jews and Christians about Levinas. In the attempt to keep our attention on the *Sache*, I shall not identify a specific paper or papers, even when quoting or paraphrasing. My hope is that instead of thinking "N. N. said . . ." we'll be thinking "One might say . . ."

2. For example, such sacraments as baptism and the Eucharist.

3. Biblical citations are from the New Revised Standard Version. In this and subsequent citations I have italicized 'world' and 'all nations' for obvious reasons.

4. This means that, while the term 'supersessionism' is usually restricted to the relation between Judaism and Christianity, the issue is by no means so limited. The New Testament claim for the universal significance of Jesus as Savior and Lord "so that at the name of Jesus every knee should bend . . and every tongue should confess that Jesus Christ is Lord, to the glory of God the Father" (Phil. 2:10–11) means that every world-view, whether eastern or western, northern or southern, religious or secular, is, at best, incomplete without such a confession.

5. That is why I have argued in *Suspicion and Faith: The Religious Uses of Modern Atheism* (New York: Fordham University Press, 1998) that Christians should take seriously the critiques of Christianity found in Marx, Nietzsche, and Freud and rooted in the hermeneutics of suspicion. These critiques have been and still are all too true all too much of the time. Their religious uses are Lenten self-examination, personal and corporate, and repentance.

6. See Richard Mouw's plea for civility in *Uncommon Decency: Christian Civility in an Uncivil World* (Downers Grove, Ill.: Inter-Varsity Press, 1992).

7. At least in their biblical forms. We shall see that this cannot be taken for granted from either side.

8. In context, one can substitute "righteous" or "intellectually brilliant" for "numerous." God's covenantal initiative is the basis of election, not human superiority in any mode.

9. In a closely related passage, Jesus rebukes the disciples' search for prestige and the power that comes with it, reminding them that "I am among you as one who serves" (Luke 22:27).

10. On Heidegger, see my discussion in the title essay of *Overcoming Ontotheology: Toward a Postmodern Christian Faith* (New York: Fordham University

Press, 2001) and "Aquinas and Onto-theology," *American Catholic Philosophical Quarterly* 80, no. 2 (Spring 2006): 78–93.

11. This is why Adriaan T. Peperzak can argue that Levinas does not repudiate ontology as such but rather offers an alternative account of how things are, suggesting that *"ontology has not yet properly begun" (Beyond: The Philosophy of Emmanuel Levinas* [Evanston, Ill.: Northwestern University Press, 1997], 84–85).

12. Here I skip over the internal limitations of this knowing suggested by Plato's idea of the Good as *epikeina tes ousias* and Descartes' presentation of the idea of the Infinite.

13. On Levinas's reading, Heidegger makes a significant but insufficient break with this tradition. See esp., Emmanuel Levinas, "Is Ontology Fundamental?" in *Basic Philosophical Writings*, ed. Adriaan T. Peperzak, Simon Critchley, and Robert Bernasconi (Bloomington: Indiana University Press, 1996), 1–10.

14. Emmanuel Levinas, *Totality and Infinity*, trans. Alphonso Lingis (Pittsburgh: Duquesne University Press, 1969), 118. Cf. 134 and 33.

15. And the primacy of freedom over responsibility.

16. Levinas, *Otherwise than Being*, 121; my emphasis.

17. Cf. ibid., 197n25: "Thus theological language destroys the religious situation of transcendence. The infinite 'presents' itself anarchically, but thematization loses the anarchy which alone can accredit it. Language about God rings false or becomes a myth, that is, can never be taken literally." But if the critique of thematization is nothing more than a rejection of literalism, there is nothing new or very interesting in it. Of course, to talk about prayer is one thing, to pray another. But that does not mean that the former reduces religion to mythic literalism.

18. Ibid., 120.

19. Thomas à Kempis, *The Imitation of Christ* (Oxford: Oxford University Press, 1900), bk. 1, chap. 1. The passage continues: "If thou didst know the whole Bible by heart, and the sayings of all the philosophers, what would all that profit thee without the love of God, and without His grace?"

20. Emmanuel Levinas, *Of God Who Comes to Mind*, trans. Bettina Bergo (Stanford: Stanford University Press, 1998), ix. Of course, Levinas elsewhere makes it clear that this recuperation can never be completed due to the structure of the trace an its anarchic temporality. See Emmanuel Levinas, "The Trace of the Other," in *Deconstruction in Context*, ed. Mark C. Taylor (Chicago: University of Chicago Press, 1986), 345–59.

21. Thus Levinas refers us to Rosenzweig's claim "Judaism saves Christianity from becoming Gnosis" (Emmanuel Levinas, *Is It Righteous to Be? Interviews with Emmanuel Levinas*, ed. Jill Robbins (Stanford: Stanford University Press, 2001), 263.

22. Levinas, "God and Philosophy," *Of God Who Comes to Mind*, 75. The passage continues: "said to the neighbor to whom I am given over." Why these

words are not to be spoken to God, as with Abraham (Gen. 22:1), Jacob (Gen. 31:11–13, 46:2), Moses (Exod. 3:4–60), Samuel (1 Sam. 3:4–10), and Isaiah (Isa. 6:8) is a question to which we shall turn in the next section. It is in this tradition that Mary responds to the words of annunciation, "Here am I, the servant of the Lord; let it be with me according to your word" (Luke 1:38). This is the posture both of prayer and of theology.

23. John Llewelyn, *Emmanuel Levinas: The Genealogy of Ethics* (New York: Routledge, 1995), 150.

24. Charles Stevenson, *Facts and Values: Studies in Ethical Analysis* (New Haven: Yale University Press, 1963), 32.

25. For this reading of the two, see my *Transcendence and Self-Transcendence: On God and the Soul* (Bloomington: Indiana University Press, 2004), chaps. 2 and 3. Reference to these two shows that the fundamental issue here is not one *between Jews and Christians.* Persuasive redefinition can occur within either horizon.

26. Spirit is " 'I' that is 'We' and 'We' that is 'I.' " (G. W. F. Hegel, *Phenomenology of Spirit*, trans. A. V. Miller [Oxford: Oxford University Press, 1977, 110).

27. Levinas, *Otherwise than Being*, 5, 8, 45, 154, 185.

28. Levinas, "Enigma and Phenomenon," in *Basic Philosophical* Writings, 77.

29. Annette Aronowicz, translator's introduction to Emmanuel Levinas, *Nine Talmudic Readings* (Bloomington: Indiana University Press, 1990), xxiii.

30. Levinas *Totality and Infinity*, 74–75. Cf. Levinas, "Freedom and Command," in *Collected Philosophical Papers*, trans. Alphonso Lingis (Dordrecht: Martinus Nijhoff, 1987), 20, and Emmanuel Levinas, *Alterity and Transcendence*, trans. Michael B. Smith (New York: Columbia University Press, 1999), 33, 126, 139.

31. Jacques Derrida, *The Gift of Death*, trans. David Wills (Chicago: University of Chicago Press, 1995), 68, 77–78, 82, 84.

32. Levinas, *Otherwise than Being*, 93–94; my emphasis. Cf. Levinas, "The Trace of the Other," 355–56.

33. Levinas, "God and Philosophy" in *Collected Philosophical Papers*, 165.

34. Levinas, *Totality and Infinity*, 79; my emphasis.

35. Ibid., 78.

36. The reduction of religion to ethics may be a betrayal equal but opposite to the reduction of religion to metaphysics (onto-theology).

37. For the face that speaks, see Levinas, *Totality and Infinity*, 66; for the commandment, see ibid., 199, 216, 262, 303; cf. 171.

38. Martin L. Smith, *The Word Is Very Near You: A Guide to Praying with Scripture* (Cambridge: Cowley Publications, 1989), 10. Smith also writes, as if in conversation with Levinas, "Religion is supremely responsive. . . . In prayer, as in life, we are the ones who answer. God touches us, God speaks to us, God moves us, God reveals truth to us, and life and prayer is our response. . . . Prayer is primarily attentiveness to God's disclosure to us and the heart's response to that disclosure" (18–19).

39. Perhaps this is the significance of certain biblical name changes: Abram to Abraham and Sarai to Sarah (Gen. 17) or Simon to Cephas = Peter (John 1).

40. A similar view of the subject is found in Kierkegaard's description of the self as "a relation that relates itself to itself [in self-consciousness and responsible freedom] and in relating itself to itself relates itself to another" (*Sickness unto Death*, trans. Howard V. Hong and Edna H. Hong [Princeton: Princeton University Press, 1980], 13–14).

41. We might say that the potential psalmist in Levinas is overshadowed by his Kantian instincts.

42. 1 John 4:18. Thus the title of Jamie Ferreira's splendid book, *Love's Grateful Striving: A Commentary on Kierkegaard's Works of Love* (New York: Oxford University Press, 2008).

43. In *Divine Discourse: Philosophical Reflections on the Claim That God Speaks* (New York: Cambridge University Press, 1995), Nicholas Wolterstorff presents a theology of a God whose personal character shows itself in performative speech acts, of which the two most typical are promises and commands.

44. In the Second Meditation, Descartes defines a thinking thing as "a thing that doubts, understands, affirms, denies, is willing, is unwilling, and also imagines and has sensory perceptions." In Principle IX of *The Principles of Philosophy* he defines intentionality as "understanding, willing, imagining, but also feeling."

45. For my analysis of Levinas's critique of Husserlian phenomenology, see chap. 7 of *Transcendence and Self-Transcendence*.

46. Levinas, *Otherwise than Being*, 53, 141; cf. 47, 101, 111.

47. Derrida makes this figure of the gaze that sees me without my being able to see it the true significance of transcendence in *The Gift of Death*; see 2, 6, 25, 27, 31–33, 40, 56, 91, 93.

48. We do well to remember that Moses' first instinct was to flee. In Exodus 3–4 his response to the call of God was "Here am I; please send someone else."

49. This is how we might read Sartre's account of our reaction to the Look in *Being and Nothingness*. See "The Look" (Three, One, IV) and "Concrete Relations With Others" (Three, Three, I-II).

50. See my essays "The Trauma of Transcendence as Heteronomous Inter-subjectivity," in *Intersubjectivité et théologie philosophique*, ed. Marco M. Olivetti (Padua: CEDAM, 2001), 87–110, and "Transcendence, Heteronomy, and the Birth of the Responsible Self," in *Calvin O. Schrag and the Task of Philosophy after Postmodernity*, ed. Martin Beck Matustík and William L. McBride (Evanston, Ill.: Northwestern University Press, 2002), 201–25.

51. Levinas, *Totality and Infinity*, 23.

52. I do not know enough to speak here of Jewish theologies.

53. See, esp., Jean-Luc Marion, *Reduction and Givenness*, trans. Thomas A. Carlson (Evanston, Ill.: Northwestern University Press, 1998); idem, *Being Given: Toward a Phenomenology of Givenness*, trans. Jeffrey L. Kosky (Stanford: Stanford University Press, 2002), and idem, *In Excess: Studies in Saturated Phenomena*, trans. Robyn Horner and Vincent Berraud (New York: Fordham University Press, 2002).

54. In Augustine and Aquinas, metaphysics is not so much replaced as teleologically suspended or *aufgehoben*. See my "Aquinas and Onto-theology." Andrew Louth laments the divorce between metaphysics and spirituality that permits even Augustine's *De Trinitate* to be misread "as an exercise in speculative theology rather than as an attempt to give an account of the ascent of the soul to God, the God whom it knows from Scripture to be God the Holy Trinity" (*The Origins of the Christian Mystical Tradition* [New York: Oxford University Press, 1983], xii).

55. Levinas can help us understand why Marion suggests that both phenomenologically and religiously speaking the subject is *der Angesprochene, l'interloqué, l'adonné*. He treats the first two of these as synonymous. See Marion, *Reduction and Givenness*, 181–205. The third, which is the theme of part 5 of *Being Given*, is translated "the gifted," though Kosky suggests as an alternative "he who is given over," like an addict or devotee. Robyn Horner renders the term "the devoted one" in her *Rethinking God as Gift: Marion, Derrida, and the Limits of Phenomenology* (New York: Fordham University Press, 2001), 149–50, though the passive, responsive dimension gets muted in this rendering.

Words of Peace and Truth: A-Dieu, Levinas, by Michael A. Signer

1. Jacques Derrida, *Adieu to Emmanuel Levinas*, trans. Pascale-Anne Brault and Michael Naas (Stanford: Stanford University Press, 1999), 1–13.

2. Emmanuel Levinas, "Judaism and Christianity after Franz Rosenzweig," in *Is It Righteous to Be? Interviews with Emmanuel Levinas*, ed. Jill Robbins (Stanford: Stanford University Press, 2001), 255–67. The original was published in *Zeitgewinn: Messianisches Denken nach Franz Rosenzweig*, ed. Gotthard Fuchs and Hans Hermann Henrix (Frankfurt am Main: Josef Knecht, 1987), 163–84. An abbreviated version appears under the title "Judaism and Christianity" in Emmanuel Levinas, *In the Time of Nations*, trans. Michael B. Smith (Bloomington: Indiana University Press, 1994), 161–66.

3. Levinas, "Judaism and Christianity after Franz Rosenzweig," 255.

4. Ibid., 257.

5. Ibid., 258.

6. Ibid., 267.

7. The statement was written on May 23, 1973, and subsequently published in *Revue des Études Juives* 160 (2001): 495–97.

8. Jacob Katz, *Exclusiveness and Tolerance: Jewish-Gentile Relations in Medieval and Modern Times* (New York: Schocken Books, 1959), describes the approach to—avoidance of Christianity within the boundaries of traditional Jewish law.

9. John Paul II, *Crossing the Threshold of Hope*, ed. Vittorio Messori, trans. Jenny McPhee and Martha McPhee (New York: Alfred A. Knopf, 1994), 35: "In gaining some distance from positivistic convictions, contemporary thought has made notable advances toward the ever more complete discovery of man, recognizing among other things the value of metaphorical and symbolic language.

Contemporary hermeneutics—examples of which are found in the work of Paul Ricoeur or, from a different perspective, in the work of Emmanuel Levinas—presents the truth about man from new angles."

10. John Paul II, *Spiritual Pilgrimage: Texts on Jews and Judaism, 1979–1995*, ed. Eugene J. Fisher and Leon Klenicki (New York: Crossroad Herder, 1995), contains the public documents. The material from 1996 to 2000 can be found on the Vatican website, www.vatican.va.

11. Darcy O'Brien, *The Hidden Pope: The Personal Journey of John Paul II and Jerzy Kluger* (New York: Daybreak Books, 1998).

12. John Paul II, *Crossing the Threshold of Hope*, 36.

13. Ibid.

14. Ibid., 210–11.

15. Johann Baptist Metz, "Facing the Jews," in F. Schussler-Fiorenza and D. Tracy, *The Holocaust as Interruption*, Concilium 175 (May 1984), 26–33.

16. Joseph B. Soloveitchik, "Confrontation," in *A Treasury of Tradition*, ed. Norman Lamm and Walter S. Wurzberger (New York: Hebrew Publishing Company, 1967), 55–80. All quotations are taken from this essay. Papers from a conference at Boston College on the occasion of the fortieth anniversary of the essay may be viewed at www.bc.edu/cjlearning.

17. Zvi Kolitz, *Confrontation: The Existential Thought of Rabbi J. B. Soloveitchik* (Hoboken, N.J.: Ktav Publishing House, 1993).

18. Ibid., 73.

19. Heschel's role at the Second Vatican Council is described in Edward K. Kaplan, *Spiritual Radical: Abraham Joshua Heschel in America* (New Haven: Yale University Press, 2007), 239–67.

20. Both essays are reprinted in Abraham Joshua Heschel, *Moral Grandeur and Spiritual Audacity*, ed. Susannah Heschel (New York: Farrar Straus Giroux, 1996), 235–67 and 268–85.

21. Emmanuel Levinas, "Dialogue: Self-Consciousness and Proximity of the Neighbor," in *Of God Who Comes to Mind*, trans. Bettina Bergo (Stanford: Stanford University Press, 1998), 137–51.

22. Emmanuel Levinas, *God, Death, and Time*, trans. Bettina Bergo (Stanford: Stanford University Press, 2000), 117, trans. modified; the second, summarizing quote is by Derrida, in *Adieu*, 13.

Contributors

Leora Batnitzky is Professor of Religion at Princeton University. She is the author of *Idolatry and Representation: The Philosophy of Franz Rosenzweig Reconsidered* (2000) and *Leo Strauss and Emmanuel Levinas: Philosophy and the Politics of Revelation* (2006). Since 2004 she has been the co-editor of *Jewish Studies Quarterly*, as well as the editor of the forthcoming *Martin Buber: Schriften zur Philosophie und Religion*. She is currently writing a book on the philosophical and historical relations between modern religious thought (Jewish and Christian) and modern legal theory (analytic and Continental).

Jeffrey Bloechl is Associate Professor of Philosophy at Boston College. His teaching and research centers on questions arising in Continental European thought, philosophy of religion, and Christian theology. He is the author of *Liturgy of the Neighbor: Emmanuel Levinas and the Religion of Possibility* (2000); editor of *The Face of the Other and the Trace of God: Essays on the Philosophy of Emmanuel Levinas* (2000) and *Religious Experience and the End of Metaphysics* (2003); and the editor of *Levinas Studies: An Annual Review*.

Richard A. Cohen is Professor of Philosophy and Director of the Institute of Jewish Thought and Heritage at the University of Buffalo (SUNY). He is the author of *Elevations: The Height of the Good in Rosenzweig and Levinas* (1994); *Ethics, Exegesis and Philosophy: Interpretation* *after Levinas* (2001); and numerous articles in modern and contemporary Continental philosophy. He is the translator of three books by Emmanuel Levinas, *Ethics and Infinity* (1985), *Time and the Other* (1987), and *New Talmudic Readings* (1999), and the co-translator of *Discovering Existence with Husserl* (1998). He has also edited *Face to Face with Levinas* (1986) and co-edited *In Proximity: Emmanuel Levinas and the Eighteenth Century* (2002).

Paul Franks is Senator Jeramiel S. and Carole S. Grafstein Professor of Jewish Philosophy in the Centre for Jewish Studies at the University of Toronto. He has also taught at the University of Michigan, Indiana University, the University of Notre Dame, and the University of Chicago. With Michael L. Morgan, he translated and edited, with commentary, *Franz Rosenzweig: Philosophical and Theological Writings* (2000). He is the author of *All or Nothing: Systematicity, Skepticism, and Transcendental Arguments in German Idealism* (2005) and of many articles on post-Kantian philosophy and Jewish thought, including most recently "Jewish Philosophy after Kant: The Legacy of Salomon Maimon," in *The Cambridge Companion to Modern Jewish Philosophy* (2007).

Robert Gibbs is Professor of Philosophy and Director of the Jackman Humanities Institute at the University of Toronto. He has also taught at Princeton University and St. Louis University. He is the author of *Correlations in Rosenzweig and Levinas* (1992) and *Why Ethics: Signs of Responsibilities* (2000), as well as co-editor, with Elliot R. Wolfson, of *Suffering Religion* (2002) and co-author, with Steven Kepnes and Peter Ochs, of *Reasoning after Revelation* (1998). He has published widely on modern Jewish philosophy and is currently engaged in a major project on law and ethics.

Kevin Hart is Edwin B. Kyle Professor of Christian Studies at the University of Virginia. He is the author of, among other books, *The Trespass of the Sign: Deconstruction, Theology and Philosophy* (1989; rpt. 2000), *The Dark Gaze: Maurice Blanchot and the Sacred* (2004), and *Postmodernism: A Beginner's Guide* (2004). He is the editor of *Counter-Experiences: Reading Jean-Luc Marion* (2007) and *The Oxford Book of Australian Religious Verse* (1994). With Geoffrey Hartman, he has co-edited *The Power of Contestation: Perspectives on Maurice Blanchot* (2004); with Yvonne Sherwood, *Derrida and Religion: Other Testaments* (2004); and with Barbara Wall, *The Experience of God: A Postmodern Perspective* (2005). His seven collections of poems are gathered in *Flame Tree: Selected Poems* (2002), and a new poetry volume, *Young Rain*, appeared in 2009.

Dana Hollander is Associate Professor in the Department of Religious Studies at McMaster University. Her research interests are modern Jewish thought, twentieth-century French and German philosophy, and German-Jewish history and culture. She has published *Exemplarity and Chosenness: Rosenzweig and Derrida on the Nation of Philosophy* (2008), and she is currently at work on a study of Hermann Cohen's writings on love of the neighbor.

Robyn Horner is Senior Lecturer in Theology at the Australian Catholic University. Her interests include the works of Jean-Luc Marion, Jacques Derrida, and Emmanuel Levinas, and she explores the intersections of theology and post-structuralism. She is the author of *Re-Thinking God as Gift* (2001) and *Jean-Luc Marion: A Theo-Logical Introduction* (2005).

Jeffrey Kosky is Associate Professor in the Department of Religion at Washington and Lee University. He is the author of *Levinas and the Philosophy of Religion* (2001) and the translator of several works by Jean-Luc Marion, including *On Descartes' Metaphysical Prism: The Constitution and the Limits of Onto-Theo-Logy in Cartesian Thought* (1999) and *Being Given: Toward a Phenomenology of Givenness* (2002).

Jean-Luc Marion is Professor of Philosophy at the University of Paris IV—Sorbonne and the John Nuveen Professor of the Philosophy of Religion and Theology in the Divinity School of the University of Chicago, where he also teaches in the Committee on Social Thought. His books in English include *God Without Being: Hors-Texte* (1991); *Reduction and Givenness: Investigations of Husserl, Heidegger, and Phenomenology* (1998); *On Descartes' Metaphysical Prism: The Constitution and the Limits of Onto-Theo-Logy in Cartesian Thought* (1999); *Cartesian Questions: Method and Metaphysics* (1999); *The Idol and Distance: Five Studies* (2001); *Being Given: Toward a Phenomenology of Givenness* (2002); *In Excess: Studies of Saturated Phenomena* (2002); *Prolegomena to Charity* (2002); *The Crossing of the Visible* (2004); *The Erotic Phenomenon* (2007); *On the Ego and on God: Further Cartesian Questions* (2007); *The Visible and the Revealed* (2008); and *Descartes' Gray Ontology: Cartesian Science and Aristotelian Thought in the Regulae* (forthcoming).

Michael Purcell is Senior Lecturer in Systematic Theology in the School of Divinity at the University of Edinburgh. His research focuses on the relation between phenomenology and theology, particularly the possibility of an ethically inspired fundamental theology. He is the author of *Mystery and Method: The Other in Rahner and Levinas* (1998). His most recent book, *Levinas and Theology* (2006), explores the possibility of "doing theology with Levinas" and its limits, with particular attention to the theology of grace and sacraments.

The late **Michael A. Signer** was Abrams Professor of Jewish Thought and Culture in the Department of Theology at the University of Notre Dame. He edited *Humanity at the Limit: The Impact of the Holocaust Experience on Jews and Christians* (2000) and co-edited *Christianity in Jewish Terms* (2000); *Jews and Christians in Twelfth-Century Europe* (2001; with John van Engen); and *Coming Together for the Sake of God: Contributions to Jewish-Christian Dialogue from Post- Shoah Germany* (2006).

Merold Westphal is Distinguished Professor of Philosophy at Fordham University. He is the author of *God, Guilt, and Death: An Existential Phenomenology of Religion* (1984); *Kierkegaard's Critique of Reason and Society* (1987); *Hegel, Freedom, and Modernity* (1992); *Suspicion and Faith: The Religious Uses of Modern Atheism* (1993, rpt. 1999); *Becoming a Self: A Reading of Kierkegaard's "Concluding Unscientific Postscript"* (1996); *History and Truth in Hegel's Phenomenology* (3d ed., 1998); *Overcoming Ontotheology: Toward a Postmodern Christian Faith* (2001), and *Transcendence and Self-Transcendence: On God and the Soul* (2004), and *Levinas and Kierkegaard in Dialogue* (2008). He has served as President of the Hegel Society of America and of the Søren Kierkegaard Society and as Executive Co-Director of the Society for Phenomenology and Existential Philosophy. He is editor of the Indiana Series in the Philosophy of Religion, published by Indiana University Press.

Elliot R. Wolfson is the Abraham Lieberman Professor of Hebrew and Judaic Studies at New York University. His main area of scholarly research is the history of Jewish mysticism, but he has brought to bear on that field training in philosophy, literary criticism, feminist theory, postmodern hermeneutics, and the phenomenology of religion. His publications include *Through a Speculum That Shines: Vision and Imagination in Medieval Jewish Mysticism* (1994), which won the American Academy of Religion's Award for Excellence in the Study of Religion in the Category of Historical Studies, 1995, and the National Jewish Book Award for Excellence in Scholarship, 1995; *Along the Path: Studies in Kabbalistic Hermeneutics, Myth, and Symbolism* (1995); *Circle in the Square: Studies in the*

Use of Gender in Kabalistic Symbolism (1995); *Abraham Abulafia— Kabbalist and Prophet: Hermeneutics, Theosophy, and Theurgy* (2000); *Pathwings: Poetic-Philosophic Reflections on the Hermeneutics of Time and Language* (2004); *Language, Eros, Being: Kabbalistic Hermeneutics and Poetic Imagination* (2005), which won the National Jewish Book Award for Excellence in Scholarship, 2006; *Alef, Mem, Tau: Kabbalistic Musings on Time, Truth, and Death* (2006); *Venturing Beyond—Law and Morality in Kabbalistic Mysticism* (2006); and *Luminal Darkness: Imaginal Gleanings from Zoharic Literature* (2007).

The late **Edith Wyschogrod** was J. Newton Rayzor Professor Emerita of Philosophy and Religious Thought, Rice University. Her books include *Saints and Postmodernism: Revisioning Moral Philosophy* (1990); *An Ethics of Remembering: History, Heterology, and the Nameless Others* (1998); *Emmanuel Levinas: The Problem of Ethical Metaphysics* (2d ed., 2000), and *Crossover Queries: Dwelling with Negatives, Embodying Philosophy's Others* (2006).

Index

Perspectives in
Continental Philosophy Series
John D. Caputo, series editor

Karl Jaspers, *The Question of German Guilt*. Introduction by Joseph W. Koterski, S.J.

Jean-Luc Marion, *The Idol and Distance: Five Studies*. Translated with an introduction by Thomas A. Carlson.

Jeffrey Dudiak, *The Intrigue of Ethics: A Reading of the Idea of Discourse in the Thought of Emmanuel Levinas*.

Robyn Horner, *Rethinking God as Gift: Marion, Derrida, and the Limits of Phenomenology*.

Mark Dooley, *The Politics of Exodus: Søren Keirkegaard's Ethics of Responsibility*.

Merold Westphal, *Overcoming Onto-Theology: Toward a Postmodern Christian Faith*.

Edith Wyschogrod, Jean-Joseph Goux, and Eric Boynton, eds., *The Enigma of Gift and Sacrifice*.

Stanislas Breton, *The Word and the Cross*. Translated with an introduction by Jacquelyn Porter.

Jean-Luc Marion, *Prolegomena to Charity*. Translated by Stephen E. Lewis.

Peter H. Spader, *Scheler's Ethical Personalism: Its Logic, Development, and Promise*.

Jean-Louis Chrétien, *The Unforgettable and the Unhoped For*. Translated by Jeffrey Bloechl.

Don Cupitt, *Is Nothing Sacred? The Non-Realist Philosophy of Religion: Selected Essays*.

Jean-Luc Marion, *In Excess: Studies of Saturated Phenomena*. Translated by Robyn Horner and Vincent Berraud.

Phillip Goodchild, *Rethinking Philosophy of Religion: Approaches from Continental Philosophy*.

William J. Richardson, S.J., *Heidegger: Through Phenomenology to Thought*.

Jeffrey Andrew Barash, *Martin Heidegger and the Problem of Historical Meaning*.

Jean-Louis Chrétien, *Hand to Hand: Listening to the Work of Art*. Translated by Stephen E. Lewis.

Jean-Louis Chrétien, *The Call and the Response*. Translated with an introduction by Anne Davenport.

D. C. Schindler, *Han Urs von Balthasar and the Dramatic Structure of Truth: A Philosophical Investigation*.

Julian Wolfreys, ed., *Thinking Difference: Critics in Conversation*.

Allen Scult, *Being Jewish/Reading Heidegger: An Ontological Encounter*.

Richard Kearney, *Debates in Continental Philosophy: Conversations with Contemporary Thinkers*.

Jennifer Anna Gosetti-Ferencei, *Heidegger, Hölderlin, and the Subject of Poetic Language: Towards a New Poetics of Dasein*.

Jolita Pons, *Stealing a Gift: Kirkegaard's Pseudonyms and the Bible*.

Jean-Yves Lacoste, *Experience and the Absolute: Disputed Questions on the Humanity of Man*. Translated by Mark Raftery-Skehan.

Charles P. Bigger, *Between* Chora *and the Good: Metaphor's Metaphysical Neighborhood*.

Dominique Janicaud, *Phenomenology "Wide Open": After the French Debate.* Translated by Charles N. Cabral.

Ian Leask and Eoin Cassidy, eds., *Givenness and God: Questions of Jean-Luc Marion.*

Jacques Derrida, *Sovereignties in Question: The Poetics of Paul Celan.* Edited by Thomas Dutoit and Outi Pasanen.

William Desmond, *Is There a Sabbath for Thought? Between Religion and Philosophy.*

Bruce Ellis Benson and Norman Wirzba, eds., *The Phenomoenology of Prayer.*

S. Clark Buckner and Matthew Statler, eds., *Styles of Piety: Practicing Philosophy after the Death of God.*

Kevin Hart and Barbara Wall, eds., *The Experience of God: A Postmodern Response.*

John Panteleimon Manoussakis, *After God: Richard Kearney and the Religious Turn in Continental Philosophy.*

John Martis, *Philippe Lacoue-Labarthe: Representation and the Loss of the Subject.*

Jean-Luc Nancy, *The Ground of the Image.*

Edith Wyschogrod, *Crossover Queries: Dwelling with Negatives, Embodying Philosophy's Others.*

Gerald Bruns, *On the Anarchy of Poetry and Philosophy: A Guide for the Unruly.*

Brian Treanor, *Aspects of Alterity: Levinas, Marcel, and the Contemporary Debate.*

Simon Morgan Wortham, *Counter-Institutions: Jacques Derrida and the Question of the University.*

Leonard Lawlor, *The Implications of Immanence: Toward a New Concept of Life.*

Clayton Crockett, *Interstices of the Sublime: Theology and Psychoanalytic Theory.*

Bettina Bergo, Joseph Cohen, and Raphael Zagury-Orly, eds., *Judeities: Questions for Jacques Derrida.* Translated by Bettina Bergo and Michael B. Smith.

Jean-Luc Marion, *On the Ego and on God: Further Cartesian Questions.* Translated by Christina M. Gschwandtner.

Jean-Luc Nancy, *Philosophical Chronicles.* Translated by Franson Manjali.

Jean-Luc Nancy, *Dis-Enclosure: The Deconstruction of Christianity.* Translated by Bettina Bergo, Gabriel Malenfant, and Michael B. Smith.

Andrea Hurst, *Derrida Vis-à-vis Lacan: Interweaving Deconstruction and Psychoanalysis.*

Jean-Luc Nancy, *Noli me tangere: On the Raising of the Body.* Translated by Sarah Clift, Pascale-Anne Brault, and Michael Naas.

Jacques Derrida, *The Animal That Therefore I Am.* Edited by Marie-Louise Mallet, translated by David Wills.

Jean-Luc Marion, *The Visible and the Revealed.* Translated by Christina M. Gschwandtner and others.

Michel Henry, *Material Phenomenology.* Translated by Scott Davidson.

Jean-Luc Nancy, *Corpus.* Translated by Richard A. Rand.

Joshua Kates, *Fielding Derrida.*

Michael Naas, *Derrida From Now On.*

Shannon Sullivan and Dennis J. Schmidt, eds., *Difficulties of Ethical Life.*

Catherine Malabou, *What Should We Do with Our Brain?* Translated by Sebastian Rand, Introduction by Marc Jeannerod.

Claude Romano, *Event and World*. Translated by Shane Mackinlay.

Vanessa Lemm, *Nietzsche's Animal Philosophy: Culture, Politics, and the Animality of the Human Being*.

B. Keith Putt, ed., *Gazing Through a Prism Darkly: Reflections on Merold Westphal's Hermeneutical Epistemology*.

Eric Boynton and Martin Kavka, eds., *Saintly Influence: Edith Wyschogrod and the Possibilities of Philosophy of Religion*.